FIRST CLASS

FIRST CLASS

Women Join the Ranks at the Naval Academy

SHARON HANLEY DISHER

Sharon Hanley Disher

USNA '80

BLUEJACKET BOOKS

NAVAL INSTITUTE PRESS

Annapolis, Maryland

Naval Institute Press
291 Wood Road
Annapolis, MD 21402

First Bluejacket Books printing, 2005
ISBN 1-59114-216-4

The Library of Congress has cataloged the hardcover edition as follows:
Disher, Sharon Hanley, 1958–
       First class : women join the ranks at the Naval Academy / Sharon
Hanley Disher.
          p. cm.
       ISBN 1-55750-165-3 (alk. paper)
       1. United States Naval Academy. 2. United States. Navy—Women.
I. Title.

V415.P1D57 1998
359'.0071'173—DC21

                                                              97-51652

Printed in the United States of America on acid-free paper ∞
12 11 10 09 08 07 06 05   9 8 7 6 5 4 3 2
First printing

To Tim, my inspiration . . .
. . . and to the three most patient children in the world,
Alison, Brett, and Matthew
"Believe in yourself"

CONTENTS

PREFACE

"Someday you can write a book," my mother told me weeks before I entered Halsey Field House at the United States Naval Academy on 6 July 1976. She urged me to keep a journal and write in it every day. I knew she was right, but I never made the time. Nevertheless, I made a promise to myself that someday I would write that book.

After graduation, I packed up memorabilia that I hoped would one day help me recollect the events of those four years. As time moved on, I routinely watched the bookstores, confident that some other woman graduate would beat me to the publishing punch. Oddly enough, years passed, and no books from the first women appeared on the shelves.

At Homecoming in 1992 I heard stories of women midshipmen with eating disorders and of continued nonacceptance by their male classmates. How could this be? I wondered. It had been sixteen years since women were admitted to the Naval Academy. How could the same problems we faced still be surfacing at such a highly esteemed institution? Had the harassment we suffered all been for naught? I was disturbed and energized. I hoped that what I was hearing was the same type of rumor that had permeated Bancroft Hall when I was a midshipman. The time had come for our story to be told—a story about the first class of women to graduate from the Naval Academy.

A survey that I sent to all the women in my class questioning the need to write this book evoked an overwhelming "Yes!" Anecdotal stories poured forth from a number of them. Others remained silent. It was not until I approached one of my dearest friends from the Academy that I understood their apprehension.

Reliving those four years was too difficult—almost impossible for some. The scars were too deep, the skeletons too painful to drag out of the closet, even sixteen years later. What could be so bad? I remembered the taunts and the insults. I remembered the defeminizing uniforms and haircuts. But I love the Naval Academy. I always have and always will. It reinforced in me self-confidence, leadership, and assertiveness. What could have happened to these women to silence them?

And then we got together at a reunion in 1993. More told me their stories and gave me permission to include them.

The following story is true. Real names have generally been changed to protect individual privacy, innocence, or guilt. The names of publicly recognizable individuals—such as the Academy superintendent, the Marine Corps commandant, and the chief of naval operations, as well as James Webb and Heinz Lenz—have not been changed; however, Mildred Dietrich is a pseudonym. Reconstructed conversations are based on contemporaneous journals, letters, interviews, and recollections. Some dates are approximations. One of the two main characters is real. The other is a composite based on several female classmates. Everything that happens to her in this book happened to one of the women of '80; minor characters associated with her are based on real individuals. (Originally there was another main character based on an individual who is still on active duty. When I called her to schedule a final interview, she expressed sincere regret that she could no longer be part of the story. She feared that her career in the navy, which is going well, would be jeopardized. And so that character was deleted.) As points of correctness, there were no women from the Class of 1980 in Seventh Company, and there was a female regimental commander for Second Set, plebe-summer detail, 1979, not First Set.

It pains me every time I see a newspaper headline defaming the Naval Academy. It is not my intent to inflict more pain. I write this book to document history. The events depicted in this book took place nearly thirty years ago. If the issues seem too fresh or the events appear too similar to modern-day occurrences, then it is time to stop repeating them.

ACKNOWLEDGMENTS

No author is alone when endeavoring to complete a literary work. I relied on the love, encouragement, and assistance of numerous individuals to help me turn my manuscript into a book. For the part they played in making my dream a reality, I thank the following special people.

For their love, encouragement, and support: Jan and Ed Hanley, Grams and Bump, JJ, Todd, and Chris, Jane and John Disher, and other members of my family—most especially, my wonderful children and husband.

For getting me started: Paula James.

For their stories, patience, and/or best wishes: Kathy Slevin Rondeau, Charlie and Patti Meyers, Peggy Feldmann, Marjorie Morley Bachman, Elizabeth Belzer Rowe, Bill Stulb, Tina D'Ercole Jaskot, Pam Wacek Svendsen, Carol Burbage, Mark Breckenridge, Dave Kish, Doug Heimbach, Mike Hawley, Sarah McGann, Joe Grace, Pat and Mary Ann Lefler, Susan Welch, Jennifer Smith Holzapfel, Sandy and Willie Taylor, Kathy Shanebrook Garcia, Kathy Karlson Ozimek, Nancy Burke Sullenger, Susan Stapler Cabral, Susan Cox Unger, and Jennifer Schulze.

For their friendship and editorial expertise: Mary Collins Dietrich, Billie Spencer, Sarah Johnson, Jean Ebbert, Diane Willard, Cliff Credle, Trisha Resevic, and Mark Gatlin.

For being the best company in the brigade: the Thirty-third Herd.

For never giving up: the women of the Class of 1980. It is my wish that each of you find a bit of yourself in this book, and that you allow the healing process to finally begin.

Women Graduates of the Class of 1980

Linda Bartlo

Elizabeth Belzer

Nancy Burke

Janice Buxbaum

Catherine Carlin

Elizabeth Cox

Sandy Daniels

Carol Desmarais

Tina D'Ercole

Robin Druce

Elizabeth Durham

Peggy Feldmann

Maureen Foley

Barbara Geraghty

Stefanie Goebel

Cynthia Grubbs

Sharon Hanley

Melissa Harrington

Jenefer Hawkins

Kathleen Henderson

Barbette Henry

Sandra Irwin

Jamesina Jimenez

Kathryn Karlson

Susan Keller

Karri Kline

Janet Kotovsky

Beth Leadbetter

Chrystal Lewis

Beth Lindquist

Janie Mines

Marjorie Morley

Barbara Morris

Patricia Murphy

Rebecca Olds

Patricia O'Neill

Susan Presto

Lynn Rampp

Catherine Rayhill

Claire Sebrechts

Kathy Shanebrook

Sharon Sheffield

Kathleen Slevin

Jennifer Smith

Paula Smith

Cheryl Spohnholtz

Susan Stapler

Ann Stencil

Elizabeth Sternaman

Patricia Taylor

Carol Thompson

Patricia Thudium

Pamela Wacek

Kathleen Walsh

Susan Welch

PROLOGUE

To prepare midshipmen morally, mentally and physically
to be professional officers in the Naval Service.

Mission of the United States Naval Academy, 1976

Friday, 20 October 1989

The leafless trees swayed in the unusually warm fall breeze while squirrels raced around the Yard searching for winter stores. Some of the bolder ones begged for their day's meal from the occasional cluster of tourists traversing the Yard or a single midshipman hurrying from class. Others played among the green park benches guarding Stribling Walk. Monuments honoring fallen war heroes stood securely surrounded by cannons recently painted green to protect them from the elements. All four seasons visit the United States Naval Academy—humidity-drenched summers, cool crisp autumns, unpredictably snowy winters, and flower-filled springs—and each marks a major passing in the life of a midshipman.

The slight, sandy-blonde lieutenant purposefully parked her red rental car at the other end of the Yard beside the Naval Academy Officers and Faculty Club. She wanted to walk the long way to Mitscher Hall. The Naval Academy public-works officer had invited Lt. Sarah Becker to speak to the first- and second-class female midshipmen at a service-selection roundup where each navy community would be represented by a female officer wearing navy designators available to the women midshipmen upon graduation. Lieutenant Becker was here to promote the Civil Engineer Corps, in which she had served for the past nine years. The public-works officer had been impressed by a standing ovation given to a female Supply Corps officer of the Class of 1980 at this roundup the year before and insisted on presenting one of his own.

Sarah Becker rounded the corner of Preble Hall and continued past the stately architecture of Mahan Hall, with its infamous bell tower and the auditorium that hosted all Masquerader theatrical productions in years past. Now,

1

behind it, a larger and more contemporary amphitheater was under construction, budding from the foundation seeds of Isherwood, Griffin, and Melville Halls. The physical appearance of the Yard had certainly begun to change, Sarah thought. Crossing the street, she stepped onto the beige bricks of Stribling Walk where Bancroft Hall came into full view. "Mother B," they called it, even though it was named for a man: Secretary of the Navy George Bancroft, who founded the Naval Academy in 1845. Bancroft Hall, built in 1901, had been Sarah's home for the four years she lived here, and it still served as home to all midshipmen who attended this military institution. Looking up at the colossal stone structure, she recalled the innumerable times she had traversed its passageways and immense yellow-bricked courtyard, Tecumseh Court. She had not done so in over nine years. Funny, she thought, gazing to her right at the enormous anchors flanking the embellished bronze doors to the Cathedral of the Navy; you never appreciate the beauty of this place until you've been away from it for a while.

But the beauty around her could not dispel the anxiety she felt. Initially Sarah had shrugged it off as nerves brought on by this opportunity to talk to young women for whom she had prepared the way. Yet, slowly strolling up Stribling Walk, she knew better. This place evoked a nagging quandary within her. It always had. Despite her overall positive experience at the Naval Academy, the question of her acceptance as one of its first women, one of its pioneers, dragged her down. It was something she would admit to no one, not even herself. She should not feel this way.

She was the officer in charge of Construction Battalion Unit 414 at the Naval Submarine Base in New London, Connecticut, which under her leadership had been chosen "Best in the Atlantic Fleet." She attributed her qualities as a dedicated and fair leader to her Naval Academy experience. This institution had nurtured her self-confidence, graduating her into a world that consistently questioned the presence of women leaders in its military. She hoped that her squared-away, competent demeanor, combined with a pleasing personality, had changed many men's views of the military woman. So why did this setting make her question herself? What was it about this environment that now unleashed self-doubts?

Looking down at the two half-inch gold lieutenant stripes adorning the sleeves of the same service dress blue uniform that had been tailored for her during plebe summer of 1976, Sarah shook her head. She remembered a day when those sleeves were empty.

"Good afternoon, ma'am."

The deep voice startled her. She glanced up to the salute of a young face that seemed barely old enough to shave. The third classman, obviously in a hurry, held his salute at his brow, as required, waiting for its return by the senior officer before he dropped his arm. Sarah snappily returned the salute and responded with a smile. "Good afternoon. How're you doing?"

"Fine, thank you, ma'am," he answered with an uncomfortable smile that seemed to ask, Is it okay for me to smile at you? She remembered how officers had evoked fear in midshipmen. It appeared that they still did, even if the officer was a woman. Maybe it was a good sign. Sarah suddenly recalled Lt. Marie Lennox, the sole woman officer thrust among the Brigade of Midshipmen as adviser to the administration when the women were admitted: "Mean Marie," the "Bitch of Bancroft." How lonely she must have been— hated yet distinctly feared by both male and female midshipmen, and denigrated by male fellow officers who denounced her credibility because of her lack of a warfare specialty. And we thought *we* were lonely, thought Sarah.

"By your leave, ma'am." Behind her a voice of higher pitch interrupted her thoughts this time.

"Carry on," replied Lieutenant Becker, returning the salute of a second-class female midshipman hurrying past her at a steady pace.

"Good afternoon, ma'am," the second class continued, respectfully.

"Good afternoon," replied Lieutenant Becker professionally, suddenly yearning to reach out and stop the young woman, to turn her around and ask her face to face, without any mental reservation, how things were going. How was life here for her as a woman? Had her way been paved smooth, or were the roads still rocky? Things had to be different now. It had been thirteen years since women had been admitted to this fraternity. Things had to have changed.

Wednesday, 16 June 1976

"Kate Ann Brigman," the principal announced.

The clamor was spontaneous as Kate stood and walked to the stage to receive her high school diploma. "Kate Brigman is one of the first women recipients of a full scholarship to the United States Naval Academy in Annapolis, Maryland," he continued. "We're very proud of her."

Everyone was standing now, including the Class of 1976, cheering and applauding one of their own: student body vice-president, varsity cheerleader, and yearbook editor. "Best all-around," the yearbook had labeled her. Kate held her head a bit higher and paused to look at them. *I've earned their admiration,* she realized, tears welling in her eyes. *I hope I can continue to earn it.*

The applause diminished as she returned to her seat, holding her diploma high, shooting a thumbs-up to her family in the standing-room-only crowd. Taking her seat, she noticed that there were no reporters in sight. That was fine. The newspaper stories and television interviews had been exhilarating, but they were prompted more by the novelty of her achievement than by the achievement itself. *I worked so hard to get the ROTC scholarships and appointments to the Coast Guard Academy and Annapolis,* she thought, *but I got all that attention because I'm a girl.*

Her doubts and fears came rushing back. *But I'm from a small farming community. Can I really compete with the "best and the brightest"?*

Her visits to the Naval Academy growing up had awed and humbled her. She had read about the athletic and academic requirements. Math and science had always been her strong suits, but had the courses she'd taken been equal to those of students from bigger high schools in other parts of the country? Athletically, she feared she couldn't come close to the men there, despite running a mile a day since she'd been accepted. *What had she gotten herself into? Was she really ready to meet this challenge?*

As she reached the top of the stairs, Sarah Becker saw her mother leaving the bedroom looking at something in her hand. *She looks worried,* Sarah thought. "Is something wrong, Mom?"

Startled, Jan Becker turned quickly. "Oh, Sarah. I was looking for you." She hesitated, then held out a small box. "I want you to have this. Your father bought it for me when he was deployed to the Far East, and. . . ."

Her voice trailed off as Sarah opened the box. Inside was a pearl ring. Sarah looked up and saw tears forming in her mother's eyes. "Oh, Mom, it's beautiful."

Mrs. Becker looked at her daughter, only seventeen, petite, bright, full of fun. *She's been a cheerleader, student council president, a gymnast, and a top student too,* thought Jan. *She doesn't even realize what a sacrifice she is making to enter the military—even if it is the Academy. And I don't know how to tell her.*

She reached out and ran her fingers through Sarah's hair. "You had to cut off almost all your hair. It's so short now."

"I know," Sarah answered. "Remember when I found out I'd have to cut it and said, 'That's it. I'm not going?'" She laughed and shook her head.

"It's cute, honey," replied Mrs. Becker, her doubts increasing to panic proportion. I'm sending my first-born girl to one of the largest fraternities in the nation, she thought. How will she ever survive alone?

She tried to blink back the tears, but it was impossible to contain her anxiety about the impending departure any longer. "Sarah, I don't want you to leave." It was a lament, not a request, for she knew Sarah's resolve. She pulled her daughter close and hugged her tightly, not wanting to let go.

"I love you, Mom," Sarah whispered, clinging just as strongly, adding to herself, I'm not sure I want to leave, either.

Yet deep down she knew she was doing the right thing.

Sarah had always wanted to join the military after graduating from college. The equal pay for women and the travel attracted her, and her dream was to become a pilot, like her father. She refused to believe the ophthalmologist's diagnosis that the only thing her lack of depth perception would restrict her from would be flying. Ingrained in her nature was the desire to pursue anything placed off-limits.

Mrs. Becker let go first. "We'd better get ready," she said, stroking Sarah's hair once more.

"For what, Mom?"

"Your father's taking us out to dinner tonight at the yacht club." She smiled and wiped her eyes. "Go on. I'll be fine."

Sarah was not prepared for the crowd that greeted her at the yacht club that evening. Friends, family, fellow class officers, and band members succeeded in surprising her with a cake that read "Move over Fellas, Here I Come" and camouflage bikini underwear labeled "MILITARY PROPERTY." After a last toast to Sarah, her friends ceremoniously picked her up, carried her out to the pier, and despite her protests dropped her into the chilly Piscataqua River for her first wetting down.

Monday, 5 July 1976

It seemed to Kate a thing of great beauty, just across the Severn River, resplendent in the afternoon sun. Sparkling blue water and lush green fields surrounded the massive contemporary buildings of beige stone and smoky brown glass thrust amid older buildings of gray-white stone and sea-green roofs. The tremendous copper dome of the chapel, green with the patina of years of service, rose higher than all as if symbolizing the supremacy of faith, honor, and respect. Kate did not yet know the names of all the buildings, but together they formed an architectural monument called the United States Naval Academy.

She stood with her family at the scenic overlook on Ritchie Highway, pausing on this final leg of their drive from Virginia. Tomorrow, 6 July 1976, Kate Brigman would be embarking on her future as one of the first women in history admitted to the United States Naval Academy. She had worked toward this goal long before President Ford signed the bill that opened the military academies to women. She had earned a 4.0 grade-point average and had received nominations for appointment from her congressman, her senator, and the vice-president. She had trained herself physically, but the emotional preparation had been the most difficult.

Kate's friends and family had been supportive, although apprehensive about her decision. Others around her held widely differing opinions. Her jaw tightened as she recalled the taunts of "lesbian" flung at her by some students at her school. Some claimed she was trying to catch a husband: so many men, so few women. Her mother had even been rebuked by another woman who said, "I'd never let a daughter of mine go near a place like that. She'll be pregnant in less than a month!"

How could they be so narrow-minded, Kate wondered. How hard is it to believe that I want to serve my country, too? I don't want to prove anything for all women. I just want to be the best officer I can. I can't let their prejudice get me down. Midshipmen are officers and gentlemen. They'll see I can do it, intellectually and even physically, and they'll accept me.

This was indeed a glorious moment, but Kate knew that the real triumph lay nearly four years in the future.

She studied the buildings a moment longer. They looked so immaculate, so pure—wholly dedicated to the moral, mental, and physical preparation of professional officers for the navy. They promised enlightenment, challenge, and hard work. The satisfaction of giving her utmost in the service of her country would be the highest reward. Churchill's words flashed through her mind: "I have nothing to offer but blood, toil, tears, and sweat. . . ."

No, she corrected herself. No tears.

FOURTH-CLASS YEAR
1976–1977

One of our most successful midshipmen, who could have gone to nearly any school in the country, told us that he chose the Naval Academy because it "offered the most options." He . . . realized that he could major in a subject which interested him, play any one of 21 varsity sports against the best teams in the country, and graduate as a trained leader with a commission in either the Navy or the Marine Corps. He could then serve in the air, on the sea, on the ground or under the sea. He could become a skilled naval officer or marine and at the same time prepare himself, through further education and training, for a second profession for service assignments ashore. The Naval Academy meant maximum choice as he went along with new and exciting options opening before him all the way.

This opportunity can be yours if you have had a good secondary school education, have done well in the opportunities open to you both in and out of school, are physically active and seek challenge. If you are a woman, you are not permitted by present law to serve in Navy ships other than hospital ships and transports or in aircraft on combat missions, but the other options open to men are yours as well.

Leadership, scholarship, fellowship; this is the Naval Academy. Is it for you?

United States Naval Academy Catalog, 1976–77

CHAPTER ONE

Induction Day

The first day of plebe summer is a day that most midshipmen will remember for many years. This is scarcely surprising, for in one short day, civilians become midshipmen. They are given haircuts, issued uniforms, taught the basics of marching, and served their first meal in the vast Midshipmen's Wardroom in Bancroft Hall. Their military indoctrination gets off to a fast start, but they are too busy to have time to worry about it. Civilian ways and days soon seem far behind.

United States Naval Academy Catalog, 1976–77

Tuesday, 6 July 1976

The heat of the day grew steadily to match the fever of Induction Day excitement. According to the well-ordered plans of the Naval Academy, the appointees arrived on a rolling schedule throughout the morning. In front of Halsey Field House, Public Affairs Office representatives escorted reporters as they darted from group to group seeking interviews. Cameramen crouched or climbed to get the best angles while film crews dragged cables in a frenzy to document the end of 131 years of tradition. One thousand two hundred ninety-one plebes reported for duty as usual, but for the first time in history, eighty-one of them were female.

Sarah nervously shifted from one foot to the other, clutching an empty overnight bag to be used later for shipping home the sleeveless brown print dress and suede sandals she was wearing. She only half-heard her parents tell her again how proud they were. Her sister reminded her to write, but she kept watching the other plebes as they disappeared into the cavernous field house.

"Scared?" asked Donnie Phillips, her boyfriend of the past two years, as he squeezed her hand warmly.

"Nervous," she replied, smiling up at him. Donnie had driven down with Sarah and her family, holding her tightly for the first two hours of the trip as she sobbed. Her weeping had been sparked by the farewell to her grandparents; the anxiety of leaving behind her childhood and trepidation about what lay ahead sustained the rest of her tears.

Sarah looked up at her dad and smiled. This is what I want, she thought: a career in the military. I want to be a pilot just like Dad. She shifted her gaze to her mother, and the smile evaporated. I just don't want to say goodbye, she silently admitted. All the months of dreams and dread culminated in this one moment.

"I'd better go in," she said to her parents. "Next time I see you, Dad, I guess I'll have to salute."

"I'll salute you, honey," he replied, pride evident in his voice.

She kissed them all goodbye and walked quickly into the field house.

Kate's first impression of the field house was not pleasant: glaring lights, incessant noise, and obnoxious odors. But finally being here was even more exciting than the Bicentennial fireworks displays that had fueled her patriotism just two nights ago. She got in line at the table marked A–F. Smiling with anticipation, she looked across the table to where first-class midshipmen in short-sleeve white uniforms with red nametags were showing other plebes how to line up properly, stand at attention, and salute. Most of the plebes were dressed in civilian clothes as she was, but a few were in navy or Marine Corps uniforms. America's finest, she thought with pride, and I'm going to be one of them.

"Name?" Behind the table sat a midshipman whose tone was gruff.

Kate smiled at him, politely. "I'm Kate Brigman, from Virginia."

He wasn't impressed. He looked through a stack of computer cards, pulled one out, and handed it to her along with three black and yellow nametags imprinted "Brigman '80." Pointing to the row of numbers on the computer card he told her, "That's your alpha code, company, platoon, and squad. Memorize them! Delta Company is over there. Look for the guidon, uh, flag, with the *D* on it." He gestured toward the end of the field house.

"Next."

. . .

As Sarah wandered through the crowd looking for her company's guidon, she heard someone behind her calling her name. Surprised, she turned and saw a reporter watching her, then realized that Gail Tome, an appointee from Maine whom she had met several months earlier, was standing ten feet away, waving. "Gail, what company are you in?" she called.

"Kilo," answered Gail. "How 'bout you?"

Sarah smiled flirtatiously. "Romeo."

Gail laughed and yelled, "Look out, Romeo, here comes Juliet!"

Sarah shook her head and grinned, then turned and spotted a flag with an *R* on it. She walked toward it, excitement mixed with apprehension. Beside the guidon two upperclass midshipmen appeared to be the official "welcoming committee." The short, stocky redhead spoke first.

"Have a seat." His rosy face beamed at Sarah and another plebe as they sat down beside one another in the middle of a row of chairs.

"You guys want to take it easy while you can. This day is going to get long, hot, and bothersome. In fact that's how the next four years of your life will be if you stick around this place." He was warming up to his audience. "They call me 'Cheese,' but you guys have to call me Mr. Randolph," he said pointing to his nametag, "for the next year, anyway." He shook his finger playfully at them for emphasis. "And don't ask me why they call me 'Cheese.'"

Sarah found his rambling refreshing, unlike the stifling regimentation she had felt when she passed the other first-class midshipmen on her way to Romeo Company. When he paused to greet another plebe, Sarah turned toward the guy beside her. Tall, black, and muscular, he stuck out his hand. "Denzel Simmons," he said in a deep voice.

"Sarah Becker," she replied, firmly returning the handshake. Denzel was a football recruit from Oakton, New York, and the two discovered they were both in the first squad of Thirty-third Platoon.

As other plebes sat down, Mr. Randolph resumed his monologue. "There'll be twelve of you plebes in each squad. Three squads make up a platoon, and two platoons form a company. Romeo Company will exist only during plebe summer. When the brigade returns in the fall, Thirty-third Platoon will become part of Thirty-third Company, and Thirty-fourth Platoon, the other half of Romeo Company, will become part of Thirty-fourth Company. You'll all be reassigned to different platoons and squads then."

Sarah and Denzel looked at one another with confusion and shrugged. "We'll figure this all out sooner or later," said Sarah.

"I don't know, man. All this stuff makes me a little nervous," Denzel con-fided in a husky tone.

Another young woman approached the company and sat down in the row behind Denzel and Sarah. Short, with brown hair and freckles, she seemed nervous and shy. Sarah turned around and introduced herself.

"I'm Tammy Leland from El Paso, Texas," the other woman said with a Southern drawl. "I'm really nervous."

"You aren't alone," Sarah admitted. "The guy with the red hair over there seems pretty nice so far. But I haven't figured out the other ones yet. They've been pretty quiet."

A third young woman approached.

"Hi, I'm Donna Carter." Tall and heavy-set, with deep blue eyes, she smiled at them as she sat beside Tammy. The three women compared computer cards and discovered that they were all in the same squad. Donna announced that she was from Tennessee and had been a junior at Memphis State.

"Really?!" Sarah was amazed. "Then what are you doing here?"

"Looking for a challenge," Donna answered with confidence. "Something new and different. They weren't accepting women when I started college. So when I heard they had changed the law, I knew it was my chance, since I'm twenty-one, still a year under the age limit. Besides," she added, "my dad's a retired navy captain, and I've always liked the military life."

"Me, too," agreed Tammy. "And my dad's in the air force."

Sarah smiled. "Then that makes two things we all have in common. We're all military brats, and I don't think any of us are sure what we've gotten our-selves into."

Kate reported to Seventh Platoon, Delta Company, and thankfully set down her cumbersome suitcase. No civilian clothes were allowed for fourth-class midshipmen, but the Academy had informed her that some personal items could be brought, noting that only hand-held hair dryers were allowed and undergarments had to be 100 percent cotton because of the laundry system. Kate and her mother had dutifully packed their interpretation of "personal items": white cotton bras, white cotton underwear, socks, slips, pantyhose, pajamas, comb, hairbrush, blow dryer, toothbrush, toothpaste, toiletries, makeup, feminine hygiene products, alarm clock, camera, stationery, address book, and pens. Just to be on the safe side, they had included a manicure set, slippers, and a bathrobe.

Kate introduced herself to the dark-haired girl already there and to the next girl who arrived, taking it for granted that they would be her roommates. Terrie Micheals was also from Virginia, and Michelle Mead was from Oregon. Terrie started to ask Kate where she was from in Virginia, but the midshipman in charge of them cut her off and began speaking to the whole group.

"All right, now, listen up," he said gruffly. "I'm your squad leader, Midshipman Ensign Daniel. You will address me and all other first classmen as sir or mister. Now, line up shoulder to shoulder in front of the bleachers!"

The thirteen squad mates did as ordered while Mr. Daniel showed them the correct way to salute and execute the facing movements that would become part of their everyday language. "Abooout face!" "Paraaaade rest!" he snapped.

The squad pivoted on their left heels to face 180 degrees from their previous direction, then stood with their hands flat behind their backs with feet shoulder-width apart. Kate found it harder than it looked. She kept trying to turn on her right heel.

"What's the problem down there?" barked her squad leader, walking toward her end of the squad. "This is pretty basic stuff, you guys."

"Okay, Miss Brigman," he said, glancing at her nametag. "Abooout face!"

Kate bit her lip and concentrated while awkwardly placing her right toe behind her left heel, spinning around with a prayer that she wouldn't land on her face. She wanted to do so well, and here she was already being singled out. "Not too bad," her squad leader commented as she finished the facing movement with a slight bobble. "We'll work on it."

Kate smiled as if to say thank you. "Wipe that smile off, miss!" he growled. "You think this is a party?" She swallowed her smile with a hard gulp. *I was just trying to be polite,* she thought, *but now I'm messing up again.*

"Got it!" she heard someone call as she turned to face the same direction as the rest of her squad. *Oh, no,* she lamented, coming face to face with a television camera. *Please don't tell me they got that episode on film!*

Next, Mr. Daniel led them to one of the side rooms in the field house, where the new plebes were handed two large white laundry bags at the first table in a line of many. Proceeding from one table to another, they filled their bags with white uniform shirts and trousers, white Keds sneakers, hats, T-shirts, black rayon neckerchiefs, smaller laundry bags, and other items. At each position a staff member asked for the plebe's size or gave a hurried fitting if necessary.

When they arrived at the underwear tables, Kate and her roommates bypassed the men's shorts and headed for the women's "lingerie" table.

"Bra size?" the attendant inquired nonchalantly. Kate was completely embarrassed.

"Excuse me?" she asked.

"What's your bra size, honey?" the woman repeated.

"Ah. . . ." Kate leaned over and whispered.

"How's that?" the woman asked again, impatiently.

Kate wanted to die. "It's 34A," she answered, louder this time, through clenched teeth, feeling her face burn with humiliation. *Must they ask us in front of the guys? Why did they tell me to bring my own if they planned to give these to me anyway? How do I know they will fit without trying them on?*

She shoved the boxed bras into her laundry bag.

At the table of women's underpants, she quietly and hurriedly informed the attendant of her size and held out her bag for the attendant to toss them in. She glanced at them just long enough to identify them as plain white cotton briefs. *We'll be in uniform down to the skin,* she thought.

The first-class midshipman directed the first squad of Thirty-third Platoon out the side door of the field house. Having changed into the just-issued socks, sneakers, blue-collared T-shirt with nametag, and blue-rimmed white hat called a "dixie cup," Sarah followed Tammy with her laundry bag slung over her left shoulder and her overnight bag in her right hand. She heard her mother's voice off to her left and looked up to see her entire family behind a roped-off area in the parking lot, yelling and waving to get her attention. Her dad was aiming his camera, and although slightly embarrassed at their commotion, she was warmed by the sight of them.

The squad walked single file toward Bancroft Hall, where Midshipman First Class Lincoln told them to leave their bags on the pavement. He led them up a ramp outside Bancroft Medical Clinic and ordered them to stand fast while he disappeared for a moment into Medical. While he was gone, one of her squad mates kept edging closer to Sarah, forcing her to move closer to Tammy. She tried smiling politely. He smiled back and moved nearer still. She glared at him and backed away. He frowned and took another step toward her. Finally she spoke. "Hi, I'm Sarah Becker."

"Hello. Tom Summers."

"Hi, Tom. Listen, is there some reason you keep trying to stand so close to me?"

He frowned as if she should know. "For the press."

Sarah didn't understand. "But the press wants to talk to the women."

"I know." He lowered his voice. "If I stick next to you, chances are I'll get my picture in the paper, too."

Sarah smiled ruefully. "Sorry, I'm not planning on being in any papers."

The first classman walked out of Medical and ordered the squad inside, guiding them to an area where other plebes were already being weighed. A first-class midshipman operating the scales looked unamused as he interrogated each new plebe. When it was her turn, Sarah stepped onto the scales.

"How much do you weigh?" the firstie bellowed.

"One hundred and eighteen," Sarah replied.

"One hundred and eighteen, what?" he snapped loudly.

"One hundred and eighteen pounds," Sarah corrected herself. She turned and grinned at Tammy.

The midshipman leaned into her face and yelled, "One hundred and eighteen pounds, WHAT?"

Sarah's eyes grew wide. "I don't know what you want me to say," she stammered.

The midshipman looked at her with contempt. "SIR!" he shouted. "One hundred and eighteen pounds, SIR!!"

"One hundred and eighteen pounds, SIR!!" she yelled back.

"All upperclassmen are *sir* to you, plebe! Don't you forget it!"

Don't worry, she thought, shaken. Especially when I see you coming.

Inside a cubicle in Bancroft Medical, a nurse with gold officer's stripes on her cap lectured Kate briefly as part of the routine I-Day introduction to the medical facility. "If you are on any medication now, or if you regularly use any kind of medication, you must turn it over to the clinic. If you are on birth control, you can set up an appointment to discuss it with a doctor." She paused, questioning Kate with her eyes.

Birth control? What kind of girls do they think we are? thought Kate. She shook her head emphatically.

Satisfied, the nurse continued sternly. "While you are here, if you ever have any medical or physical problems or illness you are to report to Sick Bay. Don't treat yourself with over-the-counter medication. Is that clear?"

Kate nodded and turned to leave, then remembered her period due to begin any day. "What about Midol?" she asked.

"Not even Midol. If you have any problems, come see us."

Kate left the cubicle and rejoined her squad as they waited for others to complete the I-Day medical routine. When they had all received their shots, another firstie marched them toward their new "home." He pointed out the different wings of Bancroft Hall as he led them to their summer company area on what he called deck 5-1.

Kate felt the sweat trickling down her right arm, collecting in her palm around the already slippery handle of her suitcase. I should have known better than to bring this clumsy old thing, she thought. Even empty it weighs a ton, and it's stuffed full.

Everyone marching beside her was carrying a small overnight bag. She tried to keep her steps even and in rhythm. The handle's too big. Why didn't I bring my new bag?

She tried to tighten her grasp on the suitcase, but her fingers couldn't close around the handle. She shifted her laundry bag slightly and lost both her concentration and her grasp on the suitcase.

It hit the pavement with a deep thud that surprised everyone, interrupting the rhythm of their steps. What a jerk! Kate wiped her hand quickly on her T-shirt and grabbed the slick handle again as the platoon resumed marching. They're going to think I'm a weakling, she scolded herself. Just hold on. It can't be much farther.

Her face grew red from determination as they marched, but she felt the handle sliding out again, her fingers uncurling despite every mental effort to the contrary. No, she commanded, not again!

She tried to jerk the suitcase up, but the sudden move unbalanced her and sent the suitcase flying. It narrowly missed the person in front of her and skidded to a stop a few feet ahead as the squad halted again. Take me now, Lord, Kate prayed. "Aw, for Pete's sake!" someone groaned in the back of the squad. Several shook their heads in disbelief.

The first classman turned on them instantly. "Listen up, people!" he yelled. "This is a classmate! You don't bilge your classmates, you help them—whoever they are!"

The inductees were shocked into silence. There was no mistaking the disapproval in his voice. Even if they didn't know what bilge meant, they knew they were guilty of something.

"Now, somebody help your classmate. Forward march!"

Kate grabbed for her suitcase just as the guy ahead of her picked it up with a huff of disgust. She tried to take it from him, but he wouldn't release it. There was no choice but to surrender it and keep marching.

. . .

Sarah, Tammy, and Donna followed their first classman down the passageway on 3-1. "Becker, Leland, Carter, over there," he said, pointing to their room. "Fall out."

Their room was across the hall from the women's "head," which they figured meant restroom. On their door were three white placards with their names engraved in black letters followed by "80," their class year. Sarah glanced across the hall at the door of one of her male classmates and noticed that all the men's names were white letters engraved on black placards. Makes the girls' rooms easily identifiable, she thought. Wonder why?

The girls went inside and dropped their bags of gear onto the beds.

"I'll take a lower bunk," said Donna.

"Okay, I'll take the top," said Tammy.

Sarah flung her white laundry bag on the remaining single bed and looked around.

All three racks, as they were called in navy lingo, were covered with well-worn six-inch mattresses. Beige walls matched the faded linoleum floor. Two sets of floor-to-ceiling pine cabinets bordered the foot of the beds. Each had three doors, only one of which could be locked. In the corner stood a gray marble walk-in shower with a single sink beside it. Over the sink was a built-in mirror and a metal medicine cabinet sunk into the shower side of the wall. Sarah wondered how the three of them were supposed to share that small space.

Across the doorway from the sink opened a small walk-in closet sporting a clothes rack, gun rack, and floor-to-ceiling shoe rack. Sarah decided that the room had originally been intended for two midshipmen and had been poorly retrofitted to hold three.

"Well, girls, looks like this is home for a while," Tammy remarked. "Not exactly paradise, but it's not so bad, huh?"

"I don't know," said Donna, looking in the full-length mirror at her shorn locks, compliments of the men's barbershop earlier that day. "Somehow, I think I'd rather be home."

By late afternoon the plebes-to-be had eaten their first meal in the midshipmen's dining hall: submarine sandwiches, potato chips, sodas, and ice cream. All twelve hundred had been served family-style in a matter of minutes, but Kate was too nervous to eat. What was coming next? So far the upperclassmen had been fairly easygoing. However, the first classman at the head of her table warned them of things to come.

"Enjoy this while you can, people. This will be the last meal you eat in peace, and the last time you can walk around skylarking." Their blank looks led him to explain. "Looking around, stargazing, checking out the scenery. After the swearing-in ceremony this afternoon, you'll be required to keep your eyes 'in the boat'—straight ahead, no looking around. Eventually you'll have the best peripheral vision ever. No talking in the halls, either. You may only talk in your rooms.

"And no more walking," he continued sternly. "You're going to 'chop' wherever you go. That means run in the center of the hall and outboard of all ladders—what civilians call stairs. Whenever you turn a corner you will 'square it' with a facing movement and 'sound off.' That means yell something spirited like 'Go Navy!' or 'Beat Army!' Starting tonight at evening meal, you will be required to make sure that all food is passed immediately to the first classmen at the table so that they can draw their food first. Keep their plates full, and you can hope their mouths will be full, too. Then they may not ask you as many rates."

What are rates? Kate wondered.

The first classman paused briefly for a bite of his sandwich. "Another thing. You will sit at attention during all meals. You will not use the back of your seat at any time, and you will keep your eyes in the boat except when you're passing food. Make sure when you take your portion you don't bilge your classmate that hasn't taken his yet. Or hers. Leave enough so everybody gets some." He took another bite. "Any questions?"

Kate's stomach churned as she picked at her sandwich. How am I going to remember all this? There's so much to know. I wouldn't dare ask a question. I wish I could eat, but I know I'll be sick if I do.

The first classman finished his sandwich and saw that the plebes were finished eating. "Let's go! Time to learn how to wear your uniform."

He led the twelve of them back to their company area on 5-1 and brought them to a halt in the passageway.

"First thing you need to do is find your *Reef Points*. It's the plebe's bible, and you'd better start learning it. You'll also find a thick blue binder somewhere on your desks. This is the *MHP*, or *Midshipman Held Publications*. It outlines all midshipman regulations and ways to properly wear and stow your uniforms. Look up uniforms and find out how to wear white works 'charlie.' Get dressed as it says, and I'll be around to each room to make sure you're doing it correctly. While you're at it, start stowing your gear. Fall out!"

The twelve plebes scattered. Inside their rooms, Michelle began paging through the *MHP*, looking for the uniforms section, while Kate emptied the contents of her laundry bag onto her bed. Shoe polish, Brasso, cleaning rags, a can of Pledge, a whisk broom, scrub brushes, belt buckles, and a book of navy songs tumbled out in a heap with the uniforms and shoes issued that morning. On the top of the pile was a small plastic-covered book entitled *Reef Points 1976–77*.

She picked it up and studied its cover: three rows of male midshipmen in white uniforms stood at parade rest, white spats over their shoes and trouser legs, each one gripping a rifle with bayonet in his right hand. The plebe's bible, she mused, opening the book to the first few pages with pictures of the Academy. The title page declared it to be the annual handbook of the Brigade of Midshipmen, and a few pages later she found the mission of the Naval Academy: "To prepare midshipmen morally, mentally and physically to be professional officers in the Naval Service." She flipped past the messages from the superintendent and the commandant of midshipmen but paused at the page containing the Prayer of a Midshipman:

> Almighty Father, whose way is in the sea, whose paths are in the great waters, whose command is over all, and whose love never fails. Let me be aware of Your presence and obedient to Your will. Keep me true to my best self, guarding me against dishonesty in purpose and in deed, and helping me so to live that I can stand unashamed and unafraid before my shipmates, my loved ones, and You. Protect those in whose love I live. Give me the will to do my very best and to accept my share of responsibilities with a strong heart and a cheerful mind. Make me considerate of those entrusted to my leadership and faithful to the duties my country has entrusted to me. Let my uniform remind me daily of the traditions of the service of which I am a part. If I am inclined to doubt, steady my faith; if I am tempted, make me strong to resist; if I should miss the mark, give me the courage to try again. Guide me with the light of truth and keep before me the life of Him by whose example and help I trust to obtain the answer to my prayer, Jesus Christ our Lord, Amen.

The words leaped out at her again: "Make me considerate of those entrusted to my leadership and faithful to the duties my country has entrusted to me." This is about much more than simply joining the navy to see the world, she thought. This is about leadership and duty to my country.

For the briefest moment she panicked. I don't know if I am ready to lead anyone.

. . .

Further down on 3-1, the women of Romeo Company were doing their best to cope with the men's-size white works: a heavy, plain white version of the classic "Cracker Jack" uniform. The drawstring-waist trousers were shapeless and sized for men's waists and inseams. The girls remedied the problem by shortening their trousers with a stapler. They did the same to the sleeves of their white works "blouses" but discovered that the bottom hem, cut straight for men, would not slide down over their hips.

Sarah gave up trying to ease her blouse down over her hips and, like Tammy and Donna, folded the extra length of fabric underneath. They were at least presentable. These minor imperfections would hardly be noticeable among the sea of plebes at the Induction Ceremony.

"Ladies!" The girls recognized the sonorous voice of their squad leader. Sarah spun around as he walked into the room. Her roommates stopped in their tracks, unsure of what to expect.

"How are you coming?" Mr. Wyman asked.

"Uh, fine, sir," Tammy answered softly. "Except for these shirts, which don't fit very well."

"Those are called blouses, Miss Leland. We'll get you down to the tailor shop as soon as we find time. Uh, ladies, I need to instruct you on a few, well, uh, women's regulations."

Sarah was puzzled. She glanced at her roommates, but they were staring at their squad leader.

Mr. Wyman held out his left hand and pointed to it as he spoke. "Okay, now, the regulations do not allow your fingernails to extend beyond the tips of your fingers, and you are not allowed to wear fingernail polish at any time." He jerked his hands down. "Now, what is that stuff that you put on your eyes?"

"Mascara? Uh, eye shadow, sir?" Donna was trying not to smile. Was this for real? No one in the room was wearing makeup or nail polish. Why was he talking to them?

"Yes, eye shadow, that's it. No bright eye shadow is allowed, and no bright stuff on your cheeks." He cleared his throat and shifted uncomfortably. "Now, let's see. Hand me one of those." He pointed to a boxed bra. Sarah obeyed, trying not to catch his eye.

"All your clothing must be stenciled with your alpha code for the laundry. The alpha code goes in a specific place on each article. Also, each article of clothing is folded in a particular way." He gingerly pulled the bra out of the box. A pink flush rose to his cheeks as he held the brassiere between his thumb and forefinger as if it were contaminated. *He looks so wholesome,* Sarah thought, wondering if he had ever handled one before.

Mr. Wyman cleared his throat again and went on in a slightly strained voice. "Your alpha code goes across the strap on the back. And you fold it like, well, uh . . . uh. . . ."

He stopped short, dropped the brassiere onto the desktop in the middle of the room, and pulled a white sheet of paper from his pocket. "Look. Just read this and follow its instructions," he sputtered, handing the sheet of paper to Donna. Beet red, he wheeled around and left the room in haste.

The three girls grabbed the paper and burst out laughing as they read the title: "Addendum to *MHP:* Proper Marking and Stowing of Women Midshipman Underwear."

Bancroft Hall was not merely a backdrop for the ceremony. She was a participant, representing the glorious traditions of the United States Naval Academy. The stone crest above the massive bronze doors proclaimed the Academy motto, *Ex Scientia Tridens:* From Knowledge, Seapower. Flanking the doors, pale gray granite columns gleamed in the afternoon sun, and antique cannon stood guard beside the stone steps. The broad, curving ramps embraced the proceedings as if "Mother B" were beckoning her newest children to enter.

Over two hundred white-uniformed first-class midshipmen assigned to the First Set of plebe detail stood at parade rest on these sweeping ramps, while the superintendent and the commandant of midshipmen seated themselves in front of Bancroft Hall. The inductees took their position in rows of chairs arranged in Tecumseh Court. Throngs of family and friends were seated behind them.

The ceremony was identical to those in the past. Even the participants appeared the same, dressed in their baggy white works, white tennis shoes, and white sailor hats with distinctive blue rim. Only slightly longer hair peeking out from beneath some of those caps revealed that a 131-year tradition had ended.

The command chaplain asked God to bless the Class of 1980, and to bless the members of the Class of 1977 who would be their leaders as members of the plebe-summer detail. Then he asked God to give the parents of the new plebes the strength to let go, to let their sons and daughters give themselves wholeheartedly to the task that lay ahead. When he finished, the superintendent rose to make a few remarks. Sarah listened intently and obeyed him when he said, "Look to your right. Now, look to your left." She was eye to eye with a male classmate when the superintendent's next words caught her by surprise.

"One of those persons will not be with you four years from now when you graduate and receive commissions in the navy or the Marine Corps," he said solemnly.

Sarah stared at the guy with determination. I'll be here, she promised herself.

The superintendent ordered the inductees to stand as he administered the Oath of Office. "I . . . state your name . . ."

The candidates responded.

". . . having been appointed a Midshipman in the United States Navy . . ."

". . . do solemnly swear or affirm . . ."

On my honor, Kate added.

". . . that I will support and defend the Constitution of the United States against all enemies, foreign and domestic . . ."

". . . that I will bear true faith and allegiance to the same . . ."

My country, the United States of America, thought Sarah. Tears began to form in the corners of her eyes.

". . . that I will obey the orders of the officers appointed over me . . ."

So that I can be just like them, one of them, pledged Kate.

". . . that I take this obligation freely, without any mental reservation or purpose of evasion . . ."

". . . and that I will well and faithfully discharge the duties of the office on which I am about to enter; so help me God."

As they dropped their right hands, Kate mentally added, I will do my best no matter what the hardships, I will never complain, and I will work harder than my male classmates to show them that I can do this.

True to her word, Sarah gave her father a smart salute when she found him and the rest of her family. Her arms throbbed from the vaccinations, and she discovered that there were tears trickling down her face when she tried to say goodbye. She turned to her dad and hugged him tightly.

"Just remember, 'I can!'" he reminded her. "You can do it! I love you, honey." She nodded and turned to her mother.

Jan wanted to be sure Sarah knew how she felt. "I'm very proud of you," she began. "I love you, and you can come home anytime you want. Call collect, and we'll come get you. I'll be there if you call, anytime. I'm not leaving home."

They hugged each other tightly. Jan stroked Sarah's short hair for a moment. Sarah pulled away reluctantly, unable to speak for fear of breaking down. She wiped her face, turned to wave at her family one last time, and purposefully strode into Bancroft Hall.

Once her eyes had adjusted to the dim lights in the corridor, Sarah realized that she had no idea where she was. She could not even identify any room numbers as she chopped down the middle of the corridor with her eyes in the boat as required. A few other plebes were running along too, but there was no one to offer assistance. Unbeknownst to them, Bancroft Hall encompassed over four and a half miles of corridors. It was the largest single dormitory at any university.

I'm going to have to look at a door sometime or I'll run all night, she thought, almost panicking. She glanced at a door out of the corner of her eye. There, 41-something. What does that mean? My room is 3142. How do I get there?

She ran on aimlessly, feeling more and more helpless as she went. She ran through a passageway that seemed like a glass-encased covered bridge and then glanced at another door. 2-1? Oh, no! How did I get here? I must have missed 3-1, but I couldn't have!

She turned around and retraced her steps through the bridgelike passageway.

"Plebe, halt!" The deep voice rumbled through the hall. Sarah kept running. Please don't let it be me.

"PLEBE, HALT!" There was no mistaking the command. She stopped, her heart pounding, and turned to face the firstie.

"What's your alpha code?" he demanded.

"802863, SIR," she gasped.

"What's your company, platoon, and squad?" He was yelling directly in her face now.

She tried not to shrink back. "Romeo Company, Thirty-third Platoon, First Squad, SIR." Please don't ask me anything else. That's all I know.

Satisfied, he backed off and became calm. "Where're you headed?"

"Room 3142, SIR."

"You're on the wrong side of the Hall," he began. "You're not really supposed to use this passageway because of the commandant's offices, but go ahead and cut across here." He pointed her toward two pairs of closed double doors. "Walk across the carpeted area and then cross the Rotunda to the First Regimental side of the Hall. 3-1 is over there." Sarah took off, silently thanking him. In a moment she was running across a patterned marble floor with a broad staircase rising to her right and immense bronze doors on her left, the Rotunda. She recognized Tammy—one of her roommates—ahead of her, obviously just as lost, and quickened her pace to catch up as she didn't dare call out.

"Plebes, halt!" Someone from an office to the left stepped out as they obeyed the order. "Haven't you been told not to chop in front of Main Office?"

"No, SIR," they called out in unison, fear evident in their voices.

"Well, I'm telling you," he paused, then sighed. "Where are you headed?"

"Three one four two, SIR."

"You're almost there. Take a left at the next shaft."

They looked confused. "Shaft, sir?"

"Uh, passageway."

"Oh, yes, sir. Thank you, sir," Sarah told him gratefully.

"Don't thank me, plebe," he answered with disgust.

They walked away, breathing hard, turned at the next hallway, and resumed chopping. They found their room a few seconds later and collapsed inside, where Tammy burst into tears.

Give me a break! thought Sarah, disgusted. I've got a wimp for a roommate! "Stop it right now!" she snapped. "That's exactly what they expect us to do, cry and carry on. They think we can't handle the pressure, but we're going to."

Tammy stared at her, stunned by her forcefulness.

Sarah let out a long sigh before she continued more gently. "Look, Tammy. Dry your eyes. There's probably worse to come."

First Squad, Thirty-third Platoon marched to their table in the wardroom and stowed their covers (hats) on the built-in shelf under their chairs. Dinner that evening was "Surf and Turf," a true delicacy, but Sarah wasn't very hungry. This place had become all too real.

She sat at attention, eyes in the boat, at a table with nine other classmates including Denzel Simmons, Tammy, and Donna. Four firsties sat at the table including Mr. Randolph and Mr. Schluntz, their platoon leader. The plebes had been yelled at constantly since entering the Hall after the Induction Ceremony, and their nerves were on end.

A wardroom steward delivered the meal to the table on a large gray metal tray. He held it above Tammy's and Sarah's heads as Schluntz yelled at them, "Take the food from the server and get it on the table! Now!" The girls turned around in their chairs and began lifting the dishes off the tray. They set them in the middle of the table while Schluntz roared at Denzel. "Get the shovels in that chow and get it down here! Fast! Let's get a move on, people. What's the problem here?"

Sarah was petrified and sensed similar fear from her classmates. This guy was mean. His Adam's apple protruded from his long neck like a mogul on a ski slope. She was desperate to catch Donna's eye across the table but deathly afraid to take her eyes out of the boat.

"Listen up, people!" Schluntz continued with disdain. "No plebes eat until all upperclass have been served. The sooner you get us the food, the sooner you'll eat. I want that stuff off those trays and on my plate ASAP, understood?"

"Yes, SIR," they answered him in unison like whipped puppies.

"So, Mr. Simmons," continued Schluntz. "Tell me, were you in your girlfriend's podunk last night?" Randolph and the other firsties snickered.

Denzel dropped his fork, looking confused and shocked. "Excuse me, sir?"

"You hard of hearing, Mr. Simmons? I asked you if you were in your girlfriend's podunk last night."

Denzel played along. "Hell, yes, sir! I wore it out!" The firsties busted up.

"Miss Becker." It was Schluntz again. "Were you in your boyfriend's podunk last night?"

What the heck was a podunk? Schluntz implied sexual context. Was this guy just trying to be funny, or was he trying to shake them up? She wanted to show him she could play along as well as any of the guys, but she was too scared to think of a smart comeback. Remembering one of the five basic responses they had been taught that afternoon, she simply replied, "I'll find out, SIR."

"How about you, Miss Carter?" Schluntz wouldn't let up.

"No, SIR, but he was in mine," Donna responded completely unrattled. The table of firsties burst into laughter again. Randolph almost choked on a piece of steak.

"A podunk is a hometown. Check your *Reef Points,*" said Randolph when he regained his composure.

The firsties must have wanted to see how the girls would react, Sarah decided. She knew this was only the first of many similar tests, and she prayed she would be able to hold her own. Donna could obviously play along, but Tammy appeared naive. Some of the men at their table also appeared uncomfortable with the conversation. Maybe this wasn't just a "girl thing," she decided.

Sarah's appetite was now nonexistent. What was the line they were supposed to use to ask to be excused? She couldn't remember. Request permission to *something.* To be excused? To push off? To shove off! That was it, she thought gratefully.

"SIR, request permission to shove off?" she cautiously leaned over her plate and looked at Mr. Schluntz, not really sure who she was supposed to address.

"Miss Becker, did you stick your arm out so I could call on you? You don't just blurt out whatever you feel like saying without receiving permission first. You wait until you are called on. In addition, you are to request permission from the senior man at the table who, in this case, happens to be Mr. Vernon, the company subcommander. Is that understood?"

"Yes, SIR," she responded loudly, feigning strength in her voice, praying to get out of there without further confrontation. She stuck out her arm with a balled fist at its end and looked at the subcommander.

"Keep your eyes in the boat, Miss Becker, until you are called upon!" he yelled. She turned her head forward.

"What is it, Miss Becker?"

"Request permission to shove off, SIR."

"Yeah, go on! Get out of here!"

She pushed her chair back, stood up and nervously retrieved her dixie cup from the platform beneath her chair. As she turned to leave the wardroom, Mr. Schluntz ordered her to halt. She froze.

"Miss Becker, what is the menu for morning meal?" They had been given the menus for the rest of the week and been told not to leave one meal without knowing the menu for the next. She honestly thought they wouldn't expect them to know that tonight, but this tyrant did. She had read it but had not memorized it. Slowly, she turned to face him.

"I, I'll find out, sir." She was trying not to cringe.

"What?!" he yelled. "Don't you know that you are supposed to know the next meal before leaving the table?" He stood up and leaned over the table, his balled fists straddling his plate.

"Yes, sir," she answered meekly.

"Ahh," he chided her. "Let's get something straight, Becker. I don't like you here. I don't like women in my school, so I'm going to be on your butt every waking minute. Don't let me ever catch you not knowing anything again, or I'll burn you bad. If my plan works, you're gonna be long gone before I graduate. Is that clear?"

Marvelous, she thought. How am I supposed to answer that? "Yes, sir," she answered quietly with respect.

"Anyone here want to help Miss Becker out?" No one raised their hands. He looked around at all of them. "None of you guys knows the menu for morning meal?!" Still no answer. "I don't believe this! My own platoon. You're off the hook, Becker, since none of your classmates know it either. Now, get out of here!"

Deeply shaken by his words, she left the wardroom briskly, understanding his potential to make her life absolutely miserable.

"You are expected to know your rates. Once something has been assigned, you rate knowing it from that time on, for the rest of plebe year." The firstie was explaining the Plebe Indoctrination System to Seventh Platoon in no uncertain terms.

"Tomorrow, you will know your alpha code, your social security number, the names and hometowns of your squad members, and the five basic responses. They are: 'Yes, sir'; 'No, sir'; 'Aye, aye, sir'; 'I'll find out, sir'; and 'No excuse, sir.' You will use the five basic responses and *only* the five basic responses when answering a question from a senior. And since you are plebes, *everyone* is senior to you! Is that clear?"

"Sir, yes, sir!" Seventh Platoon barked.

"What's that?" yelled the firstie.

"Sir, yes, sir!!" they shouted.

"I can't hear you!" he yelled back at them.

"SIR, YES, SIR!" They strained their voices to produce more raw sound.

"I STILL can't hear you!" He taunted them.

"SIR, YES, SIR!!"

What's the point of this yelling match, thought Kate, yelling nonetheless with the rest of her classmates. This is like some kind of bizarre game. We haven't done anything wrong, so why is he yelling? Why can't he just tell us what he wants us to do and see if we can do it?

Satisfied with the volume of the response, the firstie went on. "At reveille and whenever your squad leader calls 'plebe ho' you will hit the bulkhead outside your room, stand at attention with your eyes in the boat, and sound off with your name and rank."

Hit the bulkhead? What on earth is a bulkhead? Kate wondered.

"And I *do* mean outside your door—not in the middle of the passageway or down by your classmate's door, but right next to your own doorway."

Stand against the wall, she thought. *Bulkhead* must mean wall.

"You will also come to attention and sound off whenever a superior officer enters the room."

Sound off? Kate's back was beginning to ache, intruding on her thoughts. What was sound off? Oh, yeah. Name and rank.

"You will not enter a room without first requesting permission to come aboard, and when you do enter a superior officer's room you will immediately sound off. No more than six plebes shall be in one room at a time. Any more than that constitutes a mutiny, and I don't need one of those on my hands." The firstie seemed calmer now, but his anger was still there, simmering while he completed his list of directives.

Kate's backache was now accompanied by cramps, and she found it difficult to concentrate. This day has been completely different from what I expected, she thought. There's so much to learn, and the pressure is incredible.

"You will be in a complete uniform at all times when outside your room from reveille until taps—a complete uniform includes your cover. The door to your room will be open, and the window blinds will be at half mast at all times, unless you are showering or changing. There will be no exceptions, period!"

Period! Oh my gosh, Kate groaned inwardly. That's why I'm having cramps. My period is about to start—and I'm standing here in a white uniform surrounded by guys!

"Your lights will be off and you will be in your racks at taps, but you may not be near your rack at any other time of the day."

My rack? I'm wracked with pain and he's talking about sleeping on a rack? This is too much! I'll die if my period starts right now. Kate's face contorted with pain involuntarily as the cramps grew worse. There seemed no way out of her predicament. How can I excuse myself privately with only the five basic responses?

Just then, the firstie stopped abruptly. He looked sternly at the new plebes and decided that this was enough. "You will muster back here at 2055 for an honor concept lecture. Dismissed!"

I'm saved, thought Kate. Thank you! Thank you! Thank you, Lord! As she chopped down the hall, it occurred to her that the firstie might have noticed that she was having some kind of discomfort, and the thought troubled her. I'm glad he let us go, but I hope he didn't do it on my account. I don't want any special treatment. I'll just have to be better prepared in the future.

"The honor concept is just that: a concept, a philosophy on which to base all your future actions and decisions. It is based on three principles: Midshipmen will not lie, cheat, or steal, nor will they mislead or deceive anyone as to known facts.

"Midshipmen are presumed to be honorable at all times and to possess moral integrity in the fullest sense, and will be treated accordingly, unless they prove otherwise by their words or actions.

"Finally, midshipmen should neither permit nor accept anything which is not just, right, and true."

The first classman paused to let the idea sink in. "As a midshipman, you should do the right thing simply because it is the right thing to do, not because you fear punishment. Each one of you has an individual moral responsibility to act honorably in every situation, to be truly trustworthy."

His earnest demeanor impressed Kate.

"Here at the Naval Academy is where you must learn to put these principles into practice so that they become an ingrained part of you. When you get out into the fleet, people will rely on you. You can't lead people if they can't trust you."

Yes, she thought, you have to be able to trust each other, and people have to be able to trust you. She remembered a quotation she had read in the Academy catalog: "There are some upperclass I would follow through fire; there are others I feel like pushing in."

Sarah lay awake in her rack, pondering Schluntz's words from evening meal, which echoed repeatedly in her mind: "I don't like women in my school. . . .

If my plan works, you're gonna be long gone before I graduate."

She had known she would encounter opposition based on her sex; she just hadn't expected it quite so soon. *You're wrong, Mr. Schluntz,* she whispered to herself. *Nobody is going to run me out of this place, especially not you. I'll be here long after you graduate, and I'm gonna make you eat those words. In fact, I'll personally shove 'em down your throat.*

CHAPTER TWO

Plebe Summer, First Set

Y ou are now beginning a new way of life. The naval profession is
both an important and a demanding one. To prepare you for it,
the Academy must be a military, nautical, and aeronautical as well as
an educational institution. You will have to make many adjustments
to meet its requirements; these are neither unreasonable nor impractical, but they are demanding and at times difficult. Therefore, you
should put your mind and heart to those things that are new, different, and difficult and master them completely.

Reef Points, 1976–77

Wednesday, 7 July 1976

"Thirty-third Platoon, First Squad, plebe ho!"

Busy organizing the gear they had been issued the day before, Sarah,
Donna, and Tammy disregarded the interruption. It was only 0700. An hour
ago, day two of plebe summer had erupted with the excruciating scream of
the reveille bell right outside their door. The girls had leaped out of their
racks, thrown on their men's wool bathrobes, and slammed their backs against
the bulkhead in the passageway as their squad leader took muster.

"Thirty-third Platoon, First Squad, plebe ho!" The voice sounded again,
louder and more agitated this time. Sarah peered around the edge of the door
frame to see what the commotion was. It was her squad leader.

"First Squad, Thirty-third Platoon, GET OUT HERE!"

"That's us!" Sarah turned quickly to face her roommates. "Mr. Wyman
wants us out in the hall."

"Again?!" Tammy exclaimed, exasperated.

Sarah ran into the hall along with several male classmates. Tammy followed

Donna, who abruptly turned around to grab her cover. Her squad leader saw her.

"Let's go, Miss Carter!" he yelled. "It's come as you are, unless you are in your birthday suit! There's no time for makeup or nail polish!"

Once the entire squad was in the hall, Mr. Wyman told them to line up in front of his door at the end of the hall. They chopped into position.

"Ladies and gentlemen, you have just experienced your first 'plebe ho.' This is where you are to line up every evening before formation for come-arounds. Remember, by tonight you are to know the names and hometowns of your fellow squad members."

Sarah's squad had been ordered the night before to seek out and memorize this information by tonight's evening come-around, an instruction period scheduled before every evening meal during which they would be drilled on rates—the often useful, sometimes trivial professional facts they were required to memorize. The girls had managed to complete a list of the thirteen names and hometowns the night before but had not yet begun memorizing them.

"This morning you are to order either the *Washington Post* or the *Baltimore Sun* for daily delivery to your room. Starting Monday, you will be required to read and be conversant about two articles on the front page and one article on the sports page by every morning meal. You will also be responsible for all articles written about Navy.

"I prefer the *Post* but receive them both. Order the one you want. Any questions?" There were none.

"Also, each of you is required to write at least one letter home by Sunday. This is not optional, this is required. Letters in envelopes are to be turned in to me for mailing by Sunday evening. Your mommies and daddies need to know you are still alive.

"Okay, formation for marching over to the chemistry placement exams is at 0750 in front of Mitscher Hall. Fall out!"

The plebes scurried like mice back to their rooms. It was 0710 already. Only ten minutes before morning meal formation. Sarah was beginning to realize how precious time was and how much this place could pack into one day. When were they supposed to memorize these names and hometowns or write a letter home? She decided she'd better take her list of names with her and tucked them into the plastic pocket on her *Reef Points*. The girls finished stowing their gear and had just enough time to check each other's uniforms before falling in for formation.

Ten hours later, sticky with the sweat of a day spent in and out of air-conditioned spaces, Sarah stood stiff at attention in the middle of her squad at their first come-around. Despite having practiced throughout the day between scheduled events, Sarah felt sick with nervousness.

Her squad mate beside her was the first to be asked. "Mr. Dupont, let's begin with you." Mr. Wyman spoke casually, strolling back and forth in front of his squad, no notes in hand. "Where is Miss Becker from?"

"SIR, Miss Becker is from. . . ." Dupont paused. "Uh, Miss Becker is from Portland, Maine, sir."

Sarah cringed. She knew he was guessing and strangled her desire to whisper the correct answer to him.

"Are you sure, Mr. Dupont?" their squad leader asked matter-of-factly.

"Uh, no, SIR," Dupont despondently replied.

"Are you guessing, Mr. Dupont?" Mr. Wyman now stood face to face with the floundering plebe, his voice rising an octave.

"Uh, yes, SIR," Dupont answered.

"Mr. Dupont, we do not guess at the Naval Academy or in the navy. Guessing gets men killed. It can get you and your shipmates killed. Is that clear, Mr. Dupont?"

"YES, SIR!"

"Miss Becker." Their squad leader was pacing again. "Was Mr. Dupont correct?"

"No, SIR!" Sarah's momentary glibness was dashed by his next remark.

"Miss Becker, we do not guess at the Naval Academy, and we do not bilge our classmates," he said disgustedly. "Do you know what bilging a classmate means?"

"No, SIR!"

"Using a mistake by your classmate to make yourself look good. Understood?"

"YES, SIR!" Sarah now felt bad that she had done just what he described.

"Listen up, people! If you don't know something, *don't* guess! Say, 'I'll find out, sir.' You'll get in trouble for not knowing your rates, but you'll get in a lot more trouble for trying to bullshit somebody. It's also very important for you guys to pull together as a team. I don't ever want to see any of you bilge a classmate, understood?"

"YES, SIR!" the squad bellowed out harmoniously.

The most important lessons had been taught, and Sarah fell asleep that night vowing never to bilge a classmate again.

Friday, 9 July 1976

Two evenings later, twelve hundred exhausted plebes popped to attention as the commandant of midshipmen left the stage. He had welcomed them once again to the Naval Academy and reminded them that the keen, competitive spirit that had brought them here would repeatedly be called upon to sustain them in the coming days. Imploring them to maintain the deepest sense of personal honor, integrity, and loyalty, he ended by wishing them smooth sailing.

This day had been similar to the past two. Mornings occupied by chemistry, foreign language, and mathematics placement and validation exams. Afternoons filled with more gear issue from the Midshipman Store, measurements for fall and summer uniforms, PPD (tuberculosis) shot readings, chapel orientation, honor concept lectures, dental appointments, and eye examinations. Some companies were already learning to sail on the knockabout sailboats.

They were exhausted, and there was still one more lecture this evening. A lieutenant commander walked onto the stage and signaled the plebes to take their seats.

"At this time, all women midshipmen report to Michelson Hall, room 103, for their medical hygiene lecture. All male midshipmen stand fast."

It was the first time they had been singled out. Sarah was so tired, she wasn't sure if she cared, but a tiny nerve ending quivered. Having sat through coed sex education classes since eighth grade, Sarah wondered what they could have to tell them that was now so private. Besides, if women were now at the Academy to stay, shouldn't rules pertaining to either sex be common knowledge? She and her roommates stood and awkwardly knocked the knees of male classmates as they made their way to the end of the row.

"Have a good time, girls," one of them offered good-naturedly.

"Yeah, we're going to learn how to wear those regulation bras they issued us!" Donna joked.

Michelson 103 was a medium-sized modern amphitheater. After hanging her dixie cup on one of the hat hooks at the back of the room, Sarah found a seat near the end of a middle row and saved two for her roommates.

She suddenly took a strong interest in her female classmates. So far everyone had been kept so busy, there had been no time to meet any of the other women. She took time to study their faces. What did they look like? Were they pretty? Were they homely? Were they fat? Were they thin? Where was the one they called "Bionic Woman"? Where was Meredith Britain, the really cute one from California? The rumor mill was already producing stories about the women that reached her via her male company mates.

The women she saw looked tired and sweaty, relieved to be in an air-conditioned space. Some rubbed at the pink ring on their foreheads where the heat from the walk over had swelled the skin around their dixie cups. Others uselessly tried to revive their matted bangs. Funny, Sarah thought, we're like a bunch of snowflakes, looking so similar from a distance yet unique up close.

Suddenly one snowflake stood out because of her color, and Sarah began to think that perhaps her analogy was ill chosen. She watched the sole black woman in their class enter the room and thought how truly alone she must feel.

"Good evening, ladies." Sarah's attention was diverted by a somber female lieutenant with short brown hair, dressed in tropical white long, with skirt, addressing them from the stage. "I am Lieutenant Lennox, assistant Foxtrot Company officer, and I will be instructing you this evening." Sarah recognized her from pictures in the *MHP* modeling the women midshipman uniforms.

"Ladies, I am here to give you guidance on how you are to behave as women midshipmen," she began pompously. Sarah disliked her immediately. *What makes her the expert? I thought this was a medical hygiene lecture. So what is she doing up there?*

"There are some regulations I would like to highlight that pertain particularly to you as women. Number one, hair length. At no time will your hair be longer than the top of your collar. A woman's beauty shop has been made available for you in the basement of the Seventh Wing. Use it. Often!"

Lieutenant Lennox walked back and forth across the stage as she spoke, wringing her hands. "Makeup is to be conservative, if worn at all. Lipstick, faint eyeshadow, and light rouge are appropriate if they are generally unnoticeable in appearance. Brassieres are to be worn at *all* times!" She stopped to emphasize her point. "They are part of the uniform! Any woman caught without a brassiere will receive demerits for being out of uniform."

What was this woman's point? The lecture was becoming demeaning. The women were being spoken to as if they were a bunch of tramps who needed etiquette lessons instead of women who had graduated with honors from their high schools!

"Now, it is my pleasure to introduce the Naval Academy's senior medical officer, Captain Dion."

At last, Sarah thought. Captain Dion walked onto the stage. He was a heavy-set elderly gentleman dressed in tropical white long who continually repositioned his black-framed navy-issue glasses against the bridge of his nose. He could have been anyone's grandfather.

"Good evening, ladies, and welcome to the Naval Academy." His smile was warm and sincere. "I am the senior medical officer here and a gynecologist by profession. Therefore, I will be your gynecologist. You may approach me with any medical or gynecological problems you encounter. Some of you may find with the added stress and physical activity of plebe summer and plebe year, your menstrual cycle may be interrupted, changed, or missed altogether. This is normal, but please feel free to make an appointment to see me if this happens.

"Contraceptives are available through my office. Diaphragms and birth-control pills are among those methods available at the clinic. Pregnancy is grounds for expulsion. Please come by and let me help you prevent any problems if you are, or even think you may become, sexually active."

Sarah leaned over to Donna. "Pretty amazing, huh? The Naval Academy distributing birth control!" Donna nodded and smiled.

"I strongly urge every one of you to schedule an annual exam with me to include a Pap smear and pelvic examination. All of you had an examination in the past year for entry into the Academy, which included a Pap test. However, it will be your responsibility in the future to schedule exams. Every woman midshipman should be performing self breast examinations. If you do not know how to perform one, please come by my office and I can give you some literature or schedule an appointment to show you how." He concluded, "We are very happy to have you with us."

Lieutenant Lennox resumed her role as emcee. "Ladies, it is imperative that you watch your weight while at the Academy. Food here is incredibly abundant. Over 3,400 calories are available for your consumption every day. That is almost twice what you normally need to consume. During plebe summer you will need to eat more because of your increased physical activity, but watch it! Don't starve yourselves, but don't eat more than you need. You must maintain a physically fit appearance. It will not be as difficult during the summer, but once academic year arrives, your activity level will decrease considerably. So beware.

"The last part of the lecture is a film on hygiene, and then we will have a short question-and-answer period."

She left the stage, and the lights in the room grew dim. A film flickered on the screen on the stage, and the women sat back, most struggling to keep their eyes open.

The main character of the film was a tall redheaded female naval officer. Sarah could immediately tell it was an outdated film, like something out of the fifties. The officer's day began with a soft alarm-clock chime beckoning her to rise and open a sun-filled, lace-curtained window to the sweet chirping of birds. Far cry from the blast of the reveille bell, thought Sarah. As the female narrator reminded the women midshipmen that they should take a shower every day, the redhead stepped into her own pink-tiled shower and leisurely cleansed her face and shoulders. Sarah snickered. Whenever she found time to take a shower, she had only a minute, max, from start to finish as her two roommates waited impatiently to take theirs. The narrator went on to remind them of the importance of good hygiene, to brush their teeth after every meal and so on and so forth. Sarah turned to Donna and rolled her eyes.

The best part was when Lieutenant "Redhead" sat down at the breakfast table. Before her were two fried eggs with several strips of bacon, toast with jam, a bowl of cereal with a banana, a glass of milk, a glass of juice, and a sweet roll. Sarah almost burst out laughing. If I ate that much for breakfast, I'd blow up. So much for watching how much you eat, huh, Lieutenant Lennox?

Across the auditorium, Kate uneasily watched the lieutenant in the film eat her breakfast. Food. Why did it play such a significant part in one's life? She had struggled with this dilemma since junior high school, when her father had made one brief statement that etched an indelible impression she had never been able to erase. After helping herself a second time to a heaping spoonful of mashed potatoes and butter, he had remarked, "Katey, you're going to be as big as a barn if you keep eating like that."

She should have dismissed the statement as she would have any other off-the-cuff remark, but she had not. She lived with those words as if they were doctrine. They meant, "If you get fat, I won't love you anymore, and neither will anyone else." It wasn't true, and deep down she knew that, but she couldn't take the chance. At school she would skip lunches. At dinner, when her parents weren't looking, she would feed hers to the dog or slide it down the garbage disposal. At other times she would gorge on her favorite foods only to force herself to vomit them up to rid her body of the calories. It was a sick, painful existence that she learned to hide over the years. No one knew what anguish food caused her. Now she wondered anxiously, Will it still torment me here?

When the movie was over, Lieutenant Lennox took questions. One female mid asked where they were supposed to carry sanitary napkins during the day, when they were not allowed to return to their rooms between classes. Tammy looked at Sarah as if to say, "Good question." Sarah used Tampax, and being short on modesty she figured she would stick one in her sock and hope she didn't sweat too much. "Let me get back to you on that one," Lieutenant Lennox responded. There being no more questions, she dismissed the women.

"That movie was a joke," said Tammy on the way out.

"What a way to spend a Friday night! Which century did they dredge that up from?" Sarah questioned. "You'd think the Naval Academy could have found a more up-to-date film."

"Maybe not," said Donna. "We're quite a novelty, you know. They probably don't have a repertoire of women's training films—yet. Give 'em time."

"Yeah, we can be their first leading ladies." The three chuckled as they headed back to 3-1.

Saturday, 10 July 1976

Their first Saturday at the Naval Academy passed like another weekday, with a physics validation examination, reams of administrative paperwork, and an indoctrination on PEP, the physical exercise program, which was to begin at 0615 the following Monday. Since attendance at the physics exam had been by invitation of the academic dean and they had not been on the invitation list, Sarah and her roommates had time to study their rates and visit with some of their squad mates. Denzel lived just two "squared corners" away with three other guys. Next door were Rick Burns and Kurt Loper, "Fric and Frac." Tall and muscular, Rick towered over Kurt, who was of frail frame. Kurt had a natural acting streak and began performing the moment Sarah chopped into their room.

"Hi, guys! Whatcha got to eat?" Might as well break the ice early, she decided. Sarah could always eat.

Rick handed her a box of cheese crackers.

"Thanks!" She reached in and pulled out a handful. "Ready for the inspection tomorrow?" she asked.

Kurt hopped up onto the desk and did a little dance as he waved a dust rag and answered. "We will be, sweetie. Working on those venetian blinds right now. They are gross!"

Denzel walked in the door behind Sarah.

"Yo, what it is, fellow plebes?" He spied the box of cheese crackers and helped himself. "Ahh, chow!"

"Hey, Denzel, you guys started cleaning yet?"

"Nah. We'll start tomorrow afternoon. It'll just get messed up before then."

The thought of guys scrubbing their rooms made Sarah smile.

"Well, boys, Cinderella's gotta get back and scrub those floors. See ya!" She headed for the door and peeked out, looking both ways to ensure that she wouldn't run into anyone as she bounded into the passageway. Leaning out the door, she felt Denzel's eyes on her behind. Embarrassed only for a moment, she was glad that she and her squad mates were becoming so close. Although all the guys in her squad accepted the presence of Sarah and her roommates, Kurt and Denzel were becoming particularly special to her.

Sunday, 11 July 1976

When Kate returned from an early-morning chapel service, she found Terrie and Michelle already hard at work cleaning for the impending formal room inspection that evening. Although they were entitled to Yard liberty (time off) until evening meal formation, none of them felt like strolling through the Naval Academy grounds to be ogled by tourists. They had begun the task yesterday, scrubbing the blinds until they seemed two tones lighter, risking a taps violation to finish the floor by the light of the moon. It was almost funny.

I can't believe I'm scraping soap scum off a shower wall with a razor blade on a Sunday afternoon, Kate thought. The powdery flakes clung to her hair and filled her nostrils so that she sneezed every few minutes. I can't believe anyone actually lived with his shower in this condition. She sneezed again. "This had to be an upperclass room," she said aloud. "It's so gross! Can you imagine a plebe even daring to keep his room like this, let alone getting away with it?"

Terrie laughed. "Really! He would've been fried for sure!"

Kate stepped out of the shower and wiped her face with the back of her hand. "It's so hot in there, I'm drenched." She looked at her roommates, who were both flushed and perspiring, too. "We're all going to have to use it again before the inspection."

"We can wipe it down with a towel," Michelle suggested, "and then Beau said we should wax it with Pledge."

"Pledge?" Terrie was skeptical.

Kate wasn't sure about that either, but she was more interested in the source of the advice. "Beau?" she asked. "You mean Mark Beauclair?"

Michelle grinned. "Of course! Don't you think that's a good nickname for him? He's such a hunk!"

"Michelle," Kate protested, "you have a boyfriend at home!"

"Yeah, I know. But there's no harm in looking around when there's so much to look at!" Michelle shrugged her shoulders. "Beau was prior-enlisted, so he knows a lot of this stuff. He showed me how to fold our dixie cups. He seems quiet, but he's really nice and funny, too. So are his roommates. There's something special about Beau, though. Don't you think he's good-looking?"

Kate had to admit he was. In fact, she had noticed several classmates who were attractive, but who had time for a relationship? Besides, she wasn't here to get her "MRS degree," and she certainly didn't intend to break the rules against fraternization and "dragging" (dating).

"He *is* nice," she agreed. "He carried my suitcase the first day, when I kept dropping it, and he's never said anything about it. You know, he hasn't tried to rub it in like some other guys might have."

"You mean like Dirk Walker?"

"Yeah."

Terrie looked up. "Dirk came up to me after the math placement exam and told me that I 'stole' an appointment from some fully qualified guy who probably dreamed of this his whole life—as if I'm not qualified and haven't had the same dream. Can you believe it?"

"I know," said Michelle, giving the sink a final, extra-hard scrub. "He told me that, too. We'll show him."

Kate smiled. Dirk had given her the evil eye several times already although he had not said anything to her. She would show him. She would show all of them.

After evening meal the girls dressed in crisp, clean white works fresh from the repair tailor shop. A triangle of white sheeting had been inserted on either side to accommodate their hips for a "tailored" fit. They gave the room a last once-over, smoothing the dark blue bedspreads and blotting stray drops of water from the sink and shower. Freshly tied black neckerchiefs and glistening black Corfams (shoes) completed the uniform, white works "alpha." They stood nearly motionless in front of the window, hoping to catch a breeze while trying to avoid marring the floor with their shoes. Kate swiftly wiped away a bead of sweat racing down her forehead and then stuffed the Kleenex into the upper band of her sock, not wanting to clutter the trash can. When they heard their classmates down the hall sound off, they knew they would be next.

"Don't forget to sound off all at once as loud as we can," whispered Kate, remembering how Mr. Daniel had chewed them out the first day when they sounded off politely, accusing them of sounding like ladies introducing themselves at a garden party. In less than a week he had inculcated a curious mixture of desire to succeed and fear of failure that had little to do with professionalism. It was survival.

Footsteps approached. "Attention on deck!" Mr. Daniel shouted the order just outside their door.

The three girls snapped to attention and barked out their names and rank simultaneously.

"Midshipman Brigman, fourth class, sir!"

"Midshipman Micheals, fourth class, sir!"

"Midshipman Mead, fourth class, sir!"

Lieutenant Griffith, their company officer, entered, followed by Mr. Daniel, both dressed in well-pressed whites and white gloves. Kate had seen the lieutenant a few times around the company area. When he spoke to the company, he seemed pleasant.

He looked a bit flushed as he began his inspection, surveying the contents of their shelves and looking into their personal lockboxes, which stood open on the desks, to be sure that the contents were neatly arranged. Satisfied, he walked toward the three girls and lowered the blinds from their half-mast position. He ran his right index finger across one and nodded ever so slightly in approval when it came up clean. The girls continued to hold their breath. This was just the beginning.

He lifted one corner of the mattress off the frame of Terrie's rack. Unimpressed, he let the mattress drop back into place. Terrie's hospital corners were ruined.

The lieutenant opened cabinets and desk drawers, then examined the sink and shower. He seemed pleased when he could find no trace of soap scum on the walls and was about to leave when he suddenly reached up to check the shower curtain rod. Kate knew what he would find even before his finger touched the rod, and a pang of failure swept through her. How could I have forgotten to wipe that after we showered? she scolded herself.

His finger came up damp and slightly gray. Mr. Daniel glared, but Lieutenant Griffith smiled. "Had to find some dirt somewhere," he said, drying his finger on a towel hanging beside the sink. "Excellent work, ladies! Well done."

Well done! Kate could hardly believe it. She bit her tongue to keep from shouting "Thank you, sir," until he and her squad leader left the room. The three girls erupted with joy and relief the moment they were alone. They grabbed each other in a three-way hug and cheered, "We did it! We did it! We passed!"

Mr. Daniel was back in the doorway instantly. "Ladies! Please," he reprimanded, trying to sound serious, but a slight grin gave him away.

"Yes, sir," they replied, trying to look properly chastised but not succeeding in the least. They had passed. He was pleased. Life, for a few moments, was good.

Monday, 12 July 1976

At 0605 on Monday, training day number seven, Sarah and her roommates bounded out of bed at the first scream of the reveille bell, threw on a pair of navy blue shorts and their white T-shirts, neatly folded and stowed their nightshirts, ran out the door, and chopped down the hall out of Bancroft Hall to form up with the rest of Thirty-third Platoon on the Third Wing mezzanine. Today was the first day of PEP, the physical exercise program.

Mr. Schluntz, their platoon leader, marched them down the granite ladder, around the tailor shop in Fifth Wing, and through the glass walkway of Mitscher Hall, over to the Astroturf at the end of Farragut Field behind the Eighth Wing of Bancroft Hall. Ten platoons of thirty-six plebes were already in place, stretched out in single file perpendicular to the grid lines striping the Astroturf. All plebes were dressed in navy blue shorts, white T-shirts with blue-ringed collars, white athletic socks, and white Keds. Firsties were dressed in the next closest thing. A slightly damp morning breeze blew off the Chesapeake Bay, forcing several plebes to jump in place and rub their upper arms to keep warm while waiting for the rest of the Fourth Class Regiment to arrive. Sarah took a deep breath of the salty bay air and looked toward the historic Annapolis harbor, where fleets of power and sail boats were moored in the marina. The water was perfectly calm, devoid of any disturbance other than a lone seagull looking for breakfast. For a moment the hustle around Sarah disappeared.

"Class of '80, are you out there?" A strong, unmistakably German accent hailed them. Sarah looked up at the three platforms at the head of the field. On the middle platform stood a short, muscular elderly gentleman wearing blue polyester shorts and a white T-shirt with the letters *PEP* emblazoned in blue. Jack Lalanne in miniature.

"I said, Class of '80, are you out there?" he repeated loudly.

"Yes, sir!" twelve hundred–plus voices boomed back at him.

"I can't hear you!"

Not him too! thought Sarah.

"YES, SIR!" they roared.

"Class of '80, I am Coach Heinz Lenz. I will be your instructor for this first of many days you have been given to excel in physical fitness. Not only do we train your mind at Navy, we also train your bodies. For the next forty-five minutes I want you to give me everything you have. Push yourself harder than you ever thought possible, and by the end of the summer you will look like one of these gentlemen." He gestured right and left to two young men built like Arnold Schwarzenegger perched atop the other two platforms dressed in PEP T-shirts as well.

Studs! thought Sarah.

"These are two of the first classmen at Navy who will assist me in demonstrating the exercises every morning. Are you ready, '80? Let's begin!" He started them out with jumping jacks, then pushed them to their individual limits with sit-ups, push-ups, leg lifts, squat thrusts, running in place, and more. It had been two years since Sarah had been captain of the junior-varsity gymnastics team in her high school. In April, when she received her appointment to the Naval Academy, she had joined the women's track team for their cross-country workouts to try to get into shape. She had natural upper-body strength, but nothing had prepared her for these PEP endurance workouts.

Throughout Coach Lenz's sadistic drill, he encouraged "supers" to perform push-ups with one arm or sit-ups with hands in front of their chests instead of behind their heads. Sarah was proud to perform ten men's push-ups like her male classmates. On the tenth time she pushed herself away from the fake grass, she sensed someone staring at her. Elbows locked, she looked up, her eyes meeting Denzel's stare.

"Keepin' up with the boys, huh, Studette?" he remarked with a smile. She smiled back.

"Wanna race?" she asked good-naturedly.

"Hell, no! You'd probably kick my black ass! Embarrass me in front of the boys."

She started to laugh, and her elbows buckled, dropping her onto the dew-damp Astroturf and soaking the front of her T-shirt and shorts.

"Aha!" observed Denzel as she stood up. "Wet T-shirts! There may be something good about this PEP stuff after all."

"Eyes in the boat, sailor!" she ordered smiling, pulling her soggy shirt away from her chest and turning toward the end zone and the PEP instructors.

"Bounce, '80, bounce!" Coach Lenz had them back up, bouncing from the balls of their feet. "Higher, '80! Higher!"

After forty-five minutes of torture, he ended the workout with each platoon jogging the length of the field in an elongated circle around orange cones. Although winded, Sarah found the workout exhilarating. I don't know how I'll feel at the end of the week, she thought, but right now, I feel great. I really want to show these guys that girls can do it, too. And I think I've proven it to at least one of them.

Tuesday, 13 July 1976

At Tuesday's morning meal formation they got the news from their company commander: all women were to carry purses. Although in formation, standing at parade rest, Sarah glanced at Donna, confused. Donna returned the look.

"Eyes in the boat, down there!" their company commander reprimanded.

Whipping her head forward, Sarah groaned silently. Purses? Why the heck do we have to carry purses?

The Thirty-third Company commander continued speaking. "Form up here for the background and psychological testing at 0800. Bring eyeglasses, if you need them, two sharpened number-two pencils, and *Reef Points* to study in any free time. And all women carry purses."

The girls couldn't speak to one another until after morning meal, in their room preparing for the 0800 formation.

"Carry purses?" cried Sarah to her roommate. "What for?! Did they ask us how we felt about it? I'll bet this came from that hygiene lecture where that girl asked where we should carry Tampax."

"Actually, it may come in kind of handy," said Tammy, filling the hideous black vinyl purse with a brush, comb, Kleenex, *Reef Points,* and two number-two pencils.

"You really gonna carry all that stuff in there, Tammy?"

"Might as well."

"Well, not me. I'm not carrying anything in it. I'm going to hang my *Reef Points* on the top of my trousers like the guys."

Donna placed her *Reef Points* in her purse and slung it over her shoulder. "Come on, girls. We need to get to formation."

They ran out the door, purses banging against their sides and slipping off shoulders as they ran.

Sarah heard several male classmates snicker as the girls arrived for formation "carrying purses." She rolled her eyes and stuck out her tongue at them as they bit their bottom lips. Boy, this is a stupid idea, thought Sarah for the hundredth time that morning. They have *got* to change this rule.

Late that night Sarah and her roommates fell into their room sweating, exhausted from the past hour, which the plebe-summer schedule identified as "squad leader instruction time." After a day full of infantry training, honor code lectures, and lectures on Morse code, the Romeo Company upperclass decided that their plebes also needed instruction on how to expediently change from one uniform to another, and so they held uniform races from 2055 until 2150.

"I can't believe he asked us where our sports bras were!" Sarah sounded exasperated as she pulled her drenched sweatshirt over her head and looked at Donna. "Working uniform 'sweatbox,'" they had called it: navy-issue bathing suits covered by blue shorts and plebe T-shirt, layered under gray sweatshirt and sweatpants, topped by a vinyl raincoat and cape. It was the hardest, hottest uniform race yet.

"I just can't believe that jerk Schluntz made us go back and put a bra on under all of this stuff after we already had it on!" Sarah was angry as she peeled her sweat-soaked bathing suit from her body.

"'Uh, Mr. Simmons,'" she mimicked Mr. Schluntz, their platoon leader, raising her chin to stick out her Adam's apple as far as possible. "'Mr. Simmons, do you have your jockstrap on under your swimsuit?' I thought Denzel was going to die." She smiled at Donna as she thought of what had happened next. She lowered her voice and chin and held her shoulders up to look like Denzel's. "So Denzel says, 'Uh, sir, how do we wear our jockstraps under this? There really isn't much there.' Denzel meant the bathing suit, of course, but I thought I was going to die laughing when you said, 'Guess that's how we'll separate the men from the boys.' Man, Donna! If Denzel weren't black he'd've been beet red!"

"I just didn't want 'em to think they could embarrass us with all that talk about jockstraps," Donna answered defensively.

"Well, that backfired, didn't it? Schluntz turned around and pulled the same stunt on us!" She stuck her chin up again. "'Uh, Miss Becker, do you have on your sports bra?' Now what the hell is a sports bra? We don't even have such a thing! He just wanted to make us run all the way back here, take off all this gear and sweat to death. Did you see how he even made me show him my bra strap to prove that I put it on?"

"Of course, Sarah, what else would you expect from that guy? He wants to make everyone's life as miserable as possible while he's here!" Donna wasn't happy with the whole ordeal, but she now realized it was part of the game. Tammy undressed and got into the shower.

"Well, good thing we have personal time where they can't bug us till morning. That uniform race was unbelievable."

Tammy finished her shower and Sarah hopped in. The hot water was relaxing, but she scrubbed up quickly so that Donna could have her turn. After pulling on her nightshirt, Sarah returned to the mirror to cover her face with Clearasil. The tan-brown masque made her look like she was halfway through a facial.

Within fifteen minutes all three girls were showered and dressed in nightshirts sitting at their desks studying *Reef Points* for the last ten minutes of personal time. A knock on the door interrupted their concentration.

"Who is it?" called Donna, expecting it to be one of their classmates at this time of night.

"Open the door!" an unfamiliar voice commanded. They could tell it was an upperclass but didn't recognize the voice as one of their firsties.

"Just a minute, sir," Donna called back.

"Oh, my word!" said Sarah, appalled. "Look at my face!"

"Look at your nightshirt!" replied Donna. "Put on your b-robe, fast!"

The three of them tied up their bathrobes just before the door swung open. In walked two upperclassmen they did not recognize. Sarah couldn't help it. Her hands flew up to cover her face. She sounded off through her fingers. What are they doing here? she despaired. Plebes had a measly twenty-five minutes of personal time at the end of every day where no one was allowed to bother them. She peered between her ring and baby fingers at the first classman who seemed to be in charge of this expedition and recognized him as one of the hunks who performed up on the platform with Coach Lenz during PEP. What was he doing here? She wanted to melt into the linoleum.

"Midshipman Becker, what are you doing?" he yelled. How did he know her name?

"Please, sir, please don't make me take my hands down, sir," she pleaded. He looked at his classmates with incredulity.

"Take your hands down, Miss Becker! Now!"

"Please, sir, request permission not to take my hands down." She knew she was only making him angry, but she didn't care. She was begging for mercy.

"Miss Becker, I order you to take your hands away from your face." She had to obey. Slowly, she dropped her hands and lowered her head hoping he couldn't see her face. "Stand at attention!" he ordered. She gave in, wondering if the Clearasil masque covered the dark pink flush of her face underneath.

"What is on your face?!" he asked with disdain.

"Clearasil, sir," she replied, wondering if that was a slight smirk she saw.

He began to pace around their room. His classmate followed. "Who are the officers of the day?"

He can't do this, she thought. He can't do this during our personal time, but she knew she could not say anything.

"Sir, the officers of the day are . . . the officer of the day is Lieutenant Van Dorn, scheduling officer, the assistant officer of the day is Lieutenant j.g. Mitchell. . . ."

Before she could finish, he had started in on her roommates. The three of them were regurgitating rates when the Romeo Company subcommander walked by their door, saw what was going on, and stormed in.

"What the hell is going on here?" he demanded.

"Just a little fun and games," the firstie joked. "No harm done, John."

"Yeah? Well hit the road, guys! You're treading on thin ice drilling our plebes after hours!"

The two first classmen shrugged and left the girls' room.

Sarah was so happy to have been rescued from this impromptu come-around that she forgot what she looked like. The subcommander turned to the three of them still standing at attention.

"Fun and games are over, ladies. Hit the rack! By the way, Miss Becker, nice face!" He pulled the door shut behind him.

Tammy and Donna burst out laughing. Sarah grinned, feeling the Clearasil masque crack.

"Sports bras, Clearasil, come-arounds after hours. Is nothing sacred?" She shook her head and jumped into the rack.

Lieutenant Credle, Romeo Company officer, walked back to his office and sat down at his desk. He usually didn't stay this late, but he was glad he had witnessed this particular uniform race. Miss Carter had done it again, he thought. The men had tried to embarrass the girls, and she had turned it around on them, just the way she had challenged their bulletin board of "Company Cuties" by putting up some "cuties" of her own from *Playgirl* magazine. Miss Becker had stood up rather well, too. She didn't bat an eye when Schluntz asked for proof that she had put on her "sports bra," whatever he thought that was.

Credle chuckled for a moment. We've done so much planning and preparation for this first class with women, but it seems so superficial now. All those lectures about what to expect from the girls.

He pulled out a file labeled "PREPARATION FOR WOMEN AT USNA—Information and Education Programs" and flipped through it.

Physiological Differences: Data to support standards must be gathered covertly.

Everyone knows we give physical tests to all the plebes, Credle mused, so why keep the results secret?

Uniforms and Grooming Standards: Men do not know these standards or procedures, e.g. how to rig a woman's combination hat, what is "conservative" mascara and when should mascara not be worn. Add to Plebe Detail Training (Pre–I Day).

They had spent an inordinate amount of time on that—several lectures on the rules about makeup and allowing more time for the women to wash their hair because it's longer than the men's. Ha! Not by much. And the ordeal with brassieres. Credle shook his head as he recalled how the administration had called in the Judge Advocates General, the navy's lawyers, to determine how to legally write and enforce a regulation requiring women to wear bras under their uniforms at all times. He laughed to himself as he remembered all the meetings held to discuss the issue. The administration did not want to write a regulation to single out the women, so they wrote a general regulation requiring all midshipmen to wear upper and lower undergarments as appropriate.

Experience at US Merchant Marine Academy indicates that men will perform and behave better when women are a part of the organization.

Hmmm. That remains to be seen. The men still think standards are being lowered, and they resent having to wear b-robes in the hall, no matter what anyone says.

Assertiveness is discouraged among women and is viewed by society as unfeminine. Women will need more support and guidance than men in learning assertiveness. Women must be held to the task early in their training.

Miss Carter and Miss Becker certainly don't need any help here, Credle thought.

Socialization processes cause women to become noncompetitive with men at about age fifteen.

That certainly doesn't apply to these girls. You don't challenge the firsties to run the O'Course (obstacle course) like Sarah Becker did—and beat them— if you're noncompetitive.

Women have difficulty working with other women in a team or supportive effort. Roommate disagreements can be expected; perhaps even serious problems of roommate incompatibility.

Credle frowned. I haven't noticed them having any problems working with each other—or with the men, for that matter. As for roommate problems, I don't think they'd tell me.

Chivalry: In a primarily male environment, there is a tendency by the men to overprotect the women. Women must be allowed and MADE to share the load. Not doing so through considerations of chivalry will lead to resentment by the men and deprive the women of their fair share of opportunities and education. Those few women who will expect consideration will react such that if held to the line any tendency to ask for consideration will disappear in two or three months.

Our girls haven't asked for any special treatment, and I doubt that they would accept any. If anything, there's a chance the upperclassmen will push them harder to make sure they're not getting any special breaks.

Men will pay inordinate attention to pretty women and will be more willing to assist them than women less physically attractive. Selection for cheerleaders et al. must be on basis other than a beauty contest.

We're fighting societal issues here, but with their hair chopped off, no makeup, and those baggy white works, it's hardly obvious that they're women.

Lack of Straightforwardness: Side-stepping issues is encouraged by women's sociological role. Will honor be a problem? Probably not. Allow no loopholes for women—especially in first few days. Men leaders should accept no excuses.

Well, Credle thought, Carter certainly doesn't lack straightforwardness! None of them has come to me with any problems, as some of the men have, but they haven't sidestepped any direct questions or given any excuses that I'm aware of.

Women are less conditioned than men to show affection except in a sexual relationship. There is evidently a greater fear of demonstrating something which could be construed as homosexual tendencies by women than men. This can become critically important in establishing a compatriot attitude in the class. Women do not express affection or temperament by "wise cracks" or "zingers."

I've heard wisecracks out of all of them, and not very affectionate ones at that! If they do show affection, how do we know if it's sexual or not? How do we make the distinction between camaraderie that builds esprit de corps and fraternization that threatens it?

Crying: Tears are a normal and socially approved method of venting frustration and anger for a woman. Crying should be expected and ignored.

I haven't seen one of these girls cry yet and doubt that I will.

Feminine-like Traits and Stereotypes: "Mother of the group," "pet" or "mascot," "seductress," "iron maiden."

Credle shook his head again. We expected a bunch of belligerent feminists or wanton sexpots, but any one of these girls could be your sister or the girl next door.

He shut the folder and looked at his watch as he yawned, glancing at the stack of routine paperwork that lay unfinished on his desk. This plebe summer is anything but routine, he thought, and this is going to be quite a final year for me here. I'll be glad to get back to teaching engineering, and let the regular company officers oversee this transition period. There really shouldn't be any problems in the academic world with the records of these girls. They did very well competitively in the admissions process, since SATs and high school performance are by far the most heavily weighted areas in the "whole man" concept—there's another name that will have to change, I suppose.

Names. He smiled. It's quite a coincidence that Carter happens to be my wife's maiden name. What's a nice girl like that doing here? Why do any of them want to be here? he wondered as he shut off his office light and locked the door behind him.

Thursday, 15 July 1976

Complaints about the black purses came from both male and female midshipmen. The women despised lugging the bulky shoulder bag when marching and chopping. The men felt that the women had an unfair advantage since they could fill the purse with extra notes from which to study their rates. Within a week the order had been rescinded and a new order issued: women were to report to the tailor shop for issuance of a pocket belt in which they could carry feminine hygiene products.

At Thursday morning meal formation, the Romeo Company commander passed the word: "Formation for yawl sailing instruction is at 0800. Uniform for yawls is white works 'charlie' over PT gear." He turned toward Sarah and her roommates. "Women no longer need carry purses."

Sarah glanced sideways at Donna and smiled. Hallelujah, she thought. Somebody came to their senses.

Tuesday, 20 July 1976

On Tuesday morning, preparing for drill, Kate struggled to fasten her belt properly without losing the "tuck" in each side of her white works blouse. She finally gave up trying to master the technique alone and asked her roommate for help.

Once it was in place, she quickly placed her cover on her head and checked carefully in the mirror to be sure it was just two finger-widths above her eyebrows, as regulations required. The reflection that stared back was that of a tired, pimply-faced young girl. Zits again, she fretted. If Charlie ever saw me like this, he'd probably break up with me. Lord, I miss him and my family so much.

She tightened her jaw to fight off the sting of tears forming in her eyes. I can't cry now, she told herself. Save it for tonight after my roommates are asleep, or when I'm alone in the head.

Kate found herself crying all the time. She was constantly depressed but told herself that she wasn't homesick. How could she be? This was her home now, wasn't it? It couldn't be because they yelled at her all the time, since they yelled at everybody.

No, what made her cry was the happy memories of years past. Memories of her boyfriend, Charlie, and all the good times they had spent together her senior year of high school when he had been a plebe. How had *he* survived all this pressure? She must not be as strong as he. Now that he was home from his summer cruise she fought the urge, every night, to call him. I have to be strong, she reminded herself. I'm only going to call home once a week. But I miss him so much!

"Let's go!" said Terrie, interrupting Kate's self-pity. "Got your socks in?" she asked, referring to the thick athletic socks the girls had learned to secure, one under each bra strap, to prevent the sore shoulders they had endured the first time they had to carry their rifles at "right and left shoulder arms." It was one of the few advantages of being female.

"Got 'em," called Michelle as the three girls chopped into the passageway carrying their rifles diagonally across their chests at "port arms" position.

In the parking lot, Kate took her place at the rear of the platoon with the rest of the "sandblowers" (shorter members of the platoon). Most of the girls in the class were relegated to this position, she noticed.

The firsties, dressed in short-sleeve khaki uniforms, arrived and took their positions ahead of and beside the plebes. "Platoon, atten-hut!" The platoon leader's voice echoed off the walls of Bancroft, and in unison with her class-mates Kate snapped to attention and stood with her piece beside her at "order arms."

After the order "Right shoulder arms!" the firstie bellowed, "Platoon, for-ward march! Left, left, left right left. . . ."

At Farragut Field the plebes stopped and stood at attention. Recorded mil-itary marches blared from the loudspeakers to give the novice marchers a steady tempo for practice.

"First, we're going to practice the manual of arms," declared the platoon leader, pacing before them, holding his sheathed sword against his left thigh. "Now, I've said this before, but some of you still don't seem to get it. The idea is to try to move in unison; to think and act like a team so there's only one motion and one sound, not a ripple. There shouldn't be any bouncing or jig-gling around: this is a military unit, not the Dallas Cowboys cheerleaders. Move together on the count, but don't count out loud." He took a deep breath. "Seventh Platoon, port arms!"

There was a special trick to flicking one's piece off the right shoulder just far enough and turning it 90 degrees with the right hand so that it landed with a slap in the palm of the left. Too far, and you knocked out the guy in front of you. Not far enough, and you knocked yourself out. The platoon executed the maneuver simultaneously. Good, Kate complimented them silently. We sounded together on that one.

"Or-der . . . ARMS!"

Kate grabbed the tip of the barrel with her right hand and lowered her piece to her right side, striking the ground with the butt of the rifle.

The boom of thirty rifles pounding the ground in concert would have been embarrassing enough, but the sound emitted by Seventh Platoon was more like the uneven rumble of a major earthquake. The firsties were livid. "No! No! NO, people!" they yelled. "Ease it down! Ease it down the last couple of inches. Don't bang the deck!"

Kate saw the marine drill sergeant, on the field to help instruct, shake his head in disgust. That was clumsy, she scolded herself. Don't be so eager to set it down next time.

"Do it again—only do it right!" her platoon leader yelled. "Port arms! Order arms!" The thud was softer, and he commended them. "Right shoul-der arms! Right face! Forward march!"

The plebes stepped out in unison and marched along the perimeter of Farragut Field, the marine drill sergeant close behind. Halfway around the field the platoon leader gave the order, "Port arms!"

Swinging her rifle off of her shoulder, Kate momentarily lost control of the barrel and almost hit the classmate in front of her. She lunged for her rifle and immediately fell out of step with the rest of the platoon.

"Miss!" she heard someone call from behind. Afraid to take her eyes out of the boat, she ignored the call and concentrated on getting back in step. "Miss!!" The call was louder, and Kate knew it was directed at her.

Oh, wonderful, she thought. So much for doing well today.

Kate turned to face the marine drill sergeant, whose forefinger signaled her to fall out of ranks and stand beside him. Humiliated, she obeyed.

"Miss . . . Brigman," he said, glancing at her nametag. "Was that an accident, or was that your way of moving up in the ranks?"

"I'll find out, sir," she responded, not quite sure what he meant.

"Let's practice the manual of arms together."

Completely humiliated at being singled out, Kate practiced the manual of arms with the drill sergeant for five minutes until he was satisfied that she had better control of her rifle.

"Before you go," he instructed, "there's one other thing you need to watch." She looked at him questioningly.

"Stop wiggling your hips so much. This is a drill field, Miss Brigman, not the Miss America runway. Is that clear?"

Already sweating profusely from the heat and humidity, Kate felt her temperature rise with embarrassment. She bit her tongue and respectfully responded with the standard "Yes, sir." But as she turned to rejoin her platoon, her thoughts slipped out in a muttered "What were you doing looking, sir?"

An hour later, Seventh Platoon marched back to Bancroft looking and feeling a bit less like raw recruits. Kate's arms throbbed as she tried to keep her piece perfectly aligned.

My T-shirt is soaked, she thought with amazement. I've sweated so much that my bra is actually saturated! I wish I could shower. But what's the use? I'll only get sweaty again when we go sailing.

"Mr. Random," called one of the firsties, "give us a song."

"Aye, aye, sir," Mr. Random obliged. "Oh, it's beer, beer, beer that makes you wanna cheer. . . ." The rest of the platoon joined in:

... in the Corps, in the Corps.
Oh, it's beer, beer, beer
That makes you wanna cheer
In the Quartermaster, Quartermaster Corps.

My eyes are dim.
I cannot see.
I have not brought
My specs with me.

Oh, it's gin, gin, gin
That makes you wanna sin. . . .

Although still crestfallen at having been singled out at drill, Kate sang along, enjoying the cleverness of the song. She had already learned several cadences and marching songs, including one about a drunken sailor and another about the marines and Parris Island. They kept everyone in step and helped pass the time in an entertaining way. It seemed as if someone always had a new verse to add to "The Quartermaster Corps."

Oh, it's chocolate cake
That makes you wanna layer. . . .

That doesn't rhyme, thought Kate. Oh, I get it! Layer means "lay her." Ha, ha, she thought sarcastically. They won't make me blush, and since they don't want me to be Miss America, I guess I'll just be one of the boys. She joined in loudly as someone else started a new verse:

Oh, it's hot roast duck
That makes you wanna—

"All right! Enough!" ordered one of the firsties sharply. He began to count cadence in the barking marine style. "Lay-uhf, lay-uhf, lay-uhf, rot, lay-uhf. . . ."

So there are limits after all, thought Kate, relieved to discover that there was some truth to the traditional description of midshipmen as "officers and gentlemen."

Saturday, 24 July 1976

It was becoming a tradition with the plebes of Thirty-third Platoon to gather on the night of a classmate's birthday and celebrate with a song and cake snuck up from the wardroom, an infraction of the regulations that could cost the perpetrator fifteen demerits.

Tonight, during personal time, the plebes gathered in Denzel's room to celebrate his eighteenth birthday. Thirty-six plebes sang "Happy Birthday" after Denzel's roommate lit the candle on the one slice of Lady Baltimore layer cake he had snuck up from dinner. (Firsties overlooked the mutinous "six-in-a-room" rule when it came to impromptu birthday parties.) Sarah smiled at the classmate standing beside her as she sang.

"Nice voice for a ploob," remarked Alan Teague as the song ended.

"Ploob? What the heck is a ploob?" she asked.

"Ploob? You haven't heard that slang yet?" he asked, surprised.

"No, and I can only imagine what it means."

"A ploob is a plebe with boobs."

"Oh, so what does that make you guys? Plicks?" she asked, smiling impishly.

Alan laughed along with several classmates within earshot.

"Plicks and ploobs. Leave it to you for a comeback, Sarah."

Monday, 26 July 1976

Monday evening, Seventh Platoon was in the middle of uniform races when their firsties suddenly instructed the plebes to empty their lockers of all uniform items. Kate, her roommates, and thirty-three fellow plebes chopped back and forth from their rooms to the front shaft carrying armloads of T-shirts, underwear, black socks, white socks, shorts, sneakers, Corfams, towels, washcloths, laundry bags, white works trousers, and white works blouses. They dumped the assorted apparel in a huge pile in the middle of the front shaft.

Kate grumbled to herself. On one trip she ran into Terrie in their room.

"What are they up to, Terrie? This is crazy!" she complained, sweeping into her arms a pile of clothes that she had meticulously folded the day before.

"I have no idea, Kate. Do you think we need to take our bras?"

"We'd better take everything. They may come and check. Man, this is ridiculous!"

On the way back to the growing pile of clothing, Kate caught the equally puzzled eye of a classmate who disgustedly shook his head and rolled his eyes.

"Let's go, people!" one squad leader yelled impatiently. "When you're finished emptying your lockers, hit the bulkhead and sound off!"

Stiff at attention, sweat streaming down her spine, Kate focused on the pile of clothes in front of her. It was at least four feet high and ten feet in diameter. She could not tell her belongings from any other except for the shoulder strap of her black purse hanging from the edge of the pile.

Her platoon leader paced in front of the two rows of glistening plebes lining the bulkheads, hands ostentatiously on his hips.

"Now, ladies and gentlemen, we will see who properly marked their uniform items with their alpha code as directed the first day of plebe summer. When I say go, you will begin sorting the items, find yours, and immediately stow them properly in your locker. Sea-bag inspections will be held at 2100." He walked over to the pile and lifted an armful of clothes as high as his head and scattered them. The other firsties in attendance joined in. The plebes groaned silently.

"We don't want this to be too easy, now, do we?"

At first Kate thought she knew generally where her clothes were, but now there was no guessing as T-shirts, underwear, and trousers were tumbled together.

Peering at the clock with her peripheral vision, Kate saw that it was 2030. They had only half an hour to sort through this mess and reorganize. These guys were insane. It couldn't be done.

"Ready, set, go!" The plebes scrambled to the pile. Clothes flew as thirty-six plebes checked each article of clothing for their alpha code and either stuffed it into their laundry bag or threw it back.

It took over forty-five minutes to sort through the pile. Firsties stopped them and drilled them on rates as they sorted. Kate forgot the menu for morning meal and was told to bring around a form two (conduct report). Every now and then she recognized the alpha code of one of her roommates and threw the article to its owner. Thank goodness Michelle had insisted that the three of them spend a few hours that first Saturday marking all their clothes.

When it was over, a small mass of unclaimed shoes and underwear remained in the passageway. Because it was late, the sea-bag inspections turned into a quick room inspection.

Kate and her roommates fell exhausted into their racks.

"Forget about how many days until Christmas leave," sighed Terrie. "I want to know how many days until Second Set gets here?"

Who knows? lamented Kate to herself. They might be worse.

Thursday, 29 July 1976

Sarah thought she was going to die from embarrassment. Mr. Randolph, on his way out into town, had stopped by the girls' room to see if they needed anything. Donna had already told Sarah and Tammy that she was going to ask him the next time she saw him, which was now, and Sarah wanted to crawl into the closet to hide.

"Yes, sir, we do need something. Could you please get us some Tampax?" Donna asked nonchalantly.

Sarah closed her eyes and shook her head. Tammy's mouth dropped open. Mr. Randolph's typically pink complexion beamed crimson.

"Oh, come on. It's only natural," continued Donna. "We've got to have 'em, and they don't carry 'em in the Mid Store. They only carry sanitary napkins, which are pretty useless during the day in this heat."

Mr. Randolph, regaining his composure, held up his hands to halt her dialogue. "Okay, okay, no details, please. Sure, I mean, I guess I can get you some, although I've never bought those things before. I'm not really sure what to look for."

"No problem," said Donna. "We'll give you a quick lesson." She took everyone's order and handed him a list.

When they returned from infantry drill that afternoon, a brown paper bag from a drugstore stood just inside their door.

Friday, 30 July 1976

Kate stood against the bulkhead outside her room while Mr. Daniel paced up and down the passageway like a judge of the Inquisition.

I have never experienced pressure so intense as come-around, she thought. Mr. Daniel allows no room for error. Everything must be absolutely correct, and it must be rattled off at lightning speed. I have to get everything right. Everything! I can't slip up or I'll have to brace up.

To be "braced up" meant you had to rig your chin against your neck and upper chest so that you created multiple chins. You then had to hold this position at all times when you were outside your room until the next meal formation. The humiliation was what Kate hated the most: everyone could see that you were braced up and knew that you had screwed up.

Kate had time to think during this come-around while Mr. Daniel harassed

Ted Zelko. It was pretty much a hopeless case. Kate and his roommates had tried to help him with memorization, but progress appeared to be infinitesimal. He was the shitscreen and would be subjected to rapid-fire questions and verbal abuse until Mr. Daniel tired of flaming on him and began roasting another victim. For the past several days the second victim had been Michelle, and this evening was no different. "Miss Mead," he demanded, "the Code of Conduct! Go!"

"The Code of Conduct," Michelle began. "One. I am an American fighting man. I serve—"

"What was that?" Mr. Daniel interrupted her angrily.

What was wrong with that? Kate wondered. She had begun it correctly.

Michelle started again. "The Code of Conduct. One. I am an American fighting man—"

"No, Miss Mead! Try it again!"

Michelle paused a moment. Kate didn't have to look at her to know that her eyes were beginning to well with tears because she didn't know what was wrong. "The Code of Conduct. One. I am an American fighting man. I—"

"You're a *what?*" Mr. Daniel was in her face, screaming at the top of his lungs.

Michelle started to tremble, and her voice faltered. "I am an American fighting man—"

"Oh, you are?!" Mr. Daniel interrupted again. "Mr. Wilson, is Miss Mead an American fighting man?"

Suddenly Kate realized what Mr. Daniel meant. It's the word *man!* He's picking on Michelle because of a word that she is not at liberty to change.

Wilson caught on, too. "Sir, no, sir!"

Mr. Daniel turned on Wilson. "Mr. Wilson, are you bilging your classmate?"

"Sir, no, sir." Now Wilson sounded confused.

"Isn't she a midshipman, too?"

"Sir, yes, sir!"

"Then she's subject to the Code of Conduct, isn't she?"

"Sir, yes, sir." Wilson's confidence was waning.

"Then she *is* an American fighting man, isn't that right, Mr. Wilson?"

"Sir, yes, sir." Wilson had no choice.

"But you just told me 'no, sir' a minute ago!" Mr. Daniel was triumphant, almost gleeful.

Wilson stepped right into it. "But sir, I thought—"

"Are you a sea lawyer, Mr. Wilson?" Mr. Daniel was flaming on. "Do you have an explanation for everything but the answer to nothing?" Mr. Daniel flared up one last time, and the blaze consumed the whole squad. "Brace up, all of you! Dismissed!"

Alone in her humidity-drenched room the following afternoon, Kate indulged her solitude with a brownie sent from home and a Pepsi from the soda machine down the hall. One of her roommates was at the movie in the Yard, and the other was at an Academy Christian Association meeting. Having never considered herself a loner, Kate suddenly realized how seldom she was able to be by herself at the Academy, and she pined for more time alone.

She had just come from marching extra duty to work off demerits she had been awarded for having an "unsat" room. Plebes without demerits had been enjoying Yard liberty: time off from the hectic daily schedule to work out or participate in activities on the Yard. They were still not allowed to go outside the gates of the Academy into the town of Annapolis. That would be the rule until Parents' Weekend, still five weeks away.

Kate thought about how well Terrie did at everything, which was a constant source of frustration. And then there was the girl next door in their sister platoon who was not only better than Kate at everything, she was also beautiful and the nicest person you would ever want to know.

And the next set of firsties would be here next weekend. Kate was very apprehensive about their arrival, finally feeling comfortable with, or at least aware of, the expectations of the First Set.

I guess that's what it's all about, though, she thought. *Growing, changing, maturing. I just hope I can measure up.*

She reached for another brownie. Chow from home always made her feel better. Temporarily, anyway. And if she ate too many, she knew how to get rid of that bloated feeling.

CHAPTER THREE

Plebe Summer, Second Set

P lebe—That insignificant thing that gets all the
sympathy and chow from home.

Reef Points, 1976–77

Sunday, 8 August 1976

The early-August heat rose from the bricks of Tecumseh Court (or "T-Court,"
as they now knew to call it) as the midshipmen of the Class of 1980 took their
places for Sunday evening meal formation. Walking smartly and confidently
before a crowd of tourists, the young men and women took their places and
stood at parade rest, apprehensively awaiting the "changing of the guard."
Tonight the Second Set of first-class midshipmen would relieve the First Set
of their plebe-detail duties.

As usual, the regimental commander called the entire formation to attention and took muster reports from each battalion. His next order was one the
plebes had never heard before: "First Set, right or left face!" Two hundred
first classmen obeyed with a two-step grit of sole against brick. "First Set,
march off!" Leaders they had known for the past four weeks marched toward either side of Bancroft Hall, leaving the regiment of plebes momentarily leaderless.

Kate's throat tightened as a new voice from the center of T-Court gave the
next order: "Second Set, forward march!" A freshly pressed group of first
classmen marched to the exact spot of their predecessors.

Maybe it's going to all begin again, she thought, watching the new leaders
take their places. What are *these* guys going to think of us girls being here?
First Set was at least bearable as far as that goes. They really didn't treat us

any different from the guys. If only I could do better athletically and when reciting my rates.

Kate mentally recounted the "Laws of the Navy," which all plebes were required to have memorized by now. They consisted of twenty-seven four-line stanzas that they might be called upon to recite at random. They were the hardest rates to learn. She and her roommates had marched around their room after taps singing them to music until they were etched in their memories. Now she prayed that she would remember them when these new firsties demanded them.

The Drum and Bugle Corps broke into "Anchors Aweigh," and Kate's new platoon leader boomed the order to "forward march." She held her head high and stepped out behind her classmates. She told herself, I'm going to prove to this set that I can be the best.

Monday, 9 August 1976

Sarah hurried into her room, slammed her *Reef Points* onto the desk, and ran to the mirror over the sink.

"Look at this butch job!" She was almost in tears. Her cute pixie cut had been sheared to a length only millimeters longer than that stipulated for male midshipmen. "I can't believe it! The one, small, last thing I had that was feminine is gone!" The tears broke free, and Donna hurried to comfort her. She put her hands on Sarah's shaking shoulders and led her away from the mirror.

"It looks great, hon," she tried to sound convincing.

"No, it doesn't," sobbed Sarah. "It looks like a butch job, which is what it is. That clown they have down there cutting women's hair has no idea what he's doing. I asked him if he had ever cut women's hair before and he said no, but he had taken a correspondence course—and he was serious!" Her sobs continued. It had taken all the courage she could muster to cut off her long hair before coming to the Academy, and now she looked like her little brother. The administration just had to do something about this mock beautician.

"When he asked me how I wanted it cut, I told him just the same as it was, it just needed to be shorter. So this guy walks around the chair, looking at my head the entire time, clueless of where to begin." Sarah's sobs began to subside as her anger grew.

"Then he finally picks up a clump of hair and begins to chop. I should've just left, but how could I? What am I supposed to do? We're not allowed to go out into town, and we're not allowed to cut each other's hair. This is bull-shit!" She paced around the room.

"So then," she continued without pause, "when he's finished, my bangs are two inches above my eyebrows!" She looked in the mirror. "Look! I've been 'whitewalled'! I can't believe I had to pay for this torture!"

"Honey, it looks okay. A little short, maybe, but it will grow."

"Oh, fine. It won't have any kind of shape or style to it. It'll look like hell. I can't believe this! Here I am trying to get squared away for Second Set, and this is what I get. Our new firsties are going to think I'm a guy!"

"She's right, you know, Donna," Tammy agreed. "That guy is a butcher down there. He's no beautician. All those fancy hair dryers and chairs in that makeshift beauty shop are great for show, but you walk out of there feeling a lot worse than when you went in."

"As soon as we get town liberty, I'm going out into town and get a real hair-cut, and I don't care how much it costs me," Tammy continued. "My one and only trip to that barbershop is my last until they get somebody in there who knows how to cut women's hair."

"Well, girls," interrupted Donna, "we've got formation in two minutes for first aid instruction. Maybe they can cover those shorn locks with ace ban-dages, Becker!"

Sarah smiled reluctantly. Forcing herself to look in the mirror once again, she straightened the cover on her head. Man, am I attractive, she cajoled her-self. Oh, who cares? I'm not here to win a beauty contest or impress anyone with my looks.

Following Tammy and Donna out the door, she squared a corner in the middle of the passageway. "Beat the barbershop, sir!" she yelled, not caring who heard her.

Wednesday, 11 August 1976

"Bounce, '80! Bounce! Bounce!" Coach Lenz commanded the plebes with crisp, stentorian orders like a benevolent dictator. "Now push-ups, '80! Push-ups!" Coach Lenz ordered the plebes enthusiastically. "Supers use one hand!"

Kate dropped to her knees on the wet, prickly Astroturf and began to do modified push-ups. These are my worst, she thought. I wish I could do real push-ups like the guys. I know what some of them are thinking: "Look at that stupid girl. What a weakling! What a bagger!" Dirk Walker and some of the others have hardly stopped saying that since I-Day.

"Sit-ups, '80! Cross your hands on your chest and do sit-ups!"

Kate grimaced even before she sat down in the cold water. This is gross! Wet Astroturf just has to be the worst thing in the world: soggy like a marsh on top, but hard as rocks underneath. Dirk is hard as rocks too, when it comes to his opinion of women at the Academy. It's as if he's never even noticed that girl in the next platoon; she's always a super at everything. He's so quick to doubt me. It's like he's questioning my honor.

"All right, '80! Run! Run!"

Oh, no, groaned Kate, standing up, her shirt and shorts dripping. At least we're staying on the Astroturf and not going out for a mile run.

She ran behind her classmates the length of the field in an elliptical course around the orange cones at either end. As her platoon mates passed her on the opposite side, she could see each one's face clearly for just a moment, recognizing not only their identities but also their emotions: excitement, fatigue, pride, boredom, determination, exasperation. Most didn't even notice her, but a few smiled back, some nodded, others rolled their eyes. She looked down briefly but when she looked up again, she saw Dirk. Everything on the field seemed blotted out by his intense expression.

It was a look of pure hate.

Sweating profusely from the march to the field house, the Romeo Company plebes stood on the indoor track and stripped down to their gold-trimmed navy shorts and white T-shirts, ready to perform the "Applied Struggle." The applied strength test, nicknamed the Applied Struggle by their firsties, was a physical fitness test consisting of a half-mile run, sit-ups, and dips for everybody, with pull-ups for the men and a flexed-arm hang for the women. Requirements for dips had been modified for the women, as had the scoring times for the run and the number of sit-ups.

"Romeo Company will do sit-ups first with Lieutenant Robertson." A male physical education instructor directed the plebes toward the end of the track. Lieutenant Robertson was a female PE instructor Sarah had had for the self-defense class the women took in lieu of the wrestling and boxing classes offered to the men.

"Pick a partner to hold your feet," Lieutenant Robertson instructed. "Sit-ups will be performed with your knees bent, hands behind your head, and a classmate holding your feet. You will have two minutes to complete as many sit-ups as possible." She looked around the mass of plebes at her feet to ensure that everyone had a partner and was positioned correctly.

Donna held Tammy's feet while Denzel grabbed Sarah's. The lieutenant held up her stop watch. "Ready . . . begin!"

Sarah cranked out 108 sit-ups in 120 seconds.

"Damn, girl!" Denzel exclaimed in amazement. "Where'd you get those stomach muscles?"

They switched partners and repeated the exercise, after which male and female classmates parted ways. Lieutenant Robertson escorted the five girls in Romeo Company to the pull-up bars to perform the flexed-arm hang and modified dips while the men in the company gathered on the other side of the track.

The flexed-arm hang was more awkward than difficult. On the pull-up bar, the women were hoisted by female classmates into a position where their hands grasped the bar as if doing a pull-up. Then they were required to brace themselves with their breastbones against the bar, chin above, not touching, while their classmates let go. They were to hold that position for a minimum of five seconds. Lieutenant Robertson started the stop watch once the classmates let go and stopped it when someone's chin touched or dropped below the bar.

One of the girls in Thirty-fourth Platoon went first. Evelyn Parker was overweight and could barely hold herself up for two seconds when hoisted up onto the pull-up bar. Another case for the "subsquad," the group of non-hackers who had to practice these tests until they passed while other plebes were playing sports in the afternoons.

Sarah vowed to pass the Applied Struggle with a grade of outstanding. The flexed-arm hang concerned her, as she would have to hold herself above the bar for sixty seconds to score outstanding.

Donna and Tammy hoisted her into position, and she nodded for Lieutenant Robertson to start the clock. Hanging with her chin two inches above the bar, she listened for the lieutenant to call out the passing time: "Fifteen seconds . . . thirty seconds. . . ."

Her arms were beginning to ache, and her chin was starting to shake. Hang on, Sarah told herself. She tried to think about something else. Her arms started to shake, and she could feel her chin starting to drop toward the bar. Hold on! Hold on!

"You can do it, Sarah!" she heard Donna call.

"Five, four, three, two, one." Sarah's chin grazed the bar as she dropped to the floor, her biceps throbbing.

"Sixty seconds," called Lieutenant Robertson. "Outstanding."

Sarah smiled, rubbing her throbbing upper arms. "How am I gonna do dips after that?"

Male plebes performed dips by lowering and raising themselves between two shoulder-width parallel wooden rods protruding a foot and a half from the wall. The women's dips were performed on an inch-and-a-half steel bar about a foot and a half from the wall, installed parallel to the wall on a set of brackets. The bar was about three feet long and about four and a half feet off the ground. The women hoisted themselves onto the bar with both hands until the pubic bone rested against the bar. They lowered themselves until their fists met their armpits and then raised themselves by straightening their arms.

Evelyn went first. She struggled to complete only one. The minimum requirement was three. Donna and Tammy made the minimum. Sarah wanted to do ten. She had developed solid upper-body strength, and ten turned out to be no problem as, she thankfully found, she used a different set of muscles.

The half-mile run was next. The instructors ran the plebes by squads. Sarah hated to run, but a half-mile was nothing compared with some of the multiple-mile runs they had completed during PEP. She lined up with the rest of her squad and completed the run easily in the time allotted, keeping up almost the entire time with the men in her company.

Dressing back into white works, Sarah turned toward a deep voice behind her.

"Hey, Buns. Did you ace it?" It was Denzel.

"I think so," she called confidently.

"What a stud! Or should I say studette?" he replied, laughing as the two fell into formation to march back to the Hall.

Friday, 13 August 1976

As her platoon leader ordered the plebes to halt in the middle of T-Court, Kate immediately felt the sun scorching the toes of her black patent-leather shoes.

If only we didn't have to wear these stupid black Corfams! They look great—shiny black all the time without having to be spit-polished—but the plastic makes my feet sweat. And the three-inch heels are absurd! Some man must have assumed we would want high heels because we're short. Or maybe they figured that higher heels would somehow transform a basic masculine oxford into a ladies' shoe—no matter how impractical they are for marching and chopping. I can't believe they make us run in high heels! My legs ache every time I have to wear them. I think they're partly to blame for the high number of shin splints and sprained ankles among the women.

Suddenly she heard the whirring and clicking of cameras as Seventh Platoon began marching again toward Chauvenet Hall, and Kate's stomach began to churn. Please don't let them shout anything, she prayed, knowing that only a miracle could change the behavior of the tourists. There was no miracle today.

"There's one!" someone to the left shouted as she passed Tecumseh. The cameras clicked furiously, like hundreds of castanets.

"Why is she all alone at the end of the line?" a young woman asked. "Do the girls always have to walk behind the men?"

"No, look! There are three of them!" another woman shrieked. "Get a picture!"

Enough already, thought Kate, resisting the urge to shout back at them. We're not deaf, and we're not freaks. We're just midshipmen. Why can't you leave us alone?

Sunday, 15 August 1976

Sarah studied the front page of the Sunday *Baltimore Sun* for an article she could read and be conversant about at noon meal. Tammy and Donna had just left to attend chapel services in the Yard. Sarah preferred to spend her Sunday mornings napping, writing letters, or doing nothing.

Tammy's Sunday morning was a ritual. Her shower was first. Deodorant, powder, perfume, makeup, then pantyhose. She spent at least a precious twenty minutes blow-drying her hair, releasing herself from the pervasive masculine environment that surrounded them every other moment of the week. Donna was more matter-of-fact about the ordeal; a simple shower and some makeup satisfied her. Every now and then Sarah considered joining them. They looked so feminine going off to church in skirts, which were mandatory for women going to chapel.

Sarah had worn a skirt only twice during the summer. The first time was a Sunday noon meal formation when the women had been required to wear skirts. The event proved disastrous when they could not keep stride with the men marching into the wardroom because of the narrow circumference of their hems. Pants were the uniform of the day from then on.

The second time was when the entire Fourth Class Regiment had been bused to the Kennedy Center in Washington, D.C., for a performance of *Fiddler on the Roof.* Women were to wear skirts with their tropical white longs. After taking a full half-hour to get dressed, primping and indulging in light makeup, the three roommates sauntered out the door into the passageway to be greeted with catcalls and whistles from Denzel and four other male squad mates. It was the first time the guys had seen their classmates dressed as "real girls." The girls had been elated at the unsolicited response.

Engrossed in the newspaper, Sarah didn't hear him enter the room. By the time she sensed his presence and came to attention, preparing to sound off, he was holding up his hand, signifying that it was unnecessary.

"Carry on, Miss Becker," Midshipman Nolde, her new squad leader, told her.

"Yes, sir," she replied, still standing rigid at attention.

"Carry on." He repeated the order to relax her stance.

She knew it was his turn to stand weekend duty, but she didn't know why he had come to her room. She fell out of attention but remained at parade rest as her heart began to pound. Is he here to ask me rates? she wondered. I don't think he can do that on Sunday mornings during personal time.

Still, Mr. Nolde was new, and she wasn't sure how he operated just yet. Although he was extremely good-looking, she found his demeanor imposing, even icy during come-arounds. Uniformly tough on everyone in the squad, he obviously meant business. Without being a flamer, he displayed a quiet, firm disappointment when anyone choked on their rates, making them feel worse than if he had just gone ahead and yelled.

"I read your birthday cards yesterday when I inspected your room," he said, pointing to the cards tacked to the bulletin board over Sarah's rack. "Happy birthday. When was it?"

"Oh. Thank you, sir. It was August second, sir," she replied, feeling mildly violated. Was anything written in them that she might not have wanted him to read? The card from her best friend, Anne, sprang to mind. She and Anne were always joking around about how much they missed being together. Sarah was sure Anne must have written something about that. She started to blush. Maybe he hadn't really read them. She could only hope. . . .

"Or maybe I should say, Happy birthday, 'Toots.'"

She wanted to die. He *had* read them, at least Anne's card. All through senior year of high school, the two of them privately referred to themselves as the "two Tootsies." They called each other Toots all the time. A silly, private thing they did—until now. Now her nickname was in the hands of the enemy.

"'Miss Becker' will be fine, sir," she replied, trying unsuccessfully to dim the pink in her cheeks. "That card is from my best friend from high school. She and I are always kidding around, sir."

"Hmm. Home is New Hampshire?"

"Yes, sir."

"I'm from South Carolina. Most beautiful place in the world. Ever been to the South, Miss Becker?"

"Texas, sir."

"Not that South," he said. "You need to go. It's beautiful country." He phrased it almost like an invitation.

"Uh, yes, sir." Where is this conversation going? she wondered, not sure that she wanted to know.

"Well, study that newspaper. You never know who may be asking for the latest news." She saw him smile for the first time and noticed that only one corner of his mouth rose. Cute, she thought. He turned to leave.

"Sir?" He stopped and turned back to face her. "Please don't tell anyone about that nickname, sir."

"Then take it off your bulletin board, Miss Becker."

"Uh, yes, sir," she answered, realizing that the discovery was actually her fault. I guess I put them on public display, she decided. Our room is open for inspections by anyone at any time.

She watched him walk slowly from her room. Funny, she thought, that was painless. So why is my heart still pounding?

Monday, 16 August 1976

After evening meal come-around Monday night, Midshipman Nolde told Sarah to stand fast as he let the rest of the squad shove off for evening meal formation.

"Miss Becker."

"Yes, sir?" she called, still standing at attention.

"Congratulations on being selected for the cheerleading squad." Tryouts had been held two days earlier, and Sarah was one of six women chosen. In previous years the administration had recruited women from local colleges. This was the first time they had selected women from among their ranks.

"Thank you, sir."

"Also, we got the results of the applied strength test today, and you did very well. In fact, you ranked 125th out of the entire class."

Her eyes lit up. Out of twelve hundred plebes! She knew she had scored outstanding, but she had not realized that they were going to rank the men and women together.

"Thank you, sir."

"You're quite a jock, huh? What sport did you play in high school?"

"None, sir."

"Oh, just comes naturally, huh?" he said sarcastically.

She didn't know how to respond and resorted to one of her five basic responses. "I'll find out, sir."

"Don't give me that. You've never played sports?"

"I was on the gymnastics team as a sophomore, but for the past two years I was in the band, sir. It must be PEP, sir."

"Yes, I've noticed you out at PEP," he remarked. "You seem to hang in there with the best of them. That's good. Keep it up." He phrased it like an order. She took it to heart. Show these guys that some of the girls can make it, she thought.

"You can go now."

"Aye, aye, sir," she said, squaring a corner and heading to formation. Sarah was elated. One hundred and twenty-fifth! A warm feeling of pride overtook her. Then she paused.

Why hadn't he announced it in front of *everyone?*

Wednesday, 18 August 1976

Arrow-straight at attention, Kate silently reviewed her rates, only half-listening as Mr. Marshall questioned her classmates at this evening's come-around. She had not yet figured out her new squad leader, despite applying herself to the task for more than a week. He was not a flamer like Mr. Daniel, but Kate sensed that he possessed a reserve of quiet anger that could be just as demeaning as Daniel's bombast. There seemed to be a fun side to him, evident when he reminisced about his "extracurricular" exploits, such as "going over the wall" the previous year with a classmate, which had earned him a "Black N" award: seventy-five demerits and two months' restriction. He was quite open about it, almost proud, and it struck Kate as an odd example for a leader to set.

"Brigman!"

Kate broke off her private study. "Yes, sir?"

"Tell me about the . . . F-4."

"Sir, the F-4 Phantom is an air-superiority fighter manufactured by McDonnell Aircraft of St. Louis, Missouri. It has a crew of two, a speed of 1,600 knots, and a range of 2,300—"

"All right. That's enough." Mr. Marshall interrupted her as if her recitation bored him. "Mead!" Kate was disappointed that he had cut her off.

"Yes, sir," Michelle answered.

"How about. . . ." He flipped back a few pages in the *Reef Points* that he had borrowed from one of the plebes in the squad. "Um . . . how are minesweepers named?"

Michelle recited her answer, and Mr. Marshall asked a few more questions to which he received quick, correct responses, although he did not make any positive remarks about the plebes' performances. In fact, he seemed to find the whole exercise rather tedious. He closed the *Reef Points* and handed it back to its owner. "Brigman, stand fast. The rest of you, dismissed."

What have I done? Kate wondered as her classmates scattered to their rooms. She tried to squelch the sense of foreboding she felt. Mr. Marshall waited until the din of her squad mates' chopping and squaring corners had ceased. "Report to the company officer, Brigman," he ordered. "He wants to talk to you."

"Aye, aye, sir," she replied, wanting to ask him why. An order to see the company officer was ominous. What could she have done to merit Lieutenant Griffith's attention?

She chopped down the center of the passageway toward his office, her consternation mounting with every step. She caught her breath before knocking on the door. "Request permission to come aboard, sir?"

"Come aboard," Lieutenant Griffith called.

Kate opened the door and removed her cover. "Good morning, sir. Midshipman Fourth Class Brigman, sir."

The lieutenant smiled and nodded. "Good morning, Miss Brigman. Please come in and sit down." He gestured toward a chair in front of his desk.

"Looking forward to academic year?" he asked, as she took a seat.

"Yes, sir," she replied, relieved, so far, at his even tone.

"You've validated quite a few courses, which will help you out considerably." (Midshipmen took tests in certain courses. If they tested high enough, they "validated" the courses and were not required to take them.)

Was this all this was about? she wondered. "Yes, sir, and thank you for the note, sir." She had received a congratulatory note from him after validating two semesters of English and one of French I.

He looked at her a moment as if contemplating another question, then looked down at his desk. When he met her eye again, he was not smiling. "Miss Brigman, I've received a report from out of company that you were seen dragging."

Kate was aghast. Dragging? She hadn't dated anyone here! Plebes weren't allowed to date. Anyway, she wondered, who'd want to date me? She struggled to give a proper response. "No, sir. I haven't been dragging, sir."

Griffith pressed further. "You were seen walking through the yard with two of your male classmates last evening, Miss Brigman."

Two of my classmates? Kate searched her memory for an explanation. Where was I yesterday? She thought out loud. "Sir, I was at choir rehearsal last evening in St. Andrew's Chapel with. . . ." She stopped midsentence as the explanation hit her.

"Go on, Miss Brigman," Griffith prompted. "With whom?"

"With my classmates, Midshipmen Fourth Class Peeper and Chipping." The truth was so innocent, Kate would have laughed aloud had it not been for the fear of demerits—or worse. "The first class used to march us to rehearsal, but now they let us straggle over, sir. The three of us walked together because we're in the same squad, sir."

Griffith raised his eyebrows. "Choir practice?" He bit the corner of his lip to keep from smiling. "That's all it was?"

"Yes, sir." Kate wanted to clear herself completely. "I know we're not allowed to date, sir. I mean, these guys are my classmates."

ʳGriffith could hardly hide his relief. "Yes, Miss Brigman. I understand. There seems to have been a misunderstanding." He thought a moment. "Perhaps in the future you could be more careful how you walk to rehearsal."

"Sir, do you mean I can't walk with my own classmates?"

Griffith was obviously taken aback by the question. Of course classmates should be able to walk together. The men had always done just that, but somehow it was different when the classmates were men and women—suspicion

outweighed logic. "What I mean is, of course you can walk with your classmates," he said, his voice betraying his uncertainty and discomfort. "You just
need to be careful about how you walk together, so that no one gets . . . suspicious."

Suspicious. The word echoed in Kate's mind as she chopped away from
Griffith's office. Suspicious is right, she thought angrily. Suspicious minds anxious to catch a female doing anything wrong. If I walk with my classmates,
I'm suspected of dragging them, but at the same time I'm supposed to
develop esprit de corps and teamwork with them. How can I be part of the
team if I can't even walk with my teammates without being accused of
improper behavior? It just doesn't make sense. What kind of girls do they
think we are?

Saturday, 21 August 1976

On Saturday evening the Class of 1980 was scheduled to attend a Baltimore
Orioles baseball game. At 1710 all fourth-class midshipmen, dressed in tropical white long, formed up and boarded the blue and silver Naval Academy
buses.

At the stadium, Sarah, Donna, Tammy, and Denzel sat near one another in
the stands. In the middle of the second inning, Midshipman Rhodes, their
company commander and one of the duty midshipmen, joined them. He
spoke to them for several minutes, paying particular attention to Donna.

Since Donna was the same age as most of the firsties and more mature than
her roommates, she had a different rapport with the upperclassmen. While
playing the game of subservient plebe, she also managed to converse with the
upperclass in a more friendly manner. She wasn't afraid to speak her mind
and was quick to relay day-to-day problems the girls might be having that
could be corrected by the administration.

For instance, she had immediately gone to see Mr. Nolde about the problems they'd had with the women's barber. Mr. Nolde called them in one by
one, questioned them about it, and set up an appointment for them to discuss
their recommendations with the Fourth Class Regimental commander, the
summer's highest-ranking first-class midshipman. No changes had been made,
but they felt confident that some were forthcoming.

Mr. Rhodes stood up to leave as two men dressed in civilian clothes
approached. "Hey, Danny-boy!" one called. Sarah looked up and saw Mr.

Nolde and another squad leader from Thirty-fourth Platoon standing on the stairs, beers in hand. What are they doing here? she wondered. They're "off-duty" and could be anywhere else.

"What are you guys doing here?" she heard Mr. Rhodes ask.

"Thought we'd come buy ice cream for our plebes," Mr. Nolde answered. "Paul, go get the 'scream." The squad leader from Thirty-fourth Platoon turned and walked up the stairs.

"Ryan, you'd better watch yourself with these plebes. You don't want to get fried for fraternization." Sarah heard Mr. Rhodes quietly warn Mr. Nolde.

"Don't worry, Danny-boy. We're just having a little fun." He pushed his way past Donna's knees and sat between Sarah and Denzel.

"Hey, Mr. Nolde. What's happenin', sir?" It was Denzel.

"Hey, Mr. Simmons. How the hell are ya?" He turned to Sarah. "And how are you, Miss Becker?"

"Fine, sir." Her heart picked up rhythm. He was here to see her. She was flattered yet afraid that her classmates might have guessed the same. That he had not come alone was not enough to conceal his real intentions.

Mr. Nolde greeted each plebe sitting nearby and attempted friendly conversation with each. They responded respectfully, but only Denzel conversed comfortably with him.

The squad leader from Thirty-fourth Platoon showed up with a vendor box full of ice cream cones and distributed them to the plebes.

"Good job, Paul." Mr. Nolde stood to help hand out the cones. When everyone in his squad had one, he sat back down beside Sarah and Denzel. His cohort went to distribute ice cream among Thirty-fourth Platoon.

"Who else is here, sir?" asked Donna.

"A couple of other firsties you haven't met yet. They're sitting in 'bird land,' the cheap seats." He continued conversing with Denzel and the girls as they ate their ice cream cones until their conversation was interrupted by a tall marine second lieutenant.

"Excuse me, sir." He gestured to Mr. Nolde.

"Oh, shit." Sarah heard Mr. Nolde mutter under his breath. "Yes?"

"Excuse me, sir, but the young lady is not allowed to drag, uh, have a date at this game. I am afraid I am going to have to ask you to leave."

"I'm not a date!" answered Mr. Nolde, irritated. Sarah was suddenly fearful. Why had this lieutenant singled her out? She knew she had been talking freely with Mr. Nolde, but so had Denzel and all the plebes around him.

Mr. Rhodes thankfully appeared out of nowhere. "Can I help you, sir?" he addressed the marine.

"I was just telling this gentleman, the young lady here does not rate dragging."

"Uh, sir, this gentleman is a midshipman, and he was just talking to some of the plebes in our company," Mr. Rhodes explained.

"He's a midshipman?!" The marine was incredulous. "He doesn't rate sitting with fourth classmen in civilian clothes. You'd better take your business elsewhere, mister!"

Mr. Nolde told everyone to enjoy the rest of the game and left. Sarah's heart was pounding. The marine watched Mr. Nolde climb the stairs and walk through the opening to the backside of the stadium. Satisfied that he was gone, the marine left.

Sarah quickly whispered to Donna, "Let's go find the head."

Donna accompanied Sarah up the stairs to the back of the stadium. The women's restroom was around the corner.

"Can you believe that guy?" Sarah asked Donna, meaning the marine.

"Yeah, well, Mr. Nolde really shouldn't be over here with us," said Donna.

"So why didn't *you* tell him that?"

"I don't know. It seemed harmless at the time. And right, I'm going to tell our squad leader where he should be! You know, Sarah, I think Mr. Nolde has the hots for you."

"Oh, please, Donna. That's just great! And what am I supposed to do about it? Tell him to go away? He's our squad leader, for Pete's sake!" Sarah didn't want to expose the fact that she was also attracted to Mr. Nolde, because she was extremely anxious about the precarious position their mutual attraction put them in.

Although it was still unclear if male and female plebes could date one another, it was written in black and white that plebes were not allowed to fraternize with upperclass. Sarah was not sure what the punishment would be if two people were caught fraternizing. Expulsion? She guessed that the punishment would be worse for the upperclassman, who should know better, but she certainly did not want to find out. It wasn't worth being expelled over, yet these feelings were so hard to suppress.

"Just be careful, Sarah—that's all I'm saying." Donna tried to sound comforting. Sarah followed her out of the head, glad that Mr. Nolde was gone and she could enjoy the rest of the game.

Sarah's contentment dissolved when she saw Mr. Nolde sitting once again in her seat. Her eyes opened wide as she looked at Donna, who just shrugged.

"He's a big boy," she said and started down the stairs.

"Hey, ladies!" Mr. Nolde greeted them both.

"Hello again, sir," offered Donna. Sarah smiled and remained silent. They both sat down. Sarah had no choice but to sit beside Mr. Nolde. Denzel was on his other side. She felt Donna's glare but didn't dare look at her. This was not her fault. What did Donna expect her to do?

The conversation between Mr. Nolde and the plebes around him remained animated for the next twenty minutes. It was during the seventh-inning stretch when the marine second lieutenant reappeared. He said nothing, merely stood at the end of the row, pointed to Mr. Nolde and jerked his thumb, motioning for the midshipman to leave the area ASAP.

Sarah watched Mr. Nolde stand and walk sideways.

"Didn't I tell you once to leave this area, mister?" The marine was irate, veins raised across his forehead.

"Yes, sir, you did, but for no good reason," Mr. Nolde replied, in a tone bordering on disrespect. He knew that this guy was a recent USNA graduate and was pulling a power play now that he was a "real" officer.

Sarah couldn't believe Mr. Nolde's remark and attitude. She grew frightened. She knew the marine believed that Mr. Nolde was there on her account, and she was sure this was going to lead to trouble.

After Mr. Nolde had left again, Sarah wondered what would happen to him. Would the second lieutenant make him leave the game? Was he going to be fried? Was *she* going to be fried? She tried convincing herself that she shouldn't really be in any trouble, since she was a victim of circumstances, but the second lieutenant's angry stare was imbedded in her mind, and it turned into a long bus ride back to the Academy.

Sunday, 22 August 1976

Kate walked down the chapel steps Sunday morning feeling refreshed and at peace. She wanted the sensation of tranquillity to last as long as possible. Other plebes rushed down the stone steps and hurried back to Bancroft for noon meal formation, but she moved slowly, admiring the flowers lining the red brick walkways. Between Chauvenet and Michelson Halls, she could see the Severn River decorated with the blue and gold stripes of Naval Academy spinnakers.

Back home, we'd be getting ready for Sunday dinner right now, she mused. Then we'd all sit around and watch the Olympics. She visualized the scene and drew comfort from it but did not give in to the temptation to be homesick.

She reached the bottom step and walked to the curb, where she waited for an approaching car to stop or pass. There were several young men in it, and as the car neared the crosswalk it slowed as if it were stopping. Kate started to step off the curb, then hesitated, waiting for the car to pass. The driver leaned out his window, his face contorted with anger, and shouted at her, "Get the hell out of my school!"

Kate jumped back onto the curb as the car sped off. She stood there, trembling. Obviously they were upperclassman back from summer cruise. How can you say that to me? she wanted to yell. You don't even know me! This is my school, too!

She turned and looked at the chapel, but the serenity was shattered. They've ruined it, she thought bitterly. They wrecked my feeling of peace. She fought to blink back tears as her mind settled on one terrifying thought.

What if that guy is in my company?

At 2130 on Sunday night, Sarah, Donna, and Tammy returned to their room after a lecture on the rudiments of sailing given to the company by their sub-commander. They would begin sailing training on knockabouts the following day.

Sarah had her feet propped up on the desk when she heard Mr. Rhodes yelling at the top of his lungs, "Thirty-third Platoon, PLEBE HO!"

"I knew an extra hour of personal time was too good to be true," Sarah told Donna as they ran out the door, hit the bulkhead, and sounded off.

Once all plebes were present, Mr. Rhodes paced before the platoon lining both sides of the passageway.

"Tonight, ladies and gentlemen, we will perform carrier landings. Anyone know what carrier landings are?" He looked around. There were no outstretched fists. "All right, then. Tonight, two of your squad leaders and myself will teach you bums how to land on an aircraft carrier." He gestured to Mr. Nolde and Mr. Cordere standing at the end of the hall, dressed in T-shirts and white works trousers.

"All right, you clowns, listen up. This passageway is the carrier deck. You get a running start at the end of the hall here, about halfway down throw yourselves belly first onto the floor, then slide the rest of the way until you slam into the mattress propped up at the other end there." He gestured to the striped mattress at the end of the hall. Sarah wondered who it belonged to.

"Extra points are given for creative sliding. On the way down, if you crash and burn we'll have a Fire Team ready to put out your flames as they deem necessary. No one is required to land on the carrier unless they want to. Any pussies who don't want to play may go back to their rooms at this time."

The entire platoon accepted the challenge, except the girls.

"Hey, we fall into that category," said Sarah to Donna and Tammy with a big smile. "Let's bag it. I'd like to keep what small chest I have." The three giggled and turned to go to their room.

"Whoa, whoa, whoa," said Mr. Rhodes, chasing after them. "What is this? The girls don't want to play?"

"Not really, sir," said Donna, turning to face him. "We can't land on carriers by law anyway, sir."

"Good point, Miss Carter," retorted Mr. Rhodes. "How 'bout you girls being the Fire Team, then?"

Donna looked at Sarah and Tammy. "Okay, sir," said Sarah. "I'm game. What do we have to do, sir?"

"Step into your room," said Mr. Rhodes. The girls obeyed.

Once inside, he told them that they were responsible for maintaining buckets of water and shaving-cream foam to put out fires on any guys that crashed and burned.

"Sounds like fun, sir," said Tammy. "Are you going to land on the carrier too, sir?"

"No, but Mr. Nolde and Mr. Cordere are."

"Great!" exclaimed Sarah. "Our chance to get back at Mr. Nolde for all the rates he asks."

As Mr. Rhodes left their room, which, conveniently, was in the middle of the passageway, Sarah turned to Donna and Tammy. "Let's dress the part," she said.

The girls pulled out their nightshirts and printed "Fire Team" across the front and back. Sarah grabbed their cleaning bucket from under their sink while Tammy left to borrow shaving cream from some of the guys.

The carrier landings began. Plebe after plebe sprawled headfirst down the passageway, arms groping and stretching to reach the mattress at the end of the hallway so that their imaginary flames would not be doused by the Fire

Team. It was all to no avail, as the floor was too dry to allow them to slide freely. Sarah and her roommates doused and sprayed those who landed short, and in no time the passageway became flooded with water and shaving cream. It wasn't long before the plebes were having a hard time stopping before they slammed into the mattress.

"Somebody's going to get hurt," warned Tammy. "It's really slippery out there."

"Nah," said Sarah. "Besides, Nolde is up. Let's get him!"

Mr. Nolde took his place at the head of the passageway and ran down the hall. A third of the way down, he let his feet go out from underneath him and began sliding on his back in a fetal position, turning in circles as he slid. As he passed their room, the three girls seized the opportunity. They ran out of their room, each with a bucket full of water, and drowned him. He stopped spinning and struggled to get up, reaching for a bucket, looking for retaliation.

As he stood, however, he lost his footing in the inch of water covering the floor and fell headfirst onto the hard tile. The dull thud of his head hitting the linoleum was sickening. Sarah was sure he would be unconscious. She ran to his side followed by Tammy and several nearby plebes as, surprisingly, he struggled to stand up. Blood ran down the side of his face, and Sarah yelled to Donna for a towel.

Mr. Rhodes carefully made his way down the hall, smiling and shaking his head. "Way to go, Ryan. Thank goodness it was *your* head and none of these plebes'." He helped Mr. Nolde stand. "Let's get you down to Medical. Thirty-third Platoon, carrier landings are secured! Get this mess cleaned up!"

Monday, 23 August 1976

At 2200 on Monday, a form two signed by Second Lieutenant Moran was delivered to Sarah in her room by Mr. Rhodes and Mr. Nolde. She was scared. The form two placed her on report for a plebe indoctrination violation. It stated, "Miss Becker was behaving in a non-professional manner by fraternizing with a male midshipman. Midshipman 1/C Ryan C. Nolde was placed on report for the same offense." The normal penalty for this type of offense was thirty demerits to the accused if found guilty.

"What is this, sir?" she stammered. "I don't understand." She looked questioningly at the two of them.

"I know." It was Mr. Rhodes trying to sound reassuring. "I can't believe he fried you, too. I was there, and I know what happened. You were not in the wrong by any means."

"Uh, thank you, sir," she told him, "but I'm still not sure that others are going to see it that way."

"I think they will. I've already spoken to the battalion commander about the incident. He wants a full investigation done, but you need to understand that as part of your rights you may make a written statement to attach to the form two to explain your innocence. We'll help you write it, if you'd like."

It almost sounded like she was under arrest. It was crazy. She couldn't believe this was happening to her. Mr. Nolde had paid just as much attention to her male classmates that evening as he had to her.

"Is anyone else being fried for this?" she asked.

"No, just you. That is why this is so ludicrous. Mr. Nolde was acting informally with all of the plebes, but I don't feel he was fraternizing with any of them."

Sarah knew that Mr. Nolde and Mr. Rhodes were close friends, but she knew that Mr. Rhodes believed what he said, because that was what had happened.

"How do I make a statement, sir?" Sarah was scared. How did she get herself into these predicaments? She wanted to do well here. Nothing spectacular, just keep her nose clean and graduate. Now she was being fried by an officer for fraternization. Thank goodness her company commander was on her side.

She signed the conduct report indicating her intent to make a statement. Mr. Nolde and Mr. Rhodes left her room, telling her not to worry, she was innocent.

Of course I am, she told herself for the hundredth time that night, lying in bed. Exhausted from the day's activities, she still had trouble falling asleep. When would she know the verdict? She decided that her attraction to Mr. Nolde had to be suppressed even though she wasn't convinced that she had let it surface. If this was what happened when she was innocent, imagine if she were ever caught in a situation where she was guilty.

Tuesday, 24 August 1976

The men's voices drifted in through the shower vent from Craig Random's room next door. Kate couldn't quite understand all the words, but she was sure they were talking about female midshipmen. She had talked to Craig and his roommates several times and thought she was developing a friendship with them.

I think I'll go visit Craig for a while, she decided. He really is a nice guy. She left her half-polished shoes on her desk and chopped to the room next door.

"Hi guys!" she said brightly. "What's up?"

The four guys looked up quickly and abruptly stopped talking.

"Uh, we were just, you know, talking," said a dark-haired midshipman whom Kate did not recognize.

"Mind if I join you, Craig?" she asked.

Craig shrugged. "Come on in."

"Thanks." She sat down on the edge of a desk. "Don't let me stop the conversation."

Craig looked at the other guys then leaned back in his chair. "We were just trading stories, you know."

Kate nodded. "Like what?"

The dark-haired plebe gave her a hard look. "Well, I heard that one of the girls in Starboard Battalion went berserk, and they had to cart her off to the mental ward at Bethesda."

"What?! I never heard that. That's probably just some stupid rumor."

The dark-haired midshipman shook his head. "Well, I know something that isn't a rumor. Some girl got turned in for fraternization last weekend, for riding in a car with one of her firsties."

"How do you know that?" Kate challenged.

"That's not all," he went on, ignoring her. "They both tried to lie about it at first, but when they finally admitted it, the administration put the guy up for an honor offense and only gave the girl some demerits."

"No kidding?" Random asked. This was earth-shattering news to the guys as well as to Kate. "They just let her off like that?"

"That's right."

"No way," said Kate. "Besides, it doesn't work like that. She'll go to the Honor Board too—if it's true."

The dark-haired plebe looked annoyed. "It's the double standard," he said as if explaining the obvious to an idiot. "They lowered the standards to let you in here, and now they have to bend the rules to keep you here."

"That's not true," Kate nearly shouted. How dare he talk like that?

"Oh, don't listen to her," said Craig. "What do you expect from a girl anyway?" The other guys snickered.

Kate stared at him, incensed by his sudden reversal. She turned and left the room without a word, her cheeks burning. *I guess I just can't trust anyone.*

They were studying rates after evening meal when the mate knocked on their door. Tammy was across the hall in the head.

"Decent?" he called inside as he pushed it open several inches.

"Yeah, come on in," Donna told him.

"Mr. Nolde wants to see Miss Becker in his room ASAP."

"Okay, thanks." Sarah didn't dare ask what for. Too much attention had been drawn to her and Mr. Nolde lately. She glanced in the mirror to check her hair before leaving and caught Donna's reflection behind her.

"I don't know what's going on between you two," she warned, "but you better be damned careful about what you're getting into. Don't think people don't notice what's going on, because they do."

Sarah started to reply defensively but realized it was useless. Donna was looking out for her best interests. "I know," she replied as she headed out the door. Sarah knew that Mr. Nolde was attracted to her. But she also knew that she would be crazy to get involved romantically with anyone at this point in her new career. Doing so could permanently alienate her from her classmates. She had worked too hard to fit in with them to lose their friendship and support over some guy. It was just so hard to squelch these feelings.

It was after 2000, the time after which plebes no longer had to chop. Sarah walked down the middle of the passageway toward her squad leader's room dressed in gym gear, trying to calm the drum in her chest, wondering why he wanted to see her.

After receiving Sarah's statement concerning the fraternization charge, her company officer had completed an investigation into the alleged offense and recommended to the battalion officer that he find her not guilty. Several midshipmen present at the game had testified in her behalf. The company officer declared that although the pair had been acting informally, no fraternization had taken place, and Midshipman Becker had been treated no differently from her male classmates. The battalion officer concurred with the recommendation, and the form two had been canceled.

Sarah almost hugged both Mr. Nolde and Mr. Rhodes when they had delivered the news the night before. There was some justice. So why would he want to see her now?

As she reached his room, she pivoted on her right foot to face his open door, knocked, and requested permission to come aboard.

"Come in," he told her. She walked into his room and began to sound off. Before she could utter a word, he cut her off and told her to sit down.

Sit down? she silently questioned. Plebes don't sit down in firsties' rooms. What's going on?

He calmly offered the chair beside his desk, and she obeyed his directive. He stood beside her, slim, tanned, and shirtless, with only his tropical white trousers on. She tried not to stare at the soft, thin line of hair growing from his belly button to the top of his fly but found herself unable to avert her eyes. Before she could catch her breath, he took her chin with one finger, drew her face up to his, and softly kissed her.

This isn't happening, she begged. This is my squad leader, my senior. We're not allowed to do these kinds of things. I don't want this to happen. This isn't the time or the place.

She pulled back, afraid. What if someone saw us? What if we were caught?

"Is that okay?" he asked modestly, reading her confusion.

She searched his eyes for the right answer. What did he mean? What could she say? No, sir, that's against regulations? Please take it back?

"I, I guess so," she stammered, unconsciously shaking her head in the negative.

"I don't know what it is about you. I just. . . ." He stopped, obviously unsure about what he had done.

Sarah stood and asked for permission to shove off. He looked at her curiously and nodded.

She had to keep playing the game. She didn't want any special treatment. This was so unfair. Why had he done this? Now, everything was different.

She walked briskly from his room to the women's head down the hall, her mind reeling. She had to be alone. She couldn't face Donna right now. The guilt would be written all over her face.

The darkness of the head hid her from herself, and she left the light off. Seated on the cool floor, leaning against the wall, she tried to sort things out. She had worked so hard to be accepted by her classmates, not to be alienated. She didn't want to have them think she was receiving preferential treatment from her squad leader. She would talk to Mr. Nolde and tell him to stop singling her out—maybe even brace her up to show he wasn't partial. Her thoughts returned to the scene in his room. Why had he kissed her? Inexplicably, the memory sent a warm rush through her chest, and she bit her lip. He found her attractive. To him, she was a real girl. She was flattered.

Then an inner voice screamed, Are you crazy? This whole place is complicated enough without you throwing a major wrench into the works. You want to make it on your own without a "sugar daddy" to pave the way.

It was too complicated to resolve. She had to get back to her room or Donna would be suspicious.

When she walked in, Tammy and Donna were lying on their racks studying their rates.

"What took you so long?" asked Donna.

"I went to the head," Sarah replied, her heart picking up pace again.

"What'd Mr. Nolde want?"

"Nothing much. Performance stuff," she replied, hoping it would be enough of a signal to Donna not to ask any more questions. It was, she didn't, and Sarah crawled into her rack with her *Reef Points* and pretended to study.

Wednesday, 25 August 1976

"Seventh Platoon, First Squad, PLEBE HO!"

"Oh, no!" sighed Michelle. "What now?"

"Let's go!" called Kate, already heading out the door.

Terrie and Michelle chopped behind Kate down the passageway. Uneven tapping of soles on the linoleum behind them was reassurance that they would not be the last to arrive at the impromptu come-around.

An off-beat chorus of voices sounding off greeted Kate and her roommates as they slammed their backs against the bulkhead and added to the clamor by yelling their ranks and names. Sweat rolled down Kate's spine, gluing her T-shirt to her back as she watched classmates fall into place across the twenty-foot passageway. The entire company had been summoned to the front shaft, where the air temperature was only a few degrees less than the sweltering 96 outside.

Everyone was dressed in white works "alpha." Some plebes had removed their neckerchiefs, but most were still fully dressed from evening meal.

If they have us all out here, thought Kate, they must have a full evening planned. And she had thought she might have had time to clean her room and study rates.

The five firsties on duty, dressed in their tropical white long uniforms, slowly paced around the passageway between the two rows of plebes. One squad leader casually chewed on a toothpick. Another bounced the sword he had worn during the outside evening meal formation against his left palm.

"Okay, boys and girls, it's time for fun and games," the company subcommander proclaimed with an insidious smile confirming that there would be nothing fun about tonight's activities. "Let's see. . . ." He paused with both hands on his hips and swung around to face the two squad leaders behind him. "What shall it be, guys? White works Batman?"

"Nah," one of them answered. "Sweat gear Batman."

"How 'bout both?" declared another.

Kate silently groaned. She could imagine what uniform items comprised "sweat gear Batman." Shorts and T-shirt topped with sweatpants and sweatshirt, followed by raincoat and rain cape, and who knew *what* they expected you to wear on your head—probably double jock straps or brassieres for ears.

"Shit!" somebody exclaimed softly. It had come from a plebe across the passageway from Kate; she was not sure which one. The squad leader chewing the toothpick stopped in midchew. Two other firsties looked at each other in disbelief. The man with the sword froze and clasped its sheath tightly in his left hand.

"Who said that?" Delta Company's subcommander angrily demanded, his face reddening, the veins on his neck beginning to bulge. No one spoke. "I said, WHO SAID THAT?" he repeated, yelling this time. Again, no one claimed the vulgarity.

The firstie carrying the sword drew it from its sheath.

"What are you going to do with that?" Kate heard her squad leader ask his classmate. The sword bearer did not reply. He walked slowly toward the plebes across from Kate, sword held high in front of him, and stopped in front of David Rollins, a cherub-faced boy from Tennessee.

Placing the sword's point against David's Adam's apple, he asked gently, "Mr. Rollins, did you say that?"

"No, sir," David drawled gently, eyes wide, fear evident on his face.

"I'm only going to ask you one more time, Mr. Rollins. Did you say that?"

"Sir, no, sir." David throatily answered, his chin tipped up slightly to keep his Adam's apple from being cut.

The subcommander approached his sword-bearing classmate and placed his hand on his shoulder. "Bruce." Bruce turned his head over his shoulder. Their eyes met. He dropped the sword and walked to the center of the passageway.

"All right, people! We want to know who just said 'shit.' Come on! Let's have it! Who said it?" The subcommander was growing impatient but was trying to control his voice, to keep things from getting out of hand.

The silence remained as thick as the humid air filling the hall. Sweat glistened on the brow of every plebe still standing stiff at attention.

"WHO SAID IT?" The subcommander's composure remained intact, but his patience was gone. Silence replied. "Okay, nobody want to own up? Complete sweat gear with full rain gear, NOW! You've got thirty seconds!"

The plebes scurried back to their rooms, stumbling in the effort not to run into one another. Blasts of "Go Navy!" and "Beat Army!" boomed through the passageways.

Michelle beat both Kate and Terrie back to the room. "Man, oh, man," Kate announced. "Somebody is in deep trouble."

"Yeah? So why are they taking it out on us?" asked Michelle, pulling on a pair of sweatpants.

"Heck, they were going to do this to us anyway," said Terrie. "Now they just have a good excuse to be real flamers about it."

Kate was ready to go and impatiently waiting at the door. Leaving without her roommates would have been bilging them, and she had finally learned, from watching other classmates, that bilging was an infraction that could cause one to become a target for excessive abuse.

"Come on, you guys. Let's go!" She tried to hurry them along. Sweat was already running down her temples and beginning to pool in the small of her back. She fanned herself with her hand.

"We're coming, Kate." Terrie joined Kate at the door.

"Go! Go!" said Michelle as she finished buttoning her rain cape and dashed behind them out the door.

At the front shaft, they hit the bulkhead and sounded off for the second time that night. Kate's sweat gear was drenched underneath her vinyl raincoat.

As the last plebes arrived, the subcommander gave the order. "Delta Company, brace up!" The Delta Company plebes obeyed instantaneously. As they stood in this awkward position, two firsties disappeared down the middle shaft while the other two split and went down the two sides of the front shaft. Where are they going? wondered Kate, her chin beginning to ache.

Four minutes later the four returned with no indication of where they had been. They positioned themselves at the beginning and end of the two lines of plebes and began yelling.

"Mr. Smith, give me a ten-minute chow call until I tell you to stop!"

They moved to the next plebe in line.

"Mr. Hareld, what article did you read on the front page of the newspaper today?"

"Miss Brigman, what are the enlisted ranks of the Marine Corps?"

They continued down the line until the entire company was shouting rates and no one could understand anybody else for the noise. It sounded like a bull pit on Wall Street.

Sweat streamed down the face of every plebe. Bottoms of sweatpants were wringing wet. Some plebes were so drenched that pools of water began forming around their Keds.

Kate stood across the passageway from David Rollins. He was making faces as if trying to ward a fly off his nose. He kept opening and shutting his eyes, squinting, and then arching his eyebrows. The firstie carrying the sword noticed.

"What's your problem, Mr. Rollins?" he yelled. Unable to hear the response, the sword bearer signaled to the subcommander, who yelled for silence.

"I said, What's your problem, Rollins?"

"My eyes, sir," David answered angrily. "I wear contacts and they're floating in sweat. I can't get them back in place." David's tone told Kate he would have added "you asshole" if he had been pushed much further.

The unsympathetic sword bearer shook his head and turned away. He took two steps and quickly caught himself as he slipped on a two-inch stream of water running from the bulkhead to the middle of the passageway. He followed the stream with his eyes and saw that a small pool of water was forming in the middle of the shaft where two streams of sweat now met. He yelled to Delta's subcommander and pointed. They looked at one another in disbelief.

"All right, people, fun's over for tonight. Fall out and clean up your rooms!"

Kate was too angry to feel grateful for finally being dismissed. As she brusquely turned the corner into the passageway leading to her room, she heard a classmate down the hall cry out, "Fuck!" Michelle, chopping in front of her, risked a turn to send a questioning glance back at Kate, who shrugged her shoulders in reply and ran on. They were nearing the room from which the agonized cry had come.

"Fuck, fuck, FUCK!!" It exploded again as they ran by. Peering in, Michelle and Kate saw three squad mates standing helplessly in the middle of their room surrounded by the contents of their three lockers. Kate immediately heard Michelle gasp. "Oh, no!" she cried with similar anguish.

Suddenly Kate knew where the four firsties had gone during the uniform races. Her fears were confirmed as she and her roommates arrived at their room.

"Oh, you guys. I'm so sorry," Michelle was in tears. "I forgot to shut my locker and oh, God, I'm just so sorry!"

Kate was too shocked to reply as she entered their room. She could barely see the floor. Shorts, T-shirts, underwear, sweatshirts, black socks, white socks, sheets, towels, the entire contents of their lockers were scattered everywhere. Terrie and Kate stood motionless as Michelle began sorting through the clothes, tears streaming down her face.

"Get to work, ladies," their squad leader called from the door. "In case you haven't figured it out, while you were in the front shaft, the ship rolled. You girls left your lockers open, and that's what happens."

Plebes had been warned to make sure that their locker doors were closed before leaving their rooms during a uniform race, but Michelle in her haste had forgotten. Terrie was forgiving and told Michelle not to worry about it. It could have happened to any of them. Kate, however, was furious and could not bring herself to offer words of solace to her roommate despite the fact that she had rushed Michelle and had not checked the room before leaving. She was enraged at having lost precious study time. Was this supposed to build camaraderie? Kate didn't buy it.

The girls meticulously replaced the contents of their lockers, then quickly and silently showered and dressed for bed.

"I'm really sorry, Kate," Michelle offered one last time as the three girls lay in their racks, exhausted from the day's activities.

"Uh-huh," replied Kate, still upset about the lost study time but having tempered her anger toward Michelle. "It wasn't your fault, really. We just have assholes for firsties again. Only two more days until plebe summer is over. Thank goodness they can't pull this stuff during academic year."

CHAPTER FOUR

Parents' Weekend

Your sons and daughters have undergone an impressive transition in recent weeks. They have been severely tested throughout the summer, and they have worked hard to master every challenge.

The summer's intensive military-professional indoctrination program has been planned and carried out by officers assigned to the Office of the Commandant. Some 430 members of the first class (seniors) have assisted. It is now almost over. Your midshipmen have marched and marched again. They fired pistols, mastered a battery of physical tests and drills, and sailed. They were introduced to Navy lore and ways.

Parents Open House Class of 1980 Catalog, 1976

Friday, 27 August 1976

Parents' Weekend, the celebration and culmination of fifty-three days of basic training to become midshipmen, began after noon meal formation on Friday, 27 August 1976. Seven weeks of mental and physical anguish were over. Twelve hundred plebes desperate for two days of freedom formed up in Tecumseh Court in tropical white long.

Today, even though they wore slacks, it was not difficult to distinguish the women from the men. They generally stood at the end of each squad, organized by height. Their combination covers were distinctly unlike the men's—white inverted "buckets" with upturned black cloth brims. The men wore flat, round "airline pilot's" covers with black patent-leather brims. Their tunic-shaped blouses hung loose over their trousers instead of being tucked in tight like the men's. Parents, family, and friends squeezed tight against the stone walls edging Tecumseh Court, straining to see their son, daughter, sister, or brother.

Romeo Company formed up on the bricks between Second and Fourth Wings, far to the right of the viewing audience. Sarah could not see her family from where she stood, but she knew that her mom, dad, sister, and two brothers, her best friend, Anne, her boyfriend, Donnie, and another girlfriend were all there somewhere in the crowd. Today was incredibly special. In the plebe-summer schedule Tammy and she had scrawled, with a red Magic Marker, "Right On!!!" and "Max, Wicked, Psyched!!!" across the pages outlining Parents' Weekend. They had waited for this weekend with great anticipation, as had all their classmates. Sarah could not wait to be reunited with her family and friends, and this time, unlike summers of the past, she was ready for the summer to be over.

The Drum and Bugle Corps broke into a Sousa march as the regimental staff marched across the middle of Tecumseh Court and posted in front of the Fourth Class Regiment just inches from the edge of the crowd. As had been done over a hundred times this summer, the regimental commander called for the two battalion commanders to report absences. "Nineteen men absent," the Port Battalion commander boomed. "Seventy-seven men absent," the Starboard Battalion commander reported. The numbers, merely a formality, symbolized the commanders' graduation year: 1977.

The patriotic music suddenly made Sarah realize how incredibly proud she was of her accomplishments. She was proud to be wearing her crisp white uniform and to be part of this impressive display of military pomp and circumstance.

As she searched the crowd once again, she grew apprehensive about seeing Donnie. What would he think of her in uniform? How would he deal with her as a member of the military? Would he find her less feminine? Would it bother him that she was going to a school that was predominantly male? She had written to him only twice, while he had written to her at least every week.

With the Fourth Class Regiment present and accounted for, the midshipmen marched into Bancroft Hall to the beat of the band and down to the wardroom, where they were required to listen to the podium announcements. Immediately afterward they flooded out the main doors of Bancroft Hall, down Stribling Walk, searching for familiar faces. The Academy had directed parents to stand under signs bearing the letter of their last name placed along the walkway between the statue of Tecumseh and the chapel.

Sarah walked briskly until she recognized her parents waiting by a park bench, and then she broke into a run. Her brothers were perched on the back of the bench, and her mom, dad, sister, and friends stood close by, still straining to see her.

Sarah reached her mother first and flung her arms around her. Her father wrapped his arms around them both, and Sarah finally let go of her emotions when she felt her mother sobbing.

Kate strode briskly out of the wardroom and climbed the stairs to Smoke Hall two at a time, swept along by the surge of plebes hungry not for food but for liberty. Stepping into the sunlight and onto the yellow bricks of T-Court, she fought the urge to run to the area designated for plebes with a last name beginning with *B*.

Her mother saw her first and was running to engulf her in a tight hug when Kate heard the click of a camera and tensed.

"What's wrong?" asked Mrs. Brigman, sensing her daughter's discomfort and stepping back.

"PDA, Mom," she replied. "Public display of affection. I could get fried if someone sees you hug me out here in public."

"Fiddle, faddle," retorted Mrs. Brigman. "Just let them try. I haven't seen my little girl in seven weeks, and they aren't going to let me hug her? I think not." She pulled Kate toward her, and Kate surrendered. She had missed the smell of her mother's perfume. In fact, she had missed everything about her.

Mrs. Brigman stepped back and looked close at her daughter, who turned to hug her father. "Have you seen this, Katie? I can't find a picture of you in it."

Kate accepted the blue booklet from her mother, glanced at the title, *Parents Open House Class of 1980,* and quickly opened it. She gulped when she saw the first page. It was a copy of a famous World War I recruiting poster depicting a young woman in a man's blue Cracker Jack uniform beside the words "GEE!! I WISH I WERE A MAN, I'D JOIN THE NAVY." Oh, no, she thought. We're going to get a lot of grief from this. Besides, we *don't* wish we could be men! Her anxiety rose as she flipped through the rest of the book. It seemed as if nearly every page had at least one picture of a female midshipman on it, grossly misrepresenting the proportion of women to men.

The guys are already sick of hearing about us in the press, Kate thought, and now this! Why draw more attention to us? It's like driving a wedge between us and the guys, making them feel like no one cares about what they do when we're all in this together.

Her parents wouldn't understand. "I see a lot of girls I recognize, but not me," she said, thankfully handing it back to her mother.

Kate shook hands with the rest of her family, not wishing to push her luck with PDA. "It's great to see you!" she gushed. "I can hardly wait to jump in the car and get out of here."

She glanced over her shoulder and came face to face with Dirk Walker, who sneered. "Look," he said snidely to his parents, "this is what we have to look at. Isn't that lovely?" His parents smiled nervously and continued walking.

His criticism stung. You jerk, thought Kate. Couldn't you have left it alone in front of my family?

"Kate, do you know that boy?" her mother asked.

Kate struggled not to appear upset. "Yeah, Mom," she said. "He's in my company."

"Well, really, Kate." Mrs. Brigman sounded both insulted and worried. "What an awful thing to say. They don't talk like that all the time, do they? I mean, are you all right?"

Am I all right? Kate asked herself. I wonder. How can I possibly tell her how hard it's been? I've been yelled at, insulted, braced up, and fried—not just me, but every single one of us, male and female. How can I tell her how I am? How *am* I?

I'm different.

She smiled at her mother. "I'm fine, Mom, really. They're not all like that."

Mrs. Brigman wasn't convinced. "Well, I know it's been tough for you. You look thinner, Kate."

"It's all the exercise, Mom," Kate said, hoping her mother would drop the subject. "Really."

After their tearful reunion, Sarah walked with her family to the Midshipman Store parking lot. Jan Becker reached in the rear of their blue Chevrolet Suburban and handed Sarah several Care packages of cookies and brownies, her stuffed walrus, and a plastic jar containing five hundred pieces of Bazooka bubble gum. "Do you want your clothes now, honey?" Jan asked Sarah.

"Oh, no, Mom. Not now," she hurriedly answered, looking around cautiously to see if anyone had heard her mother. It was against regulations for plebes to wear or store civilian clothes until they went home on Christmas leave. Despite the regulation, last week Sarah had asked her mother to bring her some civilian clothes to change into once they arrived at her uncle

George's home in Washington, D.C. She couldn't imagine hanging around all weekend in a uniform.

"I'll put them on when we get there. Keep them hidden for now, or I could get fried," Sarah told her mother.

Plebes were granted town liberty from the moment they met their parents until midnight on Friday. Although town liberty meant that the plebes were to stay within a seven-mile radius of the Academy chapel, Sarah, family, and friends arrived in D.C. early that afternoon.

Sarah immediately changed into blue jeans and a short-sleeve shirt. It felt so good to be wearing clothes designed for a woman's body.

Talking excitedly with her girlfriends, Sarah realized that Donnie had remained silently in the shadows most of the afternoon. There had been so many people around that the two of them never had any time alone. She was sure he sensed a big change in her and her attitude toward their relationship. She didn't intend to act differently toward him, but she felt very distant. Although she had missed home and had not particularly enjoyed the hazing and harassment of plebe summer, she had enjoyed the challenging environment with new friends and was looking forward to the next four years. It wasn't that she wanted Donnie out of her life; she just didn't see a place for him in this new one. Sarah knew he could never relate to her experiences. They were losing common ground.

When they finally found a few moments to talk, they both found it awkward.

"I've missed you," he told her as they sat on a bench on her uncle's patio.

"I've missed you, too," she replied. "At least when I could find time to. I mean, every moment of my existence for the past two months has been so busy."

"You're different, Sarah."

"I know, Donnie. I've been through quite a bit these past few months. I've learned a lot about myself and my ability to deal with unbelievably stressful situations. This whole experience is like nothing I've ever been through. It's really hard, but I like the challenge. It's going to be worth it in the end, I think."

"Do you think about 'us' very often? You haven't written much."

"Sure I do," she said. "But I hardly have time to call my parents, much less write to anyone."

"Yeah, but if I really meant something to you, you'd find time, Sarah."

"Donnie, please don't do this. I'm sorry I didn't write. I've been incredibly busy. You can't begin to understand how hard it is here."

"You're right, Sarah. I can't begin to understand, and I probably never will. You're doing something I could never do. You're moving forward, and I'm still trying to figure out where I'm going." He looked down. "We're drifting apart. I can feel it."

"Donnie, I still want to be friends. I mean, you're right, things have changed, but that doesn't mean we can't keep in touch and be close."

"Is there someone else, Sarah?"

Her abbreviated silence was answer enough. "No," she stammered, "not really." It wasn't a lie. There really was no one else. She knew how she felt about Ryan Nolde, but certainly nothing would come of the two of them. He was a firstie. She was a plebe. It was forbidden. It had to stop.

"Sarah, I'll always love you."

"Me, too," she replied. Don't you always somehow love your high school sweetheart?

"No, don't say it if you don't mean it."

"Donnie . . . please. Let's not do this now." She took his hand. "Look at me." He did. "You'll always be special to me, no matter what, okay?"

He nodded. "It's over, isn't it, Sarah?"

"It's different," she said trying to smile. "We'll keep in touch. But you start dating other people, okay?"

"What about you?"

"I don't think they even let us date at that place," she joked. They both smiled. She reached to hug him. No, she thought, this doesn't feel right anymore. We need to be just friends.

Saturday, 28 August 1976

Kate was slow-dancing with her father in Dahlgren Hall, and the feeling was wonderful. The Academy had scheduled a dance on Saturday night for plebes and their drags. Kate had brought her parents.

"So, how was the summer, Katie?" Mr. Brigman asked, holding his eldest daughter tightly.

"It was fine, Dad. I mean, it was hard, but I survived." She did not want him to think it had been too easy or that plebe summer had gotten softer since he had been a midshipman.

"Still holding uniform races?"

"All too often!" she replied. They laughed knowingly, sharing a secret no one else in the family would understand.

"I was ranked third in my squad," she announced proudly. "Only two other guys were ranked higher than me." She said it with hopes that the fact that two men had done better would rationalize a third-place standing in her father's eyes. Ever since grade school, she had striven to live up to his expectations.

"Well, that's not too bad, honey," he replied. "You can do better when academic year rolls around. If I remember right, I believe I found plebe summer a real challenge, too. How'd you rank in the company?"

"I don't know, Dad," she replied softly, wondering why he never seemed satisfied with her achievements. "They only tell us our squad rankings." Kate had been thrilled to learn she was ranked number three. The two squad mates ranked above her were incredibly squared away. One was even a prior-enlisted marine.

Her father had always told her that she was given special gifts by God and that in return she should use those gifts to be the best. She had heard the same thing in Sunday school, and after years of hearing the same message, she had begun to believe it. Despite trying inexhaustibly, she never felt she could measure up to the standards he had established. Nothing she ever did was good enough until the letter had arrived offering her an appointment to the Naval Academy, his alma mater. Elation had possessed his face as if he had won the lottery.

Moving around the dance floor, she hugged him tightly. Kate loved her father dearly, no matter how hard he was on her.

"You look very beautiful tonight," Joe Brigman told her.

"Thanks, Daddy," Kate blushed, not feeling beautiful at all.

She tried not to let the makeup and beautiful dresses on the girls around her affect her attitude toward herself, but it was impossible. Wearing a uniform made her feel proud of her status as a midshipman. But tonight, at a dance, dressed so military in her tropical white uniform, she felt very unappealing. Guys in uniform were one thing, girls in uniform were quite another.

She closed her eyes and savored the music. Seals and Crofts's "We May Never Pass This Way Again" brought back memories of her high school prom. Charlie had been her date, and she had worn a beautiful lavender strapless gown. Thinking back made her feel weepy, but tonight was no time for tears. She had survived the summer.

What will the entire brigade be like? she wondered. How will they treat us, and how will I cope with all the difficult academic classes, knowing my rates, and making sure I don't accidentally break any of the thousands of regulations? The anxiety brought on by these thoughts compelled Kate unconsciously to cling tighter to her father. Let me make him proud of me, she silently prayed.

Sunday, 29 August 1976

The weekend flew by. The Parents' Weekend Dress Parade began at 1400 on Sunday. Sarah marched proudly in the last row of Romeo Company, lengthening her strides to keep pace with the men. She was pleased to show her parents how well the company had pulled together in such a short time.

Town liberty commenced after the parade and expired at 1900 at evening meal formation. Sarah and her family ate an early dinner in town and walked leisurely back to the Academy. Approaching T-Court, her stomach began to churn. A huge sheet poster hanging from a balcony on the Second Regimental side of Bancroft Hall read "Hunting Season, Now Open!" She inhaled deeply. What were they in for now?

Standing beside the statue of Tecumseh, she tried to suppress her tears when it came time to say goodbye. She was doing fine until she reached for her mother. As the two embraced, tears fell, and Sarah found it difficult to pull away. Finally she reduced their embrace to two hands clinging tightly, then turned to walk solemnly beside her fellow classmates toward formation in front of Bancroft Hall.

Second classmen, back from their summer cruises, blared Bing Crosby's "White Christmas" from their windows on the Second Regimental side of Bancroft Hall, driving home the realization that the next time the plebes saw their families would be Christmas.

Sarah fell into formation. Unlike Induction Day, tonight she could imagine what awaited inside. Familiar cadence from the Drum and Bugle Corps preceded the Fourth Class Regiment's solemn march into Bancroft Hall. It was no different from any other formation, except that during the past weekend these plebes had tasted civilization, and they all wanted desperately to take another bite.

The Class of 1977 bellowed plebe ho's immediately after dinner for the entire regiment. Uniform races commenced in an effort to take the plebes' minds off their misery. Tammy's weekend had been cut short by CMOD (company mate of the deck) duty all day Sunday. Depressed and horribly homesick, she grabbed the plebe-summer schedule, and over the "Max, Wicked, Psyched!!!" note, with black Magic Marker this time, she scratched the word "SHIT!!!" across the entire page.

CHAPTER FIVE

Plebe Year, First Semester

September arrives. Upperclassmen return from at-sea training, leave, and other summer activities. Plebe summer is over, but plebe indoctrination continues. The academic year gets underway. Four years of studies have begun, paced by a demanding daily schedule.

United States Naval Academy Catalog, 1976–77

Tuesday, 7 September 1976

The Fourth Class Regiment spent the entire evening moving their gear from plebe-summer company areas to academic-year company areas.

Kate found a minute to read the academic-year schedule. "Demanding" is right, she thought, looking at it gloomily:

6:15	Reveille
6:50–7:10	Breakfast (optional for midshipmen first, second and third class)
7:15–7:30	Special instruction period for midshipmen fourth class
7:30	Quarters for muster and inspection
7:55–8:45	First period
8:55–9:45	Second period
9:55–10:45	Third period
10:55–11:45	Fourth period
12:05	Call to noon formation
12:20	Noon meal
1:15–2:05	Fifth period
2:15–3:05	Sixth period (With the exception of a few midshipmen having a seventh period laboratory, midshipmen utilize

the time from the end of the sixth period until evening
meal formation to participate in varsity and intramural
sports and other extracurricular and personal activities.)

6:30	Evening meal formation
7:45–10:30	Study period
11:00	Taps

Maybe this *isn't* going to be easier than plebe summer.

Sarah, Tammy, and Donna were assigned a room on 8-3 (Eighth Wing,
third floor), one floor below the top floor, which housed the rest of Thirty-
third Company. They guessed that the administration had decided that
women could not live on the fourth floor because of the ledge outlining its
perimeter. The ledge could support an individual climbing from one room
to another from the outside. Was the administration afraid that male midshipmen might climb into the women's rooms? The girls giggled at the
thought.

Their first classmen explained that the women had been assigned to a room
on 8-3 so that they might be near the women in Thirty-fourth Company for
support. They pointed out that two classmates and four upperclassmen were
also assigned rooms nearby on 8-3.

Sarah and Tammy each filled a laundry cart with uniforms, shoes, boxes of
books, Naval Academy luggage, boxes of cleaning gear, and toiletries. The
carts were cumbersome, but the girls found them manageable and much better than lugging stuff by hand.

As they reached a ramped breezeway, Sarah straightened her arms and
leaned into her cart to push it up the sloped deck leading into Sixth Wing.
She almost lost her foothold when Midshipman Schluntz surprised her by
entering one of the breezeway's double doors beside her. Oh, my word, she
panicked. What is *he* doing here?!

"Good evening, sir," Sarah mandatorily greeted him, mentally reviewing
the menu for evening meal lest he should begin drilling them.

"Good evening, Miss Becker. Say, can I help you with that?"

What?! thought Sarah. Schluntz wants to help me? The tyrant who hates
women being here is offering me assistance? No way! No thanks! If there is
anybody I won't accept help from, it's this guy!

"No, thank you, sir. I can handle it," she said indignantly and continued
on her way. It was a minor victory at best. He had sincerely wanted to help

her, but she didn't want any assistance from a guy who had put her through hell more than once.

Sarah and Tammy unloaded their carts and pushed them back into the passageway.

"I'll meet you back at the room, Tam."

"Okay, Sarah. I'll start loading again."

"Thanks! See ya in a minute!" Sarah squared a corner and began chopping toward the women's head. She wasn't really required to chop, since it was after 2000, but after her encounter with Schluntz she decided not to take any chances.

"Go Navy, sir!" She turned left at the corner and squared a right into the door with a white nameplate reading "Women's Head." Behind the door a large window, halfway open, revealed a scenic view of the Academy grounds and Severn River. The splash of deep blue reminded Sarah of the ocean view from her home in New Hampshire.

What a view! she thought. This head is three times the size of the one across the hall from our plebe-summer room. You can almost do cartwheels in here. Two sinks, two mirrors, two toilet stalls, and the ever-present, never-filled sanitary napkin machine.

Next to the second stall was a freshly tiled wall that last year had not existed. The Academy had converted a number of janitor closets and men's heads into women's heads. This one had obviously been part of a previously all-male head.

Sarah walked over to the window, placed both hands on the ledge, and leaned out the opening to view the tennis courts below, her call of nature forgotten for the moment. We girls got the best end of this renovation deal, she thought. This is some prime real estate.

It's a refuge, she thought. The one place they can't get to us. She shook her head and turned toward the interior of the room. Amazing. I can't believe I'm getting excited about a bathroom!

Sarah walked into the first stall and pushed the wooden door shut. She sat on the commode and was reaching for some toilet paper when the words scrawled in pencil on the back of the door took her breath away:

hang it up,
bitch!!

It was a threat. No, a warning. No, it was pure hatred.

Someone had used pencil, retracing the letters to ensure that the message would be visible without leaving a deep impression in the wood.

"You jerk!" she whispered to the unknown author. "You insolent jerk!" Who would do this, she wondered. And why? They don't even know us yet. One of the firsties? One of the upperclassmen? Who?!

She stared at the words and thought how satisfied the author would have been to see the effect he had had on her. No, she decided. It won't work. I won't let this get to me. I'll never let him know I saw it.

She read the words again and found herself empowered by them. Somehow they strengthened her resolve to stay.

Hang it up? Never, she thought. You wimp. You didn't even have the guts to carve it with a pen.

No, these words would remain with her always, and she vowed that they would remain on that door until the day she graduated.

On her way to retrieve another load from her room, Sarah decided to stop by 4-1, where Mr. Nolde was moving in. He would live there first semester as part of the brigade staff. He had asked her to stop by to get her "grease," his evaluation of her performance this set. On her way there, she decided to discuss the obscene bathroom message with no one but her roommates, hoping they would agree to leave the message intact. Mr. Nolde's room was just ahead. Although the door was open, she knocked.

"Request permission to come aboard, sir."

"Come on in and knock off that plebe talk unless, of course, someone else is in the room, okay?" he told her more brusquely than she thought necessary.

Sarah stepped inside. "Okay," she agreed, quickly scanning the room to check that no one else was there. She remained wary, not wanting to make him angry but hoping to ensure that their relationship appeared professional to others, especially her classmates. She knew they already thought she was getting special treatment from him.

The week before, she had talked him into bracing her up for the day to prove his impartiality. She had chopped around all day, braced up, for no real reason except to try to prove to her classmates that he wasn't favoring her. Deep down, she knew it was hopeless. You had to be blind to miss the friendly glances he passed her way.

Sarah knew she was a plebe—scum, lower than life—yet here was this first classman playing the dating game. She was flattered, intrigued, but frightened. The stakes were high, especially for him. She couldn't understand why he wanted to take this risk. At that moment, she would have been happy to call the whole thing off—walk away, gratified that she was attractive to an attractive upperclassman. She didn't need the stress of an undercover relationship on top of everything else, but something wouldn't let her give it up—the intrigue, the pressure because he was an upperclass. Or maybe her attraction to him was too strong to let go.

He handed her his appraisal of her performance during the second set. He had ranked her in the middle of the squad. She was disappointed, and he could tell.

"I ranked you where I believed you belonged, Sarah. You didn't expect me to rank you higher because of us?"

Us. Were they already an "us"? she wondered. "No, sir. I mean, no, of course not. I would want you to be honest. I just was ranked so much higher last set, so. . . ."

"So . . . what?" he asked her softly.

"So, nothing. It's fine." Had her performance suffered because of the fraternization charge at the Orioles game? No, of course not, she had been found innocent. Had she slacked off? She didn't think so, but maybe he had seen a change. Oh, well, she thought. Plebe summer is finally over, and I made it through. I'm not at the bottom of the squad, so I should just be happy with this.

She signed the appraisal.

"Listen, Sarah, I'm going to have a phone in my room with an outside line this semester. This is my number. You can call me from the pay phones on 8-0." He handed her a small white slip of paper just as a man in civilian clothes walked into the room carrying an armload of black uniforms on wooden hangers. Sarah's heart froze. She dropped her extended hand. They were caught! She just knew it. This guy had to wonder what she was doing there. How much of the conversation had he heard?

"Hey, George," Mr. Nolde greeted him nonchalantly. "This is one of my plebes, Sarah Becker. Miss Becker, my roommate, George Menhold."

"Good evening, sir," Sarah said.

"Hello," the roommate answered, obviously not interested in making conversation. He hung his uniform in the closet and left the room.

"I'd better go," Sarah told Mr. Nolde. She picked up his phone number from the desk. "Request permission to shove off."

"I thought I told you not to do that anymore."

"Oh, right." She was afraid not to keep up the charade. For all she knew, the brigade commander would be the next person to walk through the door.

"I'll talk to you later."

"Okay," she said and ran out the door, squaring a corner to her left, glancing both ways to see if anyone had seen her leave his room. "Go Navy, sir!"

Wednesday, 8 September 1976

As Seventh Company CMOD (company mate of the deck), Kate stood behind the mate's desk on 6-0 watching hordes of upperclassmen lug sea bags full of uniforms, innumerable boxes of books and cleaning items, and their revered stereos to their new academic rooms. Today three thousand upperclass would augment the regiment of twelve hundred plebes, collectively forming the Brigade of Midshipmen.

It was against regulations for the upperclassmen to talk to or "drill" the plebes until the following evening meal, but they were still allowed to look. Kate found their unspoken stares an unsettling prediction of what was to come. There were only a few smiles among the quizzical and threatening glances thrown her way. She knew they were checking her out because she was one of the "girls," and she attempted to appear as professional as possible. Yet she was extremely uneasy that the depth of the fear she felt was evident to everyone.

Charlie, her boyfriend from back home, had passed by the mate's desk several times, carting his belongings to his room just down the passageway. Each time he passed he shot her a quick smile, which she hastily returned. When the passageway was almost empty of other midshipmen, he approached her briefly.

"Hello, Miss Brigman." His professional tone caught her off guard.

"Uh, hello . . . sir," she answered, confused. Charlie glanced to his left and right, ensuring that they were alone before continuing.

"Kate, we have to be careful. A lot of upperclass know about our relationship, and since our companies live so close to one another we'll really have to step lightly."

"Step lightly? What do you mean?"

"I mean, we aren't going to be able to see or talk to one another in the Hall, and when we do we need to be careful how we react."

She knew what he meant, but her frustration level grew.

"Listen," he continued, "we'll get together somehow, but never in the Hall, okay?"

Kate glanced up and saw one of her first classmen approaching briskly from her right. "Yes, sir," she answered, worried that they might have been caught.

"Good. See you later." He walked off. She pretended to concentrate on the mate's log as the first classman walked up to her desk, eyebrows creased with suspicion.

"Miss Brigman, who was that talking to you?"

Kate panicked. Oh, Lord. We've been caught, and we haven't even done anything.

She drew a deep breath. "Sir, that is someone I know from back home." She recognized this firstie as the first-semester company commander.

"Let's get something straight right now, Miss Brigman. You girls had better not try to use your femininity to smack up to the upperclass, or you will be thrown out of here. Is that clear?"

"Yes, sir," she responded, "but I wasn't—"

He pointed a finger at her. "Don't give me any lip, miss. I'm just telling you how it is and that you had better watch your actions." He turned and stormed away.

"Yes, sir," Kate whispered, stunned and suddenly very depressed.

Two days later Kate stood at attention in noon meal formation. A second classman in her company, renowned as a flamer, approached the plebes in her squad and began performing an informal inspection. Kate always made it a point to ensure that her uniform and appearance were squared away before she came to every formation, and she was confident that he would find no discrepancies.

As he finished inspecting her roommate, Kate arched her shoulders and tightened her stance. I'll show this guy, she resolved as he stepped in front of her. She held her breath and stared at his black tie.

He began at her shoes, moving his head deliberately up her figure, examining every thread of her uniform. When his eyes finally met hers, he sneered.

"You need a shave, miss."

"Sir?" she asked.

"You heard me, Brigman. You need a shave." He smirked and walked away.

She stood stunned, feeling as if he had punched her in the stomach. What could she say? How should she react? Was her appearance so impeccable that he could only taunt her? Had he meant to personally offend her? Kate knew that her dark facial hair was apparent, but what could she do about it? And what did it have to do with her professional appearance? She tried to shake off the sting of his remark but found herself fighting the sting of tears instead. This was going to be a long year.

Saturday, 11 September 1976

Sarah was nervous. For the first time in Naval Academy history, cheers for the Navy football team would be led by a twelve-member squad consisting only of midshipmen, six of them women—plebe women selected to replace the coeds from local colleges who in previous years had augmented the cheerleading squad. Sarah was one of the six.

In the past, hoards of hopeful coeds from local women's colleges had made their way to the Naval Academy to try out for six cheerleading positions. Attractive, with their faces made up and their hair long, they danced and bounced around the field, entertaining the mids while leading them in songs and cheers—and they were available for dating. Then women were admitted to the Academy, and the administration made the decision to select from among their own.

None of the girls on the squad looked a day over fourteen, since regulations required that their hair be cropped to the top of their collars. They were allowed to wear virtually no makeup or jewelry, and several of them were having trouble watching their weight. Three meals a day with a total of 3,400 calories, despite all the physical activity, did not necessarily produce thin and trim midshipmen. Another dilemma was that the new composition of the cheerleading squad had plebes directing upperclassman instead of the other way around. And they were *women* plebes! In fact, prior to the women coming on board, male plebes had not been allowed to try out for the squad. Only upperclass male cheerleaders had been selected. This year, however, there were two male plebe cheerleaders.

Sarah's nervousness was compounded by excitement. She was thrilled to be able to support Navy's sports teams while doing something that she had enjoyed in high school. She also hoped cheerleading would help her feel more feminine.

Attendance at home football games was mandatory for all midshipmen. The cheerleading squad, exempt from marching to the games, rode in a navy van to the Navy–Marine Corps Memorial Stadium two hours before the game to warm up and dress.

High with anticipation, the squad arrived at the field and ran through their warmups. Box lunches were hurriedly consumed, after which the girls ran to get dressed. Excitement was abundant in the women's restroom on the backside of the sky-high bleachers where the new Navy cheerleaders put on their uniforms for the first time. They were the same outfits the cheerleaders from previous years had worn: one-piece navy blue jumpers trimmed in gold, with a white panel down the front and NAVY spelled vertically in gold letters. Underneath they wore white turtlenecks, navy blue panties, white bobby socks, and tennis shoes, but the way they primped and helped each other get ready, they might have been preparing for the prom.

"I can't get this thing pinned on, Sarah. Can you help me?" Judy Nance handed Sarah a pearl-topped hatpin and a yellow mum corsage the size of a grapefruit. "Wasn't it sweet of the guys to buy these for us?" Each of the male cheerleaders had purchased a traditional yellow mum corsage adorned with blue and gold ribbons for his cheerleading partner. Their thoughtfulness had overwhelmed the girls.

"Yeah," said Sarah, taking the corsage and pin. "I can't believe they did it. It made me feel like a real girl. I almost cried."

"Me, too!" agreed Judy, beaming at the flower now displayed on her chest.

"Everybody ready?" asked Brigette Cook, the unofficial head female cheerleader. They nodded. "Then let's go!"

They bounded down the bleacher steps, entranced by the distant music of the Naval Academy Drum and Bugle Corps signaling the arrival of the Brigade of Midshipmen.

Every home football game, the Brigade of Midshipmen marched, company behind company, from Tecumseh Court through the Naval Academy Yard and the streets of Annapolis to the Navy–Marine Corps Memorial Stadium, temporarily halting traffic. At the back of her company with the rest of the "sandblowers," Kate marched in step to the beat of the Drum and Bugle Corps.

She was exhilarated. She had attended Navy games as a civilian, but this was different. Now she was a midshipman, a member of the Navy team, and much more was riding on this game. A win could mean some kind of "carry-on," or extra benefits, for the plebes, while a loss could mean extra harassment or more rates. Plebes were convenient scapegoats, even for the performance of the football team.

She marched on the far left in the last row of midshipmen. Some upperclassmen called it the celebrity side, since midshipmen on that side had a better chance of being picked out by any television cameras that might be covering a game.

Turning out Gate Eight, Kate caught sight of civilians straining to catch their first glimpse of a female midshipman. "Tourists," she groaned. "Alumni," whispered the guy beside her. She had forgotten about the alumni. How would they react to the girls?

As they neared the stadium, the crowd thickened and cheers of "Navy, Navy!" filled the air. Kate was proud to be wearing a uniform. The tribulations of plebe year subsided for a moment, and then she heard him. Everyone heard him. There was no mistaking what the clear, loud male voice just behind her was yelling: "There goes another bitch!"

Who was it? She couldn't look—eyes in the boat. Who could it have been? She glanced left at her roommate. Michelle looked dismayed. She shook her head slowly in disgust.

Taking abuse from classmates and upperclassmen was one thing, but to be lambasted by the public, in public, was unexpected, uncalled for. The comment stung Kate as if someone had slapped her face, and she was embarrassed at the same time. She immediately wished she were in the middle of the company where no one could see her.

The brigade staff led the Brigade of Midshipmen under the scoreboard and onto the field. The thirty-six companies of approximately 130 midshipmen apiece were identified by the blue numbers sewn onto their gold guidons. Sarah imagined the view of the formation on the field in their white uniforms with white combination covers; from the balcony above it must look like a green and white checkerboard. The spectacle sent chills up her spine.

Two senior male cheerleaders were positioned to lead the brigade through the traditional "hat trick" cheer. Leaning over the balcony, they waved signal flags signaling the brigade to "stand by." When the cheerleader on the Navy side raised his flags above his head, forty-two hundred midshipmen performed an about-face, positioning themselves face to face with the fans from Rutgers, their opponent. Rutgers and Navy fans alike cheered the well-executed maneuver. Pregame activities had begun.

The Navy cheerleader in the visiting-team stands waved his signal flags. Following his signals, the brigade yelled, "K–N–I–G–H–T–S, Gooooo Knights, Fight!" At the word *Fight,* they all tipped their hats to the visiting-team fans. The Rutgers fans cheered wildly. Then the brigade performed an about-face. The roar was spontaneous. The crowd joined in the cheer: "N–A–V–Y, Gooooo Navy, Fight!" The Drum and Bugle Corps broke into "Anchors Aweigh," and the upperclassmen marched into the stands. Plebes remained on the field to form the tunnel through which the football team would explode onto the field, led by the cheerleaders and Bill the Goat, Navy's mascot.

"Let's go, guys!" called an upperclass cheerleader. "Time to lead 'em out!"

Sarah grabbed her blue and gold pom-poms and ran across the field with the other cheerleaders to the head of the tunnel. Bill the Goat, wearing a blue wool blanket sporting a gold *N,* pawed the ground anxiously. His two handlers kept his movements in check with nylon ropes. The cheerleaders lined up behind Bill and waited for the football team.

"Go!" Sarah heard someone yell, and she sprinted through the white tunnel formed by her classmates. With her sights on the end of the tunnel, Sarah made it to the end just as the football team overtook the cheerleaders and exploded onto the field. She performed several cartwheels and jumps before running back to the cheerleaders' section on the sidelines.

When they sat down, several third classmen in their company approached Kate and her roommates. "Hey, we just want you girls to know that we thought that jerk out there by the road was really inappropriate with his remark."

"Yeah, we'd like to apologize for what happened," said another. "You guys should just ignore people like that."

"Uh, thanks, sir," replied Kate.

"The guy was probably drunk and just showing off."

Kate smiled and nodded.

"Try to forget about it, okay? We wanted to let you know it bothered us, too."

"Thanks again, sir." Kate was nearly speechless. The concern of these upperclassmen meant more to her than any apology from the jerk in the street.

As they turned to leave, one mid turned around to face her. "Congress said you should be here. So that's just how it is. If they can't deal with it, well. . . ." He didn't finish before his classmate called him to get a hot dog.

Kate blushed and turned to her roommates, who grinned from ear to ear.

· · ·

Rutgers received the ball, the brigade sat down, and some of them turned their attention to the cheerleaders as the girls performed a dance routine to "The Goat Is Old and Gnarly," a Navy fight song. Sarah moved with ease, her confidence high. She had spent the evening before in her room practicing her routines, much to the dismay of her roommates, who were trying to study. So when the brigade began to boo, she was thrown completely off guard.

She looked over her shoulder, thinking that the football team had fumbled or been intercepted, and then she remembered that Rutgers had the ball. Why are they booing? And then she understood. That sick feeling in the pit of her stomach when Mr. Schluntz told her he was going to drive her out before his graduation returned.

It seemed like the entire brigade was booing the cheerleaders. It was horrible! She couldn't believe this was happening. The girls continued dancing, but Sarah looked at Brigette Cook on her right, as if to ask, Why are they doing this? Brigette looked as shattered as Sarah, who suddenly realized that they were in for a long season. The resentment they had feared individually had surfaced en masse.

At the end of the first dance routine, Derrick Ogden, the senior cheerleader, led the cheers, determined not to let the girls take any more heat. The first half became uneventful, even boring, as Navy defense spent the majority of time on the field.

At halftime Sarah and the other girls on the squad climbed the bleacher stairs to go to the restrooms to freshen up. Surrounded by other women, some of them the girlfriends of midshipmen, dressed in the latest fall fashions, they were rudely reminded of their own plain appearance. Sarah tried not to compare herself with a woman applying lipstick in the mirror. I'll have so much more than they will when I finish this place, she reminded herself. They might have a husband, but I'll have a career and a real education.

Yeah, but for the moment you look fourteen, and the mids don't even like you, her vanity retorted.

The girls waited for one another at the exit, instinctively knowing that together they would attract less abuse.

"Okay, girls, chin up!" Brigette told them. "We can't let them get to us. We're going to show them that we can be as good as those airhead cheerleaders before us!"

"Even better!" announced Judy.

The rest agreed in unison, momentarily convinced as they returned to the field.

The second half was as uneventful as the first, except for several antics by midshipmen bored with the game after Rutgers scored six more points. Several plebes rushed over to the Rutgers side, "stole" one of their cheerleaders, and "passed her up" to overly eager hands in the midshipman stands. Sarah looked questioningly at her fellow cheerleaders as if to ask, Is this routine? feeling somewhat humiliated and hurt that they were heading to the other side to get their hands on some "real" girls. It wasn't that she wanted to be "passed up" and basically "felt up," but once again the realization that they were not thought of as real girls painfully hit home.

The first game of the season ended with a Navy defeat, 13–3, and six very bruised female egos.

Friday, 17 September 1976

Walking briskly back from class on Friday of the first week of classes, Kate already felt she was way behind. Her eighteen-hour course load was similar to that of her fellow plebes: three hours of chemistry every week plus a two-hour lab, three hours of naval history, three hours of plebe English, three hours of calculus, two hours of naval science with a two-hour lab, and two hours of naval engineering. This intense schedule also included two mandatory classes of physical education each week, for which she received no academic credit.

She had known that the academics would be demanding, but she now realized that she might have taken on too much in joining the varsity sailing team and the chapel choir—all this on top of trying to remain squared away while coping with the everyday pressures of being a plebe. Tomorrow they had a formal room inspection, and she and her roommates hadn't begun cleaning.

She thought about giving something up. Sailing is too much of a release, and we're required to play some sport, she thought. I may as well take advantage of a good one open to the girls, since there are so few. Besides, I love sitting on sailing-team tables for meals where no one asks you any rates, even though my squad leader told me that I should sit on company tables at least once a week so that the guys don't think I'm bagging it.

And chapel choir is such a joy. I love to sing, everyone is so nice, and the practices don't take up that much time. Maybe I'm being too selfish. I want to do well, but am I doing the right things? My studies should come first. And I should spend more time with my roommates instead of being such a loner.

Kate arrived at the double doors leading into Bancroft Hall, where she had to begin chopping. Holding her books close to her chest she broke into full run. Several classmates were running in front of her. "Go Navy, sir" and "Beat Connecticut, sir" resounded through the passageways.

Arriving at her room, she paused to catch her breath before noticing the handwritten message on her desk.

"Midn. Brigman, Lt. Griffith wants to see you, ASAP," it read. What did I do now? She glanced in the mirror, wiped the sweat from each side of her nose, and straightened her cover. Gosh, I look terrible, she thought. No makeup, and my hair's a matted mess. Oh, well, that's what my life has become.

She moved toward the door and peered out. With the lane clear, she burst from her room, squaring a left corner. "Beat Connecticut, sir!" Chopping past the mate's desk, Kate stopped at attention in front of the company officer's open door and knocked three times on the door frame. Lieutenant Griffith looked up from his desk.

"Request permission to come aboard, sir!"

"Miss Brigman!" he greeted her with a freckled smile and waved her in. "Please, come in. Come in." Lieutenant Griffith had been her company officer through the summer, and she had had occasion to speak to him before, but she still stepped forward nervously and began to sound off.

"Relax," he said, attempting to put her at ease. "Have a seat." Kate removed her cover and sat in the cushionless oak chair.

"How's it going?" he began.

"Fine, sir," she replied, even though she didn't think she was doing fine.

"Yes, that's the word I've been getting from your upperclass."

"Sir?"

"That you're doing just fine. And that's why I want to talk to you." Kate was confused.

"I think you are in a very good position to become a striper next year. You were ranked high in your squad at the end of plebe summer and high in the platoon, and there is no reason why you shouldn't continue to excel here. I wanted to make sure you were aware of this opportunity available to you."

"A striper, sir?"

"Yes, Miss Brigman. There are leadership positions designated for each upper class of midshipmen, similar to those that the first classmen fill. There is a second- and third-class brigade commander and staff, and each regiment and battalion has second- and third-class commanders and staffs. They aren't as active as the first classmen, of course, but individuals with strong leadership abilities are identified early on by the administration to fill these positions. Striper boards are held in the spring. If someone becomes part of this striper 'pipeline,' it helps groom them to become a striper when they are a first classman."

It was too much. Kate Brigman, a striper? She hadn't even considered it. After all, it was only the first week of academic year, and he was already talking about working toward becoming a striper next year! Kate was speechless.

"Sir, I don't know what to say. I mean, I'm just trying to make it through this year. I hadn't considered anything like this."

"Well, that's why I'm talking to you now. I'm going to be very honest. I see in you the ability to be a very strong leader. You have the potential to ride a storm well and not get rattled. You absorbed an awful lot plebe summer, more than most of your contemporaries, in my opinion.

"You know, Miss Brigman, I've been at the Academy for almost four years. Two of those I spent as a company officer, and both years I've served during plebe-summer detail. After a while you can begin to see very quickly how well mids react and how they are going to be able to deal with the stresses of plebe year. I see a leader in you.

"The only small question in my mind, right now, is how well you will be able to do academically."

Kate felt her anxiety swell. How could he put this kind of pressure on her now when she already had so much to cope with?

"I'm trying my best, sir."

"And that's all I can ask of you, Miss Brigman. Just understand that you have superb leadership potential. If you can keep your grades up, you could go very far at the Academy."

"Uh, thank you, sir. I mean. . . ." She was dumbfounded by his praise.

"Don't thank me, just do what you need to do to keep your momentum going. If I can be of any service to you, just let me know. It's what I'm here for." His voice indicated that he was finished, and she stood up to leave.

"Request permission to shove off, sir."

"Permission granted."

Dazed, Kate walked out of his office and stood in front of the blackboard by the mate's desk for a few moments, pretending to read its contents, trying to absorb all that he had just told her.

How will I ever be able to measure up? she worried. The pressure that this puts on me is unbelievable! I just want to make it through the year, and he's talking about being at the top of everything. That means not only academics but conduct, PE, company spirit, spotless room, spotless uniforms—at all times. I don't know if I can do it.

The clock on the wall behind her clicked, reminding her that she had to be at the sailing center in less than five minutes, and she had not yet changed out of her uniform. With an abrupt about-face, she chopped off to her room. Please, God, help me through another day and help me to measure up.

Monday, 20 September 1976

Sarah never got used to standing watch-squad inspections. They had to be the most nerve-racking event at the Naval Academy. Everyone sweated being inspected by the officers on duty. There were countless rumors of midshipmen being fried for such minor infractions as not having tied a fresh tie, having slight smudges on their webbed belt, and the ever-popular excessive hair length.

Standing at parade rest, the incoming Thirty-third Company mate of the deck stared at the gray bulkheads in front of her and silently reviewed the classes of fire extinguishers. Her peripheral vision continually checked her right flank for signs of the officer of the day.

"Watch squad, atten-hut!" The company midshipman officer of the watch (CMOOW) relayed the order.

Stiff at attention, Sarah slid her eyes to her right and saw the officer of the day (OOD) march onto 4-1 followed by the midshipman officer of the watch (MOOW), who tonight was Midshipman Lieutenant Commander Nolde. She moved her eyes front and center as the CMOOW presented the watch squad to the OOD, who whispered something to the MOOW, and the two parted to inspect separate battalions.

Midshipman Nolde began his inspection to Sarah's far right. She stood steadfastly still, biting the inside of her lip in a futile attempt to suppress the smile she already felt forming in her eyes. He stepped in front of her, and she felt the warmth of his body. She stared straight ahead at his tie, trying desperately not to look up.

He began with her shoes, then inspected her trousers, shirt, tie, and shoulders. Just before he reached her cover, their eyes met and her closed-lip smile broke. His slanted grin reciprocated.

"Looks very good, Miss Becker!" he lauded her. "What company are you in?"

"Thirty-third, sir," she replied, biting her lip once again as she took in his double meaning. He walked behind her to inspect the backs of the first squad and then began inspection of the second. She felt his eyes on her behind and bit her lip until she was afraid she might draw blood.

Later that evening he made rounds up on 8-4.

"You looked good tonight," he told her.

"Thank you, sir," she answered officially.

"Are you cheering at the Michigan game this weekend?" He was purely making small talk.

"Yes, sir," she answered, not daring to drop the formality. Although their conversation remained professional, the chance to speak to one another freely in front of the rest of the company was exciting, although unnerving, to Sarah. She knew that the guys in her company were suspicious, and this might just fuel the fire.

Midmorning the next day, Mr. Nolde patrolled Thirty-third Company area while the majority of midshipmen were attending class. As it happened, even the company officer was not around. Sarah was sorting mail at the mail desk. She heard the doors of the second-class stairway at the end of the front shaft close and looked to her right to see him walking toward her. Her heart stopped and then raced. He was breathtaking in his service dress blue uniform, white gloves, and sword.

As CMOD she was required to chop up to the MOOW as soon as she spotted him on deck, salute him, and sound off: "Midshipman Becker, Thirty-third Company mate of the deck, may I help you, sir?" Then she was to accompany him as he patrolled the company area evaluating the CMOD's efforts to maintain the good order and security of the company area. But it was Ryan she saw, not Mr. Nolde. She had spoken with him almost every night on the phone after study hour. The part of her that knew Ryan took control, and with no one else around and without thinking, she dropped the formalities. She walked toward him and smiled. He stopped, waiting silently for her to approach. When she reached him, he did not smile, he did not speak. He stared at her in anticipation.

"Hi!" she greeted him cheerfully.

With a grim look she had never seen before, he grasped her right biceps firmly in his white-gloved hand and led her into the closest vacant room.

"What do you mean, *hi?!*" He was incredulous.

"I mean, I saw you in the hall and I said hi," she cautiously replied, recognizing the anger in his tone while attempting to rub the sting from her upper arm.

"Whatever happened to the mate chopping up to the MOOW and sounding off?"

"But Ryan, I knew it was you."

"It doesn't matter that it was me, Sarah. Right now we are both assigned to official duties. We are acting in official capacities, and you're supposed to chop up to me, sound off, and ask me if you can help me—sir!" His tone was serious and firm.

Perplexed, angry, and terribly embarrassed, Sarah silently stared at her feet and blinked back the tears. She would have felt stupid saying those things to him.

"Come on," he told her more gently, "accompany me on my tour around the company area." He tried to soften the blow.

Sarah walked silently beside him through the middle shaft and around the back shaft. He talked to her, but she hardly heard anything. This is the guy who told me at a formal watch inspection that I "looked very good" and is planning a rendezvous out in town, she grieved. I know he's right and that I should have chopped up to him, but I honestly thought he would tell me not to if I did. I don't know when to call him sir and when to call him Ryan.

What troubled her most was that she didn't even feel she could ask him about it. She was afraid he might yell at her again or think it was stupid.

They were at the end of the back shaft when she heard him calling her name. "Sarah. Sarah, are you listening to me?" He drew her out of her daydream.

"Yes . . . sir, I mean, yes."

"I almost have something worked out where we can meet out in town. Maybe next month after the Boston College game."

"Okay." It seemed so far away.

"I better get going before the OOD comes looking for me." He paused. "And Toots, I'm sorry about back there. When we're on watch, we need to play by the rules." He had started calling her by her high school nickname.

"I know," she told him as he turned to leave the deck. She walked alone down the middle passageway, glancing into rooms with open doors along the way. Back at the mail desk, she continued sorting mail while finding herself unable to sort out her feelings.

Wednesday, 22 September 1976

Kate straightened her cap on her head and inspected herself in the full-length mirror. The short-sleeve working uniform blue "delta" was so navy blue it was black, but she liked the contrast between it and the round-neck white T-shirt visible above the open collar, even if it did seem a little strange that uniform regulations required this undergarment to be obvious on males and females alike. She accepted the fact that the uniform was a man's shirt that buttoned opposite to the way she was accustomed, and she had quickly learned to thread her belt through the belt loops in the opposite direction, too. She adjusted the shiny brass buckle so that the tab of the belt just barely showed, then lined it up perfectly centered with the button placket of the shirt, achieving only half of the required straight "gig line," the only half possible on the women's uniform. She shook her head.

I don't see why they had to make our pants with these stupid old-fashioned side zippers. My jeans never had any side zippers! It would have been so easy to give us pants just like the men's. Then there wouldn't have been any confusion about how to line up our gig line with a fly front instead of a center seam. We'd also have useful pockets instead of this tiny slit at the waistline they call a coin pocket.

She heaved a sigh, then straightened her shoulders and checked her tuck. She picked up the whisk broom and finished brushing off.

"Here's some more!" The male voice came from just outside her door, loud and full of obvious disgust.

Kate crouched nervously in front of the sink where she was returning the whisk broom to its proper place. Upperclassmen, she thought. Only upperclass can wander through the halls talking.

"Brigman, Micheals, and Mead," another male voice read their nameplates on the door.

Those stupid white nameplates, Kate thought. They might as well have painted a bull's-eye on our door. I hate them! I guess they're supposed to keep the guys from walking into a girl's room by mistake, but all they do is show 'em right where we are.

"Wonder what they look like? The ones we got are all dogs."

Kate closed her eyes and clenched her teeth, tightening her grasp on the cabinet door. How dare you!

"I know what you mean," the first replied with utter contempt. "They must all be brains or dykes, 'cuz they sure ain't good-lookin'."

"Oh, I've seen a couple that aren't so bad. There's a cute little blonde over in Sixth Wing."

"Yeah, I've seen her, but that butch haircut is too short."

"They all have those," the second one laughed, "but you didn't seem to notice it on the one we just passed."

"Who could see past her bouncin' tits? Must be the one they call Treasure Chest!" They both laughed, ribald snickers that seemed to ricochet around Kate's room long after their footsteps had faded away.

I feel like an animal in the zoo, thought Kate, cowering in a corner of my cage where I hope no one will notice me! I'm just as defenseless too, because a plebe just can't go around complaining about upperclass—especially not a female plebe. What would I say, anyway: They hurt my feelings?

How can they talk about us that way? Is it our fault we can't get decent haircuts from that butcher shop? It's not supposed to be a beauty contest, anyway! I don't want to be judged for my looks; I want to be accepted as an equal. And who says brains can't be pretty, too? I can be attractive and smart and athletic, too. We're neither whores nor lesbians—and we're not dogs, either. Guys who talk like that, they're the animals.

I'm a person, a whole person, she reassured herself as she rechecked her appearance in the mirror. Half a gig line doesn't make me only half a midshipman.

"Brigade seats," the brigade commander ordered at evening meal that night. Thirty-third Company took their seats along with the other thirty-five companies, and evening meal proceeded as usual. Dinner was rolled out in large heated chests by the wardroom staff, and forty-two hundred hungry midshipmen were served a family-style dinner in under three minutes.

Sarah and Tammy grabbed the bowls and platters of food from the tray delivered to their table while Donna set to work slicing the dessert already on the table to ensure that it was ready for the upperclass when they demanded it. Experts at serving by now, Sarah and Tammy slipped shovels (spoons) and forks into the bowls and platters and immediately passed the food to their squad leader at the head of the table. He served himself and passed the bowl to his classmate, who sent it, via the plebes, down the chain of command. Leftovers were handed to the plebes, who were careful to share them equally. The upperclass squad members usually made sure that enough food was left for the plebes. Their squad leader had established this rule.

Dessert was Lady Baltimore layer cake, a dry yellow cake with white frosting covered in coconut. Sarah sat with her eyes in the boat, her mind silently repeating the menu for the next meal in case she should be asked to recite it before leaving the table.

"Which plebe wants to whammo some cake for carry-on?" The voice broke her concentration. It was Midshipman Rhodes, the company commander.

Immediately Sarah raised her hand, along with several other classmates at other tables. What plebe would pass up a chance for carry-on? No more eyes in the boat, able to use the back of your chair at meals, no chopping in the hall, but most important, no more come-arounds! How hard can it be to whammo a piece of cake? You shove the whole piece in your mouth, chew a couple of times, and swallow. Voilà! Carry-on!

"Okay, Becker," she heard, "You're up. Hanover, you're opposite Becker." Midshipman Fourth Class Earl Hanover and Sarah left their seats and were guided by the upperclass to a nearby vacant table. They sat opposite one another while the Thirty-third Herd gathered around them.

Sarah was nervous. This had become a contest between herself and a classmate. Whoever swallowed the cake first would be granted carry-on. She had not expected this to be a race. Not to worry, she thought. I can win this. I'll beat him and show all these guys we girls can perform with the best of them.

A thick slice of Lady Baltimore layer cake was laid before each plebe. Midshipman Rhodes laid down the rules. "When I say go, you plebes start whammo-ing. First one to finish swallowing, wins. Everybody ready?" They nodded.

"On your mark, get set, GO!"

At his command, Sarah grabbed her piece of cake and shoved it into her mouth. The company burst into cheers, some pulling for Earl, others yelling for Sarah. The cake was dry. It sucked all the moisture from her mouth. She tried to swallow it whole and found herself choking. The frosting compounded the problem. She looked over at Earl and saw him having the same trouble. They were both trying to swallow while gasping for air, and both were losing the battle. I can't give up, she thought, I can't give in. This is a fight for womanhood, I don't care if I'm choking. I have to show these guys the girls can do it.

But she was scared. She couldn't breathe. The competition was now between Sarah and the cake, and the cake was winning. Her gut started reacting, and she thought she might vomit no matter how hard she fought it.

"Come on, Becker!" she heard an unrecognizable voice yell. And then a deeper voice bellowed, "What's going on here?"

It was the officer of the watch. The crowd gathered around the table had sparked his attention, and carrying out his duties, he investigated.

The company parted, and Earl and Sarah were on display for the OOD. Sarah pulled the matted cake from her mouth and gasped for air. Earl leaned over and spat his onto the floor.

"Sir, I can explain," Midshipman Rhodes took charge.

"Somebody better explain pretty damn fast exactly what is going on here!"

Midshipman Rhodes directed the plebe competitors to clean up as he accompanied the OOD to Main Office.

The company began to disperse and return to 8-4. Sarah and Earl wiped the cake from their faces and sat bent over, catching their breath for several minutes. It wasn't worth it, Sarah thought. She looked over at Earl and caught his eye. They slowly shook their heads, sharing the thought, What did we think we were doing?

Four days later the form two was delivered by the CMOD. Sarah's company officer had issued the conduct report, which read, "Midshipman Becker failed to maintain good decorum and proper etiquette in the wardroom."

"I'm being fried for this?!" she yelled aloud to Tammy and Donna. "This was Mr. Rhodes's idea! I just played along. I don't believe this! I was supposed to get carry-on! How do I get myself into these situations?"

Later that evening an apologetic Mr. Rhodes stopped by and said that he thought the form two was mostly a formality, that Earl had been fried as well, and that he was going to talk to the company officer and recommend that they be given a warning in lieu of any demerits, since the whole idea of the cake whammo had been his. Sarah was grateful but still felt that she and Earl shouldn't have been fried in the first place.

Five days later the yellow copy of the form two was placed on Sarah's desk, indicating that the battalion officer had concurred with the company commander's recommendation. She had been assigned a warning with no demerits.

Saturday, 2 October 1976

Heavy rain flooded out any hopes of a football victory for Navy over Boston College. Despite a thirteen-point fourth-quarter rally, Navy was unable to wring out the extra five points needed to win on their home turf.

Sarah cheered her heart out between downpours, along with the rest of the brigade. Boston College soaked up seventeen points in the first three quarters, leaving Navy scoreless until a plebe from Thirty-fourth Company scored their first touchdown, sending Sarah splashing around the field. When Navy scored their second touchdown from the four-yard line, the brigade went wild, victory well within their reach until a two-point conversion failed and time ran out as Boston College swam away with the game, 17–13.

Back in their room, Tammy and Donna prepared for evening meal while Sarah showered.

"Want to get a pizza out in town, Tam?" Sarah called from the shower. "Or is it still raining?" Donna waited by the door, peering sporadically at the clock in the passageway so as not to be late for her next chow call. After formation, she was meeting her sister in town for dinner.

Since September, plebes had been allowed town liberty each Saturday after noon meal formation until evening meal formation at 1830. Town liberty commenced again after evening meal until midnight.

"No, the rain has let up," replied Tammy, glancing out the window. "Where?"

"I don't care. That pizza place next to McGarvey's? Ever been there?"

"Yeah, they have good pizza."

The minute hand clicked on the clock outside their door, and Donna stepped into the passageway, popping to attention in anticipation of the next click. In sixty seconds, she began her accelerated yell: "Sir, you now have five minutes until evening meal formation. Formation is inside. Uniform for evening meal is service dress blue. The menu for evening meal is: baked haddock, tartar sauce, macaroni and cheese, seasoned spinach, rainbow salad, white bread and butter, Arabian peach mold, iced tea with lemon wedges, and milk. The officers of the day are: the officer of the day is Lt. Johnson, Third Company officer, the assistant officer of the day is. . . ."

Formation was held as usual by upperclassmen on duty. After announcements, the duty company commander dismissed them, and the three girls chopped down the front shaft ladder behind fellow classmates to the bottom of Eighth Wing.

In the parking lot, Sarah and Tammy invited Mitch Prescott to join them. The trio walked Donna as far as Dahlgren Hall to meet her sister. Then they headed out Gate One toward Prizzi's Pizza Place in the Annapolis market.

Prizzi's six tables were covered with traditional red and white checked plastic tablecloths. Several were already occupied by midshipmen. At the counter, purchasing a pitcher of beer, was Midshipman Sammy English, a second classman from their company. Sammy had been restricted to the Academy for the past three weekends for poor grades. He was a nice guy and not one to hassle plebes. In fact, he was just the opposite. When he saw the three of them sit down, he uninhibitedly joined them.

"Tough game today, Mitch," he greeted them. "You guys almost pulled it out." Mitch was a defensive back on the varsity football team.

"Yeah, thanks anyway, man."

Tammy and Sarah looked at each other in amazement, reading each other's mind. Thanks anyway, *man?* This guy was an upperclass! *Man* should have been *sir.*

Midshipman English explained, "You don't need to call me sir out here. Save it for the Hall when somebody's looking."

At least he hadn't told them to call him Sammy, thought Sarah. She wasn't comfortable being spooned (told to call an upperclassman by his first name) this early in the year.

"So how's plebe year, girls?" he asked. "Troy getting you down yet?"

Ted Troy was a second classman in their squad to whom they both came around twice a day. He was a purebred flamer, and Sammy knew it.

Tammy glanced up from the menu. "We're surviving, sir."

"Yeah, hang in there. You'll be fine."

"I don't know," said Sarah. "This week at a come-around he asked me if I thought Navy was going to beat Boston College. I knew what the point spread was, so I couldn't lie. I told him what I honestly thought."

"Big mistake." Sammy shook his head as if he knew what her next words would be.

"No kidding. He asked me what kind of cheerleader I was, not believing in my team, and made me go down to Mr. Fuller's room and tell him that I didn't think they were going to win this weekend." Steve Fuller was Sammy's classmate, who played offensive tackle for Navy. "I thought I was going to die."

"So what did Steve say?"

"He just said, 'Oh, is that right?' I felt terrible, though. I felt like a traitor, especially being a cheerleader. But what was I supposed to do? If I said I thought they were going to win, Troy would have known I was lying and probably put me up for an honor offense."

"I doubt it," said Sammy. "I don't think he's out to get you as much as you guys may think."

"He had one of our guy plebes in tears the other night at come-around," said Tammy.

"See, he treats all plebes like garbage. He's not preferential."

"But he hates us girls," replied Sarah.

"Nah. He just wants to be sure you have a plebe year."

Sarah and Tammy decided to order their pizza and walked over to the counter. When they returned, Mitch and Sammy were hunched together, whispering. When the girls drew near, the two men fell silent.

"Okay, you guys, what's up? Talking about us?" Sarah was curious.

The guys glanced at one another and smiled on the verge of laughter. "No, just wondering if you guys know anyone who has their red wings."

"Red wings, sir? I mean, what are red wings?" Tammy asked, remembering to drop the *sir*. "Do you earn them at flight school?"

Sammy and Mitch burst out laughing. Sarah kept quiet. Something gave her the feeling that if Sammy and Mitch had been whispering before they arrived, then "red wings" was probably something obscene.

"You guys really don't know what they are?" Sammy feigned amazement.

"No," said Sarah and, not wanting them to think she was a prude, asked, "What are they?"

Mitch leaned over the table and whispered in her ear.

Sarah closed her eyes slowly and shook her head in disgust. "You don't want to know," she answered Tammy's inquiring look.

"Tell me," said Tammy, overly curious.

Sarah turned to Sammy and Mitch. "You guys are sick," she half-laughingly, half-disgustedly told them.

"Tell me!" Tammy insisted.

Sarah leaned close and grudgingly told her. "A guy earns his red wings when he has oral sex with a girl when she is having her period." Tammy grimaced.

"So, do you girls know any guys who have theirs?"

"Yeah, right," replied Sarah sarcastically. She should halt this conversation.

Tammy was obviously uncomfortable, and it wasn't your ideal dinner topic. Actually, it wasn't any kind of civilized topic. She found the conversation detestable but for some reason didn't want these guys to think she was some kind of puritan, so she kept talking as if it didn't bother her. Tammy remained silent.

"How about a different subject? Where's the pizza?"

Sammy and Mitch shared a slippery smile. "Yeah, let's have pizza," one of them said. They both laughed. Sarah couldn't even look at Tammy. Their appetites were lost.

They left over half a pizza on the table, with Mitch salivating as Sammy finished his pitcher of beer. On the way back to Bancroft, Tammy turned to Sarah. "Why do you think they brought that up?"

"Shock effect? Trying to make us feel like one of the boys? Who knows, Tam? Who knows?"

"Red wings" was not a closed subject. It rudely came back to haunt Sarah the following evening at come-around with Midshipman Second Class Ted Troy. Tammy had submitted a special-request chit to dine out with a relative visiting Annapolis and was absent. It seemed that Sammy had returned to the Hall and merrily spoken to several classmates about the conversation he had had the previous evening with Miss Becker. One of those classmates had spread the word to Mr. Troy, who was now furious.

When she entered, he was at his sink, shaving. Mr. Troy was always putting on the last details of his uniform when she arrived for come-around. Sarah didn't care; she hoped in some small way that it distracted him from asking her even more rates than he already did.

"So, Miss Becker," he began, pushing his arms into his black WUBA (working uniform blue "alpha") shirt, "you ran into Mr. English out in town last evening?"

"Yes, sir," she answered with dread.

"Just what was it you talked about?"

"I'm not sure what you mean, sir." She knew exactly what he meant.

"I think you do, Miss Becker. I think you know very well what foul-mouthed smut you two discussed. Is that the kind of conversation you always carry on in the presence of men, Miss Becker?" His face was inches from hers. "I can't believe you discussed such filth. What are you? Some kind of tramp? Is that the kind of reputation you want to have around this place? Does Ryan know you talk like that?" His fury escalated as he talked.

She was frightened and angry. *What gives him the right to talk to me like this? I'm no tramp. What do you mean, "my" reputation? I didn't initiate that conversation last night. I eventually ended it.*

It suddenly occurred to her that she didn't know what Sammy had told his classmates. *Maybe he had exaggerated. What was he doing talking to anyone else about it, anyway? This was unbelievable! Why wasn't Mr. Troy coming down on Sammy? Sammy was the one with the filthy mind, fraternizing with plebes.*

"Are you going to answer me?!" His anger interrupted her thoughts.

"Yes, sir! No, I am not a tramp." She ignored the comment about "Ryan." Mr. Troy was extremely suspicious of her and Ryan Nolde but had done nothing official about it. Sarah only guessed that he hadn't because of Ryan's position on the brigade staff. "Mr. English initiated the conversation—"

"Oh, so that makes everything all right?" he broke in. "Listen to me, Miss Becker. You better clean up your filthy little mouth and stop talking like some slut, or your reputation won't be worth dirt around here. Understand? Now get out of here!"

She raged as she made a right-face and ran from his room. *What a jerk,* she thought. "Beat Air Force, sir!" She turned the corner, heading back to her room. She was beside herself. Another corner. "Beat Army, sir!" *How could that incident have been blamed on her? Down the ladder. Sammy was an upperclassman. He started the conversation. What was she supposed to say— hey, sir, why don't you clean up your mouth? She was just a plebe. The upperclassmen directed the plebes, remember? Not the other way around!* "Beat Army, sir!" She turned right, entered her room, and pushed the door shut. She leaned against it, waiting for formation. Donna was still at her comearound.

Sarah fumed. She couldn't even defend herself. She wondered if Ryan had heard about it or would even care. It was beyond her comprehension, at that point, that Mr. Troy might have been genuinely concerned about her reputation and was trying to give her some good advice. She felt that he had accused her of initiating the conversation, and she wanted to know what Sammy had been spreading around.

I just have to forget about it, she decided. *There is nothing I can do about it now.* She tried to mentally review her rates before heading out for formation and dinner to avoid giving Mr. Troy any more excuses to harass her.

As she left her room for formation, she passed Sammy English.

"Good evening, sir," she reluctantly greeted him, avoiding his face.

"How ya doing, Miss Becker?" He grinned as if they were close friends.

Unbelievable, she thought. He probably doesn't have a clue what he's done to me.

Wednesday, 6 October 1976

Kate sat alone on the floor of the women's head on the third deck of Nimitz Library, sobbing uncontrollably. It had been months since she had felt the need to purge herself of an evening meal. During most of plebe summer her elevated activity level had eliminated the need, but now the continued pressure, combined with the uncomfortable bloated feeling after dinner, had forced her to vomit her meal. It solved nothing, she knew, but she could not help herself.

Yesterday she had been yelled at for not looking good enough at inspection. Today she had received a B on a naval science test when she knew she should have gotten an A, and at sailing practice this afternoon the captain of the team had told her that she was going to have to go back to her regular company tables for meals. How was she going to tell her squad leader? She knew he was going to think she was a failure.

Then, to make matters monumentally worse, Charlie had come by her room after evening meal to tell her that he was considering quitting the Academy. He had spoken inappropriately to one of the plebes in his company, was going to be fried for the infraction, and couldn't put up with the bullshit anymore.

How could he leave her? She tried to explain that she couldn't make it without him, but he just yelled at her for not understanding his frustrations and left her room in a huff. Kate felt lonelier than ever, praying for him to change his mind.

Now on the floor of the library's head, she cradled her forehead in her palm and sobbed. I love him so much, and now all of my dreams of how it could be for us are ruined. At the end of this year we could have openly dated and gone on to have careers in the navy and maybe even get married. But now he's leaving. It must be my fault. Why am I not strong enough to keep him here? My grades are a mess, my professional performance is in jeopardy, and now I've completely alienated the only person who was on my side.

. . .

After two hours of sporadic studying, Kate returned to her room just in time for taps at 2300. Michelle was leaning against the edge of their door, talking to one of the upperclassmen in their company. The conversation was professional, for the most part, but Kate knew he should be leaving. After taps no one was allowed to talk to plebes, who were required to be in the rack with the lights out unless they had a late-lights chit. If your roommate had a chit and you did not, you had better be in the rack.

Kate found it comical—college students being told when to go to bed. Upperclassmen could stay up as late as they wanted, as long as they remained in Bancroft Hall.

Michelle stepped out of the way as Kate entered their room and shot her a look that said, Doesn't he need to be leaving? although she knew it was impossible for a plebe to tell an upperclassman what to do.

The upperclassman showed no intention of leaving. Kate laid her books on her desk as Michelle closed the door halfway and peered around to continue the conversation. Terrie was already in the rack.

"Michelle!" Kate whispered. "He needs to leave." Michelle gave her an "okay" sign behind her back, indicating that she had heard, but it was almost five minutes before the upperclassman finally left and Michelle closed the door. As the girls began to change for bed by the light of their shower, someone knocked.

"Just a minute, sir," Kate called, quickly pulling on her scratchy navy bathrobe and opening the door four inches to peer around its edge. Her company commander stood cross-armed in the passageway.

"Good evening, sir," she remarked, swallowing hard.

"It's not a very good evening for you, Miss Brigman. You girls are 'down' for taps violation," he told her gruffly.

"Sir?" she responded confused. She hadn't been talking to the upperclassman, but she was the ICOR, the midshipman in charge of their room that week.

"You heard me, Miss Brigman, I saw that mid talking to you girls after taps, which is a blatant taps violation."

"Then he should be placed on report, sir. I wasn't talking to him."

"Don't play sea lawyer with me, miss. You're ICOR, aren't you?"

"Yes, sir."

"Then you're down. Let's get something straight, Miss Brigman. I told you before that you girls had better not use your femininity to get what you want, and I meant it. I expect you to adhere strictly to the rules around here. You screw up, you're going to be punished. Don't expect any favors from me or any other upperclass. Is that clear?"

"Yes, sir," she replied, controlled anger nearly surfacing.

"You and your roommate come around to my room tomorrow evening to pick up your form twos. Don't ever let me catch you violating taps again!" He stormed away.

Kate allowed the door to close on its own and stood clenching her fists as the anger she had suppressed exploded. "He fried us!" she screamed. "What a jerk! How could he do this? Is he going to fry the upperclassman who got us into this trouble? I doubt it! Who was that, anyway, Michelle?"

"Just a guy I met in chapel last Sunday," she answered. "I'm really sorry, Kate. You shouldn't have been fried. I was the one talking."

You're right, thought Kate, but the fear of alienating another person this evening kept her from saying it. "Forget it. I'm ICOR, and that guy just hates us. He enjoys tormenting us and is doing his best to try and run us out of here. Lord, we have to come around to him tomorrow. He'll rip us apart."

Michelle nodded, downcast.

"We'd better have our rates down cold," said Kate.

"You guys had better get in the rack before somebody else catches you," interjected Terrie, who had remained innocently silent through the entire ordeal.

Heeding her warning, the girls climbed into their racks. As she lay in the dark, Kate's fury peaked. *Our company commander hates us, and I just know that he is out to get me. It seems like he's lost sight of the system and its purpose. All he had to do was tell the upperclassman talking to Michelle that he had to leave, and the problem would have been solved. Then he could have reminded us not to let the situation happen again, which it wouldn't have.*

Now I'm going to have to study my rates really hard when I need to be studying for four-week exams. It seems like I can't leave this room without being punished for something. How am I going to take this for a whole year?

Saturday, 9 October 1976

Sarah couldn't wait. Navy would be playing at Air Force this coming week-end. More than the opportunity to travel far from the Academy for a weekend, more than the excitement of flying C-141s from Andrews Air Force Base to Colorado Springs, and more than playing the rival service of which her father was a member, Sarah wanted to go to the Air Force Academy to see Jacqueline Mitchell, her friend from high school.

Jacqueline and Sarah had worked closely together during senior year, when Sarah had served as class treasurer and Jacqueline was vice-president. Jacqueline received her appointment to the Air Force Academy the same time Sarah heard from the Naval Academy.

Mids dressed in black uniforms, some with arms full of books to study while in flight, chattered excitedly about the impending game on the tarmac in the cool fall air. Sarah and the other women cheerleaders posed for a picture in front of the gaping rear door of their C-141 before boarding. Half an hour later the aircraft roared down the runway, filled with seated midshipmen wedged in tight together on long strips of red nylon webbing, sharing shoulders as pillows for the lengthy flight.

The Navy–Air Force game would help decide if the Naval Academy would retain the coveted Commander-in-Chief Trophy for the fifth year in a row. The trophy, named in honor of the president of the United States as commander-in-chief, was presented annually to the winner of the football competition among the three major service academies: Army, Navy, and Air Force. Not as great a rival as Army, Air Force was still a formidable foe in football.

Clustered amid the majestic Rocky Mountains, the rectangular glass and metal buildings comprising the Air Force Academy presented a striking contrast to the gothic architecture of the Naval Academy. The famous A-framed Air Force Academy chapel stabbed the sky with its spectacular metal spires, but despite its modern beauty, Sarah decided that she preferred the traditional architecture of Navy.

Upon arrival, the four hundred–plus midshipmen were directed to the mess hall for breakfast. Sitting at a table with the other cheerleaders, Sarah looked around for Jacqueline. She saw no familiar face and felt guilty as she watched the cadet doolies, the air force equivalent of plebes, eating at attention while she and the other plebe cheerleaders ate at ease. Her guilt was quickly turned to fear by the returned glares of upperclass air force cadets.

They know we're plebes, she realized. All the women are plebes. I wonder if we're supposed to be eating at attention. She looked at Derrick Ogden, the head cheerleader, who seemed to read her mind.

"Listen, you guys, you have to play by navy rules," he said. "You don't have to obey these guys just yet. Be respectful, but don't let them bully you. You have any problems, you let me know, okay?"

They nodded. Sarah felt a little better, but she knew that the stares had not been friendly. Some were curious. Most were hostile.

Two female doolies approached the table, explaining that they were to accompany the women cheerleaders to their rooms in the women's barracks. Sarah knew she would have to start acting like a plebe again. It was a strange feeling, "playing plebe" outside the Naval Academy. At other away games, carry-on was taken for granted.

"See you on the field, girls," called Derrick. "Remember what I told you. You belong to the navy, not the air force." He smiled at the female doolies, who returned the smile.

"Don't worry, sir. We'll take care of them."

Nevertheless, Sarah felt the same dread she had felt the day the brigade had returned. Was she going to have to prove herself to the air force cadets as well? No, she thought. I have nothing to prove to them. I'll play by their rules as much as I have to, but I don't care if these guys think I should be at their academy.

Carrying their bags and books, Sarah and the five other female cheerleaders followed the two doolies around the outer edge of the brick quadrant between the mess hall and the women's barracks. As fourth classmen, they were all required to remain on the outer boundary of all walkways, eyes in the boat, allowed to speak with no one except for the mandatory greeting of an upperclassman or officer. The stares from the cadets they passed were unsettling.

Sarah anxiously followed the girls dressed in blue uniforms. The Air Force Academy housed its women all together on a separate floor of one of the barracks, unlike the Naval Academy and West Point. As they entered the rectangular building housing the women, a blonde woman officer greeted them.

"So these are the navy girls," she remarked. "Take 'em to your room and tell 'em *our* rules. We're gonna sink their ship this afternoon!" She broke into laughter. Ah, yes, welcome aboard, thought Sarah, swallowing her first taste of interservice rivalry.

"She was lovely," Sarah remarked facetiously to her new air force roommate once in the room. "Are they in charge of you guys?"

"Yes," answered one disgustedly. "They think they're really special. We all think they're jealous. Some of them are okay, but most of them are pretty bitchy."

"How do you deal with it?" asked Brigette, also assigned to the room.

"We don't have much choice," answered one doolie. "We hate it because we're ostracized from the guys. They think we're getting preferential treatment and having a slumber party over here while these women officers are trying to practice their limited leadership skills on us to make sure we have a real fourth-class year. Eventually we're going to try to convince the administration to put us in the barracks with the guys. This method is not working."

"We don't have any problems living with the guys, except for the normal plebe-year harassment stuff," said Sarah. "Wonder why the air force did it like this?"

"We're not really sure. They need to change it, though. It makes life twice as hard. None of the guys accept us here, not even our classmates."

"Yeah, I think it creates more problems than those they were trying to prevent," said the second doolie.

"I'm Sarah Becker, by the way," said Sarah. "Sorry to have gone off on that tangent without even introducing myself." The girls introduced themselves and began to swap fourth-class experiences.

"Hey, do you guys know Jacqueline Mitchell?" Sarah asked, hopefully. "We went to high school together. I'm dying to see her."

"Sure," they both answered. "She lives right down the hall. Let's see if she's in."

Sarah followed the girls out the door, squaring a corner at the other side of the narrow hallway. Unlike navy plebes, doolies were required to rub the edges of their shoulder boards against the wall as they walked. An air force doolie could go through numerous pairs of shoulder boards in that first year at the Academy.

With her peripheral vision Sarah watched three women doolies approaching them on the other side of the hallway. As they got closer, Sarah's eyes flooded with tears. The second girl in line was Jacqueline! Sarah was helpless to stop the tears. It did not matter that both girls' hair had been cropped above the ears; they recognized each other immediately.

Sarah wanted to reach out and hug Jacqueline, but air force rules forbade fourth class to cross the hall. Jacqueline motioned with her head to an empty room and slid inside. Sarah risked being seen by the two female second lieutenants down the hall and leaped across the passageway into the room, where Jacqueline waited with open arms.

They both burst into tears as they embraced, escaping from the reality of their regimented environment for only a moment. When they finally let go of one another, their tears turned to laughter as they wiped their eyes.

"How are you?" Sarah asked Jacqueline excitedly.

"Okay," answered Jacqueline. "How 'bout you?"

"Well, it's real different from high school."

"I'll say," said Jacqueline. "My mom told me you were a cheerleader, so I figured I'd get to see you today. Then when I heard you guys were here, I came looking for you. It's great to see you, Sarah!"

Sarah and Jacqueline, at this moment, felt closer than sisters. Wordlessly, each understood the trials the other had already endured and appreciated, as only one who is there can, the challenges yet to be faced.

They shared news from home, talked about going home for Christmas, and laughed at each other's short hair.

"You know, your air force haircuts look a lot better than our butch jobs," said Sarah. "Who cuts the girls' hair, Jacqueline?"

"We have a beauty salon in one of the other barracks."

"A real salon, with real beauticians?" Sarah asked in amazement.

"Yes," answered Jacqueline. "Why?"

"Well, we have a butcher, I mean a barber, who has been through a correspondence course on how to cut women's hair."

Jacqueline laughed.

"I'm serious! Look at this mess on my head!"

"Well, why don't you get your hair cut here?" offered Jacqueline. "You could probably get an appointment before the game."

"You're kidding!"

"No, I'll help you call for an appointment, but then I have class. I'll try to see you after the game."

"Thanks," said Sarah. "It was great to see you, Jacqueline." She hugged her tightly.

"Yeah, you too, Sarah. Almost like being home again. Hang in there, and let's keep in touch!"

Sitting in the slate gray barbershop now renovated into a beauty salon, Sarah closed her eyes and savored the warm air of the blow dryer against her scalp. The mirror reflected a stylish pixie cut in place of her ragged trim, making her feel like a real girl again.

On the sidelines of the football field, dressed in her cheerleading uniform, Sarah turned her face to the warmth of the fall sun. The stands behind her were beginning to fill with midshipmen and Navy fans, while on the opposite side of the field the Wing of Cadets filed into the bleachers.

While she stretched out on the sidelines, Sarah remembered the wager she had made with her dad. Each had bet $5 on their respective teams, no points given to either side. Sarah hoped Navy would win but for now was happy to be away from the Naval Academy, despite the taunts of "Beat Navy" flung at her by air force cadets.

As the cheerleaders warmed up the crowd, Sarah's nervousness mounted. The brigade had continued to display animosity toward the cheerleaders at every home game, leaving her uncomfortable in front of them. It was hard to smile at hostility. Today, however, their animosity seemed tempered by their fervor to beat Air Force. Sarah found them actually willing to participate in the cheers.

Tension ran high throughout the game, and despite Navy's ability to move the ball into Air Force territory three times in the first half, they were able to score only one field goal. Navy lost, 13–3. Sarah's dad would be $5 richer.

The tough loss was softened by the announcement that the Naval Academy Drum and Bugle Corps had beaten the Air Force Drum and Bugle Corps during halftime competition, and since Air Force had lost to Army, Navy could retain possession of the Commander-in-Chief Trophy.

After the game the Navy cheerleaders joined several of the Air Force cheerleaders for pizza. Afterward they returned to their respective barracks. Much to her disappointment, Sarah was unable to find Jacqueline. Now with taps several minutes away, she barely had enough time to get undressed.

"Hey, guys!" she and Brigette greeted their air force roommates as they returned to the room.

"Hey, Navy! Tough game!'

"Yeah. Oh, well. Win some, lose some."

"You guys looked great on the field, though."

"Thanks," said Sarah. "It was hot out there. I got a lot of sun on my face. It feels great."

"Look out, ladies! Here comes the lieutenant. You'd better hit the rack!" said the air force doolie already in bed.

The three girls jumped into their bunk beds as one of the female second lieutenants entered the room, clipboard in hand and dressed in a pink T-shirt that barely covered her posterior. She muttered something that Sarah did not understand and therefore ignored.

"Miss, I said, Are you safe?" the lieutenant repeated, directing her question more loudly at Sarah.

"Am I what, uh . . . ma'am?" Sarah wasn't sure what to call her, scantily dressed as she was. She did not present a very professional appearance.

"Yes, ma'am, she is," her air force roomie interrupted.

"What, can't she speak for herself?" asked the second lieutenant sarcastically, turning her back on the girls and walking toward the door.

"Nice game today, Navy," she tossed over her shoulder as she lifted the back of her T-shirt and bent over slightly to expose a pair of pink bikini panties. "SINK NAVY" was emblazoned across her rear end in dark blue letters.

Sarah was aghast. Is this how professional women officers act? she wondered. I know I'm a plebe and I'm for the other team, but this is incredible, even to me, the eternal cutup.

"Wow!" whispered Sarah after the flasher left. "Do you guys always have to put up with that kind of stuff?"

"Pretty much," one doolie answered. "I told you this morning these chicks are really jealous—of all of us, you guys included, it seems. Don't let it bother you."

"What did she mean by that 'Are you safe' stuff?" asked Sarah.

"Oh, it's something they ask every now and then to see if you have any contraband in your room, like alcohol. They rarely ask us that at taps, but since you guys were here. . . ."

"Where'd she get those underpants?" asked Sarah. "They're a riot, even if she was pretty rude!"

"They sold 'em in the store here a couple of weeks ago. I think I have a pair." The doolie jumped out of her rack, padded over to her dresser, and reached into the top drawer. "Yeah, here they are." She held up a pair of pink nylon panties and displayed the "SINK NAVY" on the rear. "Here, sailor, they're yours!" She tossed them to Sarah.

"Thanks, zoomie!" said Sarah. "I'll wear them under my uniform next year when we play you guys. We're gonna sink you then!" She smiled and jumped back into her rack.

Saturday, 16 October 1976

Sarah and Ryan met on the squash courts in the basement of Fourth Wing just before study hour, once or twice a week. Midshipmen rarely used these courts, especially at that time of the evening, so they were pretty safe from being caught together. They usually played several games of squash and talked, although Ryan had kissed her once, briefly, but the two remained cautious of intimate behavior in the Hall.

Once, on the phone, Ryan told Sarah he thought they should try to meet out in town after the Homecoming football game. One of his classmates had offered them his girlfriend's apartment while they went out to dinner. Despite apprehension about being caught, Sarah agreed.

After the Homecoming game, Sarah rode back to the Academy with the cheerleaders and got ready for evening meal formation. After formation, she was free to go on town liberty, which extended to a seven-mile radius from the Academy chapel. Sarah told her roommates she was secretly meeting Ryan but gave them no details. They both told her she was taking much too big a risk, even though they knew they were talking to the wall. When formation was dismissed, Sarah donned her black overcoat, exited Bancroft Hall, and walked out Gate One.

Ryan had told her to meet him behind the field house on Prince George Street, where he would park his blue Volvo sedan somewhere along the street. He promised to bring the civilian clothes Sarah's mother had sent, along with some good tunes: James Taylor, Dan Fogelberg, Jackson Browne.

The cool fall air and Sarah's apprehension caused her to walk briskly. She was scared. *What if he isn't there? What if someone sees me get into his car? What if. . . .* She considered turning back.

A sole street lamp cast a dim light on the sign for Prince George Street, where Sarah glanced cautiously over both shoulders before turning left. Convinced that no one was following her, she turned and continued slowly, squinting for Ryan's car among the dark outlines of vehicles edging the sidewalk. She began to panic when she found that she couldn't tell one from the other. She had been right; he wasn't coming. *Turn around and go back to the Hall,* she told herself just as a car door opened on her right. She inhaled, startled, but let her breath go when she saw that it was him.

Sarah pulled the door open, jumped into the car, and immediately threw herself on the floor, her heart pounding. Ryan smiled and told her to sit on the seat and keep her head down. She reluctantly slid her upper torso onto the seat, leaving her hips and legs dangling, still worried that someone might see her. The Volvo eased out of its parking space.

"Toots, you did it!" he beamed.

She smiled lamely in return. "Ryan, this is crazy!"

"Relax. It'll be fun. No one saw you. Believe me, I was watching. Did you tell Tammy and Donna where you were going?"

"I didn't have much choice. They don't approve, but they aren't going to say anything."

"Here are your clothes." Ryan reached back for a brown paper bag, which he handed to her. "Go ahead and change. How 'bout some J.T.?" he asked, sliding a James Taylor tape into the cassette deck.

Sarah awkwardly removed her uniform, folding it carefully in an attempt to keep it from being wrinkled. She slid into a familiar pair of jeans and pink blouse, only temporarily embarrassed by her partially undressed state. Dressed as a civilian, she felt less conspicuous and sat up in the seat, oblivious to where they were going. Ten minutes later Ryan turned into the parking lot of a large apartment complex.

Please let no one recognize me, she prayed. Just get me safely inside. Her face was in front of the entire brigade every football game. People I don't even know could recognize my face, she worried. A form two could be waiting for me when I get back, but it's too late now.

Ryan opened the door for her. Hand in hand they crossed the parking lot to the dark brown apartments and knocked on a first-floor door. Ryan's classmate and girlfriend had already left, but the girlfriend's roommate was home, putting on makeup while her date waited in the living room. The date answered their knock.

"Hey, guys, come on in!" he greeted.

"Thanks," said Ryan, shaking his hand, forgoing the introduction of Sarah, who silently inclined her head behind him, feigning shyness. "Where're you guys going?"

"Dinner. Maybe a movie," said the date.

Ryan turned to Sarah. "Listen, Toots, I'll be right back. I need to get that bag of groceries in the car."

He walked away before she could speak. Sarah panicked. She tried to follow him, but he was out the door before she could stop him. Retreating to the kitchen, she looked for something to do.

Suddenly the date was beside her. Sarah suddenly felt faint when she saw an Academy ring on his hand gripping a can of beer. Her fear was suffocating. She should have guessed that this guy was in the military with that crew cut. Probably a marine. He must have been at the game today and seen her on the field.

"So, where're you from?" he asked casually.

She felt the blood rush from her head. Where was she from? What should she say? New Hampshire? Annapolis? Should she lie? Could she do so convincingly? Would he turn her in for an honor offense as well as fraternization? She couldn't think straight, she was so wrought up with fear.

"Around here," she answered.

"Severna Park?"

He's trying to make me lie because he knows who I am, she despaired.

"Uh, yeah," she answered, unsure of where Severna Park even was. It could have been in Wyoming for all she knew.

"I'm back," she heard Ryan call from the living room. The blood rushed back to her extremities, and her shoulders dropped with relief. The date went to help Ryan with the door and called to his girlfriend to hurry up.

Ryan appeared in the doorway of the kitchen, and Sarah ran to him. "Don't ever leave me alone again," she pleaded against his chest.

"What happened?"

"That guy, the date, is Class of '76. What if he recognized me? He wanted to know where I'm from," she whispered. "I had no idea what to tell him."

"Toots, I'm sorry. If he recognized you, he would have said something, don't you think?"

"I don't know, Ryan."

"Have fun, guys," the date called from the living room. "We're outta here."

"Okay, thanks," replied Ryan as the front door shut. "Come on, hon, let's get dinner started." Sarah took a deep breath and went to set the table in an attempt to regain her composure.

After a quiet candlelight dinner, Sarah found herself more relaxed. The couple sat on the couch and talked, but time passed much too quickly, and in what seemed like minutes Ryan was indicating that they had to head back.

Her heart sank. The thought of returning to the Hall after such a wonderful evening was revolting. Sarah dreaded returning to the rates, the harassment, the academics, and worst of all the charade of treating Ryan like another upperclass. She was falling in love with him and didn't know how to stop.

The ride back to school was silent. When they were close, Ryan recommended that Sarah change back into her uniform. She felt like Cinderella changing back into her rags. It was difficult to make the transition from feeling like a "real" girl to putting on her drab black masculine-looking uniform and going back to being "one of the boys."

Ryan stopped the car beside those still parked along Prince George Street where he had picked her up earlier that evening. They were both silent for a moment.

"Sarah." He turned to her, sensing her despair, and reached for her hand. "Sarah, it'll all work out."

She bit her lip. "I know," she said softly, unconvinced.

He leaned over and kissed her cheek. She turned to him with eyes that pleaded for him to let her stay. "Hang in there, Toots. I'll talk to you tomorrow night." He was telling her it was time to go.

Of course she couldn't stay. Taps was in twenty minutes. She would have to hurry as it was. She nodded, unable to speak for fear of crying, and quickly opened the door and stepped out into the street. Ryan pulled away from the curb, and Sarah solemnly retraced her steps back to Bancroft Hall.

Sunday, 17 October 1976

"If I hear them say they are 'officers and gentlemen by act of Congress' one more time, I think I'll scream," Kate muttered, walking a few steps behind a group of male classmates Sunday afternoon, on the way to Dahlgren Hall. Even an act of Congress wouldn't convince me after what I've seen and heard, she added silently.

The description had its origins in the "Qualifications of a Naval Officer," drawn from letters of John Paul Jones and given a prominent place in *Reef Points,* as well as in advice to a newly appointed midshipman attributed to Horatio Nelson. To Kate it seemed that the implementation of those noble sentiments had been reduced to issuing each midshipman a copy of the current edition of *Service Etiquette,* printing occasional instructive comments in the "Brigade Bulletin," and requiring plebes to attend a Tea Dance, scheduled to begin in a few minutes.

Another group quickly overtook her, grumbling as much as the others about their prospects at the "Tea Fight." I don't like it any better than you do, she told their departing backs. What a waste of an afternoon. Busloads of civilian girls are paired up with mids for an afternoon dance, so the guys have potential dates when plebes are allowed to drag. They're not busing in a bunch of civilian guys for us, are they? They watch us like hawks to keep us from fraternizing—even with our classmates—and now they're going to play matchmaker and throw us at each other whether we like it or not. Then when it's over, everything will be business as usual, and we'll be suspect if we even talk to a guy.

Kate paused briefly and looked up once more at the doors of Dahlgren Hall, its imposing arched glass front unable to impress her today. Fleetwood Mac was playing loudly inside. She took a deep breath, squared her shoulders, and entered the fray.

Inside, Dahlgren Hall was something like an airy arcade, with lights arranged on ribs of the high arched ceiling and flags of all the states and territories of the United States displayed along the walls. One end of the ground floor housed a small fast-food restaurant, Drydock, while the central floor area doubled as the Naval Academy's ice rink in the winter and as a multipurpose facility for dances, dinners, and ceremonies at other times. A comfortable gallery with deep cushioned chairs and sofas overhung the oval area beneath. It was intended to be a place to relax, but Kate anticipated only tension this afternoon.

She walked down the broad marble stairs toward Drydock and came to an abrupt halt at the foot, suddenly feeling awkward and plain. The busloads of civilian girls fluttered around the area like radiant butterflies. Kate looked down at her own service dress blue skirt and pumps. She shook her head sadly. I used to dress like those girls, even look like them, but no one would know it now. My uniform seems so drab and severe next to those fancy dresses. And their hair! Most of them have long, beautiful hair, but even the short hairstyles are cute. Mine looks like a beautician's nightmare. This is so stupid.

She wanted to leave but knew she had no choice.

A long gold curtain hung at the other end of the hall. Multitudes of young women and the occasional woman midshipman were lining up on one side, and midshipmen—male midshipmen—were lining up on the other to be paired by upperclassmen assigned to the dance. Kate noticed other women classmates wearing grim expressions, a few trying bravely to appear at ease and others simply resigned, as she was, to their duty. Some of the civilian girls looked at her strangely as she passed, then whispered and giggled among themselves, sharing a secret joke at her expense. I'm not going to let it bother me, she told herself. They have no idea what it's like.

She reached the end of the line but did not join it immediately. This is so stupid, she repeated silently. Brains don't stand a chance against beauty today, and I really should be studying.

A group of young women approached the line, and Kate motioned to them to go ahead of her. They thanked her so respectfully that she actually smiled. They must think I'm some kind of officer too, she realized. Then she frowned. Great! Even girls my own age don't recognize me as one of them anymore.

She glanced up at the balcony level and saw to her horror that it was jammed with hundreds of upperclassmen scoping out the girls, giving a thumbs-up or, more frequently, a thumbs-down signal to indicate their opinion of a girl's appearance. The steady, thumping beat of the music mercifully drowned out their spoken commentary, but Kate was indignant. This isn't a dance, she thought, it's a livestock show, and we're meat on the hook! I heard them calling this a "pig push," but this is worse than I imagined. Disgusting! I'm getting out of here.

She turned away sharply but stopped short as an upperclassman approached, leading another group of civilians to the line. He stayed nearby, leaving her no opportunity to escape. She did, however, manage to let the civilians get in line ahead of her, and she very politely yielded her place in line to the next two groups to arrive. With a little luck, she thought, maybe I won't get matched up with anyone.

She studied the texture of the curtain, glancing up occasionally to see if she needed either to move forward or to allow others to go ahead of her, but no other civilians arrived, so soon she was not only last in line but also first. At the first classman's cue, she walked from behind the curtain to meet her date for the afternoon.

"Hi." Her classmate smiled politely at her and introduced himself as they walked a few steps away from the curtain toward the dance floor. "I'm Bill Walgorski. Twenty-second Company."

"Kate Brigman," she replied, impressed that he was at least being diplomatic about this unfortunate incident. She decided immediately to give him a polite way out. "Look. I'm sure you don't really want to be with me. I'll understand if you want to take off."

He looked at her quizzically.

Kate explained further. "Really, it's okay. You can get back in line or go try to find a civilian girl."

He smiled. "But I don't want to, unless you'd rather not be with me."

It was Kate's turn to look confused. "Are you sure? I mean, of course I don't mind being with you."

"Good!" He laughed an easy chuckle. "Why would I mind being with you? You're one of the few girls here who knows exactly what I've been through for the last few months and won't ask me any dumb questions." He offered her his arm. "Would you like to dance or just go talk, Kate?"

Kate felt almost dizzy with surprise and relief. "I think I'd rather talk," she answered, shyly taking his arm. *This isn't so bad after all,* she thought. *He's actually very nice. An officer and a gentleman. What was I worrying about?*

After dinner, the Thirty-third Company plebes met to vote on the "Brick" award. It was an annual event, performed after each year's "Tea Fight." Individual plebes could be nominated by their classmates or nominate themselves as having been matched with the ugliest date at that afternoon's social event. Sarah and her roommates had been invited to participate but were wary of being included.

Sarah had been matched up with a fair-looking prior-enlisted guy from First Regiment who had been nice enough but obviously disappointed at having been matched up with a "plebette." They spent about thirty minutes together before deciding they had nothing in common. The last place she had wanted to be was there, and she had gone back to her room disgusted with the whole affair.

Tammy's "date" had greeted her with an "Oh, shit!" The two parted company immediately.

One of the fourth-class leaders in Thirty-third Company chaired the meeting. Holding a list of nominations in front of him, he asked for any others before they commenced. There were none.

"Well," he began, "only one guy on this list got bricked with a plebette." He looked sideways at Sarah and her roommates. "Nothing against you girls," he told them, "but this chick was ugly."

Sarah forced a slight grin. Although she didn't doubt his opinion, she suddenly felt a pang of allegiance toward her as-yet unnamed female classmate.

Donna spoke up. "Listen, I saw some pretty unattractive civilian girls, you guys. And you think all the mids we got matched up with were so great? It works both ways, boys."

"Hey, we didn't say you girls couldn't get in on the vote," asserted the discussion leader. "I'm sure several of you girls got bricked, too."

Kurt Loper noticed Sarah's unease. "Toots," he whispered, "I got paired up with a real nice girl from Twelfth Company. We didn't stay together long, but she was very nice."

"Thanks, Kurt," replied Sarah softly. "The whole thing was so demoralizing. I sure hope they get rid of it next year."

Kurt smiled in agreement. "No argument from the guys, you can be sure."

"All right. Let's get on with the vote," continued the group leader, reading the nominations out loud. "Everyone ready?"

Sarah, Tammy, and Donna abstained from the final vote, sitting quietly in the back as their male classmates voted and eventually awarded the "Brick" to a classmate who had been paired with a plebette from First Regiment.

Yes, that girl was ugly, thought Sarah, and being a female mid made her twice as ugly to these guys. At least they don't feel that way about me. I mean, I think they don't. I want to be accepted, show them that girls can do it too, but sometimes I think it all comes back to one thing: sex. It doesn't matter how we perform; it's our appearance that counts. I wonder if it will ever change.

Sunday, 14 November 1976

Thirteen days before Navy would hopefully beat the hell out of Army, Sarah waited impatiently inside the Eighth Wing phone room, gnawing her thumbnail. She tried to determine which of the twenty-plus phone booth occupants might be nearing the end of a conversation, since only thirty minutes remained until she had to be back in the company area for taps.

I have to talk to him, she pined. It's been over three days since we've spoken. I'm exhausted from spending the entire weekend in Nimitz Library, but thank goodness that term paper is done. I shouldn't have left it until the last minute, but at least I only have to type it now. Come on somebody, hang up!

Another mid got in line behind her to wait for a phone as the glass door to a nearby booth opened. Sarah slid onto the round metal seat inside, picked up the receiver, and dialed his number. Ryan answered after one ring.

"Toots! Where've you been?"

"Don't ask. I've been standing here for thirty minutes waiting for a phone. I got back from the library late, and all the booths were full by the time I changed out of my uniform and got down here."

"So, are you finished?"

"Yeah, writing it. Now I have to type it. Good thing Tammy has a typewriter I can use in the room. I have a late-lights chit, and then I may just sneak out of bed to finish it."

"Don't get caught up after taps, Toots, or you'll be marching again."

"I know. But I only have one more day to get it done. It's due Tuesday, and I have other classes I need to study for, not to mention rates and everything else."

"Did the books I recommended help?" Her paper was about the Strategic Arms Limitation Talks, about which Ryan, a political science major, was fairly knowledgeable.

"Yeah, thanks a lot. They got me started on the right track. I'm so tired, though. I don't know how I'm going to finish typing that paper."

"Listen, Toots, I need to talk to you about something."

"What?" she asked with what she hoped was unnecessary alarm.

"About Army."

"What about Army?"

"I've invited someone." Sarah tightened her grip on the phone as she felt the onslaught of nausea.

"You what?" She tried to say it calmly but knew that her voice sounded defensive. "You mean you're taking a date to Army?"

"Yes."

Sarah said nothing. She was falling off a cliff.

"I didn't want to tell you before you got this term paper behind you."

How considerate, she thought facetiously. "You mean you asked *her* weeks ago?"

"Not exactly. Listen, this has nothing to do with you. I mean, actually, it has everything to do with you. I was thinking that maybe we should just lay low for a while. We certainly can't be seen together at Army, and if I take someone else, maybe it will take some of the heat off of us."

"So she's a decoy?" Sarah asked sarcastically.

"Sarah." It was a subtle reprimand.

"Oh, so she's more than a decoy. Have you been seeing her?"

"It doesn't matter, does it? I thought we agreed to see other people."

"Oh, yeah, we did, except that who am I supposed to 'see' and when am I supposed to see them? Nothing like a girl in uniform, I always say." Her eyes filled, blurring the hands on her watch. Five minute to taps. "I've gotta go. It's almost time for taps."

"Toots."

"What?" she answered coldly.

"You know people are starting to get suspicious. Besides, you should enjoy Army. It's your first one, and you should spend it with your classmates—"

"Right. I've gotta go." She cut him off before she lost control of her voice. "Toots—"

"I'll talk to you later, Ryan." Placing the phone gently on the receiver, she pushed open the booth door and ran into the passageway, thankful for the requirement to chop.

"You should spend it with your classmates," she heard him say again. Sure, she thought, chopping up the ninety-six steps to her room. All my male classmates have dates. I guess I'm supposed to just hang out with the guys. What am I doing involved with this guy?

Saturday, 20 November 1976

Kate found herself exhausted from the emotional ebb and flow of the past two weeks. It had begun with her disappointment at being selected next semester's fourth-class company subcommander instead of company commander. The idea of being number two came as a blow, especially since she couldn't stand the classmate selected to be company commander.

Then she and Charlie had gone to her sponsor's to relax on a Saturday afternoon, and she had found her relationship with him becoming more and more strained. They had broken no midshipman regulations by being together at her sponsor's house, yet trouble began when the sponsor, a retired navy captain, drove them back to the Hall. An upperclassman saw Kate get out of her sponsor's car and took her name and alpha code, with the intent of putting her on report for riding in a car. The sponsor, after seeing the upperclassman write down her name, thought that she was in trouble for being at his house with Charlie. He called the OOD to clear up the situation. Coincidentally, the OOD, who happened to be Charlie's company officer, called Kate's company commander to make sure that everything was straightened out.

Things had certainly been straightened out. Kate was not put on report for either offense, but it was now clear to her company commander that she was seeing an upperclassman. The fact that she had a retired navy captain covering for her made him furious. What she and Charlie were doing was innocent, yet she knew that her company would never believe that.

Her relationship with Charlie was becoming more of a hardship than a pleasure. He always put her down and told her how to act, making things much more difficult than they already were. Several days earlier he had even braced her up in the passageway outside the Midshipman Store for no apparent reason except that she had greeted him by his first name, even though they were alone. It was humiliating. She was disappointed in herself to find that she might have misjudged her feelings. She missed the feel of a guy's arms around her and the compliments that made her feel feminine and desirable. Charlie was treating her like a plebe.

Life began looking up on her birthday. Her morning come-around was canceled, she found out she was getting an A instead of a B in naval science, and she was interviewed on Channel 4 from Washington, D.C. The crisp air of fall had begun to envelope the Academy, and it was only twenty-seven days until Christmas leave. That afternoon the sailing team threw her into the frigid Severn River to celebrate her eighteenth birthday, making her really feel like a part of the team. Her mom and sister arrived at Main Office with a birthday cake, cider, and some Christmas albums, and her roommates gave her a birthday party in her room. When her squad leader presented her with a Marine Corps enlisted working cover as a birthday gift, her wonderful day was complete.

It was no surprise to Kate, then, when the next day fell apart. She knew that she would have to pay for having enjoyed her birthday. After receiving a 64 on her math quiz and a B on the English paper she had worked so hard on, disaster struck with her noon meal chow call at "The Pit." The worst upperclass flamers hung out there, screaming and humiliating plebes to the point of tears.

With a dry throat and churning stomach, Kate chopped to the dreaded chow-call station. With ten minutes until formation, the clock ticked, she snapped to attention, and four upperclassmen began screaming and yelling within inches of her face, their spittle bouncing off her cheeks and nose as she tried to vocally overpower them with her noon meal announcements. The pressure was too much. She choked and forgot the number of days until the Second Class Ring Dance. They ate her alive, bracing her up and chiding her as she chopped away to the women's head for a four-minute reprieve until the five-minute chow call.

At the five-minute call, she forgot to stay braced up and was ordered to come around to the toughest second classman in the company. Back in her room, she sobbed inconsolably. She was frightened to death of this second classman, who she was sure would find some reason to fry her at his come-around. Why couldn't she be tougher?

Now with only five days until Thanksgiving, Kate was depressed. If only time would stand still for a minute so I could get my head together and get back on the right track, she thought. I can't seem to do anything right. Now that sailing is over for the fall, I don't have any athletics to free up my mind. I have four tests this week—Army Week, of all times—and I can't concentrate on my studies at all. It's just terrible, and it's really gonna hurt my cumulative QPR [quality point rating]. I had so hoped that I could go on Thanksgiving vacation feeling pretty good about things, but I guess it's not meant to be.

I want to get back with Charlie, but I look so awful. I feel so ugly and pimply. Why would he want me? I need to go home and get it all together.

Saturday, 27 November 1976

The week before Navy's most intense football game of the year had been full of "recon" raids, spontaneous pep rallies, plebes decorating sheet posters, and pranks against fellow midshipmen, officers, and most especially the West Point exchange students living in the Hall. Sunday night of Army Week, Thirty-third Company had spent the entire night relocating the furniture in their company officer's office to the women's head, then stuffing his office as tight as a Thanksgiving turkey with balls of newspaper. It was filled to the ceiling; you could barely open the door. Not one with a sense of humor, he made them return it to normal as soon as he arrived the following day.

The spirit of "Beat Army" rang raucously through every course of every evening meal as table after table of midshipmen started a wave of cheers. "Go Navy! Beat Army! Whitewash the Black Knights!" It was almost impossible to eat in between yells.

Sarah's favorite cheer was the one in which the plebes at a table were ordered to stand on their chairs and "test their lungs." Prior to the admission of women, the plebes had "tested their balls," but this year the cheer had been altered. So far this semester, the upperclass had complied with the change, but this was Army Week, and Sarah joined in the thunderous applause after three plebes at the table five down from hers stood on their chairs and yelled, "AARRGH! AARRGH! AARRGH! WE'RE TESTING OUR BALLS FOR ARMY, SIR!"

Having grimly listened to plebes test their lungs instead of balls for Rutgers, Air Force, and the rest, the brigade went wild at the resurrection of the original cheer. Sarah thought it was wonderful. She secretly vowed to one day test her tits for Army. Maybe first-class year, when the Class of '80 was in charge and no one could say anything.

The brigade was fired up, and tonight Lt. Marie Lennox was the OOD. Thirty-third Company's tables were within eyeshot of the OOD's table, giving Sarah a direct view of Lieutenant Lennox seated at its head. She watched in awe as a midshipman suddenly ran up behind the lieutenant, dumped a bowl of Roquefort salad dressing on her head, rubbed it in, and ran off. Mids called it a "wild man." Sarah called it suicide to do it to the OOD. Lieutenant Lennox went crazy! She was furious! Sarah never heard if she caught the culprit or not, but she had mixed emotions about the prank. Sure, it was Army Week, but would someone have done that to a male OOD?

Two nights later, after word had been covertly passed to all fourth classmen, Sarah and Tammy joined their classmates at Halsey Field House at midnight to relocate the A-4 Skyhawk to the courtyard in front of Nimitz Library. Almost the entire class appeared in sweat gear and white works. They sawed through the stanchions anchoring the aircraft to its concrete pad and pushed it through the streets of the Yard, carrying it up two sets of stairs to its new resting place. The civilian security guards, "jimmy-legs," were defenseless against the mob.

After their successful mission, the plebes flocked to the commandant's house on the Yard and banged on his door with demands of "Over the wall! Over the wall!" Unable to suppress the spirited mob, the commandant rode the shoulders of two of the larger members of the class to Buzzy's, a renowned pizza parlor just outside Gate Three.

The penniless throng of midshipmen ordered pizzas and beer and danced on the tables. It was rumored the following week that the Naval Academy received a bill from Buzzy's for over $14,000 for the fiasco.

Now, on the bus to her first Army-Navy game played in Veterans Stadium in Philadelphia, Sarah focused on the party planned for after the game. The Philadelphia Sheraton was hosting the entire Brigade of Midshipmen to either celebrate or drown their sorrows, depending on the outcome of the game.

The Thirty-third Company firsties had invited all their plebes to a postgame party on the ninth floor, where most of them had reserved rooms for the weekend. Their liberty did not expire until evening meal on Sunday, unlike the plebes, whose liberty expired on the buses at 0100, when they would be driven back to the Academy. Rank had its responsibilities, but weekend liberty was one of its most revered privileges.

Sarah sat near Tammy and Donna. Her cheerleading uniform was in a carry-on bag in the overhead rack above her head. As they pulled into the parking lot of Veterans Stadium, her stomach churned. This was the first milestone for which the plebes had counted days. "Zero days until Navy beats the HELL out of Army!" the chow caller had ecstatically yelled this morning. The outcome of this game would decide the fate of every plebe at the Naval Academy for next semester.

A win could mean no more chopping, a reduction in rates, carry-on at meals—heaven on earth. The rumors had run rampant. But a loss would ensure that the "Dark Ages," the bleak winter months of January, February, and March, would be worse than a living hell. When Navy lost to Army, the plebes became sacrificial lambs, and upperclassmen chewed on them like hungry piranhas. Many plebe prayers were offered today that Navy would not lose.

The brigade had been primed at a pep rally the night before in the field house. Now, at the game, they were truly fired up and ready to give their all to cheer Navy on to a victory against their biggest foe. Sarah had not seen them so riled since the game against Air Force. She felt appreciated as a cheerleader once again, and besides the thrill of cheering Navy on to a victory over Army, she was excited about the possibility of being on national television. She knew that her friends at home were glued to the television set watching for her.

Her grandmother told her later that she thought she saw her briefly dancing and cheering on the sidelines as Navy danced all over Army on the field. The game wasn't even close. Navy kicked Army's ass, 38–10. Tonight's celebration would be wild!

Kate stood huddled among her company, cheering and yelling Navy on to victory, her depression of the past week displaced by the excitement of this time-honored tradition. Sustained by the excitement of the game, the cool fall air, and sheer exhaustion from the previous week, she never wanted this feeling to end. Last night had been crazy. Plebes ran all over the company area, spraying shaving cream all over each other, keeping everyone awake, and playing cards until all hours of the morning. Kate had finally fallen asleep at 0415 only to wake up less than two hours later to get ready for the 0730 bus ride to Philadelphia.

Gazing across the football field at the impressive blanket of gray uniforms worn by Army's cadets, Kate felt that Navy was almost assured a victory. It just doesn't get any better than this, she thought. Thanksgiving had been wonderful. She and Terrie had spent the day at her sponsor's with Kate's family, Charlie, and a young naval officer Terrie was seeing. Charlie had acted terrible to Kate during dinner, but afterward they talked out their differences, and she forgave him. She decided that she just loved him too much. The event was a foretaste of Christmas, which just couldn't arrive quickly enough for her.

The final cannon shot signaled the end of the game and Navy's victory over Army! Kate went wild, hugging her classmates, jumping up and down with excitement. Now the party would begin, starting with a much-needed shower and dinner at Bookbinders with her family and Charlie.

Sarah changed into her service dress blue uniform and met her folks after the game for dinner. Afterward she persuaded them to accompany her to the ninth floor of the Sheraton to her firsties' party. They said goodbye at the elevator.

Mr. Rhodes saw Sarah arrive and got her a beer, since plebes were allowed to drink after Army. She walked over to a group of classmates already there, which included Tammy and Denzel. As the group talked, Ryan approached them.

"Hey, Mr. Simmons! Good game today!" Denzel had played the entire third quarter.

"Thanks, sir!"

"And you looked mighty good down there on the field too, Miss Becker," Ryan noted. Everyone caught his double meaning.

Despite his date, Ryan had assured Sarah that his feelings for her had not changed and that he was not severing their relationship. Feeling helpless to alter the situation, she resolved to have the best time possible tonight, since she couldn't be with him regardless.

"Thank you, sir," she answered matter-of-factly, playing along as if his comment meant nothing while casually glancing over his shoulder looking for his date.

"So the season is finally over, guys," Ryan said. "You plebes should get some kind of reward for inspiring the Big Blue on to victory." Sarah's hair rose on the back of her neck as he included her in his collective "you plebes." She hated playing this game.

"Any idea what we're gonna get, sir?" asked a classmate beside her.

"Haven't heard yet, but—"

Before he could finish, a short blonde walked up behind him and put her hands on his shoulders. "Where've you been, Ryan?" she asked, glancing at Sarah. "Come on back to the room. We're doing shooters."

Sarah gritted her teeth and bit the inside of her cheek. She knew this was "the date." I could rip every hair out of your head, she thought, but I am going to remain calm because you only have him this weekend. I live in the same building with him the rest of this week, the rest of this semester, the rest of this year.

She slipped a disinterested glance at Ryan before turning to Tammy. "Come on Tam, let's go. See you back in the Hall, Mr. Nolde," she remarked coyly.

The blonde sneered and grabbed his elbow. "Come on, Ryan. Let's go back to our room."

"Let's go back to our room," Sarah snidely mimicked as she and Tammy walked down the hall toward the elevator. "I could strangle them both."

"He'll come back to you, Sarah." Tammy tried to be consoling.

"I don't know," answered Sarah, disgruntled and dejected. "Maybe it's not worth it anymore."

On the first floor of the hotel, Sarah and Tammy walked into the ballroom, where the victory dance was being held. Feeling extremely uncomfortable and conspicuous in their uniforms among classmates who had invited "real" dates—girls who looked the part with makeup, long hair, and stylish clothes— they left almost immediately. Both of them felt very out of place. Between Ryan and his date and the rest of the midshipmen and their dates, Sarah felt like the ugly duckling. She and Tammy walked around the Sheraton the rest of the night, simply killing time.

At 0015, fifteen minutes after midnight, they boarded one of the Naval Academy buses parked outside the hotel along with the other plebes and a number of upperclass who did not have the weekend off. They shook their heads at several inebriated souls already on board, knowing how they would pay for their drunkenness the following morning.

Tammy turned to Sarah, seated beside her, shook her head, and wondered aloud, "Who ever said Army was such a great time?"

Thursday, 16 December, 1976

Sitting thankfully at ease at her wardroom table, Kate read the green and white Christmas dinner program in her hand. Tonight was special. The wardroom was alive with midshipmen celebrating Christmas and their impending leave period.

Dressed in mess dress blue, the most formal of their military uniforms, Kate finally felt feminine. The long black skirt with twelve-inch slit, ruffled blouse, and short black evening jacket appeared professional as well as appealing. Her roommates and she had even put on mascara for the event. Kate thought she felt a few heads turn when she walked through the wardroom to her seat. Or maybe not. It was probably just the novelty of seeing the women in the formal uniforms that piqued anyone's curiosity.

When dinner was over, the superintendent's five-piece combo broke into upbeat Christmas carols instead of the mellow holiday selections they had played during dinner. Kate found herself swaying to the beat as she reached for another piece of fruitcake.

I probably shouldn't be eating this, she thought. I'm really starting to put on weight. Oh, well, it's the holidays, she reasoned, and took a bite. Her roommate, Michelle, was starting to get heavy as well. Kate had seen her pinning her uniform together at the waist several days ago. If she didn't stop eating, she herself might soon be doing the same.

What did the administration expect? They fitted us for these uniforms when we were so thin during Plebe Summer. Now, after 3,400 calories a day for four months, we have no option to buy new uniforms or have these altered without the original seams being perfectly obvious to all the guys, who already heckle us constantly about our weight.

Kate dropped the fruitcake onto her plate when she was tapped on the shoulder. Oh, no, she thought, more hassle about eating too much. But it was her company officer standing behind her. "May I have this dance?" Lieutenant Griffith asked politely.

"Me?! I mean, sir?" she asked. He nodded.

"Sure, sir. I mean. . . ." How could she say no to her company officer? She looked around. No one else was dancing. Of course. There were only about seventy-five girls among four thousand men. And the girls were plebes. Untouchable. Off limits. As if anyone would want to dance with them anyway.

"Shall we?" He offered his hand. She gently took it and stood up as he led her to the center aisle, which had the most open area. Her company looked on aghast.

The band played "Silver Bells," and Kate fell into step with her company officer. Thoughts of Christmas filled her mind. She couldn't wait to be home with her family. Just one more day, and half of this year would be over. The music ended.

"Thank you, Kate." Lieutenant Griffith held her away from himself before continuing. "Have a wonderful leave. You deserve it."

"Thank you, sir. I will. I can't wait to get home. Merry Christmas to you and your family." She smiled brightly, turning to walk back to her table, but her smile evaporated as one hundred angry faces confronted her. "Smack!" someone called. "Kiss-ass!" whispered another under his breath as she walked by. Kate pretended not to hear them as she walked to her seat, eyes on the floor, secretly fearing that she had now sealed her fate. She glanced up and saw Dirk Walker two tables down, shaking his head slowly.

Oh, Lord, please don't let them hold this against me. The lieutenant asked me to dance. How could I say no?

Friday, 17 December 1976

"Do you really need all this?" Ryan asked Sarah as he lifted the third piece of luggage into the trunk of his Volvo sedan.

"Yes," said Sarah firmly. "A lot of it is books." She planned on studying for finals during Christmas leave, since she had five scheduled two weeks after they returned.

"Sarah, this can't all be books. What do you possibly have to pack?"

Sarah ignored his question, realizing that she had probably taken too much stuff, but it was too late to unpack now. She was proud of being a midshipman and was taking home some of her uniforms to show her family and friends. There were also some Christmas gifts in there.

Ryan slammed the trunk and walked to the driver's side. "Ready?"

Sarah nodded and climbed into the passenger seat, ignoring the stares of nearby upperclassmen packing their own cars. It was not unusual or against regulations for plebes to catch a ride home with an upperclassman for Christmas leave. It *was* unusual, however, when a first-class male midshipman from South Carolina gave a cute little female plebe a ride home to New Hampshire.

As they drove out the Academy gates, Sarah was ecstatic. Christmas leave was finally here, and she was riding off the Yard sitting up straight in Ryan's car instead of slouching under the dashboard!

Sarah realized that she was paying a price for her relationship with Ryan. Her classmates knew that something was going on between the two of them, and although they did not blatantly ostracize her, she wasn't an integral member of the close-knit Thirty-third Herd of plebes anymore. It had been a hard call to make—whether to continue her "illegal" relationship with Ryan and risk being ostracized by her male company mates, or to break it off and play by the rules. Wanting both, she continued to see Ryan on weekends while maintaining a good relationship with her classmates by stopping by their rooms for a brief chat in the few precious free moments after evening meal. They were always receptive to her company even though she knew they resented her dating Ryan. Especially Denzel.

Ryan followed the nine-hour route north recommended by Jan Becker. He planned to stay in New Hampshire with the Beckers for the weekend, drive home to South Carolina for Christmas, and drive back for New Year's with Dan Rhodes, the company commander. Dan had been wanting to meet Sarah's best friend, Anne, ever since Parents' Weekend when he had first seen her, so the four of them planned to spend New Year's Eve together.

As soon as they were out of Annapolis, Sarah changed into civilian clothes.

"How's it feel, Toots?"

"Liberating, although I wish we didn't have to deal with finals once we get back." Sarah paused, another concern gnawing at her conscience. "Ryan, did anyone say anything to you about driving me home?"

"What could they say, Sarah? We're allowed to drive plebes home."

"I know. But after the skit last week, it's obvious that everyone knows what's going on between us."

"No, it isn't," he said. "It's obvious that Dan and I are spending too much time down by the girls' room, but that proves nothing about you and me."

Sarah wondered how he could be so oblivious to the company's obvious suspicions about the two of them. Maybe it was just wishful thinking. She thought back to the Christmas skits acted out in the company area after Christmas dinner in the wardroom last night. After dinner, each class took turns putting on satirical skits in the main passageway, harassing or belittling particular individuals or entire classes in the company. One skit performed by the youngsters had been directed at Mr. Nolde, Mr. Rhodes, and the girls.

A youngster, dressed as their company officer, was seated behind a desk. Another, dressed as Midshipman Rhodes, was seated in a chair in front of the desk:

Company Officer: Midshipman Rhodes, I am very concerned that there may be some fraternizing going on with the women down on 8-3. I think there may be some male midshipmen who are spending a little too much time down there. I really think this is something we need to look into and take action on.

Midshipman Rhodes: Oh, no, sir. Ryan Nolde and I spend nearly twenty-four hours a day in the girls' room, and I can assure you, there is no fraternizing going on!

The entire company erupted in laughter. They clapped and cheered as Sarah felt herself sinking into her seat, hoping to disappear. She had smiled but avoided any eye contact with Mr. Rhodes or Ryan.

What the youngsters had said was true. Mr. Rhodes and Ryan were often down at the girls' room. Although Mr. Rhodes had not "spooned" any of them and they still called him sir, everyone remained aware of his frequent visits to their room. He was friendly toward some of their male classmates, but not as friendly as he was toward them. Sarah rationalized the visits by the fact that Mr. Rhodes and Ryan were such close friends, and Mr. Rhodes, of course, knew what was going on between Ryan and her. He also wanted Sarah to set him up with Anne. Ryan, on the other hand, was continually stopping by their room feigning conversation with Donna, who was "his age," while actually there to see Sarah.

"Sarah, let's enjoy the time we have together and try not to worry about what goes on back there. Okay?"

"All right," she agreed, pulling out her chemistry book to study.

"Hey, am I just the chauffeur here?"

"Sorry," she said. "You're right. Let's talk." She slid the book back into her bag.

They arrived in New Castle at midnight. The Beckers were still up, waiting with a huge wrapped gift on the kitchen table, when Sarah and Ryan walked in. Sarah introduced her parents to Ryan for the first time. Jim Becker played the role of disapproving father to a tee.

Sarah opened her welcome-home gift to find a thirteen-pound Maine lobster. Jan knew exactly what her New Englander daughter would want when she got home. "They had him at the lobster pound, and I couldn't resist," Jan explained.

"Thanks, Mom . . . and Dad." Sarah hugged them both.

"Okay, guys. Let's get to bed. I know you both are tired, and it's late," said Jan. "Ryan, you're sleeping on the third floor, and Sarah, your bed is made up in your room. We'll talk more in the morning."

Sarah sighed as she dropped her luggage onto the carpet in her old bedroom. Everything was just as she had left it. Her stuffed animals still sat on top of the two antique twin pineapple poster beds, and her collection of antique doll furniture was in its case on her dresser. *It's great to be home,* she thought.

"Here's the last of 'em," said Ryan as he brought up her other two suitcases. "I'm going to hit it. See you in the morning, babe." He kissed her good night and headed for the stairs to the third floor as Jan walked into Sarah's room. "'Night, Jan."

"Good night, Ryan."

"So, what do you think, Mom?" Sarah whispered.

"He seems very nice, honey."

"He is, and so is Dan."

"Sarah." Jan paused. "Could you be kicked out if you got caught?"

"You know, Mom, I'm not really sure what they would do to us if they caught us. I guess it depends on what they caught us doing. I know we could get in a lot of trouble. But Ryan helps me keep my sanity in that place. We have a lot of fun together. He takes me away from the hazing and harassment and builds up my self-image. My biggest fear is alienating my classmates. I know a lot of them suspect something is going on and don't like it, but they don't understand how it is being a girl in that place. It's so . . . defeminizing. Being with Ryan makes me feel attractive, like a 'real' girl."

"But you *are* a real girl, Sarah."

"Not there, Mom. There, I wear men's clothes and have a man's haircut. I really like being there and have no thoughts of quitting, but it's hard to feel feminine. And anytime you do anything that makes you look or feel a little feminine, somebody tries to make you feel like you've broken the regs.

"Like just a few weeks ago, I put on a flowered long-underwear shirt and a pair of white works pants to wear during study hour. All the guys, plebes and upperclass, wear sweatshirts or T-shirts from different colleges during study hour. So I decide there's no reason I shouldn't be able to wear this long-underwear shirt.

"I go out into the hall to get a soda and this second class sees me and asks me if I rate wearing civilian clothes. I couldn't believe it! Then five second class-men spent the rest of study hour trying to decide if long underwear is civilian clothes and if they should fry me. I told them I had seen guys wearing long underwear. 'Theirs didn't have flowers on it,' they said. It was amazing.

"Anyway, they finally decided I could wear the shirt, but I never wore it again. It wasn't worth the hassle."

"Well, you know you can come home anytime you want, honey. We'll be proud of you either way."

"Mom, I'm gonna make it there. It's something I want to do. I know it's hard now, but next year it will be a little easier not having to contend with the rates and all the plebe stuff. And we won't be the only girls there, either. Some of the girls in my class make it hard for the rest of us by not being able to keep up academically or physically. My grades aren't great, but so far I have a 2.68, and I do outstanding on all the physical fitness tests. I'm going to show these guys that girls can do it. I won't be at the top of the class, but I'm going to hold my own and graduate."

Jan hugged her daughter tightly, finally accepting the realization that Sarah wasn't coming home on her own accord. She just prayed that this escapade with Ryan wouldn't send her home involuntarily.

Sunday, 2 January 1977

Ryan and Dan had arrived in Dan's tiny green Triumph convertible on a snowy New Year's Eve afternoon. Anne Kalinski, Sarah's best friend from high school, was at the Becker household waiting to meet her blind date. Anne and Dan hit it off immediately. Sarah was surprised but pleased. The foursome went out to dinner and then returned to Sarah's house to continue celebrating the New Year listening to Barry Manilow.

The two couples spent the next two days sledding, pitching snowball fights, walking on the beach, and going out to dinner before Ryan and Dan left for the Academy. Sarah was flying back the next day. Anne and Dan were distraught at the thought of having to say goodbye. They had fallen in love, and it was killing them to part, as it would be several months before they could see each other again.

Sarah and Ryan's farewell was no less tearful. Although they would see each other in the Hall, Sarah dreaded commencing their charade once again. She had enjoyed openly dating him.

"It's so hard, Ryan," she told him, leaning against him in her snowy driveway, trying not to cry.

He tipped her chin up with his forefinger. "I know, Sarah, but it's only for a few more months. Then we won't have to play our little game anymore. I love you, and I'll see you when we get back."

"I love you, too," she told him and waved as he climbed into the passenger seat. Dan's Triumph spun its wheels as he pulled out of the drive.

This semester can't be over fast enough, Sarah told herself.

CHAPTER SIX

Plebe Year, Second Semester

Y ou should remember that at all times, in or out of uniform, you
are an officer and you should conduct yourself as such. Wear
your uniform proudly, and never give cause for discredit to be cast
upon you, your Academy, or the naval service you represent.

Reef Points, 1976–77

Tuesday, 4 January 1977

Kate's family drove her back to the Naval Academy in time for the 1700
plebe curfew on Tuesday evening, 4 January 1977. She dreaded the return
and sobbed when she said goodbye to her mother and walked back into the
Hall.

Although time had gone much too fast, Christmas leave had been everything she had hoped for. High school friends had taken her skiing and partying. Her family had been together, and she felt so close to them. Charlie
had been her only disappointment. He was supposed to visit on New Year's
Eve but called to say he was unable to come because of an illness in his family. It was the first time he had called her over the leave period, and the last.
Although he promised to call her again, he never had, and Kate found herself wishing that their relationship would just end. Charlie was so wishy-
washy. One moment he couldn't be near her enough and the next he was cutting her down and giving her advice on how to be a better midshipman. Who
needed the hassle along with everything else?

Kate knew she needed to psyche herself up for the next six months. Plebe
year was half over. If she would just keep her nose to the grindstone, she felt
she could handle the second half. So many wonderful opportunities awaited

her. The plebe stuff was pretty much routine by now, and everyone else seemed to be coping. Why shouldn't she?

Do well. Be the best. I just have to, she thought. It's my New Year's resolution.

Thursday, 6 January 1977

"Plebe, halt!"

Sarah had just squared the corner after finishing the five-minute chow call when the voice she hated so well ordered her to freeze. Standing at attention, she wondered, What now?

"Miss Becker, what's the menu for evening meal?" Mr. Schluntz circled like a vulture.

"Sir, the menu for evening meal is Ham Francisco, oven-baked potatoes, peas with pearl onions, wagon-wheel salad, ranch dressing, white bread with butter, Lady Baltimore layer cake, coffee, tea, and milk, SIR!" Her recitation was flawless.

Schluntz glanced at a list of menus posted on a bulletin board inside a nearby room, checking her accuracy. Sarah pondered his motive. He had just heard her chow call.

"Officers of the day. Go!"

Sarah regurgitated her rates without error as he circled her, listening intently for any mistake.

"So, Miss Becker, have you heard the good news?" he asked, hands on his hips, legs shoulder-width apart.

"No, SIR!" Sarah focused on his tie, refusing to meet his stare.

"Seems you and I are going to be neighbors next set. I'm moving in next door when your squad leader moves upstairs to become company commander."

Sarah stiffened. Her fingernails dug into her palms. No news could have been worse. As if returning from Christmas leave had not been depressing enough, now she was going to have to put up with Schluntz through the Dark Ages. Maybe this was payback for thwarting his offer to help her move in last summer. No. He just had it in for her. He always had and always would.

"I requested it myself. I am personally going to see to it that your little boyfriend stops visiting so often, and that the three of you girls are not here when I graduate. Is that clear?"

"NO, SIR!!" she replied vehemently, not caring that he could fry her for disrespect.

"Well, it will be, miss! Now, get out of here!"

Sarah sprinted away, whispering in defiance, "It'll take a hell of a lot more than you to get me to leave this place, Mr. Schluntz!"

Sunday, 16 January 1977

Only a handful of other midshipmen dotted the second floor of Nimitz Library where Kate sat studying on this dreary Sunday afternoon, books scattered on the table in front of her. She had spent most weekends in the library since the end of sailing season. Chin in her palm, she watched a raindrop chart a course down the window pane. Final exams began on Wednesday. Why can't we take final exams before Christmas leave like other schools? she lamented.

I'm going to burst, she thought. I haven't talked to Mom or Dad for over a week and a half. They told me I didn't need to call every week anymore, so I'm trying to hold off, but I miss them. And these finals. I really need to get A's on all of them. I can't wait for them to be over, but then second semester starts, and they put me in Mr. Marco's squad. He's such a flamer! Terrie and Michelle got such easy squads.

Lord, I hate the thought of another semester of being scared all the time. My platoon leader told me the other night that I need to tighten up, that my attitude is too loose. I guess he's right, but didn't he encourage it? Always joking around with me. I'll have to change that. It's so hard to know how to act. Maybe that's why they put me in the flamer's squad—to put me in my plebe place. Who knows? All I know is that I hate this place and wish time would fly. June Week can't get here soon enough.

Unable to concentrate any longer, Kate gathered her books and reefer (heavy jacket) to go back to her room to study and listen to James Taylor. The first-semester brigade commander, in his farewell address two nights before, had told the plebes that since they had performed so well they could now have stereo privileges, meaning that they could listen to music during the day and on weekends excluding study hour. This privilege was normally reserved for upperclassmen.

There was a rumor that the brigade commander also planned on suspending chopping for the rest of the year. Although Kate hated to chop, she was glad that the requirement was still intact. The upperclassmen would blame the change in tradition on the girls. They always did. Any changes were blamed on the girls: having to wear b-robes outside of their rooms, having to watch their language, no longer writing grease evaluations on their classmates.

The men also felt that the girls always got the best of everything: the best heads, the best rooms. When the male heads were split to become male and female heads, the girls got the half with the window. Room assignments had initially been made so that no one could look or climb into the girls' rooms. Consequently, the girls got rooms with scenic views, normally reserved for upperclassmen.

In the second-floor stairwell, Kate passed two third-class midshipmen on the stairs. Their conversation stopped when they saw her. "Good afternoon, sir." She kept her eyes in the boat and held on to the handrail. They said nothing until she passed.

"Yeah, right, oinker," one called.

"There's another one with Severn River Hip Disease," replied the other. They both broke into laughter.

Kate kept walking. Her eyes stung. *Why do they hate us so? What have we done to deserve statements like that? I don't even know those guys. Have I put on that much weight?*

Her pace quickened. *I can't wait for June Week so the plebe harassment will be over, but I'm afraid that kind of harassment may never go away.*

Monday, 17 January 1977

Sarah chopped to her room after her fifth-period English class, thankful that she had sixth period free. Her rain cape flapped behind her as she ran through the passageways, and she began to sweat from the layers of obligatory clothing that she wore: T-shirt, long-sleeve shirt, raincoat and cape.

Glancing quickly at the chalkboard, she saw that all outdoor sports had been canceled because of the rain. *Hallelujah,* she thought. *No team hand-ball!* It was a sport she and Tammy were forced to play because of the limited athletics available to the women.

During the fall, Sarah had been sports-exempt because she was on the cheerleading squad. The only sport offered solely to women then had been club volleyball, which, with only thirteen open positions, left the fifty-eight remaining women (ten had resigned by this date) to qualify for the men's varsity teams, play on the men's intramural teams, or become team managers, since all midshipmen were required to participate in some sport every season.

Expecting limited success by the all-freshman women's volleyball team, the administration and the brigade were taken by surprise when the club finished their season 11–0 and won the B Division Championship at the Maryland State Collegiate Tournament in November.

Now, for the winter season, women's basketball was available to a limited number of women midshipmen, but Sarah had no interest in this sport. Some women had signed on to the men's track, fencing, and sailing teams, but once again none of these sports interested Sarah, and she had been forced to pick a company intramural sport. She and Tammy hated playing on the men's team made up of upperclassmen in her company. She felt like a token, and the roughness of the sport made her happy to sit on the bench—but then she didn't get a workout, which left her feeling fat. She had gained about five pounds over Christmas leave, leaving her uniforms feeling snug against her thighs. She constantly vowed to start a morning exercise regime, but every time the alarm went off at 0515, she reached over and slammed it off.

Occasionally the cheerleaders would cheer for the basketball team, but they were no longer sports-exempt now that the football season was over. One or two nights a week they would be allowed to eat an early evening meal so that they could practice before study hour. Such was the case this evening when Mr. Schluntz confronted her on her way down to the wardroom.

"So, Miss Becker," he began snidely, "hear about your cheerleader class-mate who thinks all mids are 'warmongers' and 'guttermouths'?"

"I haven't seen the article, sir," she responded truthfully, realizing that he was referring to an interview with one of the other female cheerleaders that had been published in the *Chicago Tribune* over Christmas leave. The brigade was abuzz over its contents.

"Bet she's catching some real flack for those choice words," he said with disgust. "She must be a real fool, shooting off her mouth like that."

Sarah knew that "she" was Alicia Catrell, from Fifth Battalion, and she hoped to get the true story from Alicia tonight. Why would Alicia have said something like that? she wondered on her way down to dinner. That just doesn't sound like her. I'll bet it's the press again. I really wonder whose side they're on.

Sarah recalled her own comment about the cheerleading squad that had been quoted last semester in a *Washington Post* article about women's sports at the Naval Academy. Asked by a reporter if she was bothered by the implication that being a cheerleader midshipman was antithetical to the goals of the women's liberation movement, which had broken the all-male barrier at the Academy, she was quoted as replying "dryly" that "when you have your own women you might as well put them to good use." She didn't remember saying that to him, and if she had said it, she had only meant it in jest. Nevertheless, it took weeks for her company to let her live it down. They clipped the tiny paragraph from the article and hung it on the company bulletin board for days. After that, she resolved never to do interviews for the media again.

When Sarah arrived in the wardroom, Alicia and several other cheerleaders were already at the table reserved for them.

"Hi, guys! How's it going?" They returned her greeting except for Alicia, who looked up and rolled her eyes.

"Haven't you heard?" she asked.

"Well, I've heard about it," replied Sarah, "but I'm reserving judgment until I hear your side of the story. I know how the press can be."

"Thanks, unlike the rest of the brigade."

"So what's this all about?" asked Sarah. "Or do you want to talk about it?"

"Wait until you hear," interrupted Judy Nance. "You won't believe it!"

"Yeah, start from the beginning," said Brigette Cook.

"Well, it started during Christmas leave. This lady from the local paper who wrote articles publicizing my mom's garden club kept bugging my mom to get me to do an interview. So as a favor for my mom, I agreed. I thought the interview went real well. She asked me if we ever talked about going to war, and I thought that I gave her a rather benign answer. That is, until I was quoted as saying that all midshipmen are warmongers."

"What *did* you tell her?" asked Judy.

"I think I just said that we talk about tactics and going to war at the dinner table upon occasion, and that once we discussed what it might feel like to kill somebody."

"You guys talk about that kind of stuff?" Sarah asked.

"Yeah, in our company we do," replied Alicia. "So I was just being truthful, and it turns into this. I hadn't even seen the article before this wormy guy in my chemistry class comes up to me and says, 'Boy, are you gonna catch it!' I didn't even know what he was talking about until I went down to dinner that night. As I walked through the wardroom, I heard rumblings of 'There— that's who did it' and 'She's the one.' At first I didn't even realize they were talking about me, but when I got to our table, my squad leader pulled me aside and explained what had happened.

"I guess the Associated Press or United Press International got hold of the article from my hometown and went a lot more public with it, like to the *Chicago Tribune,* and that's when I was screwed. Mids from all over Illinois read it and brought it back here.

"Then the other night I went to the head just after taps. When I got back to my room there was a mob of about fifty furious upperclass outside my door waiting for me."

"What?!" asked Sarah.

"I'm not kidding. At least fifty of them. They started yelling at me, 'Baby-killer! Warmonger! Guttermouth slut! Get out of my school!' It was horrifying. I was scared to death. I really thought they were going to physically hurt me!"

"What did you do?"

"Well, I managed to force my way through them and get into my room and lock the door, but I was really scared!"

"Were they guys from your company?"

"No, they were from all over the brigade."

"Didn't somebody try to stop them?"

"My company commander finally came down and made them disperse, but I could hardly sleep that night. I'm still afraid they might come back. We lock the door in our room every night now, even though you aren't supposed to."

"I would, too," said Sarah.

"I mean, I just don't understand how they could've twisted my words so badly." Alicia looked at the floor and shook her head. "I never used those words, 'Midshipmen are warmongers and guttermouths.' Now why would I ever say something like that? But all the guys believe I did! Do they really think I want more abuse at this place? The only person sticking up for me is my squad leader. He told me he understands that the women are a hot topic for the media and they want to write the juiciest article possible regardless of the consequences for us."

"No kidding," said Brigette. "In my company you would think *I* did the interview, with all the flack I'm taking about it. I mean, I'm sorry, Alicia. I don't mean to blame you. I just mean, whenever one of us does something, it's like *every* one of us did it, even if the something we are being blamed for is something we never did or said."

Judy and Sarah nodded.

"Let's go, girls," called the head cheerleader. "Time to practice and stop jibber-jabbering."

"Yeah, right, Derrick," said Sarah with a smirk, pushing her chair back. "You just wish we were talking dirt with you."

"Alicia, if we can help in any way, please let us know," Brigette offered.

"Yeah, really," echoed Sarah. "We're on your side."

"Thanks, guys," replied Alicia. "Hopefully this will all blow over soon."

Saturday, 12 February 1977

"Hey, Buns! You ready yet?" Dressed in mess dress blue, Denzel waited impatiently outside Sarah's door. Two weeks ago he had asked her to be his date for the Valentine's Formal. They were going to dinner out in town before the dance, but unless they hurried, they would be late for their seven o'clock reservation.

"Sarah—"

Before he could finish, the door opened. "Sorry, Denzel, had to keep you waiting, right?" Sarah batted her eyelashes and pushed the door wide open, engaging the doorstop as required by midshipman regulations whenever members of the opposite sex were in the same room.

"Uh, right," he said. "Yo! Hot stuff! You look great! Never thought I'd say that about a plebette in uniform!"

"Thanks, sailor. You look pretty handsome yourself." She straightened his bow tie. "Ready?"

Denzel put on his cover. "Follow me, madame." Sarah followed Denzel, both squaring corners. This is too much, she laughed. Dressed up in formal attire, squaring corners. At least we don't have to chop, and thank goodness girls don't have to wear covers with this uniform.

Sarah had taken a long time to style her short hair for the evening's festivities. She applied mascara and, at Donna's strong urging, eye shadow. Women midshipmen were allowed to wear pearl stud earrings with this uniform, so Sarah had made a special trip to the Midshipman Store to purchase a pair. She also wore the pearl ring her mother had given her. Her formal attire along with her dashing young date made her feel stunning.

Sarah had accepted Denzel's offer to go to the dance immediately. Still in love with Ryan, she knew she had to enjoy the sporadic pleasures that came with being a plebe, such as attending the formal dances. Ryan was not pleased when she told him of her date, but the two could not attend together, and he knew that she and Denzel were close friends. Sarah reminded him of the dates he had had with the girl he took to the Army-Navy game. Ryan reluctantly told her to have a good time and sent her an anonymously signed dozen red roses for Valentine's Day.

Carefully maneuvering the ninety-six stairs to the bottom of Eighth Wing, Sarah smiled. She was looking forward to tonight, content to be in the company of someone she cared about very much. She knew that Denzel suspected she was seeing Ryan, but he had never asked, for which she was grateful.

His suspicions were aroused near the end of plebe summer, and he came by the girls' room less and less. When he did, it was to talk to Tammy. During first semester, football and cheerleading kept them both busy, although Sarah watched the football game more closely when Denzel was on the field.

They renewed their friendship at the beginning of second semester, and Sarah was glad. Because plebes rated dragging tonight, once outside Bancroft Hall the couple walked arm in arm to Riordan's Restaurant in downtown Annapolis.

"Did you catch the stares of the locals on our way over here?" Denzel asked Sarah as they ate their appetizers.

"Yeah. But I'm used to it by now. We get stared at all the time. Everybody's curious to see what a girl 'middie' looks like. It must be a real treat for them to see one in mess dress on the arm of a male midshipman."

"Yeah, especially a white girl middie on the arm of a black male midshipman!" said Denzel. They both laughed.

"Seriously, Sarah. You look great."

"Thanks, Denzel. I finally started getting up before reveille and running every morning. I really started to pork out after Christmas leave. Cheerleading practices aren't enough to keep off the weight. And I was really chowing down during study hour and at meals. Now I really watch what I eat."

"Yeah, unlike some of your classmates," said Denzel.

"What do you mean, *my* classmates?" asked Sarah. "They're *your* classmates too, you know."

"Okay, okay. Sorry. You're right. I don't know why I said that. It's just hard to claim some of them."

"I know," said Sarah. "The girls who have put on so much weight have made it twice as hard for those of us who still fit into our uniforms."

Denzel nodded. "So how is cheerleading?"

"Okay. It's hard to cheer for the basketball team, since their games are on weeknights and I really need to study. Then we catch so much flack from the brigade, it's hard to get motivated to go out there and take the abuse."

"I don't know what it is with those guys," he said, shaking his head. "The football team really appreciates what you girls do. I'm sure the basketball team does, too. I don't understand why some guys act that way."

"*Some* guys? It's *all* of them. I know that a couple of the girls are a little overweight, but the abuse we take goes way beyond that. I just don't know if it's worth it anymore."

"Well, you have a few months until next September to think about it."

"Not really. Tryouts are in April. I'll probably give it another shot, though. Maybe next year will be better." Sarah then changed the subject. "So what major did you pick, Denzel?"

"Phy-si, Cuper-high!" he replied, smiling.

"Physical science, huh?" All plebes were required to select their major from among the nineteen offered by the Naval Academy near the beginning of second semester, plebe year.

"Hey, Buns, you know all us football players pick something easy. Well, maybe not all of us. But this guy is no dummy when it comes to knowing he's a dummy. You know how my grades are. With all the other courses they heap on you, I need to skate where I can."

"You're not dumb, Denzel," she told him. "This curriculum is hard for everyone."

"Yeah. So what did you pick, my main brain?"

"Systems."

"Systems engineering?! Are you out of your mind, girl?"

"I know. I didn't know what to pick. I thought about math, but my dad thought I should pick an engineering major. Computers are the way of the future, so I picked systems engineering. I may as well take advantage of the great curriculum here," she answered. "At first I wasn't so sure I wanted to take on that kind of workload, so I talked to Steve Fuller. He's a systems engineer. He told me to go for it. I figured if he can find enough time to play football and maintain a QPR over 3.0 in systems, I should be able to at least pass it."

"Yeah, but do you see how many hours he spends studying? Damn, girl! You're either brave or crazy, I don't know which. Good luck. Guess I'll be coming to you for EI" (extra instruction).

"If I have the time," she smiled. Ryan had reacted the same way when she told him her decision. He tried to talk her into choosing a "bull" major, something like English, history, or (like him) political science. He said that every midshipmen received enough navy courses in engineering and science to easily finish a technical degree after graduation at night school. Maybe he was right, but her father's advice made more sense. Sarah wasn't completely comfortable with her decision, but she was holding a strong 2.76 average and decided she would make it work. Besides, she didn't expect to graduate with honors. She just planned on graduating.

After dinner, Sarah and Denzel walked to Dahlgren Hall and met several of Denzel's friends from the football team with civilian dates. Sarah had worried about this moment, not sure how she would feel about being in the company of "real" girls in their formal gowns and coiffured hair. She didn't imagine that she would feel jealous—merely awkward. Yet when she was introduced to some "real" girls, she felt a burst of pride. Although it was less glamorous, she realized that what she was doing at the Naval Academy was something unique, something historical, and something patriotic. She was glad to be wearing a uniform. Anyone could be at a civilian college.

The opinions of the girls she was introduced to varied. One was interested in hearing all about her experiences, while two others quickly led their dates to the other end of the dance floor.

Sarah smiled. I guess I do live with these guys twenty-four hours a day. Maybe they feel threatened. What a joke! If they only knew where my romantic interests lie!

"Sarah, let's get out of the fog in here and catch some fresh air," said Denzel.

Outside they walked hand in hand toward the field house. In front of the tennis courts they stopped, and Denzel turned toward Sarah.

He's going to kiss me, she thought. Should we? What about Ryan? What about PDA, public display of affection? Would I be leading him on? My feelings for him are purely platonic.

Before she had answers, Denzel softly kissed her. Oh, well, she decided, we *are* having a good time. How can it hurt? He's my friend.

They embraced for a moment before Sarah pulled away.

"You nut," she said gently, punching him in the chest. "Did anybody see us? We'll probably get fried for PDA."

"It'd be worth it."

"Come on. Let's go back inside. We only have an hour left until we turn into pumpkins."

They danced the rest of the evening until 0010, when they headed back to the company area to be present and accounted for by 0015.

"Thanks, Denzel. I had a great time," she told him outside her room.

"Thank you, Sarah. I really enjoyed myself." He bent to kiss her, and she offered her cheek.

"Okay, I get the message," he said and walked across the passageway to his room.

"Good night, Denzel," she called.

"Good night, Buns."

"Sarah! Get up! Mr. Smythe wants to see you in the hall ASAP!" Donna was already awake and studying. She shook Sarah's arm to wake her.

"Okay, I'm up," Sarah called sleepily. "What does he want?" she asked, climbing out of the rack and pulling on her b-robe.

"I don't know. Something about last night, I guess. Be quiet, or you'll wake Tammy."

Sarah opened the door, surprised to see Denzel standing in the passageway with Mr. Smythe, a second classman in their company on duty this weekend. Mr. Smythe was a levelheaded guy, older than most of his classmates because he was prior-enlisted. Sarah respected him a lot, as he was a mentor to the plebes instead of a tormentor.

"Good morning, sir. Hi, Denzel," she greeted them. "What's going on?" Denzel shrugged.

"Listen guys," Mr. Smythe began, "sorry to drag you out of the rack, but late last night I got a call from one of my classmates who wanted your names and alpha codes because he wants to fry you for PDA."

Sarah sighed and looked at Denzel.

"You've got to be kidding me, man! I mean, sir," said Denzel. Sarah bit her lip, looked at the floor, and shook her head. Incredible! Who is this clown?

Mr. Smythe noted Sarah's distress. "I told him I wanted to talk to you both before I gave him any information."

"Mr. Smythe," Sarah stammered, "you have to be kidding! Denzel and I held hands and kissed once. Briefly! There were mids kissing their girlfriends all over the place. I mean making out, and this idiot is going to fry us? I can't believe this! We're just friends! Who *is* this guy?"

"It doesn't matter, Sarah. Now that I've heard your side of the story, I think I can talk him out of frying you. It doesn't sound like he has a lot of ground to stand on, although officially you did show some public display of affection."

"Sir, give me a break," Denzel said. "We were in the shadows of the tennis courts. It was hardly public."

"Well," continued Mr. Smythe, "it was public enough for this guy to see you. Listen, try not to worry about it. I'll talk to him and get back to you. To be quite honest, this person mentioned, with a lot of disdain, the fact that you were white, Sarah, and Denzel was black. I'm not sure that he isn't racially motivated."

"Oh, man!" said Denzel, turning as if to hit the bulkhead with his fist.

"All right, all right. Calm down. Let me get back to you." Mr. Smythe turned to go.

"Thank you, sir," said Sarah. "We appreciate your going to bat for us."

"Yes, sir," said Denzel. "Thanks a lot!"

"No problem, but no promises. Have to watch out for our plebes." He turned to go up the ladder to 8-4.

"Well, Buns, we did it this time," said Denzel with a smile. "Even if we do get fried, I still say it was worth it!"

After noon meal formation, Mr. Smythe caught up with Sarah and Denzel.

"Just wanted to let you know you're off the hook. I talked my classmate out of the form two."

"Hallelujah! Thank you, sir!" said Sarah.

"Yes, sir. Thanks!" echoed Denzel. "How'd you do it?"

"Never mind. Just be a lot more discreet next time, huh?"

"Yes, sir!" said Denzel, smiling slyly at Sarah.

"Forget it, honey," she returned with a grin. "There ain't gonna be no next time!"

Saturday, 19 February 1977

Kate and Michelle sat across from one another in Donatelli's, the local Italian restaurant, blowing on steaming plates of pasta, trying to ignore the stares of locals and tourists. Will women midshipmen always be a novelty? wondered Kate. The two of them had spent the morning singing with the Madrigal Group, watching varsity men's gymnastics, and shopping at the marketplace.

"Isn't this great?" asked Michelle. "Having a full plate and eating at ease?" She slouched for effect.

"Yes. And a long weekend, too. It's wonderful. No rates and no upper-classman harassing you for three whole days."

"Thanks for coming, Kate."

"Thanks for asking me, Michelle."

"You really should do this more often, you know. You study way too much. You shouldn't spend all your weekends in the library and in our room."

"I don't," answered Kate defensively. "I go to my sponsor's house quite a bit."

"Okay, okay. Sorry. I didn't mean to upset you."

"No, I'm sorry. You were trying to be nice. It's just that I need to study, Michelle. My grades are going downhill so fast. I have an F in chemistry."

"Well, I wish I had a 3.5," remarked Michelle. "You'll do fine, Kate. Lieutenant Griffith loves you, and you were the first girl in our company ever to be awarded 'Man of the Week' for a Thursday noon meal inspection," she said, smiling. "You're the one they always call to do interviews for the television and newspapers. Who was it the other day? The *New York Times?*"

"Yes," answered Kate, embarrassed.

Every Thursday at noon meal formation, the entire brigade of midshipmen stood a formal personnel inspection to ensure that they had put on a clean uniform and haircuts were intact. In most companies, each platoon named a "Man of the Week": the midshipman who was the most squared away at the inspection. Kate had been flattered by the announcement last Thursday. She had also done several interviews for the media, which she enjoyed.

Kate tried to lighten the subject. "Hey, last night I had to clean the company wardroom [the TV room in the company area] with Mr. Adin. Yuk! He told me I had too much war paint on, referring to my makeup. Probably because I clutched [choked, messed up] in front of him at a come-around the other day. What a jerk!"

"Yeah, he loves to ride any plebe for any little thing he can find." Michelle took a bite of salad and looked up at Kate. "So, how's Charlie? The roses he sent on Valentine's Day are still gorgeous."

"He's fine, I guess. I really haven't seen him in a while. You know, he took some other girl to the Valentine's Formal last weekend."

"Well, you went with some other guy, Kate. It's not like the two of you had much choice."

"I know. It's just that I saw him there, and it was so depressing. The girl he was with was really pretty, and I wasn't having that great a time, while he looked like he was having a blast. When I saw all those civilian girls dressed up in their fancy clothes, walking around with their mids, I could almost see myself doing the same thing last year with Charlie. I remembered how wonderful it was to be treated like you were special and pretty and appealing. I don't feel like that very often around here. I know we should be glad we're here, with what we're going to get from this place. But sometimes it's so hard."

"I know," replied Michelle, "but we're getting there. Plebe year is over in only four months. We've come so far."

"I just want to go home. Easter leave seems so far away. I miss my family."

"Me, too. At least you get to see yours a little more often since they're so close. Mine are all the way across the country."

Kate hadn't thought of that. She was lucky to have her family living close in Virginia. Still, it had been over two weeks since she last talked to them.

"After this, I'd like to go buy Charlie a birthday present. His birthday is coming up. Wanna come with me?" asked Kate. "We could go over to my sponsor's and play the piano afterward."

"Sounds great!" replied Michelle.

At Kate's sponsor's home, the girls played the piano, sang, watched television, and enjoyed milk and cookies. Kate was glad to have Michelle's company. On the ride home at about midnight, the Yard police stopped her sponsor for speeding. At first when Kate saw the flashing lights, she panicked. What have they caught me for now? she wondered. It was always scary returning to the Academy. Each time, a dreadful feeling overcame her, whether she had been away for a week or half a day.

The next day, after church, Charlie stopped by and asked her to play tennis in the Yard. She had seen other plebes playing with upperclassmen and decided that if Charlie was willing to risk their being seen together, so was she. They played until his racket cracked, and then they went running. As usual, they found something to argue about, dampening Kate's mood. Later that evening she took his birthday presents to him, hoping to make up.

The rest of the day was relaxed and uneventful until Sunday evening meal, when the second classmen in her squad began teasing her about being sly and meeting Charlie at her sponsor's house all of the time. They were good-natured about it, but it struck Kate as funny that they seemed so sure of themselves when they were so wrong. She and Charlie hadn't been to her sponsor's since last fall. They thought she was being sly. Sly? Me, Kate Brigman? I wish they would believe me, she thought.

Sunday, 6 March 1977

"Attention to announcements!" the brigade commander ordered from his podium at Sunday evening meal. The brigade quieted.

"This weekend Navy placed thirteenth out of forty-eight teams at the Women's Eastern Intercollegiate Swimming Championships at the University of Delaware. Midshipman Fourth Class Carrie Freeman of Twelfth Company swam as a one-woman team representing the Naval Academy and won the 200-yard individual medley with a pool and meet record time of 2 minutes and 11.1 seconds. She also won the 400-yard individual medley with a meet record of 4 minutes and 38.1 seconds. She placed second in the 500-yard freestyle, third in the 200-yard freestyle, and eighth in the 100-yard freestyle event.

"This represents a superlative accomplishment on her part, and Midshipman Freeman is to be heartily congratulated!"

The brigade broke into spontaneous applause. Loud cheers came from the port side of the wardroom, where athletes sat at team tables. Sarah enthusiastically joined in the applause. That is great, and even the brigade thinks so. Good for her!

"Brigade, seats!"

Sarah quickly sat and began passing food to the first classmen. Sitting at attention, she handed the parsley buttered potatoes to her squad leader. Suddenly a large group of plebes dashed behind the announcement podium, headed for the port side of the wardroom. Wonder what they're up to? she thought as Tammy passed her the peas with pearl onions.

Staring straight ahead, Sarah heard the port side of the wardroom break into cheers and applause once again but could not see what was causing the commotion. She accepted the bowl of potatoes from Tammy and helped herself.

"Your classmate did pretty well this weekend, Miss Becker," remarked her squad leader. "She must be a pretty good swimmer to place thirteenth as a one-woman team. Do you know her?"

"No, sir."

"How 'bout you, Miss Leland?"

"No, sir, but she's from Texas, sir."

"Does that make her some kind of star, Miss Leland?" asked another firstie in their company.

"No, sir, I just meant that I'm from Texas and so is she, sir."

"Oh, so you're some kind of great athlete, too. Is that it?"

"No, sir. I just meant—"

"Forget it, Miss Leland," ordered her squad leader. A group of plebes had massed in front of the podium and OOD's table, and the source of the raucous behavior became clear.

A freckle-faced, wavy-haired female plebe sat atop the shoulders of two male classmates. That must be Carrie Freeman, Sarah decided. She thought she recognized her from the plebe-summer picnic when Port and Starboard Battalions vied against one another in a number of competitive sports, one of them an all-girl tug-of-war. Carrie had been Port Battalion's secret weapon when they beat Starboard Battalion's girls. Sarah remembered seeing her pull with the men in their tug-of-war. She had broad shoulders and was obviously very strong.

The plebes received sporadic bursts of applause as they paraded a blushing Midshipman Freeman around Second Regiment. This was quite an honor. Sarah, Tammy, and Donna clapped loudly, along with a number of upperclassmen. The real clamor exploded when they carried her through the starboard side of the wardroom, where Twelfth Company ate.

Those plebes must really like her to be carrying her around like that, thought Sarah. It sounds like her entire company is proud of her. Now the men can't say that *all* the women here aren't athletic.

Saturday, 19 March 1977

The Naval Academy chapel choir, now coed, had been invited to sing on Sunday at a church in New York City. Fifty male and female midshipmen of all ranks boarded the blue and silver Naval Academy buses Saturday morning and checked in at the Essex Hotel around 1500 that afternoon. Kate was impressed with the plush surroundings. Large mirrors, crystal chandeliers in the lobby, and two queen-sized beds in the room she shared with Terrie made her feel as if she were in a palace.

That evening all midshipmen were given the unexpected privilege of going out on the town in civilian clothes. Kate, Terrie, and sixteen other girls and guys met the choir director and his wife in the lobby at 1800. They found a shabby off-Broadway theater running *The Movie Buff,* a musical, which they enjoyed despite their initial misgivings about the appearance of the playhouse.

After the play, the group went to Mama Leone's for dinner, where a male classmate Kate rarely spoke to sat next to her. Tall, with straight brown hair and laughing green eyes, Gabe Leggett was the practical joker of the group. He had always made Kate laugh from afar, so his obvious decision to sit next to her was a bit unsettling. Her unease was evident as he quickly leaped up after taking his seat. "Whoops! Maybe you were saving this for someone else?"

"No. I mean, you can sit there, if you want."

"Great, thanks!" His manner was so jovial. He offered her his hand before sitting down, which she shook firmly. "Gabe Leggett," he said. "And you're Kate, correct?"

"Yes. Kate Brigman."

"Ah, yes," he said, opening the napkin on his lap. "Kate with the beautiful voice."

"Excuse me?" she replied.

"Kate with the beautiful voice," he repeated melodically. "I've heard you from afar and listened with delight."

She sensed that he was being sarcastic at her expense, and his phony charisma was beginning to annoy her.

"Very funny."

"Funny? I'm not being funny. I'm serious. You have a lovely voice, and I enjoy listening to it during practices and performances."

Realizing that his words were sincere, Kate began to blush. She had not received a compliment like that in months.

"You're also very cute when you blush," he continued. "But you're very attractive to begin with. Especially for a plebette."

Her bubble burst. So he *was* being sarcastic. Who did he think he was? Before she could ask him to leave, they were interrupted by a waiter asking for their order.

"Uh, I'll have the fettucini Alfredo," Gabe told the waiter. "And a glass of the house chardonnay." Neither of them had looked at the menu. Kate tried quickly to decide from a long menu written in Italian. She had no idea what to order. Gabe noticed her confusion.

"May I?" he offered, taking her menu from her. She nodded.

"The lady will have the same, *per favore.*" He smiled at the waiter and handed him the menus.

There he goes being charming again, she fretted while warming to the feeling of relinquishing control. It made her feel protected.

"Listen," he said, "please don't take my last comment about you being an attractive plebette wrong. It probably was the wrong thing to say."

Kate bit her bottom lip.

"It was. I'm sorry. What I meant was that you seem different from the plebettes, I mean, girl mids I've run into. You seem like a real girl. Someone who likes to have fun. A little uptight maybe, but what plebe isn't?"

Real girl? Had he called her a real girl? Was this a dream? A classmate found her attractive? Even Charlie had never told her that. He always found something wrong with her appearance. Especially when she was in uniform.

Feeling herself blush again, Kate stared at her napkin, trying to decide on something to say. He had also called her uptight. What had he meant?

"Uptight, you said? What does that mean?" Oh, Lord, was she being too harsh? Always on the offensive. Even her squad leader had mentioned it during her last performance rating.

"Yeah, uptight. Or maybe just preoccupied. Lots on your mind?"

How could someone she had never spoken to see right through her? She wanted to break down and tell him about everything: the pressures of academics, the feelings of inferiority as a female midshipman, the uncertainty of achieving her dreams and aspirations. But she kept them concealed. This whole experience at the Naval Academy had been so different from what she had imagined.

"I'm trying to do well in academics, but chemistry is kicking my butt. My 3.8 dropped to a 3.61, and my company officer is all over my case. He wrote 'UP' in big red letters on my report card but 'Good job' on my roommates' cards, and their grades were lower than mine."

"He obviously wants you to do well," said Gabe.

Didn't he understand that she thrived on praise and so seldom received any? "I was ranked second in my platoon," she explained. "Maybe I peaked too early."

"Don't be so hard on yourself," remarked Gabe. "We have over three more years at that place."

"Don't remind me, please! I just want to enjoy tonight and my time away this weekend, even though I do feel like I should be back there studying."

He smiled, and they continued talking. Kate was impressed to learn that Gabe had selected mechanical engineering as his major. He was prior-enlisted and had attended the Naval Academy Prep School, NAPS, for a year prior to entering the Academy. He admitted being afraid that he might have bitten off more than he could chew in selecting an engineering major, but he offered to help Kate with classes giving her trouble.

They chatted through the meal, and Gabe escorted her to a discotheque, where they danced until three in the morning. He told her that he didn't even think of her as another midshipman, which made her want to hug him. They talked in her room until 0430, when Terrie finally interrupted them, begging them to let her go to sleep. Gabe left, promising to sit by her on the bus back to school.

Kate fell asleep peacefully, with the prospect of finally having found a friend.

Saturday, 26 March 1977

On a rainy Saturday night, no one felt like going out in town. Ryan was away at a lacrosse game, so Sarah was in for the evening. Denzel and Mitch Prescott came by Sarah and Tammy's room with a "K.C. and the Sunshine Band" tape. Marcy Spencer, a woman in Thirty-fourth Company, also came over, and a youngster, who Sarah was sure had the hots for Tammy, stopped by. Within minutes the girls' room was transformed into a disco.

Marcy "bumped" with Mitch, Sarah with Denzel, and Tammy with the youngster. Tammy had cranked the tunes up as loud as she dared, having seen Mr. Schluntz in his room across the passageway earlier.

"This is better than Disco Dahlgren," said Mitch.

"Cuter chicks," remarked Denzel. The girls beamed.

Two hours later, laughing and sweaty, the guys returned to their rooms for taps. Marcy did the same but snuck back later to talk.

"So, how do you like 'Club 34,' Marcy?" asked Sarah, lying sideways on her rack. Marcy sat at its bottom.

"I like it," said Marcy. She had been moved to Thirty-fourth Company because both her roommates had resigned. "The guys have been easy to break into, unlike the guys in my other company, who I don't think ever really accepted us girls. In fact, there was only one time when I felt part of my old company."

"When was that?" asked Tammy, sitting cross-legged on her rack.

"Quietly, though," reminded Sarah. "Remember, Schluntz is in his room."

Marcy began. "During Army Week, the guy plebes in our company planned a recon raid to drop a 'Beat Army' sheet poster over the main doors of Bancroft, but they never told us girls about making the poster or going on the recon raid, which they pulled off with flying colors.

"The firsties thought it was great, but when they praised us girls, we had to tell them we had nothing to do with it. Needless to say, they were shocked and proceeded to chastise us for not having any spirit. We didn't say why we didn't participate, because we didn't want to bilge our classmates."

"Oh, not like they didn't bilge you," interjected Sarah.

"Yeah, I know. Well, the three of us decided we were going to show our company that we did have spirit. So that night, after everyone was asleep, we snuck into all the rooms in our company and stole everybody's shoulder boards off their reefers. Then we snuck back in and put the wrong shoulder boards on the wrong reefers. Youngsters became second classmen and firsties became plebes.

"The next morning was great! Everyone grabbed their reefer at the last minute on their way to formation, which was outside. Most of them recognized the problem on the way downstairs when it was too late to do anything about it. Guys were wondering what the heck was going on. It was a riot!

"Our only mistake was forgetting to include ourselves in the 'Big Switch.' Since we girls were the only ones with the right shoulder boards, everyone knew we were the culprits. But it was great! Everyone thought that what we did was really gutsy and ingenious. We showed them we had a lot of spirit after all!"

"What a great idea!" whispered Sarah. "And you never got caught?"

"No, and it was really dark in their rooms. A couple of times guys would roll over and we just froze, thinking we were caught. It was kind of scary."

"So did everyone go to class with mixed-up shoulder boards?" asked Tammy.

"No, they fixed them after formation, but it took them a while. It was funny. We casually walked off to class. Anyway, the guys seemed to accept us better after that, but I like being here. It really makes a difference which company you are in."

"No kidding!" agreed Tammy. "We feel so lucky to be in Thirty-third. Our classmates are great. Right, Sarah?"

"Yeah! They treat us like sisters or one of the guys. We are really lucky."

Wednesday, 6 April 1977

Spring break was finally here, and Kate could not have been more thankful. She had just been awarded twenty demerits for answering the mate's phone several days ago while wearing earrings; she had forgotten to remove them before leaving her room. Although it was against regulations, Kate wore earrings each weekend in her room, a minor attempt at feeling feminine.

Frustrated at now having to restrict (to work off demerits by being restricted to Bancroft Hall) for the upcoming weekend, she tried to concentrate on the good things that had occurred in the past two weeks. After the weekend in New York, she returned motivated to study for ten-week tests, and despite a case of the flu she maintained her 3.61 QPR. Gabe and she met twice in the library, where he tutored her in chemistry. He was so nonjudgmental and seemed comfortable to be seen with a female classmate. Even one in uniform. How refreshing! Appreciative of his friendship, she was only slightly disappointed when she learned that he was dating a girl back home.

Other bright spots included a win for the women's sailing team at a regatta. Kate placed third in her division sailing dinghies. Congress proposed to allow women to serve temporary duty aboard combat ships and to land planes and helicopters on those ships, and the Equal Rights Amendment needed only three more states to ratify it before it would pass. Kate finally found encouragement that she might be able to serve her country in a way similar to the men.

And then the men she hoped to serve beside made it clear that the feeling was not mutual.

Half an hour before study hour was over, a group from her company knocked on her door. As she opened it, one of them threw a peach pie, salvaged from evening meal, in her face. Through the goop, she saw cameras flash.

After cleaning up, she spent the night crying in her rack, wondering how they could have done this. And why? Who could she turn to? No one. Going to the company officer would fuel their fire. Forget it. She had to carry on and keep doing the best she could. She just wasn't sure how much more she could take, especially when the Polaroid they took was hung on a company bulletin board with a quoted regulation outlining rules for wearing makeup.

Tuesday, 19 April 1977

Ryan and Sarah's meetings had become less frequent since his lacrosse games began in mid-March. Thirty-third Company was still suspicious of the two of them, but so far Schluntz was the only one who had threatened any trouble.

Ryan had an imposing personality, which Sarah was sure made many midshipmen shy away from confronting him with any suspicions they had. He once told Sarah that he vividly remembered being admonished as a second classman last year at a "pre-woman" briefing by the Second Regimental officer to ensure that the upperclassmen's behavior did not place the Naval Academy on the front pages of the *Washington Post*. Although he knew they were playing with fire, he planned for things never to go that far.

Their relationship was becoming serious. Several weeks ago Ryan had hinted at making a permanent commitment, which scared Sarah. She loved Ryan, but her life was just beginning. She was excited about what lay ahead. The challenges that the Naval Academy and the navy would offer her were endless. She wanted to be a pilot. She wanted a career. She wanted Ryan too, and she knew she could have them all without making a permanent promise to him. Not yet, anyway.

Returning to her room, Sarah saw the light blue envelope under her desk blotter. This was the second letter Ryan had written since they returned from spring break.

Ryan had begun writing after Christmas leave. No longer a member of the brigade staff, since midshipmen served in one leadership position for the first semester and another for the second, Ryan now lived in the Thirty-third Company area as a one-striper midshipman-in-ranks, responsible for no other midshipman but himself. His phone went with the striper position. Sarah mailed her letters to Ryan, but Ryan dropped his by her room.

A manila computer card reporting her academic progress also lay in the middle of her blotter. Oh, no, she thought. Bad news first.

She looked for her quality point rating for the semester: 2.89. "Not a 3.0, but not bad," she said aloud to no one. Her cumulative QPR was now 2.7.

An A in naval leadership and in computer science, C's in seapower and

English, and B's in chemistry and calculus two. That B in calc did me in, she told herself. I should've held on to my A. And this is supposed to be the easy year? She shuddered at the amount of studying yet to come and turned her attention to something more pleasant:

Hi Love,

Well, I saw the company officer today and his first question was—is there any funny business going on? I just said no and he told me that Lieutenant Munson called and talked with him about our walking to class together. We had quite the discussion of what my duties and responsibilities are. It will take a while to explain, so I'll wait till we have some time. He doesn't know anything yet, but he is rather suspicious because of incidents which go all the way back to the baseball game last summer.

All he really said was that if anything is going on, it should stop because it just wasn't worth it. Even though we didn't quite see eye to eye on anything, he made a little sense. I suppose we'll have to cool our jets for a while. The fact of the matter is that we only have two months before we can be ourselves, and I think I can make it. I'm not saying that I don't want to go out anymore, but I'll just have to be a little more devious! Well, I just wanted you to know that you're not in any trouble, yet, and that I still love you, even with your freckles!

Always. . . .

He never signed his letters.

Tears sprang to her eyes. Why am I crying? We aren't going to get fried for walking together to class. Our company officer is suspicious, but it sounds like Ryan was able to convince him that nothing is going on. It was the part about having to "cool their jets for a while" that bothered her. Last month they had been hinting at forever.

What was he trying to tell her? Was he calling it quits? Of course not. He was just being cautious. He said he still wanted to go out. They would just have to be more careful. And he did say he still loved her, so what was her problem?

This was just too hard sometimes! She had been so frightened when Lieutenant Munson approached them on Stribling Walk yesterday and asked Ryan what he was doing walking with a plebe. Ryan had told him that Miss Becker was a plebe in his company and they were going to the same academic building for class. Lieutenant Munson had remarked that it was inappropriate behavior, and Ryan had respectfully disagreed. The lieutenant then demanded his name and alpha code along with Sarah's and called their company officer.

Maybe it wasn't worth it anymore. Two more months, thought Sarah. I have to hold on. There was plenty to keep her busy between her studies and plebe rates. She picked up her naval leadership book and tried to study.

Two copies of the *Log* magazine lay on the desk when Kate returned from her sixth-period class. Michelle was reading another and laughed out loud.

"This thing really is funny despite all the grief it gives us girls," she remarked. "And 'Salty Sam' gives us plenty of grief this time."

So what's new? thought Kate, changing into shorts and a sweatshirt.

A spin-off of *Mad Magazine,* the *Log* was a satirical magazine written for midshipmen and alumni, the only people capable of comprehending its Naval Academy slang, humor, and innuendoes. It came monthly, although Kate never remembered ordering it. As with most issued items, the annual $5 subscription cost was deducted from her midshipman account.

The *Log's* editorial staff were members of the brigade, including two female plebes. Since its first publication last October, plebe "midshipchicks" had been one of the parodied highlights of the magazine, along with officers assigned to the Academy, civilian employees like the jimmy-legs and the laundry lady, plus any individual who committed some imbecilic act.

Kate flipped through her copy. As usual, it was filled with cartoons, serious articles about Navy sports, "Company Cuties" (six pages of sexy photographs of girlfriends and/or sisters voted on by members of individual companies for inclusion in this "prestigious" section), and the notorious "Salty Sam" gossip column.

"Salty Sam" was the pseudonym of an anonymous first-class midshipman who scribed the gossip column based on information left for him in his mailbox in the Steerage snack bar. Since the beginning of the year, he had published plenty of material on the "plebettes." This issue was no different:

How 'bout the diet table? Hold on now! If the girls comprise only 2% of the brigade, shouldn't they be limited to the same percentage on the varsity fat squad? Come on—25% is overdoing it. You've got to admit—only at Navy could you find your cheerleaders on a diet table.

He left them alone for two paragraphs, and then:

> There is a confirmed rumor that a plebeian princess plunged into a sleepy segundo's room after breakfast and, mistaking him for a prince, awoke him with a kiss. Unfortunately, the mid involved didn't turn into a toad as expected, but he did come close to croaking.
>
> Rumor has it that Mean Marie didn't approve of the "Hog-log" in Main-O and proceeded to remove most of the pages. Seems she took some of the remarks personally. Don't see how that could happen!
>
> Well, all the 2/C and 3/C are now fully supplied with their V-neck T-shirts. The 4/C plebettes have their special girdle issue next week.

It never ends, Kate thought. She turned to the awards section at the end of the column. The women were not forgotten:

LAW OF THE MONTH
(DERIVED FROM THE 1ST LAW OF THERMODYNAMICS)
$Mass_L + Mass_O = Mass_R + Mass_G$, or the mass of women leaving the academy added to the original mass of women is equal to the mass of women remaining added to the mass gained by those remaining.

The weight of the women was always a favorite topic of Salty's. Kate glanced at the cartoon on the same page depicting an obstinate Popeye who was yelling, "I ain't takin' a YP cruise!"

Official word had come down: Women midshipmen would spend their third-class cruise on the yard patrol boats, YPs, eighty-five-foot patrol craft. The girls were irate. So were the men.

"If it happens to me, I'm going to refuse to go," Kate overheard a male company mate tell another. "I'm not going on some girls' cruise. I came here to be on real navy ships, not some boat we use for bumper drills in seamanship. This is only happening because of the girls."

No one was happy about the administration's decision, but what options were there? Women, by law, were excluded from duty aboard navy ships, even temporary duty. Everyone hoped the law would change, but it hadn't as yet, and every midshipman was required to receive professional training during the summer.

Youngster cruise was their opportunity to experience life as an enlisted man aboard ship. Third classmen were incorporated into the enlisted ranks of navy ships and performed daily routines from swabbing decks to manning the helm. How would they gain this experience aboard the YPs, when everyone on board would be a midshipman? It wouldn't work. YP cruises would be a waste of time. This time, Salty was right.

Thursday, 28 April 1977

"You're what?!" Tammy shouted at Donna as Sarah entered their room after a tiresome six-N day. She had attended six classes in a row with no free periods and was beat.

"What's going on?" Sarah asked, removing her cover.

"You'd better sit down for this one," said Tammy. "You aren't going to believe it!"

"What is it, Donna? What's going on?"

"I'm leaving," she said calmly, seated behind her gray desk.

"You're leaving what?"

"I'm leaving the Academy."

"You mean you're quitting."

"Well, if you want to call it quitting, then yes, I'm quitting. Either way, I've submitted my resignation."

Sarah dropped into the chair behind her desk and looked out the window, dazed by the announcement.

"Didn't I tell you?" asked Tammy. Sarah ignored her.

"You've got to be kidding," Sarah said, turning toward Donna. "I mean, we've almost made it through plebe year. I don't get it. Why now? What could have made you do this?" She didn't let Donna answer. "Donna, we're a team, the three of us. We've helped each other through this place, and we need to stick together. How can you bail out on us now that the worst is over?"

"Are you through?" asked Donna.

"No. Well, okay, yes, for now but I . . . I just don't believe this!" Sarah thought she was going to cry. She looked at Tammy, who just shook her head.

"Look, guys, I'm three years older than you. I'd already completed three years of college before I came here. Putting up with the bullshit from guys the same age as me has not been easy."

"But a lot of them treat you like their equal," Sarah interrupted.

"Let me finish, Sarah," said Donna. "I don't want to put up with the regulations or the restrictions anymore. This place just isn't for me. In the beginning I thought I could deal with it all, but I just don't want to anymore."

"So what are you going to do?" Sarah asked a little more calmly, trying not to be so selfish and judgmental.

"Well, I think I've found a small apartment out in town, and I may try to get a job."

"A job? A job?! What kind of a job? A waitress? A salesgirl? This is unbelievable!" Sarah jumped up and flailed around the room. She knew she was ranting, but she didn't care. She didn't want Donna to leave, and her frustration grew as she realized she was not going to be able to change Donna's mind.

"Yes, Sarah. I might be a waitress or a salesgirl or a bartender, until I decide exactly what it is what I want to do with my life. It's not so horrible, you know."

Yes it is, thought Sarah. She could not imagine rooming with Tammy by herself. It wasn't that they didn't like one another. It was just that they were so different.

Sarah composed herself. "I'm sorry, Donna. I just don't want you to go."

"I know, Toots. I'll miss you guys, too. But I'll be right out in town. You can come see me whenever you want. You can even sneak over the wall and come visit! This place just isn't for me, Sarah. You guys are going to have to do it for me, okay? I'm counting on you."

Tammy walked over and hugged her. "I'll miss you, 'Mom,'" she said.

"I'll miss you, too. Both of you," said Donna, returning the hug and smiling softly at Sarah, who, leaning against the edge of the desk, forced a weak smile and skeptically shook her head.

The public-works personnel manned the flower beds along Stribling Walk, replacing the flowers for what seemed to be the umpteenth time that spring as the two roommates walked to class. "So it's gonna be just you and me, Tam," said Sarah.

"Yeah, I was thinking about it last night," said Tammy, hugging her books. "Do you think we can make it?"

"I suppose we'll have to make some compromises."

"Like no visitors after taps," Tammy said with a smile.

"Yeah," Sarah replied with a grin, remembering the time Ryan snuck by their room in the middle of the night. Tammy had been awake. "And no country music when I'm in the room," added Sarah. Tammy had brought her portable record player from home after Christmas leave along with thirty albums of country music, which Sarah hated. She had also brought an "illegal" twelve-inch television set, which the girls hid in the lockable security drawer in Tammy's desk.

"I'll never forget when you told me right after I-Day that the only thing you wouldn't be able to stand in a roommate would be a Southern accent," said Tammy.

"Yeah, and then I got assigned one from Texas," Sarah shook her head good-naturedly. "Well, I remember how you would never leave the room by yourself for the longest time."

"You knew?"

"Sure. Donna and I both knew. It was so obvious. You wouldn't even go down the hall and get a soda. You would always buy, so that either Donna or I would go get them."

"Gosh, I was always so scared to leave our room. Especially plebe summer. I wouldn't go anywhere without one of you guys. I remember talking you into going with me to the tailor shop one day. I think the only time I went somewhere alone was to the barbershop once, and then I walked outside so there was less chance I'd run into a firstie."

"Well, you weren't alone. Cory Morgan used to climb out his window and crawl around the ledge on 8-4 to avoid running into Mr. Troy. Isn't that crazy?"

"Maybe to you," replied Tammy, "but I know how he feels. Hey, we worked together well the night we decorated all the lacrosse team's doors together!"

"Right," agreed Sarah. "Remember, Donna thought we were nuts and wouldn't go!" The two girls had stayed up all night before Navy played the University of Maryland, their biggest rival besides Army, in lacrosse, and decorated every lacrosse player's door. Ryan gave Sarah a roster of the thirty-plus mids on the lacrosse team. Sarah got their room numbers from a directory the last time she stood Main-O watch.

They had started at 0100, outfitting rooms with balloons, streamers, and spirited posters. It had been so peaceful in the Hall with all the other midshipmen asleep, save for one who sleepily attempted to go to the head in only his underwear. The midshipman opened his eyes, dropped his hands to his crotch, and ran back to his room when he saw the two girls. Stifling guffaws, Sarah had whispered to Tammy, "We must have scared the pee right out of him!"

The next day Sarah blushed as she chopped through the Hall, listening to the comments of midshipmen walking to class beside her. "Must be the company's plebes who did it," remarked one until he walked through the adjoining wing. "Hey, somebody did it in here, too."

Sarah felt gratified. As far as she knew no one had ever decorated for an entire team before—no one in the four years that Ryan had been there, anyway. He told her later how much the guys appreciated what she and Tammy had done, despite the fact that Navy lost the game, 13–10. No one ever found out specifically who had done the decorating. The girls hoped that sooner or later word might get around that some of "the girls" had done it, and that in some small way it would help assuage the outrage at their presence at the Academy.

"Gotta go," called Tammy, heading for class in Maury Hall. "See you later, Sarah."

Sarah waved and turned toward Rickover Hall. Tammy and I are gonna make it work, she thought. We're gonna stay together so we can stay in this company.

Wednesday, 11 May 1977

Sitting at ease felt so unnatural. The night before, the brigade commander had secured the plebes, ordering them to "carry on" for the next three weeks, after which they would officially become third classmen. No more chopping, no more rates, no more come-arounds. The only remaining plebe requirements were to keep quiet in the halls, continue squaring corners, and pass food at meals.

Kate should have been elated, but several things bothered her. Finals were approaching, and she was having a hard time getting motivated to study. She hoped to raise her QPR but was not confident.

Two days ago, Lieutenant Griffith had confronted her about Charlie: he had heard a rumor about her and a third classman. She couldn't lie, but she didn't want the lieutenant to be disappointed in her, either. He had backed her so consistently all year. Kate explained that she and Charlie had met her senior year when she had come to the Academy to perform the physical fitness admissions test, and how they had dated most of his plebe year. She told him they had limited their time together to leave periods. Lieutenant Griffith expressed his disapproval and disappointment, but with plebe year almost over, there was little reason for him to take action.

"Brigade, attention to announcements!" Kate refocused her attention.

"Next year's third-class striper selections for the Class of 1980 are as follows:

3/C brigade commander, Jerome Whitaker; 3/C brigade subcommander, Jacob Terns; First Regimental commander, Nathan Miles; Second Regimental commander, Elaine Richey—"

Before he could continue, the audience erupted: "Boooo! Boooo! Give me a break! No way! No girls! Boooo!" The jeers were unceasing.

Kate was incensed. Why can't we have a girl in a striper position? She wanted to scream at the men booing, tell them to grow up and stop acting like spoiled brats. Especially her classmates. What had happened to classmate loyalty? She shook her head in disgust, feeling for this Elaine Richey.

Seated around the corner, Sarah listened to the announcement with disgust. A female regimental commander? Please! Why was the administration doing this? Why were they pushing a female into a high-ranking spot this early in the game? Not this first year. It was difficult enough getting the men to accept us just being here, she fumed. They'll never buy this!

It took only moments for someone to confirm her belief. Mr. Schluntz walked up behind her and grunted. "I have now heard it all," he whispered softly. "A woman with stripes. And she's the one whose company officer made her firsties rewrite her grease and change her company ranking. It makes me sick!"

Sarah had heard the rumor about a girl in Thirtieth Company whose firsties had been reprimanded by their company officer for ranking her below where he thought she should be. It was said that he demanded they rewrite her grease and rank her number one. For a time everyone had been talking about it.

As Mr. Schluntz walked away, Sarah wondered why the men always classified the girls together. Why did he say that to me? I'm not looking for stripes, she thought. I'm just looking to graduate. I've made it here on my own qualifications. I've had a real plebe year. Mr. Troy and he have made sure of that.

Wednesday, 1 June 1977

Kate fingered the third-class collar device one of her summer squad leaders had just presented to her. It was the same device his squad leader had given him for good luck when he was a plebe, and she was deeply touched. There was a knock on the door.

"Who is it?"

"Jacob Williams."

"Come in." Both of Kate's roommates were away, and although Jacob kept his distance most of the time, Kate found him to be one of the more pleasant classmates in her company. Ranked number two in the company, he had been selected third-class battalion commander.

"Hi, Jacob."

"Hi, Kate. Got a minute?"

"Sure. Have a seat."

"Thanks. I just wanted to talk to you about something. Kind of prepare you for it."

"Oh, no. Now what am I in for? More pie in the face?" She forced a grin, remembering the painful incident she wished she could laugh about.

"No, no, nothing like that," he replied. "That was really uncalled for, although this is almost as bad. Except it won't affect only you. It's about all the women."

"What is it, Jacob?"

He paused. "About 250 classmates have bought some T-shirts some upperclass had printed up."

"Uh-huh. . . ."

"Well, the T-shirts are imprinted with a picture of Herndon and the letters NGOH."

"NGOH?"

"No girls on Herndon."

"What?! You must be joking!"

"No joke. They're going to wear them at the ceremony, and a lot of guys say they won't let any girls near Herndon."

Climbing Herndon, formally known as the Plebe Recognition Ceremony, took place the Friday commencing June Week, the week before first-class graduation. Erected in memory of Captain Herndon, who went down with his ship, the *Central America,* when she sank in 1857, the Herndon Monument, a twenty-foot obelisk, rises from the Yard across the street from the Naval Academy chapel. Every year in order to shed the title of plebes and be "recognized" as fourth classmen, the members of the plebe class muster a joint effort to climb the monolith, greased the night before by upperclassmen with slippery green goo. The plebes retrieve a symbolic dixie cup straddling the pyramidal apex and replace it with a midshipman's combination cover. Tradition holds that the plebe who performs this feat will be the class's first admiral. The plebes looked forward to this day more than any other.

"I can't believe this!" exclaimed Kate. "How childish! It's going to take us twice as long to climb that thing if guys start pulling classmates down."

"I know. There's supposed to be a meeting late tonight to try and figure out how we can climb the thing in record time. You know, establish up front the strongest guys in the class, who should be on the bottom, and the lightest guy, who can climb to the top the fastest."

"The lightest *guy?* The girls are the lightest, Jacob."

He grimaced.

"Okay, *some* girls here are light. Not all of us have put on a ton of weight."

"Kate, didn't you hear me? They aren't gonna *let* a girl be the one to get the cover. You guys aren't even gonna be able to get near Herndon. It just isn't going to happen!"

"This is incredible!" Kate stood up and paced. "We're here because the law says we can be here. Why can't they accept that? Why do they hate us so? Why do they hate *me* so?"

"Listen, Kate. There's nothing you can do about it. Better to just let it go in one ear and out the other. You weren't really going to try to climb it, were you?"

"No, I'm not crazy. I don't want to be mauled to death. It's just the principle of the thing."

"I know, but you aren't going to change the way they feel. Just try to forget about Herndon this year."

She bit her lip and shook her head. He was right, but it wasn't fair.

"And as to how they feel about you. . . ." Kate listened intently. "Kate, the guys in our company resent you."

"But why? What have I ever done to them?"

"Hear me out. I'm on your side."

"Sorry, Jacob. It's been a long year."

"I know. The reason they resent you is not because of what you accomplish but how you accomplish it."

"I don't get it."

"I'm going to be brutally honest with you, okay?"

"Okay." She braced for his words.

"They think you're a smack because you're always in Lieutenant Griffith's office and because you danced with him at the Christmas dinner. It's so obvious how much he likes you. He doesn't act like that with the other girls in the company."

"Act like what?"

"Always calling you into his office. The way he treats you at inspections, or . . . I . . . I don't know. It's just very obvious that he's partial to you. Obvious to all of our classmates, and they don't like it." He paused. "Therefore . . . they don't like you."

Silence. She already knew this, but it hurt to hear it. Especially from someone who would know.

"Even if all that is true," she replied, "it's not my fault. That's how he acts. I've earned everything I've achieved. I don't have a 4.0 anymore, but I still have a 3.7."

"I can only tell you that they think you encourage his interest."

"So, what if I were a guy? It would be different, wouldn't it? No one would think twice."

"Kate, we both know that your being female is a factor."

"A *big* factor. It's not fair, Jacob."

"No, it probably isn't. But that's the way it is." He shook his head. "I'm sorry, Kate. If I were you, I'd try not to let it get to me too much. Thicken your skin. Don't take it all so seriously. Who cares what they think?"

I care, she thought. That's the problem. I want to be applauded for my achievements, not questioned. Is that so unnatural? I've worked so hard. It would be nice to be recognized for my efforts, or just have them accepted for what they are and not seen as the results of extensive brown-nosing.

Still, Jacob wasn't the enemy. He was trying to boost her spirits.

"Thanks, Jacob. I appreciate your coming by. I'll try to lighten up, but no guarantees. It's just not me, unfortunately."

He walked toward the door. "Hang in there, Kate. We still have three more years to go. You'll be fine."

She nodded, imparting a fragile smile. She was not convinced. If only I could quit, she thought. But that was impossible. If she ever quit, she could not go home. It was an unspoken truth between her and her parents. Resignation would be the ultimate failure. Her parents would never forgive her.

. . .

"You won't believe it!"

"What?" Sarah responded casually, reviewing the menus on their bulletin board as Tammy ambled into the room.

"It just isn't ever going to end."

"What are you talking about?"

"The guys. I mean, I thought we'd proven ourselves to them. I thought after a year of all this bullshit, they'd finally accepted us."

Sarah had never heard Tammy swear. "Tam, what happened?"

"I stopped by Bender's room to see if he wanted to study tonight, and some third class from another company was in his room.

"When I walked up to his door, the third class quickly stuffed a T-shirt he was holding under his arm like he was trying to hide it. Well, I walked in anyway and asked them what they were up to. They stammered around and told me nothing, but I knew something was up, so I asked to see the shirt. The third class looked at Bender, who shook his head and said, 'She's cool. She won't mind.' So this guy pulls out the T-shirt and shows it to me.

"Sarah, they've printed up hundreds of T-shirts with a picture of Herndon and NGOH printed on top."

"NGOH?"

"No girls on Herndon!"

"What?!"

"The upperclass are selling them to male plebes to wear when we climb Herndon. They aren't going to let us near it if they can help it."

"Was Bender buying one?" The slow, sick burn of ostracism began to upset Sarah's stomach.

"I don't know. I don't think so. But I couldn't tell. I left right after they showed me the shirt. I just don't get it. Every time I think we have the guys on our side, they punch us in the stomach."

"Well, maybe that guy was just showing a shirt to Bender. Trying to convince him to buy one."

"I know you'd like to think that, Sarah, but I think Bender would have bought one if I hadn't come into the room."

"Yeah, but would he have worn it?" asked Sarah, unwilling to believe that one of their company mates would turn on them. She had worked so hard to prove to them that at least some of the girls could meet the standards.

Sarah suddenly wished Donna were there. She would know how to handle this—maybe even stop it. Donna had been gone for only two weeks, but Sarah missed her terribly.

"I don't know if he would have worn it or not, Sarah," said Tammy. "The fact is that those T-shirts are out there. I feel betrayed. Don't you?"

"I don't know how I feel—disgusted, angry, betrayed? All three, and just when we thought we were there, you know?"

"I know. It's just so disheartening sometimes."

"Well, we're not going to let it get us down. We're going to go out there and climb Herndon. And if I see one of those T-shirts, I'm gonna rip it right off the back of whoever's wearing it!"

Friday, 3 June 1977

"Let's go! Let's go!" Sarah yelled at Tammy, who was tying her tennis shoes. "They're forming up already!"

The Class of 1980 was mustering in Tecumseh Court at 1600 for the second official event of June Week 1977. The Dedication Parade had kicked off the special week earlier that day.

In half an hour the traditional climb of the Herndon Monument would begin and then end in what the Class of 1980 hoped would be less than the record-setting twenty minutes established by a previous class. This class, more than any other, felt a desperate need to demonstrate that, even though there were girls among them, their masculinity was intact.

Two upperclassmen had been caught selling NGOH T-shirts and were charged with violating the regulation prohibiting merchandising in Bancroft Hall. Company officers confiscated all the illegal T-shirts they could find, and all midshipmen had been threatened with a punishment of seventy-five demerits and two months' restriction if caught wearing one.

As the plebes gathered in T-Court, a curious crowd of onlookers waited impatiently behind nylon rope barricades outlining the muddied foundation of Herndon. An upperclass "demolition" team had gone to extreme lengths the night before to ensure that this year's climb would be most difficult. Sod had been removed around the base of the monument, and the underlying dirt had been saturated with water, creating a sloppy, unstable foundation from which the plebes would begin their climb. The obelisk had been bathed in two inches of green, greasy slime and, unbeknownst to the Class of 1980, the dixie cup on top had been Super-Glued in six places to the concrete apex.

As 1615 rolled around, a herd of one thousand anxious plebes moved tightly together in front of Bancroft Hall, their forward motion checked only by several white-uniformed upperclassmen who would give them the signal to "go" at 1630. But the herd was too restless, their movements too severe, and at 1616 a cry of "Let's do it!" resounded through T-Court and they burst forward. The climb commenced!

Sarah felt herself swept forward by a wave of bodies as she sprinted toward Herndon, stripping off her white works as she ran. The ground behind her was covered with white laundry as her classmates disrobed down to their blue shorts and regulation white T-shirts. At the base of the monument, the sopping muck sucked the tennis shoes from her feet, leaving her, like most plebes, in muddied stockings.

In front of her, two tiers of bodies had already locked arms, forming the foundation for the human pyramid the plebes would have to build to be able to climb to the top of this monster. Sarah shoved forward, desperate to become a brick in the wall, and surprisingly found herself face-to-face with a bare-chested, mud-coated Denzel, who as one of the stronger members of the class had immediately locked arms with a classmate to form the first tier of bodies.

"Do it, Buns!" he yelled, straining upward with his eyes as several classmates stepped barefooted onto his shoulders, only to lose their balance and fall backward into the crowd. "Get up there! You're light! You can do it! Get going so we can get out of here! Beer's gettin' warm!" Tonight the plebes could drink.

Sarah put her hands on his shoulders and placed her right foot in the crook of his elbow. She heard Denzel groan as she stepped from his elbow to his shoulders and grabbed the waist of the plebe above him.

"Are you all right?" she yelled down.

"Go, Buns! Just go!"

I'm going to do this, she decided. I'm going to get up there. A third tier of bodies formed as she climbed, but as she reached for the shoulders of a classmate beside her, she felt someone pulling on her foot. She looked down but could match no face to the fingers clasped around her ankle.

Sarah shook her leg to free the grasp, but it threw her off balance. Any hope of moving up was forgotten as she struggled to keep from falling backward. Suddenly the downward pull on her leg doubled, and she realized that the hand on her ankle had become two. She clung to the T-shirt of a classmate beside her as someone grabbed her shoulder and used it as a stepping stone, which became the final thrust to throw her off balance.

She gasped as she fell backward, suffocated her scream, and prayed that there were enough bodies below to cushion her fall. Her right triceps struck someone's shoulder blade, and she grimaced as barbs of pain shot through her arm. Somehow she managed to land on her feet and pushed her way to the back of the throng, no longer intent on becoming part of the pyramid. You had to be suicidal to join in that brawl!

Searching for a way out of the mass, she heard a voice behind her: "No girls on Herndon." It was almost a whisper but intense and hateful. Sarah turned to see who had said it but could only see greasy, matted heads of hair. Now she knew. The hand on her leg had meant to pull her down.

Any girl who tries to get near the top is going to be pulled down, she thought. That's what they are going to do, and we're never going to be able to climb that thing. She was angry, hurt. Suddenly, it became symbolic.

We're never going to be able to prove ourselves to these guys, she realized. No matter how hard we try, they're just never going to let us.

Kate watched from the middle of the mass of spectators, upperclassmen, and muddied plebe bodies. She had never planned to participate in this rite of passage, and she cringed as another pyramid of bodies collapsed under the weight of those scurrying to be first to the top.

It was almost embarrassing at this point. They had been flailing fruitlessly for two hours, their emancipation as plebes seemingly minutes away at one moment and then hours away at the next. The horde around her was actually becoming bored. So much for breaking the twenty-minute record. They were now looking at setting the record for the longest climb.

After the last fall, the bottom tier remained intact and a second was now forming. Let this be it, she prayed. Kate wasn't positive, but she thought that several times she saw a female classmate being pulled down. How ridiculous, she thought. How counterproductive. We need all the help we can get!

She looked up and was surprised as, for the first time, a fourth tier of bodies had linked arms around the obelisk. Chants of "GO, GO, GO!" burst from the crowd. "Hold on!" she yelled.

Then she saw her. A female classmate from the sailing team was ascending the obelisk with steadfast determination. "Go!" yelled Kate. "Go!" This is great! she thought. A girl is going to do it! A girl is going to get the cover off!

As members of the crowd realized the same, chants of "NO! NO! NO!" broke out. On the opposite side of the monument, a male classmate began climbing with renewed vigor. Reaching the apex at the same time, the two classmates clasped hands and struggled together to tear off the plebe cap glued to the top. Then, suddenly, the female plebe was toppling backward. No, thought Kate. Please don't fall! Please God, let them do it together!

But her prayers weren't enough to support the girl against the pull of several male hands Kate saw attaching themselves to the bottom of her T-shirt. She didn't fall; she was pulled down. And watching her male classmate cling to the top of the monument, victoriously replacing the plebe cap with a combination cover tossed to him by someone in the crowd, finally stopping the clock at two hours and thirty-three minutes, Kate felt only disgust.

June Week progressed rapidly. Class rings were officially presented to members of the Class of 1978 at the Ring Dance. The prizes and awards ceremony and the Color Parade were once again the traditional highlights of the week.

Transfer of the national colors from the current year's Color Company, the company ranked number one within the brigade, to the following year's Color Company took place at the Color Parade. Throughout the year each of the thirty-six companies competed in the color competition, accumulating points for academic, athletic, and professional accomplishments. At the Color Parade, the Color Girl, selected by the outgoing Color Company commander, presented the colors to the new Color Company commander.

Traditionally, the Color Girl was the sweetheart of the Color Company commander, and the tradition had never been questioned until now. Now there were women at the Naval Academy, and some members of the administration, concerned that the term *Color Girl* might be offensive to the female midshipmen, thought the tradition should be altered. There was talk of letting the Color Company commander select a favorite male figure, such as a professor.

Sarah was tired of being the rationale or the scapegoat for every change of tradition that had taken place since July of 1976. She didn't care if the Color Girl was a girl or if the title Color Girl was retained. The fewer changes made, the better. So when the brigade commander announced the name of this year's Color Girl at evening meal two weeks earlier, Sarah cheered loudly with the rest of the brigade.

Wednesday, 8 June 1977

Graduation and commissioning of the Class of 1977 commenced at 1030 on the sunny morning of 8 June. All members of the Class of 1980 were mandatorily seated behind the graduates.

As the superintendent introduced Vice-President Mondale to give the graduation address, Kate strengthened her resolve to remain at the Academy, despite the painful ostracism.

Watching Ryan walk to the stage to receive his diploma, Sarah pictured herself three years from now taking the same proud steps. She fondled the third-class shoulder boards bearing one thin gold diagonal stripe that soon would replace the stripeless boards she had worn for a year. In minutes she would be a youngster.

Nevertheless, tears formed in her eyes as she realized that although they would now be able to see one another "legally," she and Ryan would be in two separate worlds. She only hoped that the risks she had taken to date him were worth what she had gained by it: the sanity to make it through plebe year.

THIRD-CLASS YEAR
1977 –1978

Youngster—A third classman; his Plebe Year was fruit. Fruit—Anything that insults the intelligence; easy.

Reef Points, 1976–77

CHAPTER SEVEN

Youngster Summer

After graduation in June, the newly "striped" Third Classmen embark on their summer at sea training—"Youngster Cruise." At sea they receive their first indoctrination in actual shipboard life since reaching the Academy.

Reef Points, 1976–77

Wednesday, 8 June 1977

Sarah parked about a hundred yards from the Randolphs' house. She locked the car and walked pensively down the gravel driveway toward the wedding reception on the back lawn. Searching for Ryan among the casually dressed crowd seated at picnic tables, she worried about encountering a bewildered glare from her company officer or some other Naval Academy official.

Ryan had asked her to be his date at Tom Randolph's wedding, but she had declined. She wasn't ready to make their first "legal" appearance in public at a function attended by most of the newly commissioned ensigns and second lieutenants in their company. Reluctantly, Sarah had agreed to meet Ryan at the reception. "It's all legal now, Toots," he had said. "You're a third classman, and I'm an ensign. There's nothing they can do to us."

So here she was, dressed in a strapless blue sundress, standing uncomfortably on the outskirts of the crowd, wanting to turn around and drive back to school, when a smiling middle-aged woman approached her.

"You must be Toots, Ryan's girl," she said warmly. "I'm Tommy's mother, Margaret Randolph. We're so glad you could come. Tommy's told us all about you girls. I figured you had to be Sarah since I knew everyone else here, and. . . ." She reached up to touch Sarah's short hair.

"So that's what gave me away." Sarah blushed. "Thank you for inviting me, ma'am. Tom's a really nice person. I'm sorry I couldn't make the wedding."

"So are we. Let me introduce you around."

"Actually, ma'am, I haven't found Ryan yet. Have you seen him?"

"Sure. He's right over there." She pointed to the back of the white house. Ryan was leaning against a clothes pole, drinking a beer and talking to several classmates.

"Toots! You made it!" Ryan's arms flew into the air as he trotted toward her and hugged her tightly.

She felt uncomfortable in his arms in front of these people from whom they had "hid" their secret all year.

"How was the wedding?" she asked.

"Nice, except I missed you being there."

Pulling away from him, she gasped when she saw the Thirty-fourth Company officer staring at them.

"Oh, no," she sighed.

"What's wrong?" asked Ryan.

"Major Bailey's looking at us."

"Toots, there's nothing they can do to us now."

"I know, I know, but I still feel really weird about it."

"Come on, let's get you a beer."

On the way to the coolers, Ryan was stopped by a classmate. Before he could introduce her, Sarah interrupted him.

"I'll just go get that beer, Ryan. Be right back."

"Hey, Sarah!" She turned to see Tom Randolph with a woman who had to be his bride.

"Hi, Tom! Congratulations, to both of you," she said, smiling at the bride.

"Thanks," said Tom. "I'm glad you came. Sarah, this is my wife, Madeline." Sarah smiled and said hello despite Madeline's cool silence.

"Sarah was one of our plebes, Maddy. She's the one I told you about that beat me at the O'Course!" Tom said. "I'll never forget it!" Madeline smiled sourly.

Tom hadn't been kidding when he said his fiancée didn't like women at the Naval Academy, thought Sarah.

After a tug from the bride, Tom made the new couple's excuses, and Sarah helped herself to a beer. Turning to search for Ryan, she gasped when she saw Major Bailey whispering something to him.

Sarah waited in the shade until he was finished, then raised her beer, signaling her location.

"Do I dare ask what you two were talking about?" she asked as he slipped his arm around her waist.

"It was a very brief, one-sided conversation, actually," Ryan answered without looking at her.

"Oh?"

"Yeah, he walked up behind me and simply said, 'May God help you.'"

"What did that mean?" she asked.

"I think he meant, May God continue to watch over you as he now, confirmedly, has done for the past year."

"What?"

"Toots, our presence together at this reception just confirmed all their suspicions."

"Marvelous," replied Sarah. "Can we go now? I still have three years left at that place."

Thursday, 30 June 1977

Youngster cruise was the first taste of life at sea in the navy for young midshipmen. In years past, third-class midshipmen had typically been assigned to naval combatants, where they served for four to six weeks in the capacity of enlisted men. Women, however, were excluded by law from serving on combatants. Therefore, the Naval Academy developed a summer training program aboard yard patrol craft, YPs, for the women and some of the men.

Two one-month at-sea periods were scheduled for the flotilla of yard patrol craft that would steam up and down the Intracoastal Waterway. One was at the beginning and the other near the end of the summer. Kate chose the first.

Youngster cruise on the YPs proved an unexpected professional challenge. Kate learned more about navigation, engineering, and piloting a ship than she ever expected. Everyone had been wrong about the mids learning nothing on the YP cruises. Although they did not visit exotic ports like Marseilles or Palma de Mallorca like some male classmates on combatants, the men and women on her cruise experienced every aspect of enlisted life aboard ship, and for once Kate felt accepted by her male counterparts.

In Newport, Rhode Island, they toured the USS *Buttercup,* a mock-up of a navy ship used to train sailors in damage-control procedures. The *Buttercup* floated in the middle of a huge indoor pool and could be flooded in a matter of minutes, depending upon how quickly the crew shored up its leaking hull. Here Kate first observed hostility toward the women midshipmen from an enlisted instructor.

Before they entered the *Buttercup,* a chief petty officer had instructed the group on the use of a P-250 pump, used to pump out flooded spaces. He called on Kate to demonstrate its operation. Unsure of how to start it, she knelt down and waited for his instructions. The chief looked at her as if she were stupid.

"It's not that hard!" he snapped, not offering any help. "Haven't you ever mowed a lawn?" Kate didn't see the connection between mowing a lawn and pumping out a sinking ship.

"Obviously it takes a man to figure these things out," said the chief, pushing her out of the way. He grabbed the small black handle and jerked. The pump roared to life, and Kate wondered how many individuals like this she would encounter in the fleet. She slowly edged her way to the back of the crowd.

"Don't let him get to you," someone whispered. "He's from the old school."

Kate looked over her shoulder into a pair of emerald green eyes. "Pardon me?" she said to the third-class petty officer standing beside her.

"I said, he's from the old school. I'm glad you guys, uh, girls, are part of the navy now." His smile held her captive.

"Uh, thanks, I guess."

He offered his hand. "Petty Officer Third Class Buddy Matrick."

"Midshipman Kate Brigman." She shook it.

"Nice to meet you, Miss Brigman. Are you free this evening?"

"Uh, I don't think so."

"Oh, come on. Call it on-the-job training. I'll enlighten you about the enlisted side of the navy."

"No, I shouldn't."

"Aw, come on. Just a drink."

She couldn't resist. For the next three days she spent all her free time with him, talking about everything. Buddy loved the beach, motorcycles, sightseeing, touring museums, and going to discos. The two of them danced every night away. Buddy also loved to get drunk and encouraged Kate to join him. When their carefree nights ended and her YP pulled away from the pier, Kate was sorry to say goodbye but glad to be focused back on the cruise.

Thursday, 4 August 1977

After spending summer leave with her family and two weeks with Ryan, Sarah returned to Annapolis at the beginning of August for YP cruise. The first week of cruise consisted of training aboard the YPs at the Naval Academy, with male and female classmates practicing ship maneuvers and bumper drills (docking practice alongside the sea wall) in the Severn River.

Sarah had been assigned a room in the Second Regimental side of Bancroft Hall with two female classmates whom she recognized but did not know. Marcia McCall was a tall blonde from Second Regiment, and Carrie Freeman was the champion swimmer who had been paraded around the wardroom last spring after her impressive performance at the Eastern Swimming Championships. Carrie and Sarah immediately became friends.

After-hours liberty, Sarah spent at Ryan's house. He was in Annapolis for one more week of engineering courses before heading to Orlando to Nuclear Power School for six months.

"Toots, I want you to have a good time while you're on cruise," he told her on their last night together. "Get everything that you can out of it."

"But I'll really miss you, Ryan."

"We can write. Besides, I'll be studying my buns off down there."

"I just wish we could go on a real cruise," she told him. "On a real navy ship like the other guys. This YP cruise is a joke. Nobody thinks we girls will have a real youngster cruise, and the guys who've been forced to go are furious. They want to go on a real combatant, not the 'Love Boat.'"

"More reason for you to go out there and learn all you can to prove them wrong. Listen, Toots, I remember one of my most rewarding and informative cruises was my second-class cruise when we went on the YPs for two weeks down to Norfolk. And it was a blast to boot! Give it a chance. I bet you'll be surprised."

Sarah hoped he was right. So far, the bumper drills and man-overboard drills had not proved very challenging. They did those in naval science classes. When were they going to change the law forbidding women to go to sea on combatants? It was a major source of contention with the men. What was the purpose of women being at the Academy, some of the men were asking, if they couldn't participate in the real navy when they graduated? Sarah countered that unless there were women specifically trained to go on combatants first, there would always be an argument for keeping them off. However, even now that women were getting the training, the prospect of the law changing still seemed bleak. Sarah's dream was to become a pilot, not a ship driver, but most navy planes either were considered combatants or landed on them. She had three more years to go before graduation. Hopefully a lot would happen to change the law between now and then.

Ryan drove Sarah back to the Hall that night when liberty expired. The YPs were leaving the next morning. He kissed her goodbye, promising to visit the following weekend when the YPs were in Norfolk, Virginia. As the song "Sara Smile" by Hall and Oates played in the background on his car's tape player, Sarah couldn't help wondering what would happen once Ryan was in the fleet and she was still at the Academy.

Friday, 5 August 1977

The flotilla of six yard patrol craft left the Naval Academy on Friday afternoon, 5 August, each manned by a lieutenant officer in charge, a second-class midshipman, a navy petty officer, and twenty third-class midshipmen, ten male and ten female. They steamed to Patuxent River, Maryland, for their first anchoring. After grilling steaks on the fantail, the midshipmen held swim call until forced back on board by jellyfish.

While relaxing on the open decks, Sarah, Meredith Britain, and Trudy Sellers were joined by Dave Kite and Stuart Madden. Each of the men was from one of the nine companies not assigned women. Sarah recognized Stuart from computer class and knew he was a devout woman hater.

"Those jellyfish really cut our swim call short," said Meredith. Not everyone on the boat had taken a dip, but the girls who had gone swimming wore civilian bathing suits. Meredith's bikini created an obvious stir among their male classmates.

"Yeah, you never saw them until it was too late, and then they were everywhere," responded Sarah. "I'm still stinging." She rubbed a welt on her calf.

"You were crazy to go swimming in that water," said Dave. "I told you there were jellyfish." But how nice it was to see you girls in civilian bathing suits instead of those frumpy navy-issue suits, his eyes seemed to say.

"Yeah, but you didn't say how many jellyfish," continued Sarah. "They were everywhere."

"One is too many, Sarah," said Dave, grinning. "Hey, Trudy, why didn't you go swimming?" Trudy, a member of the varsity sailing team, sat against a railing, writing a letter.

"I do enough swimming when I go sailing," she said, smiling.

"That's not true," replied Dave. "I understand you sail very well." Dave was right. The petite brunette had been sailing Navy's dinghies since plebe summer. Together with Kate Brigman and her crew, Navy's women's team had won the Middle Atlantic Association of Women Sailors' championship regatta.

"So, where're you from, Dave?" asked Sarah.

"Chicago, originally. I could have been in the Class of '79, but I had an overbite and couldn't get a waiver out of high school. So I enlisted, went to NAPS, got my waiver, and then came in with our class." Sarah sensed bitterness from Dave when he spoke of his lost opportunity.

"So you could have been one of the *'omnes viri'* bunch, but instead you're with a bunch of girls on the 'Love Boat,'" she replied. *Omnes viri* was the Latin motto adopted by the Class of 1979 meaning "all male."

"Yeah," replied Dave good-naturedly, "but we still don't have any girls in our company, so it's about the same." Stuart grinned in agreement, not quite so good-naturedly, Sarah thought.

"I suppose you guys came around in 'locks, jocks, and boondocks' last summer," said Meredith.

"As a matter of fact, we did," replied Dave, trying not to laugh as he shot a glance at Stuart, who looked smug.

"Locks, jocks, and boondocks," a uniform worn during uniform races in previous years, was now prohibited. In that ritual, plebes would fall in on all fours, dressed solely in a jockstrap and a pair of black boondocker boots, holding in their teeth the metal security box issued on Induction Day. Upperclassmen then raced their makeshift "greyhounds" up and down the passageways.

"You must have been really ticked when you were told to come on *this* cruise," said Sarah. Trudy stopped writing for a moment, interested in the response.

Dave's smile evaporated. "Yes, I was furious. My lieutenant called me in and told me that because I had experience as an enlisted man, I'd be going on this cruise to free up a spot on a real navy ship for some other male midshipman. I told him I thought it was unfair and that I didn't want to go. He didn't care. I was very disappointed. Still am."

Stuart nodded.

"But here we are, and I'm ready to get it over with," he went on with distaste. "Then to add insult to injury—" He stopped himself, as if unwilling to verbalize his feelings.

Sarah thought she knew what he had been about to say. One of the women, Alison Jacobs, had been selected by the officer in charge to serve as the operations officer, the senior midshipman on board the YP. To Dave, an experienced enlisted man, it must have been a slap in the face.

"You don't think we feel the same way?" asked Sarah.

"I think you knew what you were getting into when you came here," replied Dave. "You knew you wouldn't be allowed on combatants. I never understood why they let you girls into the Academy in the first place. There are plenty of other gender-integrated schools. Why would you want to come here?"

Trudy spoke up. "First of all, unselfishly, I want to serve my country. Second of all, and selfishly, I wanted to take advantage of the educational opportunities here, which I don't believe should be available only to men. Especially when they are paid for by federal taxes collected from everyone."

Sarah had never thought of that rationale, but it made sense.

"What about being the first and pioneering for the cause of womanhood?" asked Dave.

"Sorry, I'm here for me," replied Trudy.

"Same here," said Sarah. "I've always wanted to fly. Even though the doctors say I don't have the eyes for it, I got a waiver to get in here, and I'll get a waiver to fly, too.

"Plus, I really wanted to join the military no matter where I went to college. My dad is career air force, and I've always loved that way of life—the travel, meeting new people, equal pay for equal work, unlike many civilian jobs. Also, I didn't want my parents to pay for my college education. A full scholarship to the Academy filled all my needs."

Dave was silent. *That* surprised you, Sarah thought. You thought we were here to make names for ourselves or to look for husbands. Bet you never thought we came here for the same reasons you did. She could see that he wasn't convinced, though. Not yet, anyway.

The next day the YPs practiced steaming in formation on their way to Norfolk, where they spent several days touring naval facilities and ships. Ryan drove down from Annapolis and met Sarah for the weekend as promised. On Monday the flotilla steamed north to New York City, where they moored at the Coast Guard station on Governor's Island.

By now Sarah had made several good friends, some from her boat, some from others. Meredith and Carrie were the most fun, along with a guy from

Carrie's company, another classmate who had at first been perturbed about being selected to go on the "girls' cruise." He now agreed that this cruise was a lot more fun than going on a real ship. Days were spent touring and learning about the various naval bases. At night the YPs pulled into port, and the midshipmen, unless they were assigned duty, were free to go on liberty until the next morning.

After liberty in New York City, the cruise proceeded to Newport, Rhode Island, where the midshipmen were led deep into the bowels of the *Butter-cup*. There the damage-control team began scrambling for shoring material and damage-control plugs as the hull of the "ship" started spewing water, rapidly filling the compartment. They worked in pairs or trios shoring up holes as quickly as possible, but as soon as one hole was plugged, it seemed that two more would burst. The water was already waist-high.

Wading toward the damage-control locker containing equipment to stop the flooding, Sarah heard Dave yell, "Here's another one! It's in the bottom of the hull! It feels bad! Hurry, Sarah!"

She turned and saw him dive below the surface of the water, now chest-high. Before long she would be treading water to stay afloat. Dave surfaced. "There's a mattress down there," he yelled. "I need help with it!"

Sarah swam to Dave's side, and the two of them dove below the surface and slid the saturated mattress over the surging hole, locating it only by feel in the brown, murky water.

They surfaced, laughing and gasping for air. "I'll bet they did that on purpose," remarked Dave, treading water.

"Who?"

"The enlisted guys running this show. I bet they're back behind the control panel laughing their asses off!"

"You think they did it because of us girls, or just because we're a bunch of mids?"

"Probably both. Either way, we did pretty well. I think we all worked great as a team, don't you?"

Sarah nodded and smiled. She had enjoyed the professional hands-on training they were receiving, but even more rewarding was the growing acceptance from her male classmates. On duty one night, Dave had admitted to her his surprise that the girls' reasons for coming to the Academy were basically the same as his. He also told her of his initial reservations concerning Alison as ops officer and how impressed he had been so far with the job she was doing. They agreed that on this ship, gender was not a factor. The men and women worked together as a team, alternating duties as officer of the deck, navigator, engineer, helmsman, lookout, and cook.

After touring the Coast Guard facilities in Cape May, New Jersey, the YPs weighed anchor for Philadelphia, where they found firefighting training scorchingly exhilarating. Sweltering in boots, overalls, jackets, and helmets, the mids fought blazing fuel fires as well as fires inside burning hulls. Male and female midshipmen fought the cobralike strength of a charged fire hose and came to recognize the advantages of teamwork. They left Philadelphia feeling professionally challenged and, except for their desire to become full-fledged youngsters, wishing that summer cruise was not about to end.

Tuesday, 6 September 1977

"Right 20 degrees rudder," commanded the OOD, ordering the YP out of the Chesapeake Bay and into the mouth of the Severn River. The peaked roof of the Robert Crown Sailing Center angled into view.

Midshipmen manned sea- and anchor-detail duties, straining for a view of the Naval Academy chapel dome. Tradition held that third classmen became full-fledged youngsters upon sighting the dome on their return from young-ster cruise.

Sarah stood on the flying bridge as starboard lookout. Stuart Madden manned the port lookout. He had never come around from his hatred of the women, but Sarah didn't care. She found him strange. Below, Dave Kite, the navigator, leaned out of the pilothouse and looked up. "See anything yet?"

"Not yet. It's got to be just beyond Bancroft Hall," Sarah replied.

"I see it! There it is!" yelled a classmate on the bow of the boat, pointing in the direction everyone was already looking. The rest of the crew strained to see.

"YES! We're officially youngsters!"

When the YP pulled alongside the sea wall across from Leahy Field, moor-ing lines properly secured, the youngsters began to gather their gear. Sarah slung her duffle bag over her shoulder as Dave approached.

"It was a pleasure to meet you, Sarah," he said extending his hand.

"Same here, Dave." She returned his handshake firmly. "Isn't this a great feeling? Plebe year is really behind us now."

"Hallelujah! You know, this has really been a great time," he continued. "Something you never could have convinced me of last May. In port every night with great liberty. . . . I know the guys who went on regular navy ships weren't doing that."

"Yeah, it really was fun. We've learned a lot and met some new classmates."

"Yeah. I've met a bunch of you girls, and I must say it has changed my opinion about the majority of you. Professionally, you've done a lot better than I would have expected."

"You mean for a bunch of girls?" Sarah joked.

"You know what I mean," said Dave. "Gender never played a part in what we did on board. Whoever was officer of the deck was just that. It didn't matter that she might be a girl. We all took orders just the same. It never seemed awkward.

"And what a bunch of partiers," he added, laughing. "We sure had some good liberty, didn't we?"

Sarah agreed. She recalled several fun evenings of bar-hopping and jai alai with Carrie, Meredith, and several male classmates who had been converted to the reality that, professionally and socially, this cruise had been a turning point for them all.

CHAPTER EIGHT

Youngster Academic Year

With the completion of at-sea training and summer leave, third classmen return to the Academy to begin their second academic year. And, although the new year brings more responsibilities in infantry drills and in watchstanding, the lessened emphasis on indoctrination leaves more time for sports and other extracurricular activities. It is a welcome and deserved change!

United States Naval Academy Catalog, 1976–77

Friday, 9 September 1977

Kate stood duty as company mate of the deck, CMOD, the day after the brigade returned to the Naval Academy from summer break. Ironically, she had stood this duty almost exactly a year ago, but today as she watched midshipmen lug books and gear back to their rooms, her concerns were different. She wondered if her classmates' opinions of her had mellowed over the summer. Would they now accept her like the guys on the YPs? Several approached her, excited to relay stories about their youngster cruises or summer leave, only to shy away cautiously when someone noticed them, obviously paranoid about being seen talking to a girl.

Another dilemma was seeing Charlie again. Over the summer she had ended their relationship, tired of his head games. She greeted him this morning in the passageway, to which he offered a disinterested sneer. Buddy and she were dating steadily now, having spent a good portion of her leave together.

Kate also pondered how she would react to the new plebes. Delivering phone messages, she wondered if she would be the flamer her classmates predicted. It was not her intention.

She straightened her watch belt and knocked on the first plebe room door. This would be her first encounter with them. Her company was not to receive female plebes. The same was true of several other companies that had had women plebes last year. The nine companies that had been without women last year were now no longer all male. Every company now had women from the Class of 1980, 1981, or both.

"Come in!" the plebes called in unison. Kate entered.

The three plebes leaped to attention and sounded off.

"Midshipman Myers, fourth class, sir! I mean, ma'am!" one stammered, unaccustomed to addressing senior female midshipmen. The others did the same, mistakenly addressing her as sir, then correcting themselves. Initially taken aback by what she considered disrespect, Kate caught herself before yelling. It was an innocent error, she told herself. They didn't mean anything by it, and they corrected themselves. Besides, they looked scared to death.

"I have a message for Midshipman Stone," she announced. The three stood silent. "Who is Midshipman Stone?" she asked remembering plebes weren't supposed to speak unless spoken to.

"That's me, ma'am." He stuck out his arm. Kate handed him the white chit.

"Thank you, ma'am."

Kate turned to leave. The three plebes did not move, since she had not told them to carry on. They stood at attention until she left the room. As it should be, she thought.

The next two messages belonged to her classmates, who were not in their room, and the last was for another plebe. She knocked on his door.

"Come in!"

Kate entered, expecting the same reaction as before. Instead, a lone plebe sat with his feet propped up on the desk.

"Yeah?" he called. Kate was appalled. She looked at the door again, thinking she might have entered the wrong room, but found that it belonged to the plebe she was looking for.

"Yeah?!" she yelled, wanting to slap his feet off the desk and order him to attention. "*Yeah?!*" she repeated angrily. "What the hell kind of sounding off is that? Aren't you supposed to come to attention and sound off when an upperclassman enters the room?"

The startled plebe clambered to attention and sounded off, using *sir* instead of *ma'am* as the others had done. He didn't correct himself, though, which infuriated Kate even more. Just who did this insolent little ass think he was talking to?

"Do I look like a *sir* to you, plebe?"

"Uh, uh, no, uh, ma'am. Sorry, ma'am."

"Sorry? Sorry?! Didn't they teach you, plebes aren't supposed to apologize for screwing up?" She gave him no time to answer. "What are your five basic responses, mister?"

"'Yes, sir,' uh, I mean, 'ma'am'; 'No, ma'am'; 'Aye, aye, ma'am'; 'I'll find out, ma'am'; and 'No excuse, ma'am.'"

"What's your name, mister?"

"Midshipman Meese, fourth class, ma'am."

"Well, Mr. Meese, this message is for your roommate," she told him, flinging the note on his desk, "and here's a message for you. You'd better start taking plebe year a little more seriously, or I'll personally see to it that you do. Is that clear?"

"Yes, MA'AM!" he shouted, obviously shaken. She stormed from the room, fuming. What kind of plebe summer did these guys have? I was scared stiff as a plebe, and they're going to have a plebe year if *I* have anything to do with it!

Friday, 16 September 1977

Classes had begun this past Monday. Sarah's eighteen-hour course load scared her, but at least she didn't have to contend with rates and come-arounds this year. When Tammy's alarm clock went off at 0645, Sarah moaned. Her squad leader wanted the plebes to come around to the third classmen before morning meal formation, which didn't thrill her. She would rather have slept in for the extra fifteen minutes. Holding come-arounds now meant that she had to be dressed by the time her plebes knocked on her door at 0700.

Last year some upperclassmen had used plebes as alarm clocks, dressing as they drilled them on rates. More than once Sarah had been ordered to stare at the wall while her upperclassman unzipped his fly to tuck in his shirt.

Tammy was excited to be a mentor to the plebes, to help them professionally, which was the traditional role third classmen played, having just been plebes themselves. Sarah was willing to do as her squad leader asked, but her priorities lay elsewhere. She planned on "making up" with her classmates in the company, making sure they accepted her. She also wanted to keep her grades up, continue cheerleading, and pursue a spot on the new women's gymnastics team.

Nevertheless, she rolled out of bed, brushed her teeth, and washed her face while Tammy took a shower. The plebes had been coming around all week now, and already Sarah was tired of them, although she hoped her apathy wasn't apparent. She didn't want them to think she wasn't interested in professional topics; she just remembered hating come-arounds as a plebe.

One thing she was thankful for was that Thirty-third Company had received no female plebes. Sarah wasn't sure how she would have reacted to new girls in the company. She was afraid some of the guys might have expected Tammy and her to take them under their wings, which was the last thing Sarah would have done. In fact, she was afraid she might have gone to the other extreme, making life miserable for them to prove she was giving them no special treatment. This way she didn't have to worry about it.

Sarah decided she would ask her two male plebes about their newspaper articles, the menus, and the officers of the day and then let them shove off. She had a physics quiz today and wanted to review before morning formation. During study hour last night, there had been a birthday party for Kurt Loper, so she hadn't done as much studying as planned.

Someone knocked on the door. "Request permission to come aboard, ma'am." Sarah buttoned her shirt and zipped her pants before ordering them to come in.

Returning from class, Kate found her special-request chit approving her "weekend" on top of her desk. Buddy was coming to visit. Each semester, upperclassmen were allowed to leave the Yard after their last class on Saturday to return Sunday evening at 1830. These periods of liberty were called "weekends." Youngsters were allowed three weekends per semester, second classmen were allowed five, and first classmen had unlimited weekends.

Kate laid her books on her desk and sat down to read her mail before changing for swimming, her new sport. She had decided to try a more physically demanding sport this year and was actually enjoying the grueling workouts, relieved that she was finally starting to lose some weight.

A letter from her mom indicated that the family's move to their new farm was complete. Her grandmother had moved in permanently with them and was doing well.

Her next letter had no return address and was postmarked from Washington, D.C. Odd, she thought. Who do I know there? She opened the envelope, and a newspaper clipping taped to a small piece of paper fluttered to the ground. Kate frowned, bending over to pick it up. The note, its penmanship barely legible, began with no salutation:

> *Don't you look lovely! I hope you're satisfied now and I hope you're happy that they've turned you into the man you obviously want to be!!*

It was unsigned. Kate stared at the clipping, dumbfounded. It was a picture of her on the front page of a local paper from last year. She had been showing the photographer how to "brace up," and he had photographed her with her forefinger shoving her chin into her chest. It wasn't the most flattering picture she'd ever taken, but she certainly didn't look like a man. She even remembered putting on mascara before the interview.

Who would have written such a thing? What have I done to deserve this? Tears filled her eyes despite her efforts to control them.

The guys had not changed their opinion of her after all. Classmates and plebes labeled her a flamer because of the way she treated the fourth classmen. She couldn't help it. They were too lax for her standards. They were nowhere near as scared of plebe year as she had been, and the brigade commander had already suspended chopping. We chopped until Easter, she thought. It isn't fair. Three weeks into the semester, she felt as low as a plebe. She wasn't sure she could afford a weekend away from her studies, but her psyche and heart demanded it. And now this. She had to get away and be in the arms of someone who cared for and believed in her unconditionally.

Saturday, 1 October 1977

Sarah attended as many away football games as her grades allowed. Last week she had cheered in Ann Arbor, Michigan. Tonight she was at Duke University, to which Navy lost 28–16, but most midshipmen who had taken a weekend to come to the game were there for the partying.

Walking among the fraternity houses with another cheerleader, Sarah felt out of place. The carefree life on the civilian campus was so foreign to her, and she felt so unattractive next to the "real" girls they passed. Their long hair, makeup, tight jeans, and jewelry made Sarah with her butchered haircut feel about ten years old. Three drunk coeds passed them, staggering and laughing, and Sarah wondered if she wouldn't rather be at a college like this instead of the Naval Academy. No drinking was allowed on Academy grounds at any time. Although the regimentation got to her every now and then, Sarah decided that she didn't miss the freedoms offered at a university such as this. I need the Academy's rules and regimentation, she thought. Otherwise I'd be out partying every night. I'd never get any studying done.

The two girls finally found the two-story dormitory where they had been invited to a party. "Born to Run" by Bruce Springsteen greeted them as they entered a dimly lit room where a number of midshipmen were already drinking. Several couples were making out on the couch. The girls made their way to the keg, where they joined in conversation with several other cheerleaders.

After Sarah's second beer, she needed to make a head call and asked for directions. She glanced at her watch: 2215. The mids had to muster on the buses at midnight.

Opening the door to the women's restroom, Sarah realized that she was not alone. The last stall was occupied, so she opted for the first. Sitting in the dim light, she froze as she heard muted sobs at the opposite end of the restroom. Who is that, Sarah wondered, and what is she crying about?

When she was finished, she walked to the opposite end of the restroom. "Excuse me, but are you okay in there?"

The sobs paused, and Sarah stepped back as the lock turned. The door swung in, and Sarah faced one of her female classmates sitting on the commode, jeans around her knees, tears streaming down her face. Carla Bridwell was another youngster who had traveled to Duke as a fan for Navy. Although they knew one another's names, the women didn't know each other well.

"I have horrible cramps," said Carla. "They're killing me."

"Why?" asked Sarah. "I mean, did you start your period or something?"

"I guess so," Carla replied. "I'm bleeding badly, and it hurts a lot." She paused. "I'm really scared."

Sarah fought off waves of panic. This didn't sound like someone having a normal period. But it must be. She was just having one worse than usual. Right?

"Do you want me to get help?" she asked, wondering if Carla needed medical attention.

"NO!" Carla screamed, reaching to stop her.

"Okay, okay," replied Sarah, holding out her hands to calm Carla while feeling completely helpless. "What can I do to help you, Carla?"

"I don't know if there is anything. I just need to get through this."

Sarah straightened and inhaled deeply. "But if you're bleeding badly, Carla, maybe we should get help."

"I think I'll be okay, Sarah. It's just these cramps—"

She stopped midsentence, grimacing as another one overcame her. "Oh, Sarah, I think I'm having a miscarriage."

What?! Sarah stopped, stunned. Was Carla pregnant? Pregnancy was grounds for expulsion from the Naval Academy. No one who had ever been pregnant or had fathered a child was allowed to attend or remain at the Academy.

"Are you sure, Carla? I mean, maybe it's just a bad period." Sarah didn't know what to do.

"Actually, I haven't had a period in a while," Carla responded when the cramp had subsided. "The same thing happened plebe summer. I mean, missing my period. But the end result wasn't this. I finally got it after about six months. I'm really under a lot of stress with academics and stuff now."

Sarah nodded. "Carla, I want to help you, but I don't know what to do."

"Sarah, I need some Kotex. Do you have any change?" Sarah checked her pockets and found two quarters.

The Kotex machine was full, and Sarah bought two. She handed one to Carla and crammed the other into Carla's purse.

"Thanks, Sarah."

Sarah felt helpless. "Carla, I really think you should be seen by somebody. A doctor or somebody."

"Sarah, the bus leaves in less than an hour. I'll be okay. Thanks for your help. Really."

"How are you going to ride the bus back like this?"

"I'll be okay. Don't worry."

"Well, I *am* worried. What if you bleed too much?"

"I don't think that will happen." She didn't sound convinced.

"Well, I'm going to stay with you," said Sarah. "I'll sit out here."

"No, you don't have to do that. Go back to the party. I'll be fine."

"Carla, are you sure? I just can't leave you like this."

"Sarah, they'll miss you back at the party, and someone may come looking for you. I don't want anyone else to know about this."

Sarah understood. "All right, but I'll be back to check on you periodically.

If you need anything. . . ." She didn't continue. There was no way Carla could contact her if she needed help.

"Hang in there," Sarah called, heading for the restroom door.

Sarah checked on Carla before it was time to get on the bus. She looked pale, and Sarah wondered if anyone would notice. They agreed they would tell anyone asking questions that Carla had the flu. On the bus, Sarah sat near Carla, who slept the entire ride back. She tried to focus on her statics book, but the events of the past few hours played over and over in her mind. What should she do? She decided to persuade Carla to go to Medical as soon as they got back. They would know what was wrong with her and how to handle it.

Kate was dead tired and hit the rack as soon as taps went down at 2300. A six-N day and a rigorous swim practice had exhausted her. Michelle and Terrie considerately turned off the overhead light and studied by desk lamp. Before she even knew she had laid her head on the pillow, Kate was dreaming deeply.

She was alone, swimming lap after lap in the varsity pool. After twenty laps, she sensed a presence in the pool area and glanced toward the sideline bleachers, where a lone male she did not recognize sat staring at her. In her dream she continued to swim, hoping he would leave. His presence was unnerving. She was tired of swimming but afraid to get out of the pool. Midlap, she turned her head to take a breath. He was still sitting. Still staring. She turned her face to the water, wishing him gone. His gaze was so focused, so intense, so . . . real? No, this was a dream. But his presence felt so close. She could feel his breath. No, this was a dream. He was sitting in the bleachers, yards away. But he was touching her, pulling her covers back. Covers? She was in the pool. No, he was beside her. He was touching her. She felt his breath on her neck. She pushed him away, and the sensation of flesh against flesh forcefully woke her.

The room was dark. She tried hastily to focus on her surroundings. He was here. In her room. Sitting on her rack, leaning over her body.

She gasped at the realization and sat up abruptly, pulling her covers to her chest and shrinking into the corner of her rack.

"It's okay," he whispered. "I won't hurt you. I just want to talk." He sat on the edge of her bed.

Talk?! At 0300? Who *is* this? Kate wailed silently. What does he want?

"Who are you?" she asked calmly, telling herself not to frighten him.

"A friend," he replied, not taking his eyes from her.

"But I don't even know you."

"I know. But you could get to know me, and we could be friends. I've seen you walking to class, and I've wanted to meet you for a long time." He moved toward her.

She put up her hand to stop him. "Don't. Please. Let's just talk for now. Okay?"

"Actually, that's not all I had in mind," he told her abruptly.

"Shh, you'll wake my roommates. Listen, I don't even know you," she repeated in a low voice, trying to place his face, which she could now make out. He looked vaguely familiar. "Have we met before?" she asked.

"Not really," he whispered. "We were in plebe chemistry together."

Kate couldn't recall. She had been so lost in that class that she had made a point of sitting in the front and listening intently so that she might keep up.

"Oh, yeah," she said, feigning recollection of this intruder. "I know, you're, um. . . ."

"I know your name but you don't remember mine?"

"No, I'm sorry. I don't." She was losing patience. This guy needed to leave, but she didn't want to wake her roommates or create a scene. Who would believe that he had come here uninvited? What if he told them she had asked him in? She would be fried big time, and it wasn't worth the gossip and speculation it would cause. She had to get him out of there.

"Then it doesn't matter," he told her. "I just wanted to stop by and see you, and I finally got up the nerve. Isn't that worth a kiss or something?"

"Look, I'm seeing someone right now, and I don't think this is right. I really think you better leave, or I may have to scream for help."

"No! Don't do that!" He glanced at her roommates in the bunk across the room and held up both hands to stop her. "Just a kiss? Please?"

"No!" she answered, her heart pounding. She suddenly realized that he had been kissing her neck when she awoke and knew he wanted more than a kiss. "Please, go! Now!"

He stood and she closed her eyes momentarily, breathing a sigh of relief. He caught her off guard, leaped back onto her rack, and planted a solid kiss on her lips.

"Get out! Get out!" she hissed, pushing him off. "Don't ever come back in here, or I'll turn you in! I swear it! Leave me alone! Do you hear me?"

He ran from the room. Kate jumped up and ran to the door, slamming her hands against its metal handle, forcing it shut, locking the deadbolt. She turned and leaned against it, breathing rapidly. Her heart pounded. Oh, my God, she thought fearfully, trying to squelch the oncoming flood of tears. Oh, my God!

Lying awake the rest of the night, Kate decided she would have to tell her roommates about the trespasser—and only them—because from now on they would be locking their door at night.

Tuesday, 22 November 1977

The 1977 football season had been rough for the cheerleaders, despite the football team's improved record of five wins and five losses, up from their four and seven record of last year. Whenever the home games turned boring, the mids relentlessly turned on the cheerleaders, showering them with abuse from the stands, dashing all of Sarah's hopes that things would be better the second time around.

Homecoming had been one of the worst games. Although Navy trounced William and Mary 42–17, the brigade had been absolutely obnoxious. During the "Let's go Blue!" cheer, a small group of midshipmen in the first few rows of the bleachers yelled "Suck my cock!" instead. Appalled, the girls let the male cheerleaders perform the yells for the rest of the game, performing only the dance routines, which the brigade also booed. The girls felt a brief respite when they moved down the stands to the alumni section, where they were welcomed with cheers and applause. That night in her rack, Sarah seriously considered quitting the squad, but since there was only one more home game before Army, she decided to tough it out.

That was before the ill-fated Army-Navy pep rally.

Mandatory for the entire brigade, the pep rally was held in Halsey Field House, after evening meal on 22 November, the Tuesday before the Army-Navy game. Staging was set up in the middle of the indoor track with a backdrop of royal blue portable screens. The cheerleaders stretched out on the floor behind the screens, anxiously rehearsing the dance routines in their heads as they listened to the brigade file noisily into the field house.

High-spirited midshipmen stood in front of the stage, eager for the show to begin. Some tossed footballs across the crowd while others sat on the floor or stood at the back, having seen this show too many times before. Rumors of an over-the-wall pep rally after study hour that night were already spreading, and as the crowd size increased, some of the pent-up spirit broke out into chants of "Navy! Navy! Navy!"

"They're fired up!" said Sarah, turning to Judy Nance, who was tying her shoelace.

"Yeah! This will be great!" replied Judy. "Maybe for once they'll cheer with us instead of against us."

"We can hope," said Sarah, smoothing the pleats of her short gold skirt.

The pep band broke into "The Goat Is Old and Gnarly," and Sarah's stomach started to burn. Oh, come on, she thought. How many times have I been in front of this crowd? Why am I nervous?

The lights in the field house went out, spotlights flooded the stage, and the band broke into "Anchors Aweigh." The head cheerleader signaled the girls that they were on.

The cheerleaders ran onto the stage, flashing smiles as they fell into step with the music and the clapping of the brigade. The response was almost immediate. The music continued to play, but the clapping stopped. Sarah kept dancing, but her smile melted as she realized that the entire brigade, now on their feet, was booing.

"Get off the stage!" someone yelled. "Yeah, get 'em out of here!" called another. "BOOO! BOOOOO!" How can they do this? Sarah wondered in anguish. Why do they hate us so much?

Still dancing, she glanced at Judy, telepathically asking her the same questions. Judy shrugged, obviously distraught over the reaction of the mids. The fight song dragged on as they continued to perform. What else could they do?

Sarah grew angry. She glared back at the uncivil crowd with a phony smile, and in a pretense of mouthing the words to the fight song, she actually chanted obscenities, her words muffled by the intensity of the booing. "I hate you! I hate every one of you assholes!"

The song finally ended, and the girls filed offstage as the brigade broke into cheers once again when the head football coach was introduced. They banded together behind the blue screens, unable to speak for the shock. As they stood huddled together, the male head cheerleader approached them.

"I don't know what to say, girls. I'm really sorry! I can't believe they did that!"

"Well, we're not going back out there again tonight," said Alicia Catrell. "Who do those guys think they are? Officers and gentlemen—what a farce!"

"I understand," he replied. "Just hang back here. We'll talk about it later."

"There's nothing to talk about," said Judy as he walked away. "I quit! I've had it! This was supposed to be fun, and it's been nothing but harassment since the first football game last year."

"You're right," agreed Sarah, "I've been thinking about quitting for a long time now. I just figured I'd stick around until the Army-Navy game since we're gonna be on national TV, but now I don't know."

"It's really unbelievable that the whole brigade stood up and booed us. I wanted to cry," said Jeanette Bushing.

"At first I felt like crying, too," said Sarah, "and then I got so angry I started yelling back at them!"

"Me, too!" said Alicia. "I can't believe the things I was saying. But I was so angry! That was awful. It never ceases to amaze me how cruel mids can be."

"So, what are we gonna do?" asked Sarah. "I say if we're gonna quit, we should do it en masse and send a real statement to the brigade."

"Yeah, and doing it right before the Army-Navy game would really be embarrassing to them."

"Oh, don't give them so much credit," replied Judy. "They'd probably be happy."

The girls sat silent for a moment as they collectively thought. They ignored the speeches by the superintendent and the captains of the football team, and the skits now taking place on the other side of the screens.

"Man! We're almost there." Sarah finally broke the silence. "We've put up with their garbage all season, and the only game we have left is Army. Let's cheer that one, get on TV, and then quit. We owe ourselves that much, and I would feel kind of bad letting the football team down now."

"I was just thinking that," said Jeanette, "although the guys would still be out there cheering for them."

"Yeah, but I want to be on TV. I've already told a bunch of my friends back home to watch for me," said Sarah.

"Me, too," agreed Judy.

"Okay, then, that's what we'll do," summarized Alicia. "We'll cheer the Army game and then quit."

"What about the basketball team?" asked Jeanette.

"I'm sorry," said Sarah apologetically, "but I've had enough. The basketball team is just going to have to get along without me this year."

The other girls agreed, beginning to feel somewhat avenged, although their egos remained bruised by the unexplained assault.

As the pep rally ended, the twelve male and female cheerleaders made their way toward the front door of the field house. Outside in the cool night air, they began to go their separate ways when Sarah grabbed Judy and one other female cheerleader. "Safety in numbers, guys. Let's walk back together."

The girls walked huddled across the street, then along the fence bordering Thompson Field. Halfway back to Bancroft Hall, they heard someone running up behind them. Sarah turned to see who it was but glimpsed only a pair of white works trousers before her eyes and hair were lathered in white foam. She stopped, frightened for a moment, as she hurried to wipe the froth from her face. She realized from its smell that it was shaving cream.

Once her eyes were clear, she saw that the assailant had also covered Judy and the other cheerleader in lather before racing away. Judy looked like she was in the middle of a shampoo. Shaving cream dripped from her dark hair onto her gold cheerleading sweater.

Sarah's fury began to build as midshipmen casually walked by, glancing at the cheerleaders wiping handfuls of foam from their head and shoulders and flinging it to the ground. "What a jerk! Did you see who it was?" she asked.

"No, I didn't see anything before I was covered in this stuff," replied Judy. "This is unbelievable! This really makes me want to quit. That was no Army-Navy prank. That was malicious! I just don't get it."

Neither did Sarah. Judy was such a likable person, cute, petite, full of school spirit. Why would anyone do this to her? To any of them?

"I'm out of here," called Judy. "I'm running back to my room before something else happens."

The third cheerleader followed.

"See you guys tomorrow at practice," called Sarah. That is, if I go to practice, she thought, running up the ladder to her room.

"Sarah, what *happened?*" asked Tammy as Sarah walked into their room.

"As if booing wasn't enough, some jerk doused us with shaving cream on the way back from the field house." She started to undress and found herself unable to hold back the tears she had tried so hard to suppress.

"Oh, Sarah, I'm so sorry," remarked Tammy. "I couldn't believe they booed you guys like that, and then this."

"Yeah, we're all on the verge of quitting. We've about had it," she sobbed.

"Man, I can't believe I'm crying over this." She wiped her eyes. "At least I didn't do it in front of any guys, huh?"

"Oh, so what. You have a good reason to cry. Go ahead and get it out." Tammy handed her a Kleenex and paused. "Are you really going to quit?"

"No, but we came close tonight. If the game wasn't being televised, we would have."

"Well, I can't say I wouldn't understand, but I know the football players would be disappointed."

"Oh, I don't know. They probably couldn't care less if we're out there or not. They'd probably rather have civilian girls on the field just like everybody else. Like it used to be."

"I think you'd be surprised, Sarah."

"I can't talk about it anymore, Tammy. I've gotta get cleaned up so I can go study." Sarah showered, dressed in service dress blues, and grabbed her statics and elements-of-materials books, a notebook, and several pencils.

"Maybe we'll try to start a spontaneous pep rally when you get back," called Tammy as Sarah headed out the door. "We'll get 'em to go over the wall. Then you'll feel better."

"Maybe," replied Sarah despondently. "See ya, Tam."

Sarah walked to Nimitz Library depressed, pondering her decision to remain with the cheerleading squad. There had been so many good times, but the bad times hurt deeply. Tonight had been the worst. No one had ever physically attacked them before. Maybe the brigade wanted a change. Maybe new faces on the squad would help improve things. Maybe not. Well, at least one of the faces on the receiving end of the abuse would no longer be hers.

Sarah had joined the recently formed gymnastics team. The coach was working hard to get them official status and a season of real meets. Sarah decided that she wanted to put all of her energy into gymnastics. Now that she was an upperclass and could get away from the Academy more often, cheering just wasn't worth the abuse anymore.

On the second deck of Nimitz Library, Sarah found a quiet wooden cubicle in the corner, deciding to remain as inconspicuous as possible after this evening's events. Settling in, she opened her statics notes and began studying for an upcoming test. Half an hour later she was leaning back with her eyes closed, trying to memorize several important equations, when someone walked up beside her.

Great, someone's going to bug me here too, she thought anxiously. Sitting up quickly, she opened her eyes to find Ted Gantry, a wide-receiver for Navy's football team and one of their star players, standing before her. It was rumored that he would be one of the team captains next year.

"Hi, Sarah," he said softly, smiling.

He knows my name? "Uh, hi, Ted." She tried to sound casual despite her nervousness.

"Listen, I'm glad I saw you here. I heard you girls might be thinking of quitting the squad after what happened tonight."

What a rumor mill Bancroft Hall is, she thought. "Well, yeah," she answered, suddenly embarrassed. "I mean, we talked about it, but we decided to cheer for the Army game and *then* quit."

"Well, I know you girls have taken quite a beating this year from the brigade. The team gets it too when we don't play so well, so I kind of know how you feel. I don't want to tell you guys what to do or anything, but I did want to let you know that the team really appreciates your being down on the field. It means a lot to us to have you cheering for us and getting the fans behind us. No matter what the brigade does, the team supports you 100 percent, and we sure would hate to see you quit. I know the basketball team feels the same way."

His words left Sarah speechless for a moment. His kindness overwhelmed her.

"Wow," she finally said. "Thanks! I didn't think you guys cared if we were out there or not. It means a lot to hear you say that."

"Listen, I've gotta run. Take care, and try to hang in there."

"Bye, Ted. Thanks a lot. Hey, good luck with Army!"

"Thanks!" he called, turning the corner around a bookcase.

The intoxicating effect of his words dissolved her depression. She felt as if she had just received a big hug. What a nice guy, she thought. I can't believe he came up to me and said that. I didn't even know he knew who I was.

She tried to focus on her statics problems, but her mind repeatedly turned back to their conversation. The football players don't want us to quit. So how can we let them down? She began to feel guilty. Before this, I assumed they couldn't have cared less about the cheerleaders, but now. . . .

I've got to study, she reminded herself. We aren't going to quit until after Army, so there's no need worrying about this now. Besides, if I don't get my grades up, somebody else will be making the decision to quit for me.

Saturday, 3 December 1977

A week after Navy lost to Army, Sarah was restricted to Bancroft Hall to work off the twenty-five demerits she had earned for arriving back late after her weekend in Atlanta with Ryan. She had mistakenly thought that the limousine from the Baltimore-Washington Airport to USNA left earlier than 1800 and missed Sunday evening meal formation. She now had to muster in uniform every two hours in front of the Sixth Battalion office for inspection by the battalion officer of the watch. The only saving grace was that she was not alone. Denzel Simmons was also restricting.

Denzel had been fried ten demerits for failing to shave for a Thursday noon formal inspection. He rectified the situation by getting a "no-shaving" chit from Sick Bay, certifying that his sensitive skin broke out every time he used a razor.

Sarah spent Saturday evening in her room studying between restriction musters. After the last muster at midnight, she ran to her room and stripped off her uniform, changed into white works and a sweatshirt, and ran down to Denzel's room bursting with an idea.

"Denzel!" she called, cracking his door several inches.

"Yo, Buns! Come on in. What's up?"

"Denzel, I've got a crazy idea!"

"Oh, no!"

"Listen, taps doesn't go down for another hour and a half, and I'm going nuts in this place. I've just gotta get out of here for a while. I thought we could go over the wall to Donna's."

"Yo, Buns, that *is* crazy!"

"Come on, Denzel. It'll be fun!"

"Sarah, you always get me into trouble."

"We'll be back before taps. No one will know. Come on!"

How did he let her talk him into these things? "Okay, but how're we gonna get there?"

"Poker's here for the weekend studying. I bet I can sweet-talk him into taking us."

"Yeah, you just turn on that charm, girl."

Poker was Brian Pokerno, a first-class systems engineering major who had talked Sarah into choosing the same major. Tonight Sarah needed no sweet talk, as Poker was more than willing to take a break from the books.

On the way back from his room, Sarah invited Tammy and Mitch Prescott to join them.

The four youngsters hurried down the back steps of Eighth Wing and jumped into Poker's Trans Am on Bronson Road. He dropped the foursome in front of Donna's apartment on King George Street and went to park.

Sarah had not called ahead to warn Donna. It wasn't necessary; her apartment had become a haven for all her midshipman friends and was open to them any time. Sarah knocked, and Donna answered.

"Surprise! We're here!" Sarah called. "Have you missed me?" she asked, giving Donna a big hug. "We've missed you! This restriction stuff is the pits!"

"Hi, guys! Come on in," said Donna. "Are you on restriction, Toots?"

"Yeah, so is Denzel. Tammy and Mitch are legal."

"You are nuts, Toots!" She went to answer the second knock, which had to be Poker.

"We were going crazy in that place, Donna. We had to get away. Anyway, it's only for an hour. So where's the brew?"

"You know where it is, hon. Help yourself." Donna gestured toward the tiny kitchen.

Three beers later, at 0120, Poker announced that they needed to head back ASAP. Taps was going down in less than ten minutes. The five thanked Donna and rushed to Poker's Trans Am.

Poker dropped the other four behind Eighth Wing, and they raced up the back steps to Sarah and Tammy's room. As they bent over to catch their breath, the taps taker knocked on the door. He realized immediately that something was awry.

"Where have you guys been?" he asked.

Sarah would not lie. She took the honor code very seriously; the conduct system was another story. "We've been out at Donna's apartment." She cringed as she spoke.

"*All* of you?!"

"Yes, sir," replied Sarah, sheepishly looking around at Denzel, Tammy, and Mitch. She could hear Denzel's silent reproach, "Sarah, you always get me into trouble."

"Aren't you on restriction?"

"Yes, sir. Denzel and I are," she answered, waiting for him to chastise them.

"You've been drinking, too. Haven't you?"

"Yes, sir." She knew she was in for it. May as well try to be respectful to try and soften the blow.

"How'd you guys get out there so fast? Didn't you have restriction muster at 0000?"

"Yes, sir, but Poker drove us." She didn't want to implicate Poker but had little choice at this point.

"What?! One of my classmates took you out there knowing you were on restriction?"

"Well, yes, sir."

He shook his head. "This is gonna cost you guys big time."

Sarah's stomach sank. She couldn't imagine restricting every day for two months in a row. If ever there was a time to cry, this was it. Although this guy was somewhat of a male chauvinist, she sensed he had a soft spot for the girls. Her tears flowed. "We're . . . we're really sorry, sir. It won't ever happen again."

"Well, I'm going to have to talk to the company commander." He left abruptly.

"Sarah, are you okay?" asked Denzel tenderly. He had never seen her cry before.

"Oh, man, Denzel. What are we going to do if we get seventy-five and two? I never thought we'd get caught, did you?"

"Hell, no, or I wouldn't have gone."

"This is bullshit, man," fumed Mitch. "I'm going to go talk to somebody." He stormed out.

"Go get him, Denzel. He'll just make matters worse. We got caught. We'll have to pay the price," said Sarah, wiping her eyes. "I'm fine."

Denzel left to catch Mitch, returning a few moments later. "I stopped him. It looked like a major pow-wow was going on in the company officer's office. Somebody told me a couple of plebes and youngsters got caught drinking in the Hall."

"Oh, great!" said Sarah. "They'll fry us all. I'll never get to sleep until I hear our fate."

"Me, neither," said Denzel, plopping down on her rack.

Tammy, Sarah, and Denzel talked for the next two hours, waiting for the verdict. The company commander came to the girls' room to hear their side of the story. Poker stopped by as well, assuring them that he understood how

Sarah had had to implicate him. He thought the fact that he drove them out there might be their saving grace. If they fried Sarah and Denzel, they would have to fry him too, and classmates rarely fried classmates.

At 0430 the company commander delivered the verdict. "Listen, you two, what you did was incredibly stupid!"

"Yes, sir," said Sarah. "You can be sure—"

He cut her off. "I've convinced the taps-taker not to fry you, because we've had several other major mishaps in the company tonight, and because it was one of my classmates who took you out there. We're letting everything slide, but you are on thin ice, my friends. You'd better never pull anything like this again. Never!"

"No, sir, never again," said Sarah.

"No, sir. No way!" echoed Denzel.

"All right, then, let's hit the rack."

"Hallelujah!" she cried when he left the room. "I thought we were dead meat!"

"Must have been those tears that got 'em," said Denzel.

"Hey, if it worked, it was worth it, and it got you off too, babe, right?"

"Right. *Muchas gracias,* and good night!"

Saturday, 10 December 1977

On a windy Saturday afternoon, Kate was studying alone in her room for a physics test on Monday. The prof had given them no gouge as to what would be on the test, although before her lay several copies of tests from previous years that a classmate had shared with her. Old tests were routinely handed down from class to class. The Academy was riddled with this sort of thing, and for years the mids had relied on it.

I hate physics, Kate groaned to herself. I just don't get it. She leaned back in her chair and sighed. I have no idea how I've maintained an A in that class.

The knock on the door startled her. Who was still in the Hall on a Saturday afternoon?

"Who is it?"

"Mike Timmons."

Mike was in her physics class and lived in an adjoining company. He was shy, and she rarely spoke to him. What could he want? Gouge?

"Come in," she called.

The door swung open, and Mike waited a second to ensure that the doorstop engaged before releasing his hand. No one wanted to be caught in a room with a girl with the door shut.

"Hi, Mike."

"Hi, Kate." He walked toward Kate's desk and gently set a chocolate-frosted cupcake on the blotter. "Figured you'd be studying. Thought you might like this. My mom sent me a bunch." He turned quickly to leave.

"Thanks!" she said, stunned by the kindness of his gesture. It was the nicest thing anyone had done for her here. Mike pulled the door from its clasp, eager to leave.

"Wait!" she called. "Are you studying for this test, too?"

"Uh-huh." He paused.

"Want to study together? I have some gouge tests here."

"Yeah, I have them, too. Thanks, but I'd better not."

Kate didn't press him. He probably didn't want to be seen studying with a girl. "Thanks again," she said.

"Sure. Good luck on the test." The door slid shut behind him.

Kate peeled the accordioned pink paper from the sides of the cupcake and marveled at the warmth this single charitable gesture generated within her. Her spirits were renewed.

Friday, 16 December 1977

For Christmas, Sarah was flying to Tehran for two weeks, where her father was assigned to the Military Air Assistance Group. Roger Phillips, Class of 1979, was going there too, and out of obligation to his parents, who had met hers in Tehran, he grudgingly agreed to ensure that she got on the correct plane at Dulles airport.

Roger had to pick up his sister at a Christmas party in the D.C. area hosted by friends of his parents. Sarah went with him. At the party she was the only one in uniform, and so she decided to inconspicuously sip a diet soda in a corner chair. Within several minutes, however, two curious guests approached.

"Hello, dear," said the well-dressed elderly woman, accompanied by an even older gentleman. Sarah stood.

"Good evening, ma'am. Sir."

"Roger tells us you go to school together at Annapolis," said the woman. "So you are one of the midshipwomen?"

Sarah smiled. "Actually, ma'am, I am a midshipman. Midshipman is a rank, not a title, so gender is irrelevant."

"Oh, yes, of course."

"A lot of people think the same thing," remarked Sarah.

"Well, when I was a midshipman," piped up the gentleman, "we were all just that—men!"

"Harold, stop," said his wife, flicking her wrist in disdain. "My husband is a retired Marine Corps colonel from the old school. He's really quite harmless, so I'll leave you two military types to talk." She left Sarah alone with him. Here we go, thought Sarah. An alum who thinks we shouldn't be there. It was her first encounter.

"Yes, sir," she replied confidently, "but they changed the law two years ago."

"Well, I'm certain they don't make you girls eat 'square meals.'"

"As a plebe, yes, sir, they do. We had to sit on the edge of our seats and keep our 'eyes in the boat' at every meal, and when chopping down the passageways as well."

"Hmmph, that right?"

"Yes, sir." She enjoyed his shocked interest that there weren't separate rules for the women.

"Well, you ladies certainly don't carry rifles when you march?"

Sarah wanted to laugh and tell him no, that the men carried them for them but decided that would be rude. "Yes, sir, we do. The M-1. We carry it for all drill periods and parades."

"That heavy old thing?"

"It's really not so bad, sir." She contemplated telling him about the trick with the sock under the bra strap but again decided against it.

"Well, I'm glad to hear that there are *some* traditions left. The place has really changed since I was there."

"And when was that, sir?"

"Nineteen twenty-four, my girl. Nineteen twenty-four. Well, good luck there, young lady. Enjoy it! They'll be some of the best times of your life." He raised a wizened hand as he shuffled away.

Sarah sat down and grinned. How funny his perspective on the things we girls can and can't do.

Several minutes later, Roger and his sister ushered her off to Dulles airport, where she changed into civilian clothes and anxiously boarded the fourteen-hour flight to Iran.

Friday, 20 January 1978

Kate had spent Christmas leave with Buddy in Rhode Island, much to the disappointment of her parents. She had felt guilty at first, but that changed once they were together. Her feelings for him were stronger than ever—until he asked her to marry him.

Caught completely off guard, she explained that she had too many unknowns in her life and just wasn't ready to make a lifelong commitment at that point. This led to discussions about her frustrations with school and why she was going to the Academy in the first place.

Buddy thought she was doing it for her parents, especially her father, which she had to admit was partially true. Still, she liked the Academy, the superb education she was getting, and all the other opportunities it offered. But did she really want to be a naval officer? Was that what she wanted to do with her life?

And what if she couldn't hack this electrical engineering major? She had finished the final exam this afternoon and felt like she had done fine. But what if she had failed it?

Someone knocked on her door. "Come in," she called.

"It's the mate, ma'am. Main-O just called and said your mother wants you to call home."

"Is it an emergency?" she asked, alarmed that something might have happened to her grandmother.

"No, ma'am. They said it wasn't. I asked specifically."

"Good job. Thanks!"

Her mother reported that Buddy had called and needed her to call him as soon as possible. She immediately placed a collect call to Newport and learned that Buddy had been busted for drugs for the second time and was asking for a general discharge from the navy.

Oh, perfect, she thought. Just when the navy is starting to crack down on drug users, I'm practically engaged to one. She was angry but didn't let on, deciding that he had enough people on his back right now. How could he have done this? Now he had blown his chances to get the GI Bill and get an education. She knew he had saved no money.

She hung up, helpless and confused. I love him so much, but I can't believe he was so irresponsible. Oh, Lord, I can't think about it now. I've got four more finals to study for, and I'd better pass them, since it looks like I may become the breadwinner in this family.

Saturday, 11 February 1978

Christmas in Tehran had been wonderful. On a whim one day, Sarah had invited Roger over for a Coke and was surprised to learn that his initial impression of her had been that of a nerdy mid he wanted nothing to do with. After the Coke he asked her out, and the two dated almost every night they were in Iran.

Back at the Academy, they dated several more times, but nothing serious ensued. Sarah called Ryan upon returning to the States and flew down to see him in Orlando over semester break.

Despite an eighteen-hour credit load, and even with a D in statics, Sarah had maintained a 2.75 quality point rating for first semester. This semester she was taking advanced-level physics and differential equations, along with dynamics, leadership, introduction to systems engineering, and psychology.

Still working hard on the gymnastics team, she would be participating in an exhibition meet against the University of Maryland at Baltimore College on 26 February, which her grandparents and sister were coming to see. The team was shaping up, although the administration had given them no official status yet. This afternoon she performed a balance-beam exhibition before the men's meet and fell twice on a handstand and forward roll, in front of Admiral Lawrence, the superintendent, who had stopped by to watch the team. Nerves.

Near the end of study period, Sarah was sitting behind her desk in only a T-shirt and panties, working on a psychology paper, when an unexpected knock came on the door.

"I'll get it," she said. She opened the door partway and stuck her head around the edge. The visitor was a first classman in her company. Tammy came over to say hello.

The firstie had just come from town and had stopped by after buying a Pepsi from the machine down the passageway. He made small talk with Tammy about the varsity tennis team, which he managed.

Tammy conversed with him for another ten minutes while Sarah returned to her paper. Moments after he left, there was another knock on the door. Sarah figured it was him again and, since she had started undressing for bed, told him to hold on. The door began to open.

"Wait a minute, PLEASE!" she yelled. But the visitor did not listen. Sarah quickly pulled on her underwear and threw herself against the door, slamming it shut.

"Open this door!" a strange voice yelled. Sarah opened it and peered around the edge again. It was the officer of the day, glaring ominously at her.

"Open this door!" he demanded, pushing against Sarah's efforts to keep it closed.

"Sir, I don't have any clothes on! I'll open it in just a minute, sir."

"Open it NOW!" he ordered, still pushing. Sarah could not understand his determination. Why wouldn't he let up for a second?

Tammy grabbed a pair of sweatpants and threw them to Sarah, who pulled them on just as the door slammed open. Lieutenant Sheedy stormed into the room as Sarah and Tammy leaped to attention and sounded off.

"Where is he?" the lieutenant demanded.

"Where is who, sir?" Sarah replied, eyes in the boat.

"Where is the guy I saw come in here? Where did you hide him?" The OOD began opening closets. He pulled back the shower curtain and stormed to the window, looking out onto the ledge for the imaginary male he was convinced was in their room.

"Sir, I don't know who you are talking about. There's no one else in our room, sir." Sarah shot an incredulous look at Tammy, who shrugged in response.

"Listen, miss, don't lie to me. I saw him come in here." He jabbed his white-gloved finger at her face.

"Really, sir. We just finished talking to one of the first class in our company, but he never came into our room. He stayed outside the door because I wasn't completely dressed."

The OOD leaned down so that he was face to face with Sarah. "You're just lucky I didn't catch you, miss! You better never get caught with a man in your room!" Before she could consider a reply, he stormed out of the room.

Sarah turned to Tammy. Both were speechless. They didn't know if they should laugh or scream. Who did this guy think he was, busting into their room, accusing them of harboring a first class? Why wasn't he checking on some of the guys, like the ones who kept asking to borrow Sarah and Tammy's sweat gear so that they could sneak their girlfriends up to their rooms?

Sarah needed to vent. She grabbed a quarter from her desk drawer and stormed out of the room to get a soda and find Kurt Loper. He wouldn't believe this one.

Nothing was getting better for Kate. Tonight at dinner, her classmates in the company had performed a rousing cheer in her honor:

Rah, rah, rah!
Ho, ho, ho!
Everybody knows that Brigman blows!

Sitting in her room trying to concentrate on her studies, Kate brooded. Why me, Lord? My own classmates, my own company. I haven't done anything to them, yet they feel such malice toward me. Last night they threw a cake at me to show me how much they can't stand me. I'm so tired of it. I don't hate them, it just hurts. Maybe it will turn to hatred, and that will be easier to handle. You'd think they'd get tired of it, but they don't. They just keep doing it to me over and over again. When will it stop?

Kate looked at her watch and saw that it was almost 2030. At 2045 a classmate from her electrical engineering class was meeting her in the Steerage snack bar to help her study.

I may as well go down there now since I can't study in this state of mind, she thought. Maybe a box of crackers will make me feel better, even though I hardly need to eat.

She gathered her EE textbook, calculator, and some pencils and opened the door, checking to see if anyone was in the passageway before proceeding. She couldn't deal with any more harassment tonight.

The coast was clear. As she turned the corner into the main passageway, however, her luck ran out. Two classmates were headed her way. As soon as they saw her, their animated conversation stopped and the whispers began. Kate decided to ignore them. What more could they do to hurt her? She stared at the beige walls. Unfortunately, she couldn't block out their voices.

"Bilge-man, the bitch," whispered one loud enough for her to hear him, belching instead of pronouncing the *bilge* part of the disgusting nickname.

His companion snickered. "Looks like she's headed for the feeding trough. Gotta maintain that bulk."

"Yeah, oink, oink!" replied the other.

Tears stung Kate's eyes, although she resolved not to let them get the best of her out here in the hallway. Crying was done in her room. She bit her lip and continued as if she had heard nothing, wanting to confront them, make them tell her why they hated her so. But she didn't dare. They wouldn't tell, and it would give them ammunition for the next time. It was better to try and ignore them.

At the Steerage, she grabbed a box of Cheese Nips from the shelf and felt the accusing stares of male midshipmen around her as she stood in line to pay. Yeah, maybe I don't need to be eating this, she thought, but if only for now, it'll make me feel better, which is something no one else in this place cares to do.

Friday, 3 March 1978

Backstage, Kate's stomach churned. She had thought she was over the stage fright. She had expected to be nervous last weekend, when the Naval Academy Glee Club's production of Gilbert and Sullivan's operetta *H.M.S. Pinafore* opened, but not tonight. She was only in the chorus. It wasn't like she had the lead, and her parents and grandmother weren't coming until tomorrow evening.

Kate had been happy to start the live performances. The midshipman cast held parties after each one, and Kate enjoyed their company. Everyone helped one another, and the whole thing made her feel like part of the group. Besides, it was fun dressing up in the long lacy gowns and bonnets.

She was beginning to feel better about herself. With warmer temperatures, she was working out more often and going out with different midshipmen on the weekends. She enjoyed not being involved with any one person. Making new friends bolstered her spirits. Buddy wrote often, although she hadn't seen him since Christmas. She still cared for him but no longer felt desperate to see him.

Kate routinely saw Gabe Leggett at Glee Club practices. Last Sunday they had gone to lunch together at the Harbour House. She enjoyed Gabe's company more and more. Talking with him was so comfortable. He told her he was having second thoughts about his recent engagement to his girl back home, and Kate feared that she might have been the reason. Several weeks ago she had told him she didn't think he was ready to get married, even if his fiancée was "the one" for him. She had no real concrete reason; the two of them certainly were not romantically involved. She just felt in her heart that he was not ready for that kind of commitment, and she told him so.

Now she felt guilty and wished that someone else had brought it to his attention. He would visit his fiancée over Easter break, and Kate hoped things would work out between them. She really liked Gabe.

"Curtain's up!"

Kate glanced in the mirror to check her overly made-up face. Her heart was pounding. Maybe it was because Gabe had mentioned that he might be at tonight's performance.

. . .

Sarah sat with Carrie Freeman in the audience, watching the musical with mixed emotions. The female midshipmen on stage seemed out of place, acting so feminine, dancing around in frilly dresses. It seemed unmilitary to her, unsuitable in this professional environment. How will the guys take us seriously if we act like silly girls? Even if it *is* just an act.

She had felt the same way last year when the Glee Club produced *The Boyfriend,* in which her good friend Meredith Britain played the lead. The 1920s flapper costumes had been much more revealing than the ones up on the stage now, and some of the girls had had to act ditzy, which annoyed Sarah. It sent mixed signals to the guys. Maybe that's what I did on the football field as a cheerleader, though, she thought. I guess there's really no difference. Maybe that's why they couldn't accept us—the dual role. You can't be a feminine professional, at least a feminine military professional. You must be hard and cold and masculine—wear men's uniforms, cut your hair short, skip the makeup and jewelry. Don't try to be attractive. Attractive girls wouldn't want to come to a place like this unless they were looking for a husband.

Not me, she resolved. I want an education and a career. I want to be part of the revolution to change the way men view female officers. We can be attractive and feminine and still be taken seriously as professionals as well.

Her confidence waned only when she tried to determine *when.*

Sunday, 12 March 1978

Kate finally got up enough nerve to visit her academic adviser and hand him her request to change majors. She had no choice. The thought of descending to a C average for the next two and a half years repulsed her, especially when she was studying so hard. She had been to EI, extra instruction periods with her instructors, on numerous occasions, but the results never changed. She had done so well initially, but now her class ranking had dropped considerably. How had this happened?

It didn't matter. It had to change. Electrical engineering was too difficult. General engineering was her new request. What humiliation! What a failure! And on Kirchhoff's birthday, no less! With only eight weeks until final exams, Kate resolved to complete and pass her electrical engineering courses and put them behind her forever.

Monday, 20 March 1978

Fifteen minutes before this year's interview with the company officer, Sarah nervously brushed the few minute traces of lint from her black uniform. She wished she were spending her free fifth period some other way, but this meeting was required by regulations. What would he talk about? Like most mids, she kept a safe distance from her company officer.

Let's see. I haven't broken any regs lately. My grades are mediocre. Scored outstanding on the physical fitness test and obstacle course, and my new spring sport is going well.

Two weeks ago Sarah had begun rowing crew, now that gymnastics season was over. At the first crew practice, the coach had tried to persuade her to be a coxswain because of her small stature, but Sarah wasn't interested. She wanted to sweat and learn how to row. Tammy had been rowing since September and had been elected captain of the women's team.

So, the company officer and I should have very little to talk about, Sarah decided. She looked in the mirror, straightening her gig line, ensuring that the edge of her blouse lined up with the edge of her brass belt buckle and the seam in the middle of her trousers. Her hair was looking better. Thank goodness they had hired some women beauticians this year. She placed her grease cover (her best, inspection-quality one) on her head and left her room. The passageways were empty except for the CMOD.

Captain McCormick's office door was open. He glanced up briefly when he heard Sarah approach but turned back to his desk as if he had heard nothing. The clock on the wall read 1359. Her interview was scheduled for 1400. She stood at parade rest beside the company office door, waiting for the clock to tick.

Sarah found Captain McCormick unapproachable. He took everything too seriously. Himself included.

Tick.

Sarah performed a left-face and stood before the office threshold. She knocked and requested permission to come aboard. The captain motioned for her to enter.

She stepped inside, removed her cover, and sounded off. "Midshipman Becker, third class, sir. Good afternoon, sir."

"Good afternoon. Have a seat." He gestured to a wooden armchair in front of his desk.

Sarah sat at attention on its edge and clasped her cover with both hands. She felt like a plebe again.

"How's it going, Miss Becker?" he asked with feigned interest.

"Fine, sir," she replied with a smile, hoping to elicit the same. No response.

"I see you received a 62 on your youngster cruise exam. Not very commendable."

"Uh, yes, sir. I mean, no, sir." Great, she thought. Things are going *well* so far.

"Additionally, your grease for youngster cruise indicates that you were ranked in the lower third on your YP and that you did not seem to take things seriously."

"I believe I did take things seriously, sir, and I enjoyed the cruise as well."

"Then how do you explain your low ranking?"

"I . . . I don't know, sir." He made her feel so uncomfortable. "Maybe I should have worked harder. I mean, I feel like I learned a lot professionally on the cruise. Maybe I just joked around too much."

She couldn't tell him how she really felt. You don't talk to your company officer that way. You don't tell him that you're not looking for stripes or to make a name for yourself. That you're not willing to give up your social life to be number one. That you just want to make it through this place and graduate as one of the few women engineers, hopefully with reasonable grades. He would never understand how you're trying to be "one of the boys" so that they can see that you would make just as good a naval officer as they would. Telling him these things would be professional suicide.

"In the future, I recommend that you act more professional and improve these evaluations."

Great advice, thought Sarah facetiously. "Aye, aye, sir."

Captain McCormick picked up another form.

"This is an academic performance report from your elements-of-materials professor. He ranked you ninth out of eighteen midshipmen. You have a B in the class, and he indicates in the comments section that you maintain a good attitude and appearance, and are quiet. Quiet?!" He looked at the top of the report. "Yes, this chit is for Midshipman Sarah Becker. I just don't believe *quiet* is an adjective I would expect to see to describe you."

"Well, in class I *am* pretty quiet, sir." Sarah never spoke up in class. She wouldn't risk the embarrassment of being wrong or somebody thinking her opinion was ridiculous. Especially in a class full of men. Only if she was absolutely certain that her answer was correct would she ever speak up.

"Class participation can be an important part of your grade. You should try to speak up more."

"Yes, sir."

"One last thing, Miss Becker. I want to know about your relationship with Midshipman, rather, Ensign Nolde."

Sarah panicked. "I don't understand what you want to know, sir," she stalled. Could she be fried for something she had done last year?

"What exactly is your relationship with Ensign Nolde?"

Sarah hoped her shock was not evident on her face. She was scared. Her stomach burned. Did she have to answer this question? What did it have to do with her professional growth and development?

"Mr. Nolde and I are friends, sir."

"You're friends?"

"Yes, sir."

"And what were you last year?"

"We were friends, sir. Mr. Nolde drove me home for Christmas leave." Should she have added that? It was common knowledge and acceptable at the time. At least for the guys.

The captain paused. "Are you dating?"

"Yes, sir. Right now, we are." Oh, please, Lord, don't let him ask me if we were dating last year. Please! I can't lie, but I don't want to tell him. He'll be furious.

The silence was chilling. Sarah could tell by the anger on his face that she had confirmed what he already knew, and that he was trying to decide how far to take this interrogation.

"Very well, that is all. You may go." He turned back to the papers on his desk.

Sarah stood, hoping she didn't appear too anxious to leave. "Request permission to shove off, sir."

"I said you could go."

She placed her cover on her head and exited his office.

He didn't ask! Thank you, Lord! He must have decided that there was nothing to be gained by dragging up the past. Sarah retrieved her books from her room for her sixth-period class and quickly left the company area.

• • •

Sarah and Mick Kuroff were both early for dynamics class and had time to talk.

"Guess what's been going on in our company lately," Mick said. Mick was another systems engineering major whom Sarah found to be a lot of fun.

"What?"

"Well, last week at breakfast a group of plebes sitting at the girls' table got up and left right after they announced 'Brigade, seats.' They didn't even sit down. They just walked back to the company area."

"I don't get it."

"Okay, Collette and Amy, the youngster girls in our company, were supposed to sit with a table of plebes, but the plebes didn't want to sit with them, so they decided to leave. They didn't ask permission to shove off or anything.

"Then Collette and Amy come back to the company area, livid over what the plebes did. They go to the company officer and demand that the plebes get fried to the max and are made to restrict over spring break."

"For what?"

"For disrespect. So, the company officer doesn't know how to handle it and calls in one of our plebes who was prior-enlisted for advice. After talking to this guy, he decides that instead of frying them, he'll make the plebes who did it march for five hours with the prior-enlisted guy in charge."

"Was he one of the ones at the table?"

"No, and needless to say, Collette and Amy are bullshit over this idea. They want nothing less than the plebes restricting over spring break for disrespect. They go to the company officer again, but he doesn't change his mind. They went nuts! I saw them in his office, ranting and raving."

"I still don't get it. Why did the plebes leave?"

"They say the girls are big-time flamers and they hog all the chow. Youngsters aren't supposed to flame on plebes. You know that."

"Yeah, but plebes aren't supposed to disrespect upperclass, either."

"Well, they got punished. Except I heard that when they were out on Red Beach marching, they were actually having a pretty good time. Amy and Collette saw this and were screaming mad again. But there was nothing they could do about it."

"Plebes were having a good time marching?"

"Yeah, they were doing all sorts of fancy maneuvers like the Marine Corps Silent Drill Team. I heard it was pretty funny."

"I guess," remarked Sarah. "Don't you think the whole thing should have been taken a little more seriously, Mick?"

"Nah, those girls are out of control sometimes."

Thursday, 23 March 1978

It was the Thursday before Easter, the start of spring leave. Buddy would be arriving soon to pick Kate up and take her back to Newport, where they would spend four days together in his BEQ (bachelor enlisted quarters) room. Kate, once thrilled that he was coming, was now apprehensive.

Now that she had met guys like Gabe, she wondered if Buddy was her type. He had no concrete plans for his life, even though he would be getting out of the navy in less than seven months. Getting high and riding his motorcycle seemed to be his only goals. Unlike her, he had no drive or dreams, and it didn't matter to him whether she stayed at the Academy or quit.

Kate had made up her mind. It was time to say goodbye to Buddy, and when he met her in the Seventh Wing parking lot, she asked him to walk with her along the sea wall.

An hour later, relief and a sense of maturity surged over Kate as she watched the most carefree part of her life weaving away: Buddy burning rubber in front of Mitscher Hall on his way to Gate One.

Thursday, 11 May 1978

Red Beach was the red-tiled court between Fifth and Sixth Wings where midshipmen were allowed to sunbathe. Regulations dictated that midshipmen wear appropriate swim gear on Red Beach and appropriate athletic gear when walking to and from. Plebe year, the women wore their one-piece navy-issued bathing suits, though in fact they rarely sunbathed, since it was unwise for plebes to appear to have too much time on their hands. Besides, the blue and gold paneled suit with the small red heart on the left bottom leg was something out of the 1940s.

By youngster year, the women braved wearing colorful civilian suits, mimicking upperclass male midshipmen who did the same. Some, including Sarah and Meredith Britain, were even bold enough to wear bikinis.

After fifth period, Sarah met Meredith in her room with a towel and a physics book and waited patiently while Meredith scurried around getting ready.

"Come on, Merry. We only have an hour, then I've gotta go to crew."

"I'm coming, sweetie." Meredith ran to the mirror and dabbed her eyelashes and lips with Vaseline. She never wore mascara. "Okay, ready." She smiled.

The girls skipped downstairs and opened the doors to "the beach," where male midshipmen, spread-eagled on towels, dotted the area. There were no other women.

"You've got magazines?" asked Sarah, noticing the issues of *Woman's Day* and *Mademoiselle* in Meredith's arms. Sarah hadn't read a women's magazine in a long time.

"Yeah. I have a bunch of 'em in my room. You should've grabbed one. What'd you bring to read?"

Sarah held up her physics book and grimaced. "Got a quiz tomorrow."

"Forget it. You can study tonight. Let's lie over here, in the corner. I don't want to get too near the guys. I wore my bikini."

"Me too, you brazen woman." Sarah pulled off her T-shirt and began to slip out of her shorts. Meredith did the same as a catcall came from somewhere inside Sixth Wing.

The girls looked at each other and rolled their eyes. "Oh, please," said Sarah.

"Just pretend you didn't hear them. Don't give them the satisfaction."

Sarah spread her towel on the warm red tiles and glanced up at the five rows of windows in Sixth Wing, wondering where the voyeurs were. Almost instantly she saw them.

"Oh, Meredith. They have binoculars."

"What?!"

"Don't look! Don't look!"

"Why not? If the asses can see me, I want to see them." She looked up, and the guys waved.

"All right, Becker. We're out of here!" Meredith swept up her towel and magazines. "Let's go over by Fifth Wing. Hopefully no perverts live over there. You'd think these guys had never seen girls on the beach before!"

"They probably haven't on this beach. Especially girls in bikinis." Sarah pulled on her T-shirt and followed Meredith.

Face down on their towels, confident that they were no longer under scrutiny, the girls boldly unfastened the hooks of their bathing-suit tops to prevent tan lines. Sarah reached for Meredith's *Woman's Day*.

"Weren't you in one of these magazines before plebe summer?" asked Sarah.

"Yeah. That one."

"I've never seen the article, but I've heard all about it from guys in my company. You're quite a celebrity around the brigade, you know."

"No, I'm not."

"Yes, you are. I heard about you before I ever saw you. The cute blonde from California. I was jealous of you before I'd even seen you."

"Oh, Sarah. How ridiculous!"

"No, I'm serious."

"Well, that article cost me a lot of grief, even though it was fun to do."

"What do you mean?"

"A couple of months before I-Day, my mom saw an article in *Woman's Day* that said if you sent in a picture of yourself with long hair, they would design a hairdo for you. She sent in my picture and explained about my going to the Naval Academy with the first class with women and asked them if they could rush their response because I-Day was only four weeks away.

"The beauty editor wrote right back, all excited because they wanted to do an article on me. They flew me to New York, and for a day I got to be a model. They did my makeup and cut my hair in sort of a pageboy. The whole day was really fun. You know, I was never into watching the Miss America pageant or becoming a model. I was always encouraged to study and go to college. So this was something I would never aspire to do forever, but for one day I felt like a glamour girl. It was really exciting."

"Cool."

"Yeah. You know, it's funny, though, the gist of the article was that my hairdo was intended to be amenable to a work environment, yet in the evening you could curl it and voilà, you'd be out on the town. Like, plebes out on the town? Can you imagine? And the makeup. They put more makeup on me than I've ever worn in my life."

"So what grief did you get?"

"Well, when the story came out, my first class were at my company officer's house for a green light [an impromptu gathering, usually on a weeknight]. His wife had a subscription to *Woman's Day,* and she showed it to them. They came back after taps and were outside my door singing 'Vivacious Merrrredith, vivacious Meredith,' which is how the article described me.

"Then it was up on a lot of the bulletin boards around the battalion with faces drawn over mine and rats crawling all over my face. Things a lot worse than mustaches."

"They drew rats all over *your* face? You're so attractive. People like you. I would think the guys in your company would have been proud of you."

"They weren't. You're really lucky to have such a good company, Sarah. You just don't know. It's so different for me. Most guys in my company despise me."

Sarah could not imagine living day to day in a company intolerant of your presence. Her days of ostracism were over. She had a warm relationship with the guys in Thirty-three.

"It started first semester, plebe year," said Meredith. "One classmate who is so gung-ho it's nauseating was put in the same squad as Erica and I." Erica Tyler was Meredith's ex-roommate.

"Well, Mr. 'Plebe-of-the-Year' was going to become a marine. I don't think he ever missed a rate during plebe summer. In fact, I think the upperclass put him in our squad specifically to make us girls look bad. I always wondered if he had ever even dated a girl. Actually, I think he hated girls. Especially us.

"Anyway, Erica knew her rates pretty well but was sort of drifty, and our other roommate was never interested in her rates. Of the three girls, I knew mine the best, so the upperclass would always pit Mr. 'Plebe-of-the-Year' against me."

"Did you nail him?"

"Sometimes. The point is that there was never any teamwork or camaraderie between us. We never worked on projects together or anything. It was him against us, and a lot of times I felt like it came down to him against me. He still hates me. Erica is the lucky one."

"Why?"

"She got out of our company and into a good one." Erica had been moved to Thirty-fourth Company.

"Why didn't *you* move out?"

"I should have, but I screwed up. Near the end of plebe year, one night when Erica was CMOD, she went down to this first classman's room and was caught with the door closed, sitting on his bed. They were just talking and it was an innocent meeting, but the door was closed. I realize now that they were dating.

"Anyway, my company officer came to me and asked me if I would rather have Erica stay with me in the company or leave. We had both been in quite a bit of trouble throughout the year, and it was obvious that he thought we should be split up. Nothing big, just a bunch of little stuff.

"I told him I thought it would be best overall if we were separated, so she left, but now I think I should have asked to go."

"It doesn't sound like that was an option, Meredith."

"I don't know. I might have been able to convince him. But I felt this loyalty to my company. I still do, in a way. What the heck, just two more years. Besides, we're upperclass now.

"New subject. How's Ryan?"

Ryan was on the other side of the country, training on one of the navy's three prototype reactors. Meredith had known about him and Sarah last year, because she herself had been seeing another first classman on the sly as well. According to Meredith, they rarely snuck out together, but Ryan had often joked about trying to double-date.

"Fine. He's in Idaho at prototype. We went to Ocean City a couple of weekends ago when he finally got some time off. I'm flying out to see him after June Week."

"So you guys are still going strong?"

"Yeah. I mean, I date other people when he's away, but he's still number one." She smiled. "It's an unwritten agreement between us. I know he doesn't really have time to date, but he could if he wanted to, and it's the only way I'll ever know if he's the one, you know?"

"Is he?"

"I don't know. Sometimes I think so, but I'm just not ready for that right now. I really miss him, though. A couple of months ago, during the Dark Ages, I was ready to quit, I missed him so much. I've just got to be patient."

While the girls were talking, the officer of the day had decided to tour Red Beach. As he strolled through the bronze double doors with a male plebe "scribe" at his heels, the two bare-backed women immediately caught his eye.

Sarah's peripheral vision picked up his white uniform. "Sail ho! The OOD," she whispered to Meredith just as the toes of his white shoes slid under her nose.

The lieutenant cleared his throat. "What do you ladies think you're doing?" he asked gruffly.

Both girls hastily reached behind their backs and held their tops in place while shielding their eyes from the sun. Meredith squinted up at his silhouette. "Lying in the sun, sir."

"I can see that, miss. What I want to know is why you have your tops undone."

"We don't want any tan lines, sir," Meredith replied matter-of-factly. Sarah struggled not to laugh.

"And just what would you ladies do if the fire alarm went off right now?"

He *couldn't* be serious! The girls looked at one other and bit their lips.

"Excuse me, sir?" replied Sarah.

"What would you do if the fire alarm went off right now?"

He *was* serious.

"Sir, if the fire alarm went off, we would hook up our bathing-suit tops, put on our athletic gear, and move away from the building," said Meredith.

The OOD paused. "Well, I suggest that you two keep your tops fastened in the future." He turned and walked away, his scribe dutifully following.

"Aye, aye, sir," Sarah replied respectfully, digging her fingernails into Meredith's forearm to keep her from speaking.

Once the OOD was out of earshot, Meredith burst, incredulous. "Can you believe that guy?!"

"No," said Sarah. "But don't let him hear you. I don't want to get fried for disrespect. Isn't it amazing how some guys can't handle our femininity? That's what this was all about, you know. I checked the *MHP* to be sure before we came out: there's no reg that says we have to keep our tops done up when lying on our stomachs. And look at those guys over there with their waist-bands rolled down to their pubic hairs. You think he's going to say anything to them? 'Hey, mister,'" she mimicked. "'What're you going to do if the fire alarm goes off? Be caught with your pants down?'" They both laughed.

"What is it with these guys who can't deal with the fact that we're real girls?" asked Meredith. "They want to keep us in some freak-of-nature category so they can deal with us being here. I only dress like they do and cut my hair like they do because they won't let me graduate if I don't."

"Yeah, but they aren't all like that. Remember the Peeping Toms with the binoculars over in Sixth Wing? They were certainly looking at us as if we were real girls." They laughed again.

The bell rang. Sarah hooked up the back of her top. "Gotta get to crew."

"See ya, Toots," called Meredith, pulling on her gym shorts and T-shirt. "Stop by after study hour."

"Okay, Mer. See you later." Sarah walked briskly toward Eighth Wing. She really liked Meredith. Carrie Freeman and she were her best girlfriends here at school.

SECOND-CLASS YEAR
1978–1979

We were such an unusual mix of women who never got to know one another. We were so afraid of being seen together and labeled a sewing club that we kept our distance. We should have banded together and supported each other.

Female midshipman from the Class of 1980

CHAPTER NINE

Second-Class Summer

During a fast-moving summer, second classmen undertake professional studies at the Naval Academy and receive familiar-
ization training in the four warfare specialties which comprise the
naval service.

United States Naval Academy Catalog, 1976–77

Saturday, 3 June 1978

Kate was in love. Maybe even deep enough for forever. Gabe Leggett was the
best friend she had ever had, and the feeling was mutual. Purely by coincidence,
he called off his engagement at the same time she broke off her relationship with
Buddy. For the past month they had spent every free moment together—studying in Nimitz Library, running along the sea wall, meeting in the Steerage. And
now, during June Week, he asked her to be his date, a situation complicated by
the fact that they both were midshipmen.

Their time together, amid the numerous formations and mandatory scheduled events, was as sporadic as free time during plebe summer. Kate constantly glanced at her watch, unable to relax for more than an hour. Then,
once they were together (always in uniform), there were unsettling stares from
tourists attending the weeklong event, even though the two rarely touched,
mindful of the strict regulation against public display of affection. PDA was
typically overlooked for midshipmen "dragging" civilian dates, but Kate knew
that some mid would love to fry her for PDA, and therefore she insisted that
Gabe and she maintain a professional distance. Gabe told her she was being
paranoid but respected her wishes. Except during the dances.

On Saturday evening, a formal hop for the Classes of '78, '80, and '81 was held behind Mitscher Hall beside the Reflection Pool. Members of the Class of '79 were at their Ring Dance. Dressed in mess dress white, Gabe and Kate slow-danced to Jackson Browne's "Here Come Those Tears Again" played by the hired band.

Leaning her head against his shoulder, Kate squeezed him tightly. Although they had never seriously discussed marriage, they had talked about the future. Both were dedicated to graduating from the Naval Academy and planned on returning after second-class cruise, unlike Kate's roommate, Michelle. Michelle had decided to resign several weeks before June Week to marry a guy from the Class of '77.

After June Week, Kate would begin the first phase of second-class cruise while Gabe would go on leave. He would go on cruise in July and August, when she would be on leave. Gabe had talked her out of switching cruises with a classmate. "Let's just not make waves," he said. "We'll be together again in September."

At the time, Kate had decided he was right. She didn't want any special consideration, especially for something as trivial as a relationship. It wasn't as if she had a special event to attend like a wedding or birthday, which some classmates used as reasons to switch cruise dates. But now, so close to him, she dreaded the separation and wished she had tried to change his mind.

"Hey, Legs!" It was Gabe's nickname. Kate lifted her head.

"Hi, Brian," said Gabe. "Nice night for a hop, huh?"

"Yeah. Nice date, buddy," Brian whispered snidely, loud enough for Kate to hear. She froze. She had guessed that Gabe received ribbing about dating a female midshipman when she wasn't around, but to be this bold, this cruel? Feeling her pull away, Gabe squeezed her tighter.

"Drop it, Brian." His classmate swaggered away with an armful of pink lace and blonde curls.

"I'm sorry, Kate," Gabe whispered. She nodded, unable to respond, knowing that her voice would crack.

"He's wrong, Kate. I have the most beautiful date here." As sweet as they were, his words provided little consolation. This had happened before.

Last spring Gabe and she had been walking down Main Street in Annapolis to Burger King when a pair of mids in a green van drove by screaming obscenities out the window.

"Fuugglyy!! Can't get a real date, huh, pal?"

Neither she nor Gabe dignified the slurs with a reply. Gabe had been so sweet during dinner, trying to assuage the pain of the remarks. Kate had assumed then that the abuse was something she might as well get used to if they were going to continue dating. She just wondered when it was finally going to take its toll on Gabe and he would drop her. Each time it happened, she figured it would be their last time together.

Tonight her solace was shattered again. Sensing her discomfort, he led her to the edge of the Reflection Pool. He sat beside her as she stared despondently back over her shoulder into the colored lights anchored to the pool's bottom. Maybe this was why he didn't want them to go on the same cruise together: he was tired of the abuse. She was afraid to ask.

"Maybe it's time to go," she said softly.

"Do you want to go?"

"No, I *was* having a really good time."

He slid closer to her. "So was I, and I'd like it to continue. I'm not going to let some jerk in my company ruin my evening. Are you?"

She looked down and felt tears stinging her eyes. Thank goodness he could be so strong. She bit her lip and buried her face in his shoulder. Tears streamed.

Gabe held her close. "Hey, babe, I know it's hard, but please try to forget it. He isn't worth it."

"I know," she sniffed. "But I can't help it. What did I ever do to make him say something like that?"

"Nothing. Absolutely nothing. Some guys will just never change their opinions, and that's their problem. Not yours. Please smile and dance with me. Taps is still two hours away, and we can use all of it, since I don't have to drive you home, now that we 'live together.'" He wiggled his eyebrows like Groucho Marx.

Kate laughed, and he wiped the tears from her cheeks. She noticed light brown makeup on the shoulder of his white mess jacket. "I got makeup on your jacket. Sorry."

"Hey, I'm sure the press shop has seen it before. Now, if they saw some on *your* jacket they might have cause to worry." She laughed again. He was right. She shouldn't let cruel individuals get to her. She was so lucky to have him.

Kate's commitment to her education and career was sealed when she spent the weekend before her second-class cruise with her family in Virginia. After twenty-five years of marriage, her parents, she now learned, were on the verge of divorce. Interested in another woman, her father was moving to Oregon, and in an attempt to pull her life back together her mother was finishing her teaching degree. The shock that a marriage that had survived twenty-five years could be so fragile convinced Kate that despite her deep love for Gabe, for the moment she was prepared to commit to only one person: herself.

Monday, 3 July 1978

Second-class cruise provides specialized education and a two-phase, in-depth indoctrination in naval warfare subspecialties for midshipmen beginning their third year at the Naval Academy.

One phase, PROTRAMID, Professional Training of Midshipmen, lasts four weeks and transports second-class midshipmen to each of the four warfare-specialty capitals for one week of indoctrination: to Quantico, Virginia, for introduction to the Marine Corps; to Pensacola, Florida, for naval aviation training; to Norfolk, Virginia, for surface fleet training; and to New London, Connecticut, for introduction to the submarine service, to include a short cruise on board a nuclear-powered submarine. This year, though, because of USC 6015 prohibiting women from sea assignments, the women midshipmen would not go to New London. Instead, they would participate in a one-week special training program that would place them with a female junior officer "running-mate" in one of the navy's shore commands.

The other phase, ACTRAMID, Academic Training of Midshipmen, comprises a weeklong public-speaking course and a week of operations and tactics classes, followed by a two-week cruise to Philadelphia and Norfolk on the YPs.

At Quantico, the marines bullied the mids through an abbreviated form of basic training, culminating with an overnight ambush-and-assault exercise. Sarah had never been bitten by so many bugs, but she enjoyed the physical challenges of the marines and impressed several second lieutenants with her ability to complete their arduous obstacle course, including the rope climb.

Pensacola, home to naval aviators, introduced the midshipmen to the exciting blend of adventure and unabashed amusement so characteristic of those flying desperadoes. This was the job Sarah wanted. Her excitement mounted as the midshipmen were briefed on the prerequisites for accompanying a jet pilot in his A-4 Skyhawk.

Each midshipman was fitted for a "G-suit" and helmet, and had to fit into an ejection seat. Sarah did not. She, one other woman, and an Asian male classmate were "grounded" from flying jets for being too short. Sarah was devastated. The instructors rechecked their measurements, but her knee-to-hip measurement was too short, and her legs wouldn't reach the rudders. Trying to hide her disappointment, she jokingly asked to be allowed to strap two-by four-inch blocks onto the rudders, since she only needed an inch more to reach. The more serious problem, the instructors informed her, was her inability to fit properly into the ejection seat. If she should ever have to eject, it would probably break her back.

Sarah resolved to find a plane she could fit into. Helicopters were definitely out. Yesterday she had almost crashed the 'copter because of her lack of depth perception. She couldn't tell how far away the ground was, forcing the instructor to grab the stick from her. The same had happened last year when Tammy and she went sky-diving. By the time she realized she was near the ground, her knees had already been shoved into her chest by the impact.

With both her size and her lack of depth perception working against her, Sarah's chances of becoming a pilot began to look dismayingly slim. There has to be a way to get a waiver, she told herself. This is just a temporary setback.

Her hopes were elevated when she took to the air in the back seat of a pro-peller-driven T-34 trainer. In an olive drab flight suit and with a parachute strapped to her back, she cradled her helmet under her arm, walking toward the plane and pilot that would take her skyward. The pilot had a disenchanted look, leaving Sarah to wonder if his indifference stemmed from the fact that she was a midshipman, a girl, or both.

They flew around for an hour and a half, looping and diving, which at one point caused her to experience tunnel vision as her body "pulled two G's," enduring twice the force of normal gravity. She loved it. Soaring through the billowing clouds, she felt a sense of freedom mixed with power that she wanted to experience routinely.

Her aspirations were not even dashed by the news that greeted her when the T-34 landed on a practically deserted airfield. Sarah walked to the hanger where a surge of classmates, led by Carrie Freeman, engulfed her.

"Thank God you're back!" Carrie cried.

"Why? What's wrong?"

"A T-34 just spun out and crashed! We thought it was you!"

"Oh, great." Sarah felt the blood rush from her face. "Did they—"

Before she could finish, her pilot walked up. "No, the pilot and student both ejected safely. We must have been out of radio range and didn't hear the recall of aircraft. Well, you take it easy. You did good." He headed toward the back of the hanger.

"Thank you, sir. And thanks for the flight." He replied with a thumbs-up without looking back.

The choice Sarah would make on service-selection night was clear. Navy air, sir!

Indoctrination for the surface navy took place in Norfolk. Midshipmen toured the Fleet Combat Training Center at Dam Neck and the mock-up amphibious-assault display at Little Creek. The presence of the women midshipmen elicited a variety of stares from the enlisted men they encountered—most of them curious, some suggestive.

At 0700 midweek, the male midshipmen mustered beside a gray government bus in the BOQ (bachelor officers' quarters) parking lot. Opposite them, thirty female midshipmen mustered separately, the two groups slated for different destinations.

The women stood at parade rest, in two platoons, waiting for the plan of the day to be read. Sarah stood beside Carrie.

"Wonder what exciting tours they'll have for us today?" she whispered facetiously. Carrie grinned and said nothing.

"This is really bullshit, you know. How come the guys get to go on a ship and we don't? It's only for the day." Sarah was angry. The male midshipmen were going to sea on a guided-missile cruiser to watch a missile shoot. The women, no doubt, were bound for another boring tour.

"Title 10, Sarah," Carrie whispered. "No women allowed on combatants."

"Bullshit! They let women go on dependents' cruises [day cruises where sailors' families are taken out for a ride on the ship]. What's the difference? We're midshipmen, for Pete's sake!"

There was no difference. There was only the law excluding women from combatant duty, which the navy used as an excuse not to send female midshipmen to sea for the day. What if the ship was called to war in the middle of the one-day deployment? Why, it would have to come all the way back to port to drop them off. It would be an unnecessary hindrance to operations.

"Detail, atten-hut!" ordered the lieutenant. "Today you will be taken on a tour of several tenders here in Norfolk." The women groaned. More ship tours? Worse yet, tours on ships with no weapons systems, noncombatants. Another flying bridge. Another engine room. Another bilge. They all looked the same, and the girls had seen enough between YP cruise last year and visiting ships in the Yard back at the Naval Academy. They wanted to get under way.

"Let's go, ladies! Load 'em up!" the lieutenant barked.

"This stinks," said Sarah, climbing onto the bus.

Seven hours later, the women departed the last of three tender brows (gangplanks), bored and disgusted, cognizant of the fact that if women were ever assigned to ships, tenders would be the first to become coed.

"Hey, it's only 1400," said Carrie, standing among a group of fifteen female midshipmen on the pier beside a submarine tender. "Look, the guys aren't back yet." She pointed to a pier two down from theirs.

"Let's go meet 'em!" called Sarah.

"Let's!" agreed another woman.

The group wandered over to the cruiser's berthing area and waited for the arrival of the warship carrying their male counterparts. Forty minutes later, the sleek gray combatant docked at the pier, and a crane dropped the brow into place. The women were eager to hear about the missile shoot they had missed.

A small male form appeared at the top of the gangplank. Sarah thought he looked too small to be a classmate, and he was dressed in blue, not khaki. Behind him twelve more small forms appeared, and immediately the female midshipmen realized that these males were about ten years old. Boys?! Sarah did a double take. Young boys were bouncing down the gangplank. Cub Scouts! She looked at Carrie, who shook her head slowly.

"What in the hell were *they* doing on board?" Carrie cried. "A bunch of little *boys* can go see a missile shoot, but we can't?!" She gestured wildly as she spoke.

"You've got to be kidding me! You have *got* to be kidding me!" Sarah was flabbergasted. "How do they get away with this?!"

"Unbelievable! Friggin' unbelievable!" raged a female classmate beside her.

"Hey, we weren't supposed to see this, remember? We should have still been touring some bullshit tender," replied Carrie. "Man, this time they've gone too far. It's time to talk to the commander."

The commander had no explanation. The male mids had also questioned him as to why the women hadn't been allowed to come along.

"I can't answer you," replied the PROTRAMID officer in charge. He perched on a desk in the middle of the BOQ lobby, the female midshipmen encircling him like a tribe viewing their victim tied to the stake. "It was a bad call."

"A bad call?! Sir, that just isn't good enough." Carrie was respectfully direct, and Sarah envied her nerve. "This was a slap in the face. The administration takes Cub Scouts more seriously than female midshipmen."

"Look, Carrie, all I can say is that this trip was planned months ago. It had already been arranged for you girls to visit the tenders. Those Cub Scouts may have been invited to go at the last minute. It was probably an oversight."

"I guess I don't buy that, sir." Sarah couldn't believe she was speaking back to an officer. "I think they got caught. We weren't supposed to be waiting on the pier. We weren't supposed to know that those kids were on board."

The commander had no response. After a few seconds of silence, he spoke. "I'm very sorry this happened, ladies. But at this point there is no way to correct the situation. I will relay the faux pas to the administration when we get back to the Academy, and hopefully nothing like this will happen again."

"It shouldn't have happened in the first place," replied a woman next to Sarah.

"Enough!" called the commander. "It's over. Time for the next evolution. You are dismissed!"

The women sauntered from the room, unappeased.

"They'll never take us seriously," said Sarah.

"Yes, they will," said Carrie. "Someday they will."

"Yeah. Right after we get back from D.C. while the guys go on submarines in New London."

During the fourth and final week of PROTRAMID, the male midshipmen spent three days under way on a nuclear submarine out of New London. Submarines were the last all-male bastion that women would be allowed to infiltrate. Consequently, the Naval Academy administration had devised an alternative training week for female midshipmen.

Teamed with female officers stationed in Washington, D.C., the women midshipmen worked beside their "running-mates" to observe billets open to women in the navy. Most of them were administrative.

Sarah's running-mate was an ensign who worked in the communications center of the Pentagon. After three hours on her first day of following her run-ning-mate back and forth from her office to the message center to pick up message traffic, Sarah knew what she would absolutely *never* do in the navy. In Sarah's opinion, this woman officer was a glorified message sorter.

Midweek, she was introduced to another female officer who worked with satellites and gave top-secret briefings to the chief of naval operations. She showed Sarah several of the high-tech rooms where she performed her brief-ings. Things seemed to be looking up until this woman told them that she was currently sitting on the Navy's Uniform Board, which was revising women's uniforms. Over lunch in the center courtyard of the Pentagon, the lieutenant boasted about her recommendation to the uniform board that all the new pants for women include pant liners.

Pant liners? Sarah couldn't believe what she was hearing. She wasn't even sure she knew what pant liners were.

"They're a slip for pants," explained the lieutenant. "Then you won't be able to see through the white ones, and the black and khaki ones won't have to be made of such heavy fabric. They'll hang much better."

Sarah was aghast. What could be more impractical? Pant liners sounded like something out of the forties. Please, let there be another woman on the board, she thought. Someone out of the seventies. No wonder they had had such trouble getting women's khakis designed last year.

Last summer Sarah and a number of other female classmates had been issued several different sets of test khakis for women to wear on cruise. Sarah had liked the design of one shirt in particular, which had sewn-in military creases. The trousers were pocketless in the back and were more flattering to a female figure than the men's trousers they had originally been issued. A lot of the women found them impractical because of the lack of pockets, how-ever. The final design was pant-liner-less, pocketless khaki slacks.

At the end of the week in Washington, the female midshipmen attended an outbrief with a senior navy admiral who encouraged them to take advan-tage of the numerous opportunities open to women in the navy. "No, women are not allowed on ships yet, but we're working on it," he said. "Someday women will serve on some navy ships."

Someday. Some ships. The girls were disheartened. If a man of this rank was only at the "someday" stage, shipboard life for women was years away. The girls were glad this week was over. Most were disappointed in the jobs they had been assigned.

"We're not pursuing the rigors of the Naval Academy to end up as glorified paper pushers," they agreed, though deep down they were afraid that this was exactly what awaited them in the fleet.

Monday, 31 July 1978

On Monday morning the second classmen began suffering through the in-class phase of ACTRAMID, with a week each of speech classes and operations and tactics. Sarah was rooming with Marcia McCall, the same roommate as last summer's YP cruise. Marcia was moving up in the striper world. The announcement of her selection as second-class battalion commander at an evening meal last spring had elicited a chorus of boos from the brigade. It did not matter that they had announced her as M. McCall, excluding her first name. The men knew she was a woman and reacted badly.

Ryan wrote every four days from the Idaho prototype-reactor site. Sarah had spent a week with him in June. He'd had only three of the seven days off, so Sarah worked on her tan and practiced running for a five-kilometer race. On his days off, they went camping.

He had orders to report to the USS *Nimitz* next March, after attending Surface Warfare Officers School in Newport, Rhode Island. Ryan was ready to be out of school and part of the real navy. Sarah was happy for him but knew that the *Nimitz* was scheduled for a six-month deployment. This long-distance relationship had already proved trying. Would it survive an entire deployment?

The underway phase of ACTRAMID began on 14 August 1978. An even gender mix of twenty midshipmen cruised the Intracoastal Waterway, practicing shipboard tactics on their way to the Philadelphia Naval Shipyard. There they fought fires at the navy's firefighting school for the second summer in a row. Veteran midshipmen from last year's YP cruise eagerly allowed their unseasoned classmates to don the metallic firefighting suits in the sweltering summer heat first.

Sarah relished the camaraderie among classmates. All second-class midshipmen had to go on this YP cruise, so there was no dissension among the ranks as there had been last summer. Each boat worked as a team. Carrie's YP, of which she was the senior midshipman, selected the "Theme from Star Wars" as their breakaway song. They played a laughing box over the radio whenever one of the YPs messed up during tactics. Their officer in charge, Lieutenant Stark, was really cool.

Carrie told Sarah that Lieutenant Stark had let them have a ceremonial burial at sea for their PQS books, Personnel Qualification Standards, the practical factors they were supposed to learn on the cruise. In fact they never really finished any of them, Carrie said; the mids on her boat just put them all on a board and slid them into the water. Even so, their boat won the "E" award for excellence, since they had performed best during tactics and maneuvers. They were crazy on that YP, and Sarah was jealous. That was her kind of boat.

Friday, 25 August 1978

At the Little Creek Amphibious Base, the Officers Club hosted a barbecue dinner for the midshipmen to celebrate the completion of summer cruise. One hundred and twenty mids loaded plates with hickory-smoked chicken, ribs, potato salad, beans, and plastic cups of cold beer filled from several kegs. Carrie and Sarah shared a table with other mids inside the air-conditioned club. Although it was almost sundown, the outside temperature was over 90.

Gnawing on a chicken bone, Sarah glanced outside and noticed the O'Club swimming pool beyond a stone patio. "Hey, Carrie. Check it out." She nodded toward the pool.

"Think it's open?" asked Carrie.

"I think there's only one way to find out," replied Sarah, wiping her mouth with a napkin. She carried her plate to the trash can. Carrie followed.

Approaching the aqua and white chain-link fence, the girls saw that the pool was closed.

"Man, I could really go for a swim," said Sarah, peering through the fence slats.

"Me, too," said Carrie. "Maybe we could climb the fence." She walked around the corner by the locker rooms.

"You think anyone would see us?" asked Sarah.

"Not if we climb here." The O'Club was not visible from where they stood. Sarah smiled. "Let's do it!"

The girls left their shorts and shirts in a pile on the concrete deck near the women's shower room and slipped into the pool in bras and panties. Gently treading water, Sarah floated toward Carrie. "Is this great, or what?!" she cried. She leaned back, spread her arms, and let the water support her.

"Hey, Carrie, think this is breaking and entering?"

Carrie chuckled. "I don't know. We didn't really break in. We climbed over and slid in."

"Yeah," laughed Sarah, "and we won't stay long. When did you start swimming, Carrie?"

"When I was five. My mom just threw me into the pool, and I pretty much started swimming on my own."

"Have you always been an All-American?"

"Pretty much."

"What do you mean? You were the incredible one-woman team at Easterns plebe year. I remember being so impressed when those guys carried you through the wardroom."

"Yeah, well, unfortunately you can't qualify for All-American at Easterns. I needed to qualify at the AIWA Nationals, which took place several weeks after Easterns."

"So, did you?"

"No. I couldn't because the Naval Academy didn't register as an active member of the AIWA, so I was ineligible to compete. They registered as an inactive member."

"I don't get it," said Sarah, rolling over to perform scissor kicks to exercise her thighs. Her uniforms were feeling a little snug.

"See, for me to compete in Nationals, the Academy had to be registered as an active member of the AIWA. I specifically asked the commandant and Lieutenant Robertson at that all-woman sports meeting at the beginning of the summer if the Academy planned to pay the $1,500 fee to become an active member of the AIWA. This had happened to me once before when my high school didn't register. The two of them assured me that they would. But they didn't.

"They registered the Academy as an inactive participant, I guess, because it didn't cost anything, and they must have figured they didn't have any women good enough to compete that year."

"How could they not have known after Easterns?"

"They had to register long before Easterns. But just before I came to the Academy, I had the fourth best time in the country in the individual medley, and the seventh best time in the butterfly. They told me they would take care of it, and I just assumed they would."

"Gee, Carrie, I'm sorry to hear that."

"Yeah. Another thing, the AAU Senior National Swimming Championships were held in August of plebe summer. I qualified to swim in them in March of my senior year. But when I came to plebe summer, I didn't discuss attending them with my coach because I thought that by coming to the Academy, I had given up my opportunity to go. Now looking back, I think my coach should have taken the steps to get me there. He's the one who recruited me."

"You were recruited?" asked Sarah. "I didn't know any of us girls were recruited."

Carrie blushed. "Actually, I think I'm the only one recruited for a sport. The crew coach told me that at the beginning of plebe summer. I remember getting a couple of letters from the head swim coach, but I don't remember being actively recruited.

"Anyway, the reason I was so pissed about missing AAU Nationals is that I found out the week they took place that a football player in Eleventh Company had been allowed to go home to play in his state championship football game. Can you imagine? A state football game! Here I was, nationally ranked, missing a really important meet. Man, was I pissed—probably as much at myself as at my coach. I guess I could have asked to go, but I just figured since I was going through plebe summer I was quarantined."

An angry voice from behind the fence startled the girls. "Hey! What are you two mids doing in there?"

The girls spun toward one another in alarm.

"Oh, shit!" whispered Carrie. "What do we do?" mouthed Sarah.

Carrie shrugged and pointed to their pile of clothes half the length of the pool away.

Sarah understood and sucked in a deep breath. She slid underwater and headed for the side of the pool. Thank goodness for swim class. She had failed to swim the width of the pool underwater the first time and had been required to join the remedial swim class. It wasn't until the instructor told her that his three-year old daughter could do it that she was embarrassed into swimming the thirty yards underwater.

Carrie, of course, beat Sarah to the other side of the pool. The girls clung to the edge and glanced toward the fence where the voice originated. Through the slats they could make out two figures. One began to climb the fence.

"Hey, Carrie! It's only me. Dave!"

Carrie let out a sigh of relief. "Jesus, Dave! You gave us a heart attack!"

Dave Sher was a teammate from the swim team. "Hey, this is great!" he cried, surveying the empty pool. His cohort climbed over beside him. "Move over, girls, we're coming in!"

"Do it quietly," called Sarah. "We don't want to get caught!" Then she and Carrie glanced at one another and looked down at their half-dressed bodies. "Listen, you guys, we're in our underwear, so don't go stripping down to nothing, okay?"

"Oh, come on, girls. We'll show you ours if you show us yours!"

"Shut up, you guys, and get in the water. Quietly!" scolded Sarah. "You're gonna get us caught."

No sooner were the words out of her mouth than another group of three male and two female midshipmen appeared on the other side of the fence. "Swim call!" cried one. "Let's do it!" yelled another.

Within ten minutes almost the entire barbecue had relocated to the pool. Even two lieutenants joined them. Mids performed half-gainers off the high dive in their underwear. Two mids did surface dives, mooning each other on the way under. It was a full-fledged pool party! "If they won't open for us, we'll open it ourselves," someone rationalized. "They can't arrest us all. Right?"

Everyone left on skivvies, despite pleading by most of the males for the women to go skinny-dipping. None would, so the sides of the pool were dotted with piles of top-layer-only clothing. Sarah and Carrie stood modestly in the four-foot section of the pool, only their heads visible above water. "Man, Carrie. Look what we started!"

"Somehow I think we're going to get caught," replied Carrie, surveying the bedlam.

"Carrie, look!" Sarah pointed toward the high dive. "Is that? . . . It can't be. . . ."

"It is!" cried Carrie as Lieutenant Stark flew off the high dive, spread-eagled, his boxer shorts flapping against his thighs.

"It's out of control!" whispered Sarah. "We're all dead."

Then she heard the sirens.

"Let's get outta here!" Sarah and Carrie swam to the other side of the pool to their clothes. As they scampered out of the pool, the bullhorn blared.

"All right, everybody out of the pool! We have you surrounded!"

Carrie and Sarah froze as bedlam broke loose. Mids raced from the pool. Girls screamed and everyone frantically searched for their clothes in the dusk.

Sarah found hers, but someone had already grabbed Carrie's. She, in turn, grabbed someone else's pants and pulled them on. It was everybody for themselves. Sarah clambered over the fence and ran for cover, of which there was very little.

She hid behind a small bush and heard a "pssst" behind her. Dave Sher was hiding ten feet beyond her behind a bigger bush. Bent in half, she scurried beside him, and the two watched through the leaves as midshipmen leaped the pool fence and ran to escape base security. Some were successful; others were loaded into the base paddy wagon.

Carrie sat on the hard bench in the paddy wagon and tried to remember whose idea it had been to go swimming. She reached into the pocket of the pants she was wearing and pulled out a green military ID card. It wasn't hers. It belonged to a guy from the Class of '79 on her boat who was making up the cruise he had missed the year before.

"All right, miss. Let's have your ID card," called a security officer from the rear of the wagon.

"Sir, I don't have mine," she told him.

"Come on, miss. Don't play games with me. We're gonna find out who you are one way or another. Hand it over."

"Really, sir. These aren't my clothes. Someone else has mine with my ID card in them. See?" She handed him the ID card. He shook his head and moved on to the next mid. She smiled, thinking of the guy who had her ID card.

Back in the bushes, Sarah and Dave watched as the paddy wagon full of mids pulled away. Their sighs of relief were short-lived, though, for a white government sedan pulled up and the front door opened.

"Oh, shit!" cried Dave. "It's probably the base CO." They crouched lower behind the bush.

Sarah peered from behind a leaf and saw Lieutenant Stark standing beside the driver's door.

"Hey, guys! It's me, Lieutenant Stark. Let's go!"

The two crawled from behind the bush and ran toward the white car. As they did, four other classmates slid from their hiding spots.

"Let's get out of here!" called Lieutenant Stark, waving them in. "I'll drop you guys off at the boats, and then I've got to go down to security and bail out the rest."

· · ·

Steaming toward Annapolis, the flotilla of YPs executed their tactical maneuvers with precision. The laughing box never went off. Midshipmen worked as a team, and a spirit of camaraderie prevailed. The guys accepted the women, socially and professionally.

Everyone was exonerated of the charges of breaking and entering the pool the night before, although rumor had it that the lieutenants who had joined them were in deep trouble. As the YPs pulled away from shore, the officer in charge of PROTRAMID waved goodbye from the pier. He was not riding back with the flotilla, as he had an appointment with the commanding officer and head of base security to "discuss" the previous night's debauchery. Sarah got ready to take in the lines on her boat and saw him shake a finger good-naturedly at Carrie, who was standing officer of the deck on the flying bridge of her YP. Carrie knew the commander well.

"I know you instigated this, Freeman. I know you were involved somehow. I'm going get you for this," he called, as she ordered the mooring lines to be taken in. Carrie smiled and waved. She glanced over at Sarah and grimaced. Had they heard the end of this?

Far from land, Lieutenant Stark's YP ran a line hung with boxer shorts, panties, and brassieres from the masthead to the bow of their YP as a memorial to the night before. Mids aboard all boats cheered from the weather decks.

We can work together as equals, Sarah thought. One on one, or in groups like this, they accept us. But will these bonds be strong enough to overcome the prejudice of the entire brigade?

CHAPTER TEN

Second-Class Academic Year

Following summer leave, as the second class midshipmen return to the Academy to begin their third academic year, still greater military responsibilities become theirs. Midshipmen officers are selected and trained to direct the Brigade during periodic absences of the first class. An important role in the indoctrination of the new fourth class is undertaken by the second class. In addition to contributing to the development of the fourth classmen, this responsibility makes a vital contribution to the second classmen's growth as leaders. There is little time for watching the calendar. And, before long, another June Week has come and gone, and first class year is under way.

United States Naval Academy Catalog, 1976–77

Thursday, 7 September 1978

Second-class year—junior year, at any other college. Only two more years until graduation. Kate could hardly believe it. Standing at parade rest at Thursday noon meal formation, she waited for her company officer to finish inspecting Second Platoon. Hers was next.

Eyes in the boat, she stared at the black cotton back of the company mate in front of her and pondered the commitment she had made by mustering the first day of this academic year. That act made the navy a career for all members of her class, either as an officer for those completing the next two years or as an enlisted person in the fleet for any who opted out early. Anyone resigning from the Academy from this point on incurred an obligation of several years as an enlisted man in the navy. Kate would never consider resigning. She wanted to be a naval officer, a surface-line officer.

Lying in ditches swatting bugs at Quantico had convinced her that she did not want to be a marine, even though she recalled telling some newspaper reporter during one of her numerous interviews that she did. It had sounded so gung-ho at the time. Submarines, of course, were off limits to women, and her poor eyesight disqualified her from flying jets. She refused to become an NFO, a naval flight officer, the number two position in an aircraft. She would be in charge of the plane or not fly at all.

Her week in Washington, D.C., had convinced her that she was not going to waste her time at USNA to become a paper-pusher. She wanted to do something that her male counterparts could do. She wanted to drive ships.

The last night after flight indoctrination at Pensacola, Kate had gone to a pool party thrown by a Class of 1978 grad going through flight training who was dating a woman of '80. The party lasted all night, and Kate, uncharacteristically, got absolutely drunk. She was awed by one of the other girls there, a classmate who had a deep tan and a slim figure poured into a strapless green sundress. Annette Reason's jet black pageboy curled gently below the nape of her neck, just violating the year-old regulation allowing women to grow their hair to the bottom of their collars instead of the top. Hoping to look half as attractive as Annette, Kate recklessly dyed her hair black after the party, and the summer sun immediately turned it orange. Gabe chewed her out for the change, reminding her that he liked her the way she was. What a mess! Her natural dark brown roots were just now starting to overtake the orange.

"Platoon, atten-hut!" Kate snapped to attention with the rest of the platoon and watched her company officer inspect the squad in front of her. When he arrived at the midshipman beside her, she sucked in her stomach and pulled back her shoulders.

Lieutenant Willard had relieved Lieutenant Griffith during youngster summer. Lieutenant Willard paid much less attention to Kate than Lieutenant Griffith had done.

He started at her cover and scrutinized every inch of her uniform. "How are classes, Miss Brigman?"

"Fine, sir." Classes were easier now that she had switched from "double E" to general engineering, although she did not like the major any better. She had decided that it was better to focus on the results of her education rather than on the education itself. She tried to make herself believe that graduation was the important thing, and not being number one, but that train of thought seemed so foreign to her, and so disappointing.

"Looks like you've lost some weight, Miss Brigman. Keep it up." Lieutenant Willard pressed his lips together in a mock grin and moved on.

Kate was elated. Someone had noticed! It meant so much and gave her further resolve to lose more. Eleven more pounds, down to one-twenty-five. Then she might be satisfied with herself. At least with her physical appearance.

Monday, 2 October 1978

Sarah and Tammy were assigned taps-taking duty the first week in October. They picked up the midshipman rosters at the mate's desk.

"Confirmed my plane reservation to Newport today," said Sarah happily. "I can't wait."

"How is Ryan?" asked Tammy.

"Fine. Says SWOS is a piece of cake compared to nuke school. Although it's cold as heck up there in Newport. I pick up my ticket Friday and I'm out of here Saturday at 1300. Won't be back till Monday afternoon." Sarah was expending one of the five "weekends" second classmen were rationed during the semester to spend the Columbus Day holiday with Ryan at Surface Warfare Officers School.

"And I have duty," replied Tammy, meaning she had to remain in Bancroft Hall the entire weekend. "Oh, well, we have crew practice every day, anyway."

The girls split up to ensure that all midshipmen second class and below in Thirty-third Company were present in the company area. Sarah took the front shaft. Tammy began with the middle.

As taps-takers, the girls were required to physically see an individual before reporting him present. If a mid went to bed early, they had to knock on the door, open it, turn on the light, and physically see him in bed before marking him present.

Sarah knocked on a door, cracked it open, and called "Taps!" She marked both occupants present after visually ensuring that they were there. Three doors later, she arrived at a door to a dark room. It belonged to two youngsters Sarah knew and liked well who were known for being a couple of cutups. Asleep, she assumed and gently knocked. Receiving no response, she cracked the door and peeked in, observing the shadowy outline of two figures on their racks. She quickly switched on the lights and immediately retreated from the room, gasping at the sight that had greeted her. Both third classmen were stretched out naked on their racks. Hearing her gasp, they burst into laughter, and Sarah couldn't help but do the same.

"You guys are sick!" she yelled to the closed door.

Tammy walked around the corner. "What's going on?"

"See for yourself." Sarah cracked the door to the exhibitionists' room.

Tammy peered around its edge. "Oh, my *God!*" she cried. "Youngsters!" She looked at Sarah, and they both burst into laughter.

Sarah caught her breath long enough to crack the door one last time. "It's the *little* things that make life so interesting around here. Come on, Tam. I have a weapons lab due tomorrow."

Tuesday, 7 November 1978

It lay on the desk of every female midshipman—an official memorandum from the Naval Academy's director of professional development:

6 Nov 1978
MEMORANDUM

From: Director of Professional Development
To: Midshipman Second Class Sarah Becker, USN, 33rd Company
Subj: Latest information on career patterns and assignments for
     women officers
Encl: (1) Women Officers At Sea
     (2) 110X Women Officer Career Development

1. Enclosures (1) and (2) are forwarded to you as the latest career planning information available.

2. I expect to have a list of officer assignments in the next two weeks which will show you typical billets which will probably be available for your choice when service selection occurs for the Class of 1980 (about January 1980). I hasten to add that these will be "sample" billets. No one knows at this point what assignments will be available to you in January 1980. These decisions will be made and adjusted several times before that date by the Chief of Naval Personnel. However, without doubt you and your classmates will be able to pick some number of ship billets and aviation billets (in some "fair share" arrangement with NROTC/OCS—as yet undetermined) and among several naval officer career "designators" (i.e., such as 1110 [Surface], 1310 [Aviation], and 1140 [Special Operations—salvage & diving and explosive ordnance disposal]). In all probability, some Restricted Line and Staff billets will be open for you but that

is a "guess" not a "fact" at this point. Of course, there will be important and challenging MOS's [Military Occupational Specialties] in the Marine Corps for which you will be eligible. The policy which will determine how many of your class may select which warfare specialty or the U.S. Marine Corps is yet to be determined but will be specified in the Service Selection letter for the Class of 1980 (to be issued about November 1979).

3. When the billet list reaches my office, I will schedule a career planning meeting with you and your classmates to pass out the "sample" assignments. At that time I'll answer any questions that you have concerning the two enclosures to this memorandum or about any related subject. However, if in the meantime you have questions you would like to get answers to, contact my office at Extension 2570.

Respectfully,
RICHARD C. USTICK
Captain, U.S. Navy

Sarah read it quickly and perused the enclosures. With enactment of the fiscal year 1979 Authorization Bill, Title 10 had been amended to allow the navy to commence assignment of female officer and enlisted personnel to shipboard duty on board hospital ships (of which there were currently none), navy transports, and certain other auxiliaries that did not normally perform a combat mission. Female aviators might also, for the first time, perform non-combatant flight duties involving the landing of aircraft aboard ships at sea.

Of course, because of the limited number of non-combat-related sea billets available, only a limited number of unrestricted line (URL) women would be able to elect warfare careers, which would be distributed among the various officer accession programs: Officer Candidate School, NROTC, and the Naval Academy. Approximately 80 to 85 percent of URL women entering the navy each year would continue to follow the 110X non-warfare-career progression, i.e., administrative types, paper-pushers. Enclosure two of the memorandum was five pages long and detailed the career development of the 110X woman officer.

This doesn't pertain to me, thought Sarah, tossing the well-intentioned memorandum into the bottom drawer of her desk. I'm not busting my butt at this place for four years just to go sit behind some desk and supervise the filing clerks in a personnel department. Whatever it takes, I'm gonna be one of the 15 to 20 percent, and I'm going to fly.

The possibility that all of her fifty-four female classmates might feel the same never crossed her mind.

Kate read the memorandum, and her heart leaped. They're finally opening up ships to women! Besides Gabe, surface line was her first love. Now she just had to keep her grades up to ensure that she maintained a high enough class standing that she might be one of the first women to select ships. The pressure was on.

Thursday, 16 November 1978

Tammy was already in their room eating a bag of cookies, drinking a diet soda, and listening to Fleetwood Mac when Sarah returned from noon meal.

"You got back early," remarked Sarah, throwing her cover onto her desk. "Got a test this afternoon?"

"Oh, Sarah, I hate this place! Sometimes I absolutely hate this place!"

"What's wrong, Tammy? What happened?"

Tammy shook her head, obviously distraught. "I came back early from lunch because I was absolutely grossed out."

"What happened?"

"Well, there weren't enough seats at our table for lunch. So instead of making our plebes or youngsters roam—remember how you hated doing that?—well, I said I would roam [find a seat at another table]. I couldn't find a seat with our company, so I went to another one. I don't even know which company it was, but there weren't any other girls at this table.

"The firsties told me I could have a seat, and while we were waiting for announcements, one of them picked up the jar of peanut butter and opened it. His eyes lit up when he saw it was a new jar, and he passed it to one of the plebes and asked him if he knew how to rig it.

"Well, I can't believe that I'm hearing this—that this guy had the nerve to ask a plebe to rig the peanut butter in front of me. I know he did it on purpose to see how I'd react."

"Oh, Tam," Sarah remarked sympathetically, "you've got to be kidding. Did he rig it?"

"No, he didn't know what the firstie was talking about, so some third classman volunteered to teach him—out loud."

Sarah remembered the first time she had been told about rigging the peanut butter. Kurt Loper had been asked to do it plebe summer when forced to roam to another company's table. Back in their rooms, after incessant begging from her, he described the procedure to her. She wished she hadn't begged so hard. To rig the peanut butter, one used jelly, ground pepper, and a butter knife to make the smooth surface of a new jar of peanut butter look like a vulva.

"I just stood there stunned," continued Tammy. "As soon as he began, I grabbed my cover and left. I didn't even wait for announcements, almost hoping I'd get fried for leaving early so I could tell someone why I left."

"That's so sick, Tam! I'm really sorry."

"You know what, Sarah? I was going to start eating a balanced diet today and get some of this weight off. Now here I am eating cookies again." Tammy had been battling her weight since I-Day. "It's so disheartening."

"You'll do it, Tam. You know, I just can't believe that we've been here for three years and they're still pulling stuff like that."

"It's going to take much longer than that for some of them to change," replied Tammy. She shivered. "It makes me so angry. I wish I could have done something about it. But I was so angry and embarrassed."

"You did the right thing, Tammy."

"I just feel like I let them get to me, though, you know?"

"I know. Just try to forget about it. We'll stay away from that company and be glad we're in ours. None of our guys would do something like that."

Tammy gathered her books. "Just one more year, Sarah. Then we'll be firsties, and no one will pull that stuff on us."

Friday, 1 December 1978

Sarah flew into Providence, Rhode Island, to meet Ryan to drive to Philadelphia for the Army-Navy game, where Navy was a shoo-in to beat Army. In fact, they would most likely be going to the Holiday Bowl. Of course; now that she was no longer a cheerleader, they were burning up the field and receiving bowl bids. Oh, well. She was happy for Denzel. He had suffered a shoulder injury last season that sidelined him. This year he had been shifted from middle guard to defensive back, and although he had not started until the end of the season, he was still a formidable player.

The new set of "rah-rahs" received nowhere near the abuse of Sarah's old squad. She was happy to be in the stands this season but felt jealous of the new girls on the field, who she felt pushed the limits of Academy rules regarding hair length and makeup. Maybe that's what we should have done, she thought, knowing how infeasible that would have been.

Oh, well. Now she could concentrate on gymnastics. Her coach didn't want her on the cheerleading squad anyway. When they were out of season, Coach Durand wanted Sarah to get a strenuous workout every day. The team had two meets scheduled next semester. The coach had talked the athletic association into giving them club status; she was still working on varsity status. They almost had a real season ahead.

Consequently, Coach was requiring them to come back to school early from Christmas leave to begin practice. Plans to fly to Iran for Christmas had fallen through because of the unrest there. Her family would probably all meet in Maine at her grandmother's house instead.

The USS *Nimitz* was scheduled to deploy next Christmas, so Sarah hoped that Ryan would be able to come to Maine despite her current frustration with him over some silly little thing. Why did they have to fight, when they were only together for such a short time? Probably because they had to fit everything in during these sporadic weekends together: time to be together, time to talk, time to argue, time to make up. What a way to maintain a relationship! Just a year and a half, she thought, and all my time will be my own.

Saturday, 23 December 1978

Carrie Freeman sat on the edge of the twin bed she had slept in since grade school and gazed at the pale blue walls of her bedroom, still adorned with first-place ribbons, certificates, and trophies from her once illustrious swimming career. Life had changed. Although she was still an All-American swimmer, the captain of the women's swim team at Navy, and record holder in the 100- and 200-yard breast stroke and 200- and 400-yard individual medley, younger women recruits were now the highlight of the Navy women's swim team, but she didn't mind. She was looking forward to her new career as a naval officer, willing to let junior swimmers assume the glory.

Carrie looked at the floor and kicked the edge of the small carpet beside her bed. A deeper issue troubled her. Something her roommate Margot had warned her about before leaving school. Something that might explode when she returned after Christmas.

She shook her head. It'll ruin us, she thought. If the results of that investigation are made public, all the work to make us girls accepted will have been for naught.

"Honey?" Carrie's mother's stood at the door. "May I come in?"

"Sure, Mom."

"What's up, honey? You look pretty pensive sitting here. What's on your mind?"

"Nothing, really, Mom," she fibbed. "School, you know, same ol' stuff."

"You know, your father and I are very proud of you. You have done so well. All of you girls."

Yeah, but it's all going to be for nothing when the media gets hold of that investigation, thought Carrie.

"Thanks, Mom. It's been a long two and a half years, but we're almost on top. Half a semester and we'll be seniors." She smiled, trying to convey a sincerity she did not feel.

"Carrie, what's wrong? There's obviously something on your mind."

Carrie knew she was fighting a losing battle trying to hide her feelings from her mother. They had always been close, but she was not sure if she could talk about this with her mom.

"Nothing, Mom."

"Carrie?"

"Oh, Mom. There's some stuff happening, or going to happen at school, according to Margot, that's going to ruin everything we've done to make it through there."

"What kind of 'stuff,' Carrie?"

Carrie paused, then turned to face her mother.

"Margot is involved in a big investigation by NIS, the Naval Investigative Service, concerning a 'lesbian ring' at the Academy. They've been at it since the beginning of the year, and from what Margot says, their report is going to be released right after Christmas leave. From what I understand, they looked closely at girls on the basketball and volleyball teams and any other female athletes."

"You?" Mrs. Freeman asked with shock.

"No. Well, I don't know. I'm pretty sure I'm in the clear, only because I think Margot told them I wasn't the type. Otherwise I'm sure I would have been questioned. You know, I don't know who to hang out with anymore. If I hang out with the guys, they'll think I'm looking for a date or a husband, and now if I hang out with the girls, they'll think I'm gay. The whole thing is incredible! I just can't believe this is happening."

"Well, honey, if you're not involved—"

"Oh, Mom." Carrie stood up and walked to the window sill. "It doesn't matter if I'm involved or not. It's going to affect all of us. If they implicate any-one or if they do find a 'ring,' we'll all be labeled. The whole thing just makes me physically sick."

Mrs. Freeman sat for a moment in silence, slowly absorbing the full meaning of what her daughter was telling her. Carrie was right. This could be a horrible blow to all women at the Academy. "How did it get started?" she finally asked.

"According to Margot, last year a female youngster on the volleyball team came up to her, crying, and told her that she was being coerced into partici-pating in homosexual activity. Margot encouraged her to go to the comman-dant and report the story. She did, and so—the investigation."

"Maybe the investigation will reveal that there is nothing going on."

"Margot thinks differently."

"And what do you think?"

Carrie sat silent for a moment, cautiously contemplating her next words. "I don't know what to think. I can only imagine that there are a number of girls who feel very hated at school. Rejected. Outcast. Looking for attention or affection from wherever they can find it. So, maybe, if someone of the same sex gave them that attention—"

"But you said Margot said that this girl was being coerced into participating."

"Yeah, I know." Carrie looked at the floor and paused. "I just don't know what to think. I just know that if this story breaks. . . ."

"Was Margot certain that the report would be released? And to whom? They certainly wouldn't release it to the media without the administration approving it first."

"Mom, the media has been one of our worst enemies. What if it gets leaked to them somehow? What a story!"

Mrs. Freeman wasn't sure how to direct the conversation from here.

"Carrie, I really don't see what you can do about it, honey. If there is a ring of girls like that, they should probably be removed from the Academy, don't you think?"

"But Mom, some of these girls are from the Class of '80—the first year! The damage will be irreparable! The whole idea of us being there will become a joke."

Mother and daughter sat in silence.

"Carrie, I honestly don't know what to tell you. It seems to me that the administration has done a fairly good job promoting the presence of women at the Academy, and I feel certain that they will not want to unnecessarily blemish their reputation."

"Maybe it will all be unfounded."

"I don't think there's anything we can do about it right now, honey."

Carrie nodded.

"Ready for dinner?"

"Sure, Mom, I'll be right down. Hey, don't say anything to Dad about this, okay?"

Her mother nodded.

Watching her mother walk down the hall, Carrie still ached inside. Maybe it will all be unfounded, she told herself again. And maybe it won't.

Tuesday, 23 January 1979

It was 2200. Kate had just finished an entire package of Oreos when her room went black. Sitting alone at her desk, she immediately felt sick to her stomach. Oh, please, Lord, she pleaded, not again. What have I done to deserve this torture? When will it stop?

Never. It would never stop unless she quit, and she never would. The only way she would leave the Naval Academy would be in a body bag, and sometimes she feared so much for her physical safety that the idea was not completely implausible.

Unable to suppress the fusion of rage and fear building inside her, she bounded to the door. "Enough!" she screamed, pulling it open, knowing instinctively what would happen. It had happened twice already, and Key lime pie was on the menu tonight.

"Stop!" she yelled at the handful of classmates clustered around her door. "Just sto—"

She smelled the lime before it hit her face, stinging her eyes and nose and momentarily squelching her frenzy. Tears filled her eyes, unable to find a path down her face through the light green foam. "I hate you!" she screamed. "I hate you!"

She let go of the door and grabbed a white towel from the silver bar beside the sink, wiping away the sticky meringue. "I can't take it anymore," she sobbed out loud. "I just can't! Dead mice in my mailbox, and now this. I'm turning them in!"

Two days ago she had picked up her mail after class and between two letters in her box found a carefully placed dead mouse. She had screamed, dropping the letters and carcass and almost stepping on them as she leaped in fear. The CMOD had rushed to her rescue, picking up the rodent by the tail and depositing it in the trash can. There was no use trying to guess who had sent the gift; the list of those who might *not* have sent it would have been shorter.

Now she stood before the mirror in her room and could not stop the flood of tears surging down her face. There was no one to turn to. During Christmas leave she had put her relationship with Gabe on hold. There had been no reason, really, nothing he had done. It was her. No, it was her parents. In October they had divorced after twenty-five years of marriage. She was a wreck over the divorce. Gabe had been her champion, listening, consoling, and holding her while she cried.

Nevertheless, the disintegration of her parent's marriage left her questioning her contentment with Gabe. If even her own parents' marriage could not survive, then the euphoria she felt with Gabe was sure to be short-lived. They needed to date other people. Just to be sure. It was not that they had discussed marriage, but the prospect was there, and she wanted to be certain. Gabe understood. He saw that she needed space and stepped back. He knew that she would come back to him, but Kate was not so confident.

Now sobbing uncontrollably, she considered going to his room with her latest plight. No, she thought, his roommates will be there, and I can do this by myself. I can handle this, because it has to stop. These guys have to pay for what they have done.

She dried her tears and splashed cold water on her face. Taking a deep breath, she left her room and headed down the hall to the company officer's office, where she knew her company commander was studying. He looked up from his books and uneasily listened to her story. Then he sent the CMOD to summon her attacker, who hesitantly admitted his guilt and professed insincere remorse.

Sympathetic to Kate's case, the company commander counseled her that "boys will be boys" and questioned her desire to place her classmate on report, wondering if she might not accept an apology instead. After all, the attacker *was* willing to apologize.

Maybe that was enough, she figured. I don't want to alienate my classmates even further by frying one of them. "An apology is acceptable," she told him, "but this pie-in-the-face routine has happened to me three times now, and I don't want it to ever happen again!"

The attacker's apology was brief and of questionable sincerity, but on the way back to her room Kate felt certain that no more pies would greet her at the door. I just want to feel like I'm part of this company, she thought. Is that so terrible? Why won't they let me be one of them?

The bloated feeling in her stomach gave her one answer. My weight. I'm so fat.

She made a beeline for the women's head and stood sideways before the full-length mirror on the wall, sucking in her stomach. Eleven pounds I've lost, she thought. That's not enough. I need to lose more, and I know how to get there.

On her knees in a solitary cubicle, Kate flushed the toilet to camouflage the retching sounds she made as she vomited what she hoped was the entire package of Oreos into the bowl. Pausing for a second, she inspected her surroundings. What was she doing here? What had driven her to these depths?

Her hands began to shake as they clutched the hard enamel of the toilet seat. Oh, God, she despaired. Why am I doing this? It's so unnatural. It's so . . . sick.

She leaned limply against the cubicle wall, reaching for a piece of toilet paper to wipe her mouth. I've got to get control. This has to stop. It all has to stop. The weight gain, the eating, this hatred I feel for everyone.

She walked over to the window and looked down at the small parking area between Fifth Wing and MacDonough Hall. I could end it, she thought. I could stop this pain. I could climb four more flights of stairs and make it all go away.

The Lord gave you many talents, her father's voice called from the depths of her despair. Be sure you never waste them.

What talents? she thought. Talent for making everyone hate me? I even chased away Gabe, who said he would love me forever.

The door to the women's head opened, startling her, and Kate stepped back from the window.

"Thought I'd find you in here," called her roommate. "The mate just came by and left a message that Gabe called and wants you to call him."

Gabe, my guardian angel, thought Kate. What timing. What perfect timing!

"Thanks, Terrie," she called, hurrying to the telephone at the mate's desk. Gabe was always there for her. What would she do without him?

Friday, 16 February 1979

Sarah and Jeff Raitt, a classmate from her company, strolled down Stribling Walk toward Mahan Hall for the Masqueraders' production of *How to Succeed in Business without Really Trying*. Other midshipmen happy for the excuse to skip study hour accompanied them at various distances.

"Brrrr. It's freezing out here!" Sarah massaged her triceps with gray-gloved hands.

"I'll keep you warm," joked Jeff, reaching to put his arm around her.

"Yeah, that's what I need," replied Sarah, leaning away from him while steadying her cover, "to be fried for PDA. Ryan would understand. No problem."

"Ryan. Give him up, then you and I can get serious." He retracted his reach. Jeff and she had become good friends, although Sarah perceived a deeper interest on his part. She had dated a number of midshipmen but had no serious interest in anyone but Ryan.

"How is old Nolde, anyway?" Ryan had also been Jeff's squad leader during plebe summer.

"Fine. I saw him a couple of weekends ago. We went skiing in New Hampshire," said Sarah.

"Hey, Sarah, what do you know about this 'lesbo-ring' everybody keeps talking about?"

"What 'lesbo-ring'?"

"You know, girls on girls?"

"Jeff!"

"Hey, it's what I heard."

"Well, I don't know anything about it."

"Of course not, with all the guys you date."

She punched him. "Actually, I did hear about it from Carrie," she said. "Her roommate was involved somehow—something to do with helping an NIS investigation, but they must have found nothing, since we've heard nothing. Good thing! That's all we'd need the press to get hold of!"

"Right," agreed Jeff, opening the door to Mahan Hall for Sarah. "That'd be a nightmare."

Backstage, Kate paced nervously. Gabe had sent her a dozen roses that morning to wish her luck. Two weeks ago she had asked him to come see the play the week after opening night so that she would not be so nervous. He had surprised her and snuck in on opening night anyway, and tonight he was again sitting in the audience.

This was the first time she'd had a real part in a play. What an opportunity! Of course, I only got to do it because there are so few women at this school to try out for these productions, she told herself. Anywhere else I probably would have only been in the chorus.

She checked her makeup for the fourth time. Pressing her bright red lips together, she glanced down at the disappointing pale green blouse and skirt she wore as a costume. *Nothing like the frilly, lacy gowns we got to wear for H.M.S. Pinafore,* she thought. *That production had had a budget—unlike this one, where we have to provide our own clothes. Of course, I was in the chorus in Pinafore. It figures. They save the drab costumes for "my" play. I can never win.*

Enough, she reprimanded herself. *Think positive,* Gabe had told her. *Stop coming down so hard on yourself and looking at the bleak side of things.* His advice was finally beginning to sink in. *At least it's fun getting dressed up in dresses and makeup and feeling a little bit feminine,* she thought happily.

"Five minutes!" the stage manager called.

"Here goes nothing," whispered Kate, with a final glance in the mirror. "Wish me luck!"

They had two hours until taps after the last curtain call, and Gabe invited her out into town for drinks. Still in her costume and makeup and not wanting to change back into her uniform, Kate declined and invited him to the cast party instead. The play had once again been well received by the audience, and Gabe unceasingly extolled her performance. She blushed at his praise, secretly unable to hear enough.

Lord, she needed him. He looked beyond all her faults and understood and supported all she was doing. He lifted her spirits whenever they were together, which in the future, she decided, should be as much as possible. What had happened between her parents was not going to happen to Gabe and her. They shared so many common goals, unlike her parents. Clutching his arm tightly, she gazed proudly at this handsome midshipman who gave her the strength to go on.

Friday, 30 March 1979

"Tammy, did you get yours?" Sarah called anxiously, flinging her books onto the desk so that she could study the new ring on her finger before noon meal formation.

She had just come from Smoke Hall, where second-class midshipmen were picking up the class rings they had ordered several months earlier. They would be allowed to wear their rings for the following week to ensure that they fit properly. Then they could not wear them until the Ring Dance in May.

The administration had given the women a choice of ordering a specially designed women's Academy ring, which was just slightly smaller than the men's Academy ring, or a miniature replica of the men's ring, normally purchased by men as engagement rings. Sarah had ordered both versions, each with a Josten's blue star sapphire. The miniature ring would be a present for her mother this Christmas. The official-size ring was hers.

Tammy and she couldn't imagine why any of the girls would want to buy a miniature, which would immediately label them as some mid's fiancée. They had worked too hard to be identified as a girlfriend instead of a midshipman. Nevertheless, a number of female classmates had bought the miniatures, concerned that the official ring might look too heavy on their hands.

Now, though, Sarah wondered if she had made the right choice. The stone on her finger was beautiful. A six-pointed star flashed on the surface of the dark blue sapphire nestled between the official crests of the Naval Academy and the Class of 1980, but the ring itself was huge! If she hadn't known better, she would have thought it was a man's ring. She took it off for the third time and looked at the name engraved inside the gold band. "Sarah Nicole Becker"— that was correct, but the ring felt too big. She had paid $230 for it.

"Oh, Sarah, they're gorgeous, aren't they?" Tammy exclaimed, admiring her own outstretched hand.

"Oh, Tam. They're too big!"

"Oh, no! They're perfect. I'm really glad we got the women's ring instead of the miniature."

"But mine's huge!" complained Sarah.

"Let me see." Tammy immediately recognized the disparity in the ring sizes. "Sarah, yours is huge because you have a man's ring!"

"What?!" gasped Sarah, grabbing her ring back. "You're right! Those idiots gave me a man's ring and even engraved my name in it!" She wanted to cry. This was a moment sacred to every midshipman. It signified that you were a card-carrying member of this huge fraternity. They had waited months, years, for this day, and Sarah was deeply disappointed.

"I guess I'll have to take it back and have it redone," she said sadly. "I won't be able to wear it next week. Does 'Sarah Nicole Becker' sound like a man's name to you? I can't believe they did this!"

"Oh, Sarah. I'm sorry."

The five-minute chow call began, and Sarah took off her ring and locked it in her desk.

"Guess I'll have to return it tomorrow," she said. "Man, everybody's gonna ask to see my ring at lunch. This really sucks!"

"I'm sorry, Sarah," Tammy repeated. "But I'm sure they'll fix it."

"That's just not the point, Tammy, ya know?"

Tammy knew. They had waited a long time for this treasure. It wasn't fair. Sarah stared at the locked desk where her treasure lay buried.

"Come on, Sarah, we'd better get to formation."

"Yeah. It's just a ring, right?" Sarah announced, heading out the door.

Saturday, 14 April 1979

Two weeks later, Kate wore a different kind of ring. Gabe had asked her to marry him, and she believed that her life was finally coming together. Their announcement to family and friends was met with concern about her continued allegiance to the Naval Academy. Kate was flabbergasted. Her graduation was a goal both she and Gabe treasured. She was not going to quit to become his wife.

They set the date for June Week 1980—now renamed Commissioning Week, much to the dismay of a number of midshipmen and alumni. The change was blamed, by many, on the presence of the women. However, the academic schedule had been pushed back, and midshipmen would now be graduating the last week of May. It did not make sense to call it June Week.

Gabe and Kate decided to get married as soon after graduation as possible—the same day, if it could be arranged, but because of the number of June Week weddings, the Naval Academy generally held a lottery, drawing names to select who would go first.

Kate was overjoyed. She could survive anything now. Her grades were up, her weight was down, and she had found the man with whom she wanted to spend the rest of her life.

Wednesday, 2 May 1979

She put it on, then took it off. Standing before the full-length mirror, Sarah grimaced as she turned sideways, then frontward again, agonizing over what should have been a mundane decision to wear her gymnastics letter sweater to class. Would wearing it be worth listening to the snide comments that no doubt would be flung at her on the way to Luce Hall?

It was ridiculously unfair. She had worked two years to earn this sweater—in fact three, since she had also earned one for cheerleading, but she wouldn't be caught dead wearing that one. Carrie Freeman had been the first woman to earn a sweater plebe year. Not long after, women on the basketball and volleyball teams were issued one. By the end of plebe year, it seemed that almost all the girls were wearing the coveted blue knit apparel.

Sarah had heard too much grumbling from the guys about girls with letter sweaters. Anger erupted among the brigade, particularly among athletes who had worked hard to earn one. "Guys have to work their asses off to win a sweater," they said, "but the administration issues them to any girl who plays a club sport for one season. And the girls have the gall to wear them!"

Sarah didn't argue their point. When 20 percent of the women were wearing letter sweaters, their value decreased proportionately. Hence Sarah's current dilemma. To the guys, the value of her sweater was less than that of a male varsity athlete's. She was afraid to confront their reaction.

Oh, screw 'em, she thought. Other girls wear theirs, why shouldn't I? I earned mine, no matter what anyone thinks.

"Come on, Becker. Let's go!" Kurt Loper appeared in her doorway. They had arranged to walk to class together.

"Whoa! What is this?!" he exclaimed as she grabbed her books from her desk. "A letter sweater? Wow! I've never seen you wear that before!"

"Stuff it, Loper!" she replied. "I earned it, and I'm not taking any shit from anyone about it!"

"Hey, relax! It looks nice—even on a girl." He smiled.

She belted him with a book. "Let's go, or we're gonna be late, funny guy!"

As they arrived in T-Court, joining the migration of midshipmen returning to class, her prediction came true.

"Oh, please," groaned one. "Midshipchicks in letter sweaters! I think I'm gonna be sick!"

"Yeah?" she volleyed, "Well, go throw up somewhere else!" She was tired of the abuse.

"Whoa!" interjected Kurt. "You told him."

"I'm tired of listening to that shit. I'm a good athlete, and I worked hard as a gymnast. They can just get over it!"

FIRST-CLASS YEAR
1979–1980

I believe our main goal was survival and each of us chose our own survival technique. I chose to become "one of the boys" while some of us found religion. Others I know tried to blend into the background or wrap themselves up in their sport. Survival . . . that's what it was all about with us.

Female midshipman from the Class of 1980

CHAPTER ELEVEN

First-Class Summer

During their last summer, first classmen go to sea for training with the Fleet for their second and last time as midshipmen. Here, they have the opportunity to assume the responsibilities and perform the duties of junior officers. A number of carefully chosen members of the first class will also take part in the training and indoctrination of the new plebe class at Annapolis during the summer.

On board the cruise ships, functioning as a junior officer, the first classman is exposed to the social courtesies, amenities, and customs of wardroom life. Work in navigation, watch-standing on the bridge, exercises in the combat information center and in the engineering spaces, and lectures and studies on other aspects of shipboard life complete the summer's training with the Fleet.

United States Naval Academy Catalog, 1976–77

Friday, 20 July 1979

The first-class midshipmen of plebe-summer detail were led by Midshipman Commander Elaine Richey during formations. Wearing five thin gold stripes on each shoulder board, Elaine marched confidently into the lead position in the middle of Tecumseh Court. Her sword, pressed firmly against her right shoulder, sparkled in the evening sun. Over eleven hundred plebes and two hundred first-class midshipmen stood tight at attention before her. Her charges. Her responsibility. Let anyone be damned who thought she did not belong in this position. She had earned it as much as any male regimental commander before her.

The brigade had not been ready for a female striper, much less one who held the most senior position of plebe-summer detail. Her first company officer had been instrumental in ensuring that her impressive leadership skills were brought to the attention of the administration. Initially dubious that any female midshipman would be capable of taking charge the first year that women were firsties, Midshipman Richey's company officer found that he had an overwhelming challenge in trying to convince the administration of her innate ability to lead, which he discovered the first few days of plebe summer. His views were validated by several of her professors, who were impressed by not only her leadership skills but her superior intelligence as well. Consequently, Midshipman Richey joined the higher ranks of those with stripes early in third-class year, and she continued to be promoted year after year. As a first classman she was selected to participate in the elite Trident Scholar Program, where she was one of a very limited number of exceptionally capable midshipmen granted the opportunity to pursue independent research during her senior year on a subject of her choice.

Unlike the administration, most men and women of the brigade viewed her appointment to the position of regimental commander as pure tokenism. How could a woman be slated in a top position already? Typically, one of the two regimental commanders for plebe summer was selected to become brigade commander for the subsequent academic year. Neither the brigade nor the Naval Academy was ready for a female brigade commander. But now it appeared a possibility.

Among the ranks led by Midshipman Richey, Kate stood proudly as the leader of twelve plebes comprising the Third Squad of Seventh Platoon in Delta Company. She cringed as Midshipman Richey gave the order for the plebe regiment to "forward march!" Although clear and distinct, the high-pitched female voice sounded awkward. Kate had heard the rumors about how Midshipman Richey had achieved her status and position—the story of how her plebe-year company officer made his firsties rewrite her grease when they initially ranked her at the bottom of the company.

Kate glanced at the freshly shaven plebes. She had three women in her squad, one whom she had already labeled a smack, and she was determined to break her or run her out. She couldn't stand ratey (smart-alecky) plebes.

She took plebe indoctrination very seriously and wanted to ensure that these twelve had a real plebe summer. Especially the girls. She would be sure not to show any preferential treatment. At least three of her plebes had great potential, and she resolved to challenge them while keeping them focused on remaining at the Academy. Two others she hoped would resign early.

. . .

As the first two weeks of plebe summer ended, Kate realized that one of her three hopefuls was weakening. Six-foot-two and over two hundred pounds, this guy would sweat continually in more ways than one. He was constantly calling her sir, as did a number of plebes in her squad, but it seemed to Kate that he was being snide. She gave him the benefit of the doubt the first two times but then began bracing him up whenever it happened. It didn't help. He also had a difficult time recalling his rates. It was evident to Kate that he knew them; he just clutched (panicked and forgot them) when called upon at a come-around. Once he burst into tears when asked the menu for noon meal.

There was more to the tears than just nerves, Kate decided. He possessed such confidence when not put on the spot. She called him to the company officer's office to talk one evening. Five minutes into their conversation, he broke down again and told Kate that his grandfather had died unexpectedly two weeks before the start of plebe summer. Very close to his grandfather, a member of the Class of 1945, this young man had lived to attend the Naval Academy. Now his grandfather would never see him graduate, and the disappointment weighed heavily on him, interfering with his ability to concentrate.

Kate counseled him and told him of her confidence in him, while reminding him that despite his grief, she would cut him no slack for her remaining two weeks as his squad leader. He accepted her terms and thrived from then on, achieving the rank of two out of eleven plebes.

The night before First Set left, the plebes of Delta Company parodied their squad leaders with skits. Kate's star plebe and two others paid tribute to her with their rendition of the *Reef Points* Table Salt, replacing "Why didn't you say sir?" with "Why didn't you say ma'am?"

They stood at attention before the company of seventy plebes and nine first classmen, braced up, and bellowed the new ditty:

Ma'am, ma'am is a misrepresented word made up in the magnificent days of medieval Manchuria when many men, too masculine to say ma'am, yet mindful of mocking their mistress, mitigated this major mistake by mentioning the marvelous word ma'am by which I now belatedly address a miss mistaken for a male who mystifies me by her mandatory monitions that fourth class middies must murmur ma'am after every word they say, ma'am![*]

---

[*] Actually written by John Cerasuelo, Darren Anderson, and Kathy Bruzas of the Class of 1983.

The company cheered. Kate was elated and touched. She had been called sir too many times to recall during the past four weeks.

Although her reputation was sealed as one of the toughest squad leaders in Seventh Platoon and she knew that the plebes considered her a flamer, she hoped they had grown with the satisfaction that they had stood up to her tests. And after her discussion with her number two plebe, she now understood the importance of knowing and looking out for your people.

Monday, 23 July 1979

Sarah's desire to take charge as a leader in the company had waned over the past three years. Her goals now were to complete her studies, compete in her last year on the women's gymnastics team, and graduate. She had declined an offer to fill a squad-leader position during plebe-summer detail, even though she distinctly remembered as a plebe relishing the thought of the day when she would be in a position to get in someone's face. Oooh, the first time someone called her sir. . . . Unlike Tammy, who was gung-ho to lead a squad of charges, Sarah no longer felt compelled to make some underling's life miserable for six weeks. She appreciated the objective of plebe indoctrination but felt no calling to be part of it.

She and a fellow systems engineer planned to purchase Eurail passes for the summer to take a whirlwind tour of Europe after Commissioning Week. Ryan was not happy that she would be traveling through Europe with a guy, but he was fully ensconced in his job on the USS *Nimitz* and was not free for any extended periods of leave. Sarah assured him that her relationship with Brian was purely platonic.

Ryan remained an ingrained part of her life. Their long-distance relationship grew strained at times yet at others derived strength from shared joys and tribulations. Sarah would not see him all summer unless their ships literally crossed paths in August, when she would be aboard the USS *Dahlgren,* a guided-missile destroyer, for first-class cruise.

Early in Commissioning Week, women from the Class of 1980 had been ordered to Memorial Hall, where they were informed that the shore-based "cruises" they were scheduled to go on either in Washington, D.C., or Norfolk, Virginia, had been canceled. They would not again have to follow a female officer running-mate around for a month. Instead, they would spend first-class cruises on destroyer tenders, submarine tenders, and other noncombatants including the training aircraft carrier USS *Lexington.* Thank goodness for the amendment to Title 10 allowing such! The women's credibility with both upper- and underclass men relied on it.

In the back of her mind, Sarah wondered if the administration's dilemma of where to place the women on summer cruise, combined with their impending graduation, had somehow forced this issue of new assignments for women. After all, there was a strong argument against the presence of women who could not be assigned combat duty at a school designed to breed combat leaders.

Sarah and Justine Harper, a classmate from First Regiment, were two of only four female midshipmen assigned to navy combatants. Sarah was actually disappointed. She had wanted to spend time on board the USS *Lexington* in Pensacola, observing flight operations every day. She yearned to sit in the back seat of an aircraft catapulted off the end of the floating runway, a precursor to the day when she would sit in the front. The women drew numbers from a hat, however, and when it came time for her to pick, all billets on the *Lexington* had been chosen. News that the USS *Dahlgren* was scheduled for missile shoots in the Caribbean and port calls in Puerto Rico and St. Croix softened her disappointment.

Sarah and Justine now lugged their white duffel bags up the gangplank of the USS *Dahlgren* in Norfolk. They saluted the officer of the day and requested permission to come aboard, their nervousness compounded by stares from sailors painting the ship. Of course they're going to check us out, Sarah thought. This is new for them, too.

Sarah was informed that a female ensign would join them. Three against 350. I guess I can survive a month of this, she thought, although she felt like a plebe again. Will it always be like this? Continually proving myself to someone or some group?

She finally felt comfortable at the Academy, but this was different. This was the fleet. The real navy.

Sarah and Justine unpacked in the operations officer's stateroom, where they would room together for the next month. Justine claimed the bottom bunk as Sarah glanced around the six- by twelve-foot stateroom complete with two gray bunks, two gray sets of lockers, two gray desks, and one stainless-steel sink.

"Guess they moved the ops officer somewhere else," Justine said. "Wonder where. Maybe in with the XO?"

"Oh, great," replied Sarah. "Bet they both love that."

"What choice did they have? They couldn't put us in with the other junior officers, and we can't sleep down in enlisted berthing."

"Guess you're right. I just hope nobody thinks we asked for these accommodations."

"Well, I'm going to enjoy them," continued Justine, removing a blow dryer from her duffel bag.

"Hey, did you notice a head on your way down here?" asked Sarah.

"Out the door and to the right. They turned one of the officer heads into a 'female only' head."

"We're just taking over," Sarah joked. "I'm going to go make sure it works. Be right back."

In the passageway Sarah met the third female on board. Ensign Petersen was personable without being overtly friendly, but she was a bit too gung-ho for Sarah. She obviously wanted to maintain a professional distance from the female midshipmen, which made Sarah wonder if this was how she herself appeared to the three underclass women now in Thirty-third Company. She was cordial to them yet maintained her distance. No one could accuse her of showing preferential treatment, and she planned on treating the three incoming female plebes the same way.

Feeling adventuresome, Sarah turned left and headed toward the bow of the ship, avoiding ladders so as not to get lost. Stepping through a hatch, she almost bumped into an attractive, dark-haired lieutenant.

"Midshipman Becker?" he asked, reading her nametag.

"Yes, sir."

"How do you do?" He extended his hand. "I'm Lieutenant Harmon, the fire-control division officer. You'll be my assistant for the summer."

"Oh, nice to meet you, sir." She returned his handshake firmly. "I'm looking forward to it."

"Good, because I plan on making you work on this cruise," he remarked gruffly. "You have things way too easy back at the Academy. I know. I graduated four years ago."

"Uh, yes, sir," she replied, unsure of how to respond to the unnecessary dressing-down.

"Are you getting settled? Anything you need?"

"No, sir. I was just taking a look around the ship."

"Well, let me give you a quick tour. I'll introduce you to the men in the division tomorrow at quarters, although we may run into a few of them down in the fire-control spaces."

Lieutenant Harmon led Sarah through the wardroom where the officers ate and spent their leisure time, the bridge from where the ship was driven, and the enlisted berthing spaces, which the women were forbidden to enter unless previously announced.

On their way back to the fire-control division spaces, Lieutenant Harmon and Sarah passed through the enlisted mess, or dining area, where several groups of enlisted men sat drinking coffee or talking. Upon their entrance, several whistles from unidentifiable sources rang out.

Sarah tried to keep her eyes in the boat and ignore them. She couldn't believe the men would be so bold with the lieutenant beside her.

"All right, knock it off!" he shouted. "Knock it off!" The noise died down. "Sorry about that," he whispered. "Once they get used to you, that shouldn't happen anymore."

But it did. Four nights later, having just finished the preventative-maintenance schedules for her division in the wardroom, Sarah was forced to travel the only available route from fore to aft, through the enlisted mess; the weather decks (the ship's exterior passageways) had been secured because of rough seas. This time she was by herself, and the dining facility was almost full. The burlesque-type banter began as soon as she entered.

"Mmmm, mmmm! Hey, baby!" called one. "Come here, sugar!" cried another. The taunts came from everywhere. There was no way to identify the sources. Sarah focused on her only exit, the hatchway fifty feet in front of her. Ignore them, she told herself. You're almost there. Don't let them get to you.

She picked up her pace. Why would they do this? she wondered. I'm an officer. Why don't they give me the respect they unquestioningly give the men? But she knew the answer: They did not view her as an officer. She was the wrong gender. To be on their team, you had to be a man.

Stepping through the hatch, Sarah caught her breath and reaffirmed her previous decision. There is no way I am going on ships after graduation. No way.

Monday, 13 August 1979

Two weeks into first-class cruise, Kate still found flight ops mesmerizing. Standing beside her male running-mate, a mustang ensign, an individual who had come up through the enlisted ranks, Kate held her hands tightly over her

Mickey Mouse ears in hopes of further attenuating the excruciating screech of tires against runway as the USS *Lexington*'s number two arresting gear snagged the tailhook of an incoming A-6 Intruder.

It took her breath away. What fear, what passion must overcome these men accountable for the mission of these multi-million-dollar machines! Soaring in the heavens, racing with the angels, imbued with a feeling of immortality, only to be forced by mission accomplishment or a lack of fuel to land once again among mortals of lesser powers. Venturing this transition from divinity to temporal being must prove as challenging as guiding that aircraft onto the postage-stamp platform in the middle of the sea, she thought. Yet while most landed their aircraft safely, few successfully made the psychological transition. Such was the excuse she granted the lieutenant aviator who had "come on" to her the second night on board. What other reason would this married man have had for asking her to engage in a secret rendezvous? She didn't even know him. She might have shrugged it off as a lame effort to shock her and check her reaction, but his words had been uttered sincerely, and her resolute negative response had obviously bruised his ego.

She shook her head and smiled, remembering the reverse incident that had occurred her fourth day on board. Standing beside the enormous elevator used to hoist airplanes to the upper flight deck, Kate had watched in awe as this gigantic hydraulic platform lifted an eighteen-ton aircraft four stories into the air.

"There's one of the dykes, now," she had heard him say, "standing there with her mouth open."

With great restraint, she had closed her mouth and continued to stare at the rising elevator, not wishing to give this petty officer the satisfaction of knowing how his words had stung. Approached for a fling one day and berated as a homosexual the next, she felt humiliated until minutes later when a first-class petty officer who had been walking with the accuser approached her and apologized for his friend's insult.

Kate was astounded. She couldn't believe that anyone was apologizing to her. It was so uplifting. She couldn't remember very many voluntary apologies from anyone for remarks made about her at school, and those remarks had come from individuals who were about to become naval officers. Maybe things would, after all, be better once she was part of the fleet.

In fact, the majority of enlisted personnel on board were friendly and helpful. A number of the enlisted men appeared anxious to show off for the women mids, obviously proud of their expertise in their individual ratings. Expecting antagonism and discord, Kate was delighted to encounter professionalism and enthusiasm.

Sarah's division officer had a bark worse than his bite, and he warmed quickly to her presence as his assistant. Sarah was lucky. Justine's running-mate was a hardcore mustang officer who on the day of their arrival posted a newspaper article about the female midshipmen coming on board. It had been embellished with crude editorial comments scribbled on by a number of crew members to indicate their displeasure at having women on board.

Despite Lieutenant Harmon's acceptance, Sarah was depressed and unsettled at having no one with whom to share her feelings. Although she liked Justine, she was always busy with her division or working on her PQS, Personal Qualification Standards, and Ensign Petersen was unapproachable.

Something was eating at Sarah, something she couldn't quite grasp. They had been at sea for a week, transiting to Roosevelt Roads, Puerto Rico, completing a week of weapons shoots. Unlike school, the all-male environment here was beginning to unnerve her. Everywhere she went she felt she was being ogled by enlisted men, although no one had overtly approached her, as one had Justine.

One balmy afternoon a petty officer had approached Justine, who was enjoying the breeze on the weather decks, having just been relieved from watch in the smelly, humid engineering spaces. The crew member asked her if she had time to talk. She agreed, and they chatted pleasantly until his conversation turned from the impending weather to "Do you have a boyfriend?" and "When was the last time you got laid?"

Completely flabbergasted, Justine managed to impart that he better watch how he spoke to officers and left. In their stateroom, Sarah and she discussed approaching the executive officer about the incident, but Justine decided that she was too embarrassed. The next day the sailor found Justine and apologized profusely, leading the girls to believe that he realized how much trouble he could be in if Justine ever turned him in.

Sarah had no space. She was constantly on guard, feeling trapped by her inability to get away from all these men who she felt did not view her as a naval officer. Yes, she was friendly, but she wore the uniform and insignia of a first-class midshipman, which should have earned her the respect they instinctively gave the two male midshipmen on board.

One of the two senior petty officers in her division, who had initially taken her under his wing, was no longer speaking to her because he felt too attracted to her and was concerned about his marriage. He told the other single petty officer that he could no longer keep up the professional charade and had decided to maintain his distance from Midshipman Becker.

"Professional charade?" Sarah had been friendly to this guy, they joked around now and then, but she certainly was not attracted to him. And he knew about Ryan. She had told both of them about him, and they had introduced her to friends in the Communications Center, who helped her send a Class Easy message (the lowest class of message) to him on the *Nimitz* telling him when she would return to Norfolk. Another time they had snuck her up to an off-limits area directly behind a Terrier missile during a missile-firing exercise. The three of them were in such close proximity to the missile that when it was fired, her eyebrows were singed.

Maybe she should have maintained more of a distance from them. She was just so anxious to be accepted by the male crew members, and these two were so willing to show her the ropes.

It was so frustrating! Too friendly, and they all want to date you. Too aloof, and you're a snobby bitch. Where was the happy medium? Even the officers' wives were leery about the women on board. A group of them waited anxiously at the pier the first time the ship pulled into Roosevelt Roads. Shipboard rumor was that the wives had never done this before for a monthlong cruise.

There was only one individual on board Sarah felt comfortable approaching to discuss and sort out her feelings: the sonar officer, Lt. Brian Fern, Class of 1977. His men revered him, and Sarah felt a common bond with him since he had been one of her firsties, and his position as a striper had been one of her required rates as a plebe.

At first she wasn't sure if she should address him as sir or lieutenant, but Brian put her immediately at ease, listening to her woes, remaining completely impartial and sympathetic to her position. Having been at the Academy the summer the women first arrived, he understood the crew's curiosity and uncertainty about how to treat these ladies who were their superior officers. Brian assured her that the entire evolution of having women on board for the first time was unsettling for everyone and probably would be so for some time to come.

"Take it a day at a time," he advised. "Be professional but not unap-proachable. Remember, these guys are people too, and most of them are very good at what they do. The majority of them don't want to see you fail and don't want to get you in the rack. It's just so new to them. They're going to have to learn to sort out their feelings on their own. They also aren't used to having a female boss. I don't see why you can't be professional and friendly at the same time. A smile and a pat on the back go a long way with a guy who's been working his rear end off for you."

His words consoled her, and just knowing she had someone she could talk to made the rest of the cruise bearable. She and Justine even made dinner for the entire wardroom on one of their last evenings on board, with the assistance of the mess cooks, suggesting that each officer take one night to plan and cook an evening meal. No one took them up on the suggestion, but all enjoyed their Polynesian pork chops.

Four weeks after entering this vessel of uncertainty and male chauvinism, the girls left with the crew begging them to stay on the ship for another week of refresher training in Guantánamo Bay, Cuba. But Sarah and Justine had had enough. Anxious to see Ryan one last time before he deployed for six months, Sarah caught a military hop from Roosevelt Roads back to the Norfolk Naval Air Station a week before they had to be back at school.

Her cruise evaluation indicated that she had shown the officers and the men of the USS *Dahlgren* that she "could readily be accepted into the surface line community based largely on her professional attitude towards learning about shipboard life as well as genuine concern for the men and the mission of the Fire Control Division. Her ability to retain a tremendous amount of information and knowledge pertaining to the summer's training environment proved that she was well capable of becoming a superior naval officer in any assignment she might pursue."

CHAPTER TWELVE

First-Class Year, First Semester

It is by no means enough that an officer of the Navy should be a capable mariner. He must be that, of course, but also a great deal more. He should be as well a gentleman of liberal education, refined manners, punctilious courtesy, and the nicest sense of personal honor.

Based on letters of John Paul Jones

Tuesday, 28 August 1979

Tammy returned to the Academy after first-class cruise with a renewed vigor for Christ and a fresh love for an enlisted man she had met on her ship. Although happy for Tammy, Sarah realized that she was now rooming with a "Bible-beater."

"Listen, Tam, it's not that I'm antireligious or anything," Sarah told her. "I mean, I went to Catholic schools until I was in sixth grade. It's just that I don't practice the stuff as heavy now. So, I'll respect your beliefs, as long as you respect mine and don't try to convert me, okay?"

Tammy agreed, and Sarah tried to ignore the Bible left on the desk and the Christian readings posted on their bulletin board. If this was what Tammy needed to help her make it through this last year, that was fine with Sarah, and for the first time in the three years that Sarah had known her, Tammy seemed to be truly in love. Sarah hoped that she had finally found something to replace the hopeless infatuation she had maintained for the past two years with an indifferent football player, but Sarah worried about her dating an enlisted guy.

Rumors ran rampant about a female classmate who had been sent back to the Naval Academy by the commanding officer of her ship for getting caught in the rack with an enlisted sailor. Sarah shared the disgust of her classmates, who felt that this woman had deeply embarrassed the Academy and damaged the reputation of the rest of the women there. It was potent fuel for the argument against allowing women on navy ships. Imprudent acts by one branded them all.

Now Tammy was basically pulling the same thing, violating the navy's fraternization regulations. Sarah was also concerned because Tammy's enlisted romance sounded somewhat one-sided and extremely tumultuous. She prayed that Tammy wouldn't be hurt but realized that there was little she could do to change her roommate's stubborn heart.

Sarah folded her laundry as Tammy took her Bible from the desk drawer.

"Going somewhere?" Sarah asked.

"There's a Bible study in Mitscher Hall."

As soon as Tammy left, Sarah headed to Kurt Loper's room to tell him about Tammy.

"Beat Army, sir!" The plebe squared the corner before bounding down the ladder on his way to class. Three steps behind, Kate cringed.

"Plebe, halt!" she ordered. He obeyed.

"Why don't you try that again, mister! This time using *ma'am* instead of *sir!*"

The plebe looked confused. He glanced briefly at Gabe, standing beside Kate, for reprieve. Given none, he chopped back up the ladder and performed his steps in reverse. "Beat Army, ma'am!" He squared the corner for the second time.

"I can't hear you, mister! Let's try that again!"

Gabe stood silently beside Kate, unsure what point she was trying to make.

The plebe made an about-face. "Beat Army, MA'AM!" he yelled, pivoting on his right toe. He hurried down the ladder, hoping to move on, but Kate was still not satisfied. There was something patronizing about his tone, she thought. She wouldn't have it. Not from a plebe.

"That was just a little too snide, mister. Do it again!"

He moaned, provoking her fury, yet obeying. "Go Navy, MA'AM!"

It wasn't enough. "AGAIN!" she yelled, determined to break this guy.

"GO NAVY, MA'AM!" The plebe wanted to get to class.

"AGAIN!" Midshipmen were beginning to stare.

"Kate," Gabe whispered softly.

"Stay out of this!" she snapped.

"BEAT ARMY, MA'AM!"

"AGAIN!"

"BEAT ARMY, MA'AM!"

"AGAIN!"

"NO, enough!" Gabe ordered. "Get out of here, mister!" The plebe took his cue and chopped away, eager to be on his way to a class for which he was now undoubtedly late.

"Who do you think you are?!" Kate lambasted Gabe. "That was none of your business!"

"Kate, you were out of control."

"I was not! I knew exactly what I was doing!"

"Yeah? What was your point?"

"That plebe was being disrespectful. He needed to be shown who was boss."

"The only thing you showed him is what a flamer you can be. He did nothing to provoke the abuse you just rained on him. He was innocently on his way to class."

"Oh, sure, stick up for one of your fraternity brothers. An underclassman, no less."

"Kate, you're making no sense. I thought you worked through this flamer problem last summer. This is not how you gain their respect. We've talked about this."

"I can't help it, Gabe. I'm tired of always hearing 'Beat Army, sir!' around here. When are we going to count?"

"You count now, but you can't change the opinion of everyone overnight."

"But we need to start showing these male plebes that we girls are also in charge." She hated the way that sounded. Every time she used the word *girl*, she wished she had said *woman* instead.

"They know that. You showed them that this summer, and you'll show them next semester as a squad leader. Being a flamer like your own firsties doesn't gain respect. Remember how you 'respected' them? You hated them and vowed you would never act like them. But look at you."

Kate inhaled deeply. "You're right. I was out of control. But didn't he seem insolent to you?"

"No, he seemed like a plebe worried about getting to class late."

Now she felt bad. This was not how she had intended to behave as a firstie. What had come over her?

Tuesday, 18 September 1979

The notice leaped out at Sarah as soon as she began reading the "Brigade Bulletin":

ATTENTION ALL FIRST-CLASS WOMEN MIDSHIPMEN: All women midshipmen in the Class of 1980 are required to attend a mandatory meeting in Michelson 103, Wednesday, 19 September, at 1900. Deputy Under Secretary of the Navy Mildred Dietrich will be speaking to the Class of '80 women. Uniform is Tropical White Long.

"Oh, no, Tam," Sarah whined. "Have you seen the 'Brigade Bulletin'?"

"Yeah, the mandatory-meeting thing?"

"Yeah. Man, I hate those things. Why do they separate us from the guys like that? Why is it that we have to attend every professional lecture on the Marine Corps, or navy air, or surface line, or submarines, things that we can't even *do,* but the guys never have to attend any professional lecture of ours?"

"Well, you have to admit, we haven't had many all-women lectures since we've been here."

"Yeah, but any little thing, like a separate meeting, that calls attention to us as women seems to make life a little more difficult. On the other hand, if the guys had to go to women's professional lectures they'd bitch so much we'd never hear the end of it."

The next night after evening meal, Tammy and Sarah left the wardroom through Smoke Hall with other groups of female first classmen.

They hung their combination covers on the hooks in Michelson Hall where three years earlier they had listened to the medical hygiene lecture. By now the women were acquainted with one another, and the air was animated with voices. Sarah waved to Carrie.

"What's this about?" she mouthed. Carrie shrugged. Sarah rolled her eyes.

At precisely 1900 the room fell silent as a woman officer appeared on stage and introduced Deputy Under Secretary Dietrich. The women still did not know why they were there.

Slim and middle-aged, Ms. Dietrich walked onto the stage wearing a light brown suit.

"Good evening, ladies. It is my pleasure to be with you tonight, to discuss how you are doing and how, together, we can help the administration of the Naval Academy assist you better."

"Oh, oh, a covert bitch session," Sarah whispered. "We tried to do this plebe year and almost got fried for mutiny." Carrie's roommate had tried to organize a women's support group plebe year with a female officer on staff and was reprimanded by the commandant for attempting a mutiny.

"Let me begin by telling you that I am the first woman to hold my current post, which is the equivalent of a three-star admiral," said the deputy under secretary.

Sarah looked at Tammy and rolled her eyes. Give me a break! she thought. The only three-stars *I* know wear it on their sleeves.

Sensing the skepticism of her audience, Ms. Dietrich repeated herself. "Yes, although I am not in the armed forces, my job position is the equivalent of a three-star, and in that capacity, I wield a considerable amount of power and influence. In other words, if you women feel you are being mistreated in any way, I can help you.

"I also know how you feel being the first. As a fellow pioneer, I have been in your shoes, and I'd like to share a story with you which demonstrates the similarities of our situations." She paused.

"Shortly after my appointment as deputy under secretary, I walked to lunch with several of my male colleagues. As we approached the doors to the Navy Mess, the men stopped and looked at me oddly. When I asked them what was wrong, they told me that women were not allowed to eat in the Mess Hall, that it was restricted to men. However, due to the nature of my position, it was obvious to all of us that I should be allowed to eat with them. So, I shrugged, opened my own door, and entered the mess. From that day forward, it was open to women." She relayed this story as if she had taken a major step for womankind.

Sarah and Tammy grimaced. "You've got to be kidding," whispered Sarah. "This woman thinks that small event can even begin to equate with sitting down in the head on 8-3 for the first time and closing the door to read 'Hang it up, Bitch!' engraved in huge letters. You mean to tell me that she thinks her insignificant ordeal is the same as standing up in front of the entire brigade to perform a cheer for the football team and getting booed off the stage because you don't look like some airhead beauty queen? I don't believe this! Can we leave now? Because I'm going to throw up!"

"Calm down," Tammy whispered. "You're right, but you don't want to get fried for disrespect."

"Why not? She obviously can't respect what we've been through."

"It'll be over soon," said Tammy. "Just listen."

Ms. Dietrich continued. "I probably don't need to tell you girls that the administration is very happy with the progress you have made over the past three years. You know, 759 women applied for the Naval Academy after the law was changed in 1976. Those of you sitting here are among a very select group who not only made the cut but have survived the pioneering process. Did you know that your average entrance SAT scores were 1,253 compared with 1,223 for your male classmates?" She was reading from a "cheat sheet."

"Thirty of you will finish an academic major in the sciences, sixteen pursued a humanities degree, five will complete a major in math, and four of you will receive specific accredited engineering degrees." That's me, thought Sarah proudly.

"Your academic performance has been strong with an average cumulative quality point rating, CQPR, of 2.68, equal to that of the men.

"Your professional performance grades have also been impressive. In conduct, 81 percent of you have received an A, compared to 80 percent of your male classmates, and 13 percent of both men and women received a B.

"As far as aptitude for the naval service, 37 percent of you received an A, compared to 34 percent of the men. Thirty-nine percent received a B, compared to 34 percent of the men."

"I wish she'd stop comparing us to the guys," Sarah whispered to Tammy. "If they get wind of this, we're screwed!"

But Ms. Dietrich wasn't finished. "These figures suggest that you women have complied more vigorously with the rules and regulations of the Naval Academy and may have a stronger aptitude for the naval service than the men."

"Please!" moaned Sarah. "These figures may also suggest that we just didn't get caught as often."

"Shhh!" Tammy reprimanded.

"I'm sorry, Tam, but this is nauseating."

"It's not to me. In fact, it's nice to be built up for once."

"But what if the guys find out?"

"Screw the guys!" Tammy told her firmly. Sarah sat back and rolled her eyes.

The speech went on. "In the area of physical fitness, you have excelled as well. Twenty-five of you have won at least one varsity letter. You have an All-American swimmer among you . . ."

"Yea, Freeman!" Sarah whispered.

". . . and an honorable-mention All-American marksman in pistol who also set a new women's collegiate record in standard fire during the 1979 International Pistol Sectional Intercollegiate Championship. You boast an honorable-mention All-American sailor, who, last year, together with three other women sailors from the Class of '80, won the Women's National Sailing Championship and joined the men in accumulating enough points to win the Fowle Trophy for the overall National Collegiate Sailing Championship, which the Academy has won for an unprecedented three consecutive years. Three of you women fencers teamed to win the Region Six Championships for the past two years, and one of you was a 1979 individual champion. The women's crew team placed third in the 2,000-meter events in Philadelphia's Dad Vail regatta, which determines the small-college rowing champions for women in the eastern United States."

"Yea, Tammy!"

"I must say, I am impressed, and you should be as well. Your attrition rate has been a bit higher than the men's, with 32.1 percent of the women resigning compared to 26.3 percent of the men, although that was probably to be expected given the rigors of plowing new ground in a previously all-male environment. I'm sure it has not been easy living in a fishbowl atmosphere, exacerbated by heavy media interest and some resistance by the men to accept your presence."

Some resistance? thought Kate, across the amphitheater. I think it qualifies as a lot more than *some.*

She found the remarks by Ms. Dietrich interesting but not particularly uplifting and wondered if these statistics were being presented to the men in the brigade. Just as well not, she decided. They would only discount them as facts massaged by the administration to make this experiment with women appear to be working. She knew that there were still women who had not passed the obstacle course or the mile run yet.

Finished with her monologue, Ms. Dietrich opened the floor for questions and discussion. She called on a midshipman Sarah recognized as one of the better volleyball and basketball players. "Ma'am, I'd just like to say that I don't think this place is so bad. I'm not really having any problems here. Yeah, we take grief from the guys every now and then, but I think that's to be expected in a situation like this. We've all done well to get through the first three years like we have, and I plan on making it through this last one with no major glitches."

A small group of women applauded. Although she didn't applaud, that was how Sarah felt. For the most part, she had fond recollections of the past three years. The way she saw it was that those girls who had problems had probably brought them upon themselves by being overweight, being unable to pass the physical fitness test, or not trying to get along with the guys. She herself wasn't having any problems, and even if she were, she wouldn't tell this woman.

Around the room a few more hands were raised. Why are they talking to this woman? Sarah wondered.

Ms. Dietrich acknowledged a hand behind Sarah. Sarah looked over her shoulder. The Fifth Battalion commander and senior woman midshipman rose to her feet.

"Good evening, ma'am. I am Midshipman First Class Elaine Richey, and I have had an experience quite the opposite from the one just described. The past three years have been absolute hell for me, to say the least. I have never been accepted by my male contemporaries. I have been tormented and tortured, mentally and physically." Her voice began to shake.

"Since the day I arrived, I have tried to do my very best. I've studied hard and tried to make a name for myself to show that we women belong here, but all I receive from my classmates and other male midshipmen is constant torment and hatred. I have found dead rats in my mailbox. I have been dragged out to pep rallies so violently that I feared for my physical safety and sometimes even my life. I hardly ever sleep at night, and I always keep my door locked. Every time someone passes me in the hall, they throw taunting comments my way. You cannot imagine how horrible it has been for me here. . . ."

Sarah watched her fall into hysterics.

"And where was our senior leadership? Where was my company officer on the nights they dragged me out to pep rallies or bombed my room with shaving cream? Not as a prank, but because I was a woman. Where were they?"

I can't believe this, Sarah thought. This is the senior woman in our class! The leader among us is breaking down in front of a perfect stranger—a civilian, no less! How dare she! And who was going to do anything about Elaine's situation now, or about *any* of the abuses these women had suffered? They were the first. It was part of the game. They should have expected some obstacles.

Yeah, this place has its downside, thought Sarah. She had had moments of despair when she knew she was not wanted here, but the animosity came from guys who did not know her personally. Once some guy got to know her, he was usually glad she was at this school. "I don't think women should be at the Academy," some would say, "but I like *you* being here." If you tried to get along with the guys, be one of *them* and not set out to prove something for the feminist movement, you could get through here without a lot of hate and harassment.

This meeting was ludicrous. Here was this civilian "three-star," telling a room full of authentic trailblazers about her ridiculously irrelevant experiences of working in an all-male environment. Then the senior woman in the class practically succumbs to a nervous breakdown in front of all them all. What was happening?

Midshipman Richey sat down, drained. Secretary Dietrich, obviously distressed by the oration, recommended that Richey see her personally after the meeting and resumed her position as facilitator, asking if others had suffered similar types of harassment.

Sarah looked around the room. There were no more hands. Good! Let's get out of here, she thought. If the guys hear about this, the harassment we suffered in the past will pale next to the grief we'll take.

Kate listened with the same disgust that gnawed at Sarah. Who did this "senior" woman think she was, coming into our lives now? Where was she when that guy snuck uninvited into my room? Where was she when the cheerleaders were taking so much abuse from the brigade that they quit? Why wasn't she here three years ago to edit all those diatribes published in the *Log* magazine? Elaine Richey was right. Where were the officers? Did they think sending this senior woman to talk to them would make it all right?

Kate was angry. The *nerve* of this woman, to show up now to try and "fix" things! Things were already "fixed" as well as they could be, and the women midshipmen around her had fixed them all by themselves. She glanced proudly around the room at fellow classmates who she knew had endured personal tribulations during the past three years. Like her, most had undoubtedly succumbed to them initially, but then they found the inner strength to persevere.

Maybe this first class of women had not paved a road for future generations of female midshipmen, but they had undoubtedly cleared a path. And however rocky that path might be, it now solidly existed, and they didn't need some Washington bureaucrat, female or otherwise, suddenly to show up second-guessing their decisions or telling them how to yield a machete. They had made it. They were first classmen. They had taken charge alongside their male classmates, and no one was going to blow this year for them by reporting back to the administration that there were "problems." Whatever "problems" remained these women would fix as best they could during their last year here. Then they would graduate to face the fleet and blaze another trail.

Sunday, 14 October 1979

Sarah knocked before peeking into Carrie's room early Sunday morning. The Hall was quiet as most midshipmen slept in.

"Come on in," called Carrie. "It's just me. Margot's at church."

"Good. I need to talk to you." Sarah usually bounded in jovially, but today her tone was serious.

"What's wrong?" asked Carrie, placing the *Washington Post* on her lap.

"I need to tell you about something. Something happened to me last night that's really buggin' me." Sarah pulled a chair from behind Carrie's desk and slumped low in the seat. Carrie waited for her to begin. She had never seen Sarah so serious.

"I had a date last night. With Harry Surpoe. We went to dinner, had a bunch of drinks, went dancing, and got back here after midnight. We're both on a weekend, so we weren't worried about taps. Harry had a cooler in his car, so we sat over by the sea wall and kept drinking, although we were pretty blitzed by then, anyway." Sarah rubbed both hands over her face and looked at the floor.

"Well, Harry is a pretty good-looking guy, and we'd had a lot of fun, so we started making out. And then. . . ." She shook her head as if in disbelief. "And then the next thing I know he has me in the back seat with half my clothes off and is on top of me while I'm telling him, No! I tell him no over and over, but he won't listen." She stood up and began pacing.

"Then I'm thinking to myself, I have to sober up. This is out of control! I don't want to do it with this guy, but he won't stop, no matter what I say! He's pulling his pants down with one hand and holding me down with the other, so I start yelling for him to stop!

"But I'm too late, or too drunk, or . . . I don't know." She paused for a moment and looked out the window, biting her lower lip.

"So he did it. I really didn't want him too, ya know. But I was so drunk, or maybe I thought I'd led him on by making out with him in the first place. I don't know. I only know that I told him not to do it . . . but he did it anyway." She stopped, chewed her thumbnail, and sat down again.

"I didn't want him to do it, Carrie, and now he's probably gonna tell all the guys in his company that he scored with a WUBA, and it'll be all over the brigade! I don't want that kind of reputation. I know I date a lot of guys, but I don't go to bed with them."

"WUBA" was slang for woman midshipman. It stood for nothing that Sarah was aware of besides "working uniform blue 'alpha.'" The way she understood it, if you were a WUBA, you were considered to be one of the "cool" women. It was kind of a compliment.

"I told him no, Carrie. But what if he tells everybody? You know, I can deal with this as long as no one else knows about it."

"There's nothing you can do about that, Sarah."

"You're right. I just needed to talk to somebody. Thanks for listening."

Carrie could see that Sarah was already trying to erase the unsettling event. Effervescent Sarah—live it, get over it, and move on to the next event. She had always been like that.

"I've gotta go," said Sarah, reaching for the door. She paused. "Carrie, if you hear anybody talking about it—any guys, you know—let me know, okay?"

"Okay. But Sarah, you told him no. He should have stopped."

Sarah nodded, but Carrie could see the uncertainty on her face as she left the room.

Tuesday, 30 October 1979

Kate's 3.4 CQPR was solid. She stood in the top 15 percent of the women and the top 20 percent of the class. And she needed to stay there, with service selection just around the corner.

This semester she had been selected company subcommander, a two-striper. As such, her duties were trivial, taking little extra time. She had been interviewed to be the company commander and disappointed when the job went to a guy. Now her focus was on graduation and her impending marriage to Gabe. They had decided to get married in the Naval Academy chapel the day after graduation. It was such a crapshoot, though. The Academy typically held a lottery to determine when weddings would be held, because there were so many couples eager to tie the knot immediately after graduation.

She had joined the track team and loved it. Her coach was incredibly supportive and recommended that she run cross-country. Lengthy runs at the end of the day helped relieve the stress she brought upon herself, and her eating binges had nearly stopped. Her weight was way down, just where she thought it should be, although many teammates commented on her skinniness. She blamed it on the workouts, internally glowing at having finally achieved her goal of being thin.

Yes, first-class year was living up to its much vaunted reputation, and Kate was on top of the world. That was until the media attacked.

Carrie had borrowed the November issue of the *Washingtonian* from a classmate when Sarah stopped by after gymnastics practice. She opened the magazine to page 144 and silently handed it to her friend.

"Women Can't Fight"?! The title filled Sarah with anger. She looked up at Carrie, who shook her head. "It gets worse."

James Webb, an ex-marine and a Naval Academy graduate who had recently finished teaching a semester of English at the Academy, had rekindled a furor that was still smoldering throughout the brigade, pitting male against female midshipmen. His article had evoked a variety of piercing comments from the men, whose basic message was clear: women do not belong here, and thank God somebody finally had the balls to say so. Everyone was talking about it in class.

On the edge of Carrie's rack, Sarah eagerly read the article, which began with a riveting account of the Spartan and demoralizing conditions under which the author and his comrades had fought the Vietnam War. As the article unfolded, Webb's premise became clear: although he believed that the advances made in behalf of equality for women in the previous decade were good, placing them in the service academies was now "poisoning the preparation of men for combat command by sexually sterilizing the Naval Academy environment in the name of equality." The function of the service academies, in Webb's view, was to prepare men for leadership positions so that they might someday exercise command in combat. Any other accomplishments performed by graduates he dismissed as inconsequential or "incidental" to that primary function.

Every problem that Webb believed would arise if women were introduced into combat units had already, he said, "surfaced at the Naval Academy." Although only "three major conduct offenses of sexual fraternization" had been documented in the three years the women had been there, it was Webb's opinion that "sex was commonplace in Bancroft Hall."

"The Hall," he wrote, "which houses 4,000 males and 300 females, is a horny woman's dream."

Sarah slapped the magazine against the desk. "'A horny woman's dream'?" she yelled. "What is he basing his opinion on?"

Carrie shook her head.

"How can he write this stuff—'a horny woman's dream'?! This is awful!"

"I know," said Carrie.

"Do you know what this is going to do to us?" Sarah asked rhetorically, "us" meaning the women.

Carrie nodded. Sarah continued reading.

The article described how the administration had stifled male midshipmen's first-amendment rights by threatening them with retribution for speaking out against the women to the press, while the women were "interviewed like movie stars." Webb interviewed and quoted three male midshipmen from the Class of 1980 and one from the Class of 1979 who had served one semester as deputy brigade commander. Two of the other three were prior-enlisted marines. One was Jerome Gardner, who served as deputy regimental commander during plebe summer when Elaine Richey was regimental commander.

The four men shared similar opinions about women being given preferential treatment in all areas, particularly the assignment of leadership positions and a double standard when it came to discipline. They voiced strong concerns about the future welfare of the military and even the country. Jerome Gardner had argued that as regimental commander, "Richey was the token women. I was the token ex–enlisted marine, we had a token ex–enlisted sailor, a token black and a token high school product. That's just the way it is now."

"Can you believe this stuff, Carrie?" Sarah read on aloud:

Historically, the academies and a few other areas of the military—Marine Corps boot camp, airborne training—have provided a ritualistic rite of passage into manhood. It was one small area of our society that was totally male. Women now have a full range of choice, from the totally female— motherhood—to what was once the totally male—the academies, for example. Males in the society feel stripped, symbolically and actually. I wonder if that doesn't tie into the increase in rapes over the past decade. Rape is a crime of revenge, not passion.

"I thought rape was a crime of violence," said Sarah. She continued reading:

In any event, the real question isn't the women. The real question is this: Where in this country can someone go to find out if he is a man? And where can someone who knows he is a man go to celebrate his masculinity? Is that important on a societal level? I think it is.

"I think I'm going to throw up!" raved Sarah. "This guy can't be for real. So, where do we go to celebrate our femininity? To the labor decks and the OB wards? Oh, no, I forgot, we come to the Naval Academy—to get laid."

Carrie smiled.

"This is incredible!" said Sarah. "Ten pages of this bullshit."

On the last page of the article was a photograph of a row of midshipman covers hanging outside an academic classroom. In the middle of the row hung a solitary female cover. Webb professed a heartfelt concern for the women "emerging into womanhood almost alone, in an isolation that resembles a tour of duty on a desert island."

The symbolic lone cover, thought Sarah.

They study a man's profession, learn the deeds of men, accept men as role models.

This is not a "man's profession," thought Sarah. Women have been in the navy for years, and there are plenty of these men I would *not* accept as role models.

They seem spirited but confused, tolerated but never accepted.

He couldn't be more wrong, she thought. I know the guys don't accept some of the women being here. Heck, *I* don't think some of them should be here. But we've proven ourselves. We've made it to first-class year, and the guys I know accept me as a professional equal.

I see these women ten or twenty years from now, finally deciding that they did indeed lose something, something more intangible than mere femininity. It is easy to say these women are pioneers who are breaking barriers, moving along the fabled cutting edge of social change, and perhaps they are, and I hope that sustains them. But there is a cost, and they, along with society and the men, are paying the price.

Webb's final paragraphs offered solutions: Cease admitting women to the academies altogether. Offer them ROTC scholarships and OCS appointments instead.

Or, if it is the consensus of Congress that the service academies no longer perform their historic function of preparing men to lead in combat, but are now primarily mere academic institutions, it would be logical and cost-effective to close them down.

Webb did not recommend this alternative, but then again, he conceded, he viewed the academies "quite differently than two-thirds of the Congress did in 1975," when they changed the law to admit women.

Sarah stared dumbfounded at Carrie.

"I know," said Carrie. "Unbelievable."

"Do you know what this is going to do to us once the brigade gets hold of it? He's wrong, but they'll jump on this bandwagon in a heartbeat. It's just not fair!

"We've worked too hard to get where we are. We've put up with all the garbage for three years, and now it's our turn! We're on top now. We're first classmen. We're the leaders, and this clown comes out with an article like this, saying that women can't lead, for our plebes, youngsters, and second class-men to read! How can he get away with this?"

Carrie felt the same. Having worked diligently toward becoming company commander for the past three years, she now had second thoughts about taking the post if it were offered to her. Would she now be considered just a token? The thought was very unsettling.

Sarah sighed. "The damage is done, Carrie. I don't know if we'll ever recover from the fallout from this thing."

Thursday, 15 November 1979

Seated on gray folding chairs in Halsey Field House, the Brigade of Midshipmen listened intently to Admiral Thomas Hayward, the chief of naval operations, speaker at tonight's Forrestal Lecture. The Forrestal Lecture Series had been established in 1970, in honor of the late James V. Forrestal, chief architect of the Department of Defense and the first secretary of defense under President Truman in 1947. Each year public figures were invited to speak to the Brigade of Midshipmen to enhance their awareness and appreciation of the social, political, and cultural dimensions of the nation and the world.

Featured speakers in the past three years had included Senator William Proxmire, Gen. Alexander Haig, and the novelist Alex Haley. Although the *Log* had dubbed them the "Bore-us-all" Lectures, Kate generally appreciated the privilege of being able to listen to these quality speakers, even if their talks did cut into study hour.

Kate perused Admiral Hayward's biography in the manila program as he finished his lecture and asked for questions from the brigade. The first two questions focused on the recent extended deployments of several navy ships in the Indian Ocean and the actions the navy was taking to ease the mental and physical strain of the sailors and their families. Kate was ready to get back to her room to begin studying. She folded the program and glanced around the room, hoping no more hands would fly into the air. The sight of several more made her moan.

The admiral called on a female third classman. What could she want to ask? wondered Kate. The youngster stood.

"Sir, Midshipman Third Class Jane Mitchell, sir. Sir, I disagree with the congressional ban on women in combat and wondered if you could tell me why the Naval Academy is training women if we cannot serve in combat."

Four thousand male midshipmen burst into howls and cheers. The roar was deafening. Kate's jaw dropped as mids leaped to their feet, clapping loudly—among them, Gabe.

"Stop it!" Kate cried, trying to pull him down. She couldn't believe he was joining their display. "That's not what she meant to say! That's not what she meant!"

Admiral Hayward raised both hands to quiet the midshipmen and spoke directly into his microphone. "Are you suggesting that we don't need women at the Naval Academy?"

The mayhem doubled. For the next full minute, bedlam reigned in the field house. No one could speak over the cheering.

"Well, that seems to be the consensus of opinion, sir," the third classman replied when the cheering began to subside.

"Well, it all depends on who's voting, and I didn't clap," the admiral rejoined. He gathered the pages of his speech and turned toward stage left, indicating that the lecture was over.

"Oh, no!" said Kate, turning to her roommate beside her. "Who was that girl, and why in the hell did she ask that question?"

"I don't know," replied Terrie. "I think she really meant to ask if the CNO was doing anything to get the law changed now that we are at the Academy. She couldn't really have been questioning our presence here."

"But that's what it sounded like, didn't it?" said Gabe.

"I can't believe you clapped!" Kate shouted. "I thought you supported me being here."

"Gotta go," said Terrie, not wishing to be part of this confrontation. She made her way down the aisle, joining the throng of midshipmen filing out of the field house.

"Kate, this has nothing to do with you personally. It's just a fact. If you girls can't fight in combat, what is the purpose of having you here?"

"Oh, so are you now a member of the 'Why are you here taking the spot of some guy who really could be serving his country' club?" She was incredulous. He had never before questioned her presence at the Academy.

"No. I'm just saying that Congress should either change the law or rethink why they put you girls here in the first place."

"Well, for your information, Gabe, I'm here to serve my country, and I deserve to take advantage of one of the best military educations in the world. And if Congress won't let me serve behind the bridge of a navy combatant or the stick of a fighter aircraft, that isn't my fault. I can only hope that my presence and performance in the fleet will one day change their minds for the girls who come after me."

"Kate." Gabe reached for her arm. "I'm sorry. Please don't take this personally."

She shrugged him off. "But it *is* personal, Gabe. It's been personal for three and a half years. Don't you think it's as frustrating for us girls as it is for you guys? At least you get to *really* serve your country. You haven't had to trail behind some female officer running-mate whose job it was to make sure everyone's personnel file was in order. You think that's why I've been working my ass off at this place?"

"No. I want to drive a *real* navy ship and one day be its commanding officer. And I'm not talking about some destroyer tender or oiler. I'm talking about a combatant—a cruiser or a destroyer or a carrier. How would you feel if they told you you could only fuel the planes you want to fly so badly? See, you don't even have to worry about it. You get to do what you want."

"You mean, if I don't get drafted to go nuke," he replied.

"Exactly. If you get drafted, you don't get to do what you want, and you have no control over your career. How does that feel?"

"I'm sorry, babe. You're right. I'm sorry I clapped."

"I hope you mean that. After Webb's article and now this, it's like we have to start proving ourselves all over again."

"Kate, I'm behind you all the way."

"We're going to be in this together once we're married, you know."

He acknowledged with a nod.

"Come on, then. Walk me back to my room so no one will throw disparaging remarks my way."

"Hey, I don't deter them."

"You lessen the chances."

"You just use me," he replied, grinning as the pair walked through the field house doors.

Friday, 16 November 1979

A tradition of unknown origins, Eighth Wing Players was Bancroft Hall's amateur satire hour. First classmen of the six companies in Sixth Battalion wrote and starred in parodies performed after study hour in the Eighth Wing parking lot. In November 1979, Thirty-third Company stole the show.

Sarah initially refused to perform. Even though they were first classmen now, women in past productions had always been booed, and she was unwilling to take the chance. Once Kurt Loper explained the skit they had in mind for her, however, she acquiesced.

"Let's go!" yelled Kurt, director and choreographer for tonight's performance. The Thirty-third Company cast members rode the elevator to the bottom deck and waited by the doors to the parking lot. Kurt signaled to a company-area window, and the "Pink Panther Theme" purred from speakers on 8-4. Midshipmen hung from Sixth and Eighth Wing windows. They burst into applause as a firstie from Thirty-third Company, dressed in a bridge coat with upturned collar and a fedora low over the brow, emerged from beneath a manhole cover in the middle of the road.

He strolled to the antique lamppost beside the sidewalk and snapped his fingers. A folded newspaper flew through the air from 8-4 straight into his outstretched hand. The crowd went wild. (Although it appeared that the newspaper had flown by itself, it had actually traveled down a fishline rigged from an 8-4 window to the lamppost.) "Inspector Clouseau" snapped open the paper and leaned against the lamppost for the duration of the performance. Each Eighth Wing Players opening tried to outdo the last, and this one had succeeded.

The first skit, entitled "The Football Player Went Down to Rickover," was set to the music of Charlie Daniels's "The Devil Went Down to Georgia." The football player, representing the boy in the song, was played by Denzel Simmons. Dressed in white works, he carried a pigskin to Crystal City in Washington, D.C., for his interview with Admiral Rickover, the devil, played by Kurt Loper. Wearing service dress blues with three masking-tape stripes on the sleeves, Kurt was made up as a shriveled old man, his hair baby-powder white. He flashed the atom emblazoned on his rain cape as he waltzed around the parking lot, tempting the football player with a pair of giant golden dolphins, emblem of the nuclear navy and counterpart to the golden fiddle in the song.

Now the football player went down to Rickover for a nuclear-power interview, which would win him the golden dolphins. But the ornery old man presented him with a chalkboard full of mathematical problems. The football player examined the problems, but, completely perplexed, he conceded and punted the football. The crowd roared.

Then two beautiful girls, played by civilian girlfriends, appeared from behind a curtain with a pair of giant golden wings, representing navy air. They presented them to the hero, who walked "offstage" beaming broadly, arms around both girls. The audience screamed their delight.

The skit parodied the current rumor that the Class of 1980 was to become the first class to fall victim to a nuclear-power draft. Not enough male midshipmen had voluntarily indicated a desire to join Admiral Rickover's nuclear navy to fill his established quota. The navy, however, was prepared to use an involuntary draft to get its share of nuclear-powered ship and submarine drivers. Mids hoping to be "airdales" or conventional ship drivers were now thinking seriously of joining the Marine Corps just to avoid being drafted. The Marine Corps was thrilled. Some of the most intelligent men in the class would be yelling *"Semper fi"* come service-selection night.

The next skit was staged in the center of the parking lot, where three long tables were placed side by side, full of items typically issued to new plebes on Induction Day. A poster attached to the middle table read "Gear Issue." On another table lay an oversized set of shoulder boards with six stripes and a neatly folded letter sweater. The skit began with a plebe-detail firstie pacing before the tables. Six bewildered male plebes in civilian clothes filed up, whereupon the firstie signaled them to fill a white duffel bag with gear.

As the bumbling plebes filled their bags, an attractive female plebe vampishly entered. Catcalls rang out from the windows above her. Sarah was in her element. Dressed in an aquamarine dress, she sashayed across the parking lot, pausing until the firstie noticed her. He ran to her assistance, dropping to one knee to ask how he could be of service. The mids went crazy: everyone *knew* how male firsties gave preferential treatment to new female plebes.

He placed her arm in his and guided her to the table that was obviously "female midshipman gear issue." As the skit's male plebes watched with confusion, the firstie presented Sarah with the letter sweater and helped her put it on. The audience burst into jeers and applause. Next, the firstie placed the set of six-striper shoulder boards on her shoulders, and the applause doubled: everyone also knew that the girls were practically issued varsity letters and stripes as soon as they arrived at the Academy.

The firstie ordered the male plebes to fall in behind him as he escorted Sarah "offstage" to the theme of "The Pink Panther." The "Inspector" folded his newspaper and sauntered into the shadows. The "curtain fell."

Back on 8-4, the firsties were ecstatic. This had been one of the best Eighth Wing Players ever! Kurt was lauded for his Academy Award–winning performance as Admiral Rickover, and the entire company was on a natural high.

Tammy had watched the performance from an 8-4 window. "You looked great down there," she told Sarah, who was changing into white works and a sweatshirt.

"Thanks, Tam. It was really great, wasn't it? Kurt and Denzel were perfect! And how about that gear-issue skit? What a riot!"

"Well, I don't know about that one," said Tammy. "I'm not sure we should perpetuate that image of us girls."

"Oh, come on, Tammy. Give me a break. They're practically handing out letter sweaters to almost all the women now. The one time I wore mine I caught so much grief that I'll never wear it again."

"I got one for crew, Sarah. And I earned it."

"I know you did, Tammy. I feel like I earned mine, too. But what about stripes? You can't tell me that the girls in our class with four stripes weren't handed them by the administration."

"What about Carrie, Sarah? She's a three-striper."

Sarah paused. Carrie had certainly earned her stripes, in Sarah's mind.

"I'm just talking about the four-stripers, Tammy," she replied. "Listen, I just had a blast down there. Let's talk about this later, okay?"

Tammy said nothing.

"I'll see you later," called Sarah as she headed for Kurt's room, hoping he might have some ice cream on his ledge. If not, she might talk him into going out into town for some. She wanted to recapture that natural high.

Wednesday, 21 November 1979

The white index card containing her name, alpha code, and Social Security number lay on top of her blotter. Sarah recognized it as the one she had filled in last September indicating her first and second choices for service selection. First, navy air pilot. Second, naval flight officer (NFO—the backseater). She was afraid to pick it up. Its back would reveal the fate of her naval career, the Bureau of Medicine's decision about a waiver for her to fly. Her dream would either soar or crash and burn.

She picked up the card and stared at its front. Although she had indicated that her second choice was to be an NFO, she had since changed her mind. Sarah was going to be the one in control of the "stick" or not fly at all. She wasn't placing her life in someone else's hands. Her waiver just *had* to have been approved.

She gingerly turned the card over.

> BUMED has found you physically not qualified for flying
> because of height and excessive refractive error. PQ
> (physically qualified) Unrestricted Line. If you have any
> questions, please see Mrs. Miller, Medical Records Office.

Tears sprang to her eyes as she slumped back onto her rack, defeated. Who was I kidding? They've always told me my eyes weren't good enough to fly. I just never listened. Now what am I going to do? Be an admin officer somewhere?

She had considered no other service. First-class cruise had convinced her that surface line was too male-dominated for her liking, as was the Marine Corps. Sarah was finished pioneering. She was unwilling to break any more nontraditional ground for a while.

Submarines were excluded by law, and she was absolutely not going to be a GURL (general unrestricted line officer). She had not busted her rear end at this place for the last three and a half years to push paper or sit behind a desk. There was no one else to whom she could appeal. BUMED was the head guru in these matters. Flying was out. Now how was she going to tell her dad?

Monday, 26 November 1979

Kate was excited. Finally, a mile run she did not dread. Cross-country track had sculpted her physique into the best shape she had ever been. She felt thin, light, invincible, and today she was running the mile for graded time with her physical education class, which included Dirk Walker.

His negative opinion of women at the Naval Academy had not changed since plebe summer, and the easing of physical requirements for the women had fueled his disdain. It was Kate's goal today to beat him at his own game and run the mile faster than he. After they peeled off their white works, the instructor announced the mile heats. Kate and Dirk were in the same one.

The lieutenant blew the whistle, and they were off. On the last lap, Kate glanced back at Dirk, half a lap behind. Her lead energized her, and she sprinted over the finish line. Justice! she thought, jogging slowly around the track to cool down. She watched Dirk finish at least twenty seconds later.

As the class pulled their white works back on over their gym gear, Kate couldn't help herself. She sauntered over beside Dirk amid a group of male classmates.

"You were cooking out there, Kate," one remarked. "What was your time?"

"Six-seventeen," she replied casually.

"Good job!"

"Thanks!"

"How did you do, Dirk?" she asked.

He stared at the floor. "Six-forty."

"Hmm." Yes! I did it! she gloried silently as she turned away. I beat you, and you feel it! Ha, ha! How's it feel to be beaten by a girl?

"Good job, Kate." Who said that? Kate spun around.

Dirk.

Her glory disintegrated as she realized that she'd done exactly what had so often been done to her—humiliated someone in front of their peers for something they could not help or change. She had purposely asked him his time in front of their classmates to emasculate him, and she now felt horrible.

"Thanks," she replied meekly. She wanted to tell him he had done well also, but the damage was done. She pulled on her white works blouse and gathered her books. Gloating gets you nowhere, she scolded herself. Way to bilge my classmate.

Thursday, 29 November 1979

Toward the end of Army Week, when all hell breaks loose, Sarah sat in her room during study hour, thinking about her interview with the Civil Engineer Corps earlier that afternoon. It could not have gone worse, but she'd had no idea what questions they were going to ask.

After her receipt of the card that shattered her hopes of a flying career, officers from the Civil Engineer Corps and Supply Corps began recruiting her, promising a realm of shore billets. Both sounded intriguing, although not as exciting as being a navy pilot. The Civil Engineer Corps (CEC) sparked her interest most, since there she could use her engineering training.

The interview board consisted of one navy CEC captain, several CEC commanders, and the lieutenant who had initially talked her into considering the corps. She was the first interviewee among several NPQ (not physically qualified) classmates, the rest of them male, who attacked her like piranhas for the "gouge" after her interview.

The whole thing was depressing. The interview board had asked her the definition of *engineering ethics,* to which she babbled some unimpressive response. She had never heard the term before, as had none of her potential CEC classmates, who ran to the library to look it up before their interviews. That made her feel better, but it hadn't made her look any more intelligent to the board members, who were also concerned about her grades. Her last QPR had been a 1.76 because she had gotten a D in fluid mechanics and a systems engineering course. She felt she had been successful at convincing the board that she would bring her grades up, but now she wondered if there was any point. They probably wouldn't even let her into the Civil Engineer Corps after that interview.

Sarah knew she should be in the library, like Tammy, getting some real studying done, but she hated walking all the way over there. As she reached for her fluids textbook, there was a knock at the door. Before she could respond, the door burst open, and three guys with pantyhose over their heads rushed in.

The next thing she knew, Sarah was blindfolded and gagged. She thought she recognized the guys as classmates in her company and decided not to put up a fight. Probably another Army Week prank, she thought. Carrie, Meredith, and she had pulled their own at evening meal earlier. The three women had climbed onto chairs and made good Sarah's plebe-year vow of testing her tits for Army. The brigade loved it!

The men led her out the door and down the hall. Sarah hoped they weren't taking her out of the company area. She wondered where the CMOD was— not that some plebe was going to question the actions of three upperclassmen, even if the actions did appear somewhat out of the ordinary.

As they turned left, she started to resist, afraid that they were leaving the company area. She dug her heels into the linoleum, but they grabbed her under the arms and lifted her off the floor, carrying her another fifty feet before pushing open a door to a room.

We're still in the company area, she thought. In fact, if I mentally navigated correctly, I think I'm in the Love Grotto. ("Love Grotto" was the nickname for Denzel's room. His roommates had named it that after meeting some women from Hood College who had named their room at Hood the "Den of Foxes.")

Sarah smelled a cigar. She could tell that the room was dark, and she sensed the presence of a number of individuals. Oh, man, she thought nervously, who's here? All guys, I'm sure, but what are they up to? Are they classmates? Company mates? Should I go along with this?

They carried her to the end of the room, stood her in front of a square concrete pillar, and tied her hands behind it. Now she was scared. When they tried to tie her feet to the post, she kicked and shook her head no. They left her feet free, and her fear subsided slightly as she realized that they weren't going to do anything she didn't want them to. Or so she hoped.

I should stop this, she thought. Why am I going along with this?

Because you're afraid they'll be mad at you if you don't. You want these guys to like you, right? Besides, they're just playing around. Go along with the joke, for Pete's sake. It must be classmates. They're not going to let anything happen to you.

No, I should stop this right now. They'll understand.

But before she could speak, a male voice Sarah thought she recognized spoke first.

"Welcome to the Love Grotto, with your hosts the Duke of Depravity, the Sultan of Sensuality, the Earl of Ecstasy, and the Lord of Lust." Sarah almost started to laugh.

"If you do not resist, we will not harm you. Now, let us welcome you." Someone approached her and lifted her sweatshirt to expose her belly button. Sarah tried to tilt her head back to see under the blindfold, but the pillar kept her head in place.

She felt something cold and textured against the skin of her abdomen. A football? What are they up to? Others approached and repeated the move with what she thought was a baseball, then a soccer ball.

This is too weird, she thought. Time to quit.

But then they untied her. Someone removed her gag, then led her to the other side of the room, still blindfolded, and made her lie flat on what she could tell was a slatted bench. They must have carried one up from Stribling Walk.

Tell them to stop, she thought.

Someone lifted her shirt.

Tell them no.

They poured a liquid into her belly button.

End this now, Sarah!

Someone began licking the fluid from her belly.

She almost laughed. This was so crazy! Or was it?

The person licking her belly slowly moved toward her head. She felt his breath on her face as he began to kiss her.

"Enough!" she shouted, pushing him away. "This has gone far enough!" She stood up and pulled off the blindfold, keeping her eyes focused on the ground. She didn't want to know who was in the room. She knew where the door was and headed straight for it.

"Sarah!" someone called, but she grabbed the door handle and flung it open, not looking back. No one came after her. She walked back to her room.

Angry, invaded, ashamed, hurt, disbelieving—she couldn't decide how she felt right now. Perhaps it was a combination of all those emotions that was causing her to shake. She sat at her desk and rocked herself.

I don't understand this. I thought we were friends. I thought I had proved myself to them and they considered me their equal. Their professional equal. Maybe Webb was right. "Tolerated but never accepted"—wasn't that how he put it?

She stared into space.

No. They're just being guys. They're just joking around. It was a gag. Don't take it so personally, she thought. They never would have kidnapped Tammy. They did it to you because they knew you would take it the right way. They knew you would be cool about it. So why get so upset? Maybe you should be flattered they chose you.

She bit her bottom lip.

I don't know. Maybe they don't take any of us here seriously. Not even me.

She decided to force the event from her mind, vowing never to tell anyone what had happened, certain that no one present in that room ever would, either.

Friday, 21 December 1979

Tammy swung her new Firebird into the Andrews Air Force Base air terminal parking lot and stopped in front of its entrance. Sarah hopped out of the passenger seat, in service dress blues, and pushed the seat forward to retrieve her two suitcases in the back.

"Thanks again, Tam. I really appreciate your driving me to the airport."

"No problem, Sarah. Glad you finally got a ride in my new car. Isn't it great?"

"Yeah. It's really nice, Tammy," Sarah replied. The Firebird would not have been the car of her choice, but a number of mids had used their low-interest-rate car loans to purchase sporty Z-28s or Firebirds.

"Have a great time in Norfolk, Tam. Tell Danny I said hi!" Sarah shoved the door closed with her hip.

"Have a great time in the Caribbean! I'm so jealous."

"Hey, I told you you could come with me. My mom said we're going to decorate a Christmas tree on the beach!" Sarah beamed.

"Well, don't get too sunburned, and bring me back a shell or something."

"How about some rum?"

"Make it Jack Daniels instead. Merry Christmas, Sarah!"

"Merry Christmas, Tammy! Drive carefully." Sarah watched Tammy pull away from the curb and walked toward the terminal.

Inside, an airman behind the counter informed her that the hop scheduled to fly the first leg of her Christmas leave journey to the Virgin Islands had not yet arrived. He showed her the lounge where other Caribbean-bound midshipmen were waiting. Among them were Drew Collins and his brother, Steve, who was a plebe.

In November, Carrie Freeman had told Sarah about Drew, a second classman in her company, who was organizing a Christmas hop to the Caribbean; his family lived on the naval station at Roosevelt Roads, Puerto Rico. At a meeting in the Steerage two weeks earlier Drew had told the assembled group that any midshipman who lived in the Caribbean was eligible to sign up. There were plenty of seats, and Sarah signed on for one. She remembered working briefly with Drew last spring on the organizational staff of the Naval Academy's Foreign Affairs Conference. He was tall, blonde, and cute, but an underclassman. She never dated underclassmen.

As she looked for a seat in the lounge, Drew was suddenly at her side offering to carry her bags. What a gentleman, she thought, thanking him for relieving her of the load.

"The plane should be here in about fifteen minutes," he said. "Want to sit over here?" He pointed to a seat covered with a *Sports Illustrated*. He looks like a jock, she thought.

"Sure. Thanks!" she replied. "Man, this is going to be great! I can't wait to be on the beach and forget about finals. My last one was this morning. They about wiped me out this year." Sarah was so glad the administration had changed the schedule to allow finals to be taken before Christmas leave.

"I know what you mean," said Drew, setting her suitcases in front of her chair. "Is this your first time to the Caribbean?"

"First time since my folks moved down there," she told him. The Beckers had retired to St. Croix after leaving Iran. "My ship for first-class cruise had several port calls there. It's really beautiful."

"Yeah, and there's so much to do," agreed Drew.

"Hey, I'm going to go get a soda," said Sarah, retrieving several quarters from the pocket along the waist seam of her trousers. "Want one?"

"No, thanks," he answered. "Hurry back." His request caught her off guard, but she decided he meant nothing by it and smiled.

Sarah sipped her diet soda on the way back to the lounge, where she found Drew surrounded by his father (a navy captain), his sister, a third classman at the Air Force Academy, and his brother Steve. The cheerful family reunion kept him occupied until they were all on board the C-131.

Sarah fell asleep shortly after takeoff, exhausted from studying late the night before. An hour later, sensing a presence, she woke to find Drew seated beside her.

"Want to play backgammon?" he asked.

"Sure," replied Sarah, stretching her arms above her head and yawning. "What time is it? Have we been off the ground long?"

"Oh, about an hour or so. You've been out cold." Have you been keeping tabs? she wondered as Drew set up the black and white backgammon pieces.

"You may have to refresh me on the rules," Sarah said. "I haven't played this since I was in Iran with my parents."

"Iran?" he asked, intrigued. "Your parents were in Iran?"

The topic ignited a conversation that lasted for two hours. Sarah found Drew gentle, intelligent, and fun-loving. They spoke with the ease of old friends.

She learned that he was an aerospace engineering major and a member of the Academy's 150-pound lightweight football team, of which he had been elected one of next year's co-captains. He had also been selected as one of four midshipmen to attend the French Naval Academy on a foreign-exchange program this coming spring. He spoke the language fluently, and Sarah found herself inexplicably drawn to him.

They talked about everything. Drew was so open and self-assured. He even awkwardly admitted having spent the last three days restricting off demerits for calling one of her female classmates a "hosebag" as she walked through his company area. His confession dismayed Sarah briefly. Did he hold all women midshipmen in contempt, like so many other male mids? This seemed so unlike him. Drew made no excuses for his actions and apologized as if he had said it to her. "It was a stupid thing to do, which I really feel bad about." His sincerity impressed her.

The two talked until the plane landed at the Jacksonville Naval Air Station, where the entourage would remain overnight. At dinner Sarah and another female midshipman ran into Drew and his brother and sister at the base Pizza Shack. The pounding of her heart when she saw Drew hinted that the two were destined for more than casual conversation.

They spent the evening together at the Officers Club bar with other midshipmen on the flight consuming numerous pitchers of beer. In an effort to be alone with him, Sarah impishly suggested that she and Drew reconnoiter the Christmas tree from the BOQ lobby to take back to her room. Comprehending her intentions, he followed her from the bar. The couple had barely reached the bottom of the entrance stairs to the Officers Club when he swept her into his arms. The mutual passion of their embrace lasted the entire Christmas break.

Drew caught a helicopter from Roosevelt Roads to St. Croix three days after their arrival in the Caribbean. Sarah and he relaxed beside her parents' pool for two days. Despondent when he departed, she promised to take the same hop to Puerto Rico within the next few days to visit him.

On a moonlit evening, on the officers' beach at Roosevelt Roads, the couple agreed that their shared passion was an infatuation, fueled by the romantic setting of the Caribbean. They both had long-term relationships back in the States. Once they were back at the Academy, things would return to normal. This had been a fun interlude, nothing more—except that Drew extended his Caribbean stay for three days, when he had originally planned on leaving a few days early to meet his girlfriend. And when he finally did leave to meet her, Sarah's heart burned at the thought.

CHAPTER THIRTEEN

First-Class Year, Second Semester

F̲ar better it is to dare mighty things, to win glorious triumphs,
even though checked by failure, than to take rank with those
poor spirits who neither enjoy much nor suffer much, because they
live in the gray twilight that knows neither victory nor defeat.

Theodore Roosevelt

Friday, 4 January 1980

The strongest rebuttal to James Webb's "Women Can't Fight" article was
authored by the superintendent of the Naval Academy. Published as a letter
to the editor in the January issue of the *Washingtonian,* it granted the women
at Navy a momentary reprieve from the female-bashing. Although staunch
Webb supporters in the brigade alleged that Admiral Lawrence was merely
doing his administrative duty, his words were uplifting to the women.

"Of course he's going to support you girls," Dirk Walker told Kate.
"What'd you expect him to say?"

Kate knew better. Admiral and Mrs. Lawrence were avid supporters of the
Class of 1980. Mrs. Lawrence had even been named an honorary member.

After the mile run last fall, Dirk and Kate had agreed to disagree about the
presence of women at the Academy. Like so many other men, he admitted
that although he didn't think women in general should be at the Academy, he
thought she had proven herself and deserved to be there. Kate failed to follow his reasoning but was happy to no longer be a target of his malice.

Across Bancroft, Sarah read the superintendent's letter to the editor with great
interest and hope. Admiral Lawrence made clear that, although Webb was a

324

decorated combat veteran, his impressions of women at the Academy had been established during a brief five-month period. As superintendent of the Naval Academy, Admiral Lawrence believed that his own experience observing the women would be "useful to readers in evaluating the validity of Mr. Webb's perspective."

"Go get 'im, Admiral!" Sarah called.

Admiral Lawrence made clear that Congress had decided to admit women to the service academies because they were an integral part of the military services, and their numbers were steadily increasing. The intensive academic, physical, and professional training at the Academy had not been modified because of the presence of women except in minor ways dictated by physiology and standards of privacy. The women participated in every scheduled evolution alongside their male counterparts and were performing effectively in leadership roles.

Admiral Lawrence disagreed with Webb's theory that the physical abuse and punishment of plebes to the point of breakdown was desirable and even necessary to produce good leaders. The admiral himself had never been physically abused as a midshipman at the Naval Academy, and he still endured six years as a POW in Vietnam.

As to assertions that sex was rampant in Bancroft Hall, the admiral stated that violations concerning fraternization had been few.

"Change comes hard, particularly [change] of institutions such as the Navy and Naval Academy, because we cherish our tradition," the admiral quoted a former commandant of midshipmen, who also stated that "the process of integrating women at the Academy has suffered from the intense glare of publicity wherein every false step was quickly put on film or quoted in the press. A platform has been provided for every critic—and they exist for every institutional change." Admiral Lawrence welcomed the scrutiny as long as it was "tempered with fairness and objectivity."

As an observer of Naval Academy graduates for over thirty years, it was his professional opinion that

> the quality of graduates was as high as it had ever been and the Academy continues to produce superb leaders, fully prepared to perform all of those roles officers of the naval service have traditionally fulfilled. And the country was better off for the fact that, among these leaders, there now were women.

"Yes!" Sarah exclaimed, clenching her fist in midair. "You tell 'em, Admiral!"

She admired Admiral Lawrence. He had attended one of her gymnastics meets and personally congratulated her on her performance. For him to take time out of his busy schedule to do so had meant a great deal to her. She realized that this was the mark of a great leader—supporting the rank and file.

James Webb replied to the admiral's letter, disagreeing that the plebe experience today was similar to the physical hazing he had endured as a member of the Class of 1968. He also strongly believed that academics had always taken a secondary role to military education at the Naval Academy. As for women in the military, he wanted the readership to know that

> we are the only nation in the world doing this. The Soviet Union, which experimented with women in combat during World War II out of sheer necessity, now has only 10,000 women in a military of 4.4 million. What an enticement we must be offering them as we play our silly sociopolitical games.

Sarah shook her head. The last three and a half years had not been a game to her. She wanted to serve her country, travel, and experience those equal opportunities advertised by the military. She understood why she could not fly, but why did gender, an issue that had never held her back before, now suddenly rise to halt dreams she had set her heart on accomplishing?

Tuesday, 29 January 1980

Sarah met Drew right after study hour in the catwalks of the Rotunda, despite her exhaustion from the afternoon's gymnastics practice. It had become routine. The two tried to study at the library but always ended up talking instead. When their grades began to suffer, Sarah stayed in her room to study while Drew went to the library alone. They agreed to meet each evening for the hour before taps. Sarah usually came to see him. It was easier for her, as a firstie, to make excuses if she was a little late for taps.

Their relationship was getting more serious. Tonight, as they sat on the stairs outside Twelfth Company, Sarah sensed an uneasiness about Drew. He kept standing up to lean against the white railing, only to sit back down a few minutes later.

"What's wrong, Drew?"

"Nothing," he replied. "No, that's not true. I mean, actually it *is* true. That is, I mean nothing is 'wrong.'" Sarah warmed to his boyish stammer.

"Just tell me," she said, thinking she knew the source of his hesitancy.

"Well, I was just wondering . . . and it's okay if you say no. I mean. . . ." His foot pawed the marble floor. "Sarah, would you go to my Ring Dance with me?"

Call it woman's intuition or whatever you like, but somehow she had known that was what he was nervous about asking her, and she had been nervous that he wouldn't.

"I would love to go to your Ring Dance with you. But what about Trisha? I mean, have you told her?"

"No, but I will. I just really want to go with you, Sarah. I'm not sure what to do about Trisha."

"Well, don't do anything rash. Remember, this is only a Caribbean infatuation." They laughed at the phrase they used to describe their relationship. How she would tell Ryan was something Sarah would address later.

The bell clanged, waking Sarah to the fact that she was now late for taps.

"Oh, no! I've gotta go, sweets," she said hurriedly, turning to race up the stairs leading to the Rotunda catwalk. She had almost a half-mile to run to get to her company area.

Drew grabbed her wrist, and she spun to face him. Risking much more than a PDA violation, he pulled her to him and kissed her before letting her race to the other side of their world.

Thursday, 7 February 1980

Several weeks ago, Sarah had received word that she would be a welcome addition to the Civil Engineer Corps, excluding, of course, their naval construction battalions, which were still closed to women since they deployed to areas of conflict. So tonight, service-selection night, held no special surprise.

As class standings resounded over the Bancroft Hall loudspeakers, Sarah, Tammy, and Kurt listened from the girls' room for their numbers. Sarah had resigned herself to becoming a civil engineer instead of a pilot. It was a crushing blow, but aviation would just have been another path to pioneer. Granted, there were only several women currently serving in the CEC, and she and one other, Justine Harper, her roommate from first-class cruise, were the only two women selected from the Class of 1980. There was something about the ego and psyche of an aviator, though. They didn't want women in their ranks, while the CEC had received her so warmly.

The next set of numbers included Kurt's and Tammy's, and they stood to leave for Smoke Hall. Kurt was going to be a nuke. Tammy hoped to sign on as a ship driver. She wanted a ship out of Norfolk, where Danny was stationed. The two of them had become quite serious.

"Wish me luck, guys," she called anxiously. "I don't know what I'll do if I can't get a ship out of Norfolk. Go GURL, I guess." A list of fifty-nine general unrestricted line officer billets had been delivered to the women of '80 two weeks earlier.

"Don't you dare, Tammy! You get a ship! That's always been your dream. Long-distance romances can work," Sarah said with a confidence she didn't really feel. Ryan had been at sea since last September. Sarah didn't know what ships Tammy would find available, but she hoped her roommate would not forsake her dreams of being a surface-line officer by choosing some lesser job just to get a duty station in Norfolk. No guy was worth that.

"You pick a ship!" Sarah called out again, even though Tammy was already out of sight.

The waiting was over, and Kate's dream had been realized. Because of her high class standing she was one of the first women to choose a surface ship, the USS *Samuel Gompers,* a destroyer tender out of Norfolk. Thank goodness, her Naval Academy education would not be wasted. She was going to do what the men did. The only problem was that Gabe would be going to Pensacola for flight training immediately after graduation leave. They would not be stationed together, an issue they had discussed at length.

He wanted her to try and get stationed on the USS *Lexington* in Pensacola. She just wanted a surface ship no matter where it was home-ported. We can see each other on weekends, she reasoned. Besides, I have to go to SWOS in Newport, Rhode Island. We'll be apart, regardless. Norfolk, however, meant that their separation would be longer.

Gabe had persuaded her to meet him that night at the Class of 1980's celebration in Dahlgren Hall, despite her typical aversion to class events. Who needed the hassle they inevitably provided? Snide comments, disgusted glances from male mids escorting attractive civilian dates. But tonight she didn't care. Let 'em look, she thought. I'm on cloud nine, and I want to celebrate with the man who means the most to me.

In Dahlgren Hall, Terrie pointed toward two classmates the girls knew from Masqueraders. "Come on, Kate, let's go talk to Paul and Jeff. We can watch for Gabe there."

Kate followed her roommate and conversed excitedly about their future. Terrie was one of the five women to select aviation. Four had selected pilot and one, NFO. Terrie would begin flight training immediately after graduation and was elated over her luck.

Ten minutes later Kate felt a presence behind her, which she initially ignored until she felt a sting in her service dress blue–clad derriere. She screamed, jumped hastily aside, and faced a smirking classmate from First Regiment. Embarrassed and furious, she realized that this classmate had bitten her on the rear end. Bitten her! In public! Behind him, four other classmates were suffocating with laughter. She couldn't believe it! It must have been a dare to elicit some crazed response from her.

"Enough!" she heard herself scream. "I don't have to take this kind of bullshit from anyone!" She turned vehemently on her attackers. "Let's have it! Name and alpha code. Now!" She was furious, flaming on them as she had done with her plebes.

"What're you gonna do, Brigman?" one asked snidely. "Place me on report?" His sarcasm fueled her fury.

"You'd better believe it!" she told him. "You are not getting away with that!"

"So what's the offense gonna be?" he asked, smiling coyly to his cohorts, who were obviously intoxicated. "PDA?"

His remark sent them into rollicking peals of laughter.

"You're down, mister. Down hard! Now give me your alpha code!"

The leader of the hyenas refused, and the rest followed suit, but she knew she could get the information from someone else.

Putting a classmate on report was practically a sin, but Kate was fed up. She was sick and tired of being ridiculed to the point of tears while the perpetrators were constantly let off the hook to strike again. She was tired of acquiescing. She was ready to fight back, and if it took frying a classmate to turn the tide, then so be it.

Wednesday, 5 March 1980

Wednesday afternoon Sarah and Carrie drove to the Randolphs' house to hang out. After Ryan stayed there during Commissioning Week last year when he escorted Sarah to her Ring Dance, she had a standing invitation from them to come over anytime. This afternoon, first classmen were granted three-striper liberty (the freedom to leave the Academy grounds after their last class, with the requirement to return by taps).

"I really should be working on my project," Sarah remarked, unlocking the side door with the key the Randolphs had given her. Mr. and Mrs. Randolph were still at work. "It's nice to get away from that place for a while, though. We won't stay long."

Carrie nodded, following Sarah into the kitchen with a grocery bag containing Heavenly Hash ice cream, a bag of M&Ms, and diet soda.

Sarah pulled the carton of ice cream from the bag, opened it, and dumped M&Ms across the smooth surface. She pulled a spoon from the counter drawer and scooped out a huge bite.

"Want some?" she asked Carrie. "Anne and I used to do this after class in high school. Eat a half-gallon of Heavenly Hash with a pound of M&Ms and watch *All My Children.* We did it almost every day and never gained a pound. Now I can only do this because gymnastics is over and I ran seven miles yesterday."

Carrie grinned and grabbed a spoon. "You guys did pretty well this year."

"Won three meets and lost three. Not bad for our first season. I'm looking forward to starting crew on Monday, though."

"Me, too." Carrie was also rowing crew for her spring sport. Her swimming career had finally concluded.

"Will you miss swimming, Car?" Sarah asked.

"No. I've always wanted to try other sports, so this is my chance." Sarah opened the liter of soda and poured them both a glass.

"So, how's it going as company commander?" asked Sarah. "Who'd have thought?"

"I know," replied Carrie. "Although you know, this is really weird, but plebe summer I was walking down the hall and something just came to me, like a premonition or something, and I just knew that's what I wanted to do."

"Be a company commander?"

"Yeah. I really liked the guy we had as our company commander First Set, and I decided that was what I wanted to be. So I kind of made a commitment to myself then, although I never told anyone. But you know, it was kind of weird, 'cause my company officer never held any kind of interview sessions with the firsties in my company who were contending for the position.

"I asked the first-semester company commander about it, and he told me that it had come down to myself and another classmate. He said he recommended me."

"Everybody likes you."

"I'd like to think so. They clapped when our company officer announced his choice, but I sensed their apprehension at having a 'woman in charge.'"

"But you earned it. They know that."

"Yeah, but Webb's article did a number on the women-with-stripes issue. I don't know, I just hope I can be a good leader."

"Of course you will," replied Sarah. "Having them like and accept you is half the battle."

"Well, I didn't make any friends with the plebes before Christmas leave."

"Who cares about the plebes?" Sarah asked, scooping out another bite of ice cream.

"Well, we're up in the company area after Christmas dinner watching the skits. Our class put on skits about the plebes, and I played one of our female plebes who's a real smack. We poked fun at them, and everything was all in jest.

"Then it's the plebes' turn. Well, instead of putting on skits about the firsties, they put on skits about each other. I couldn't believe it. They're really a different breed to begin with, but every year the Christmas skits have been the plebes' opportunity to slam their firsties. Not these guys. They start slamming each other, and their first skit was about their female company mates. I couldn't believe it! One guy stood up and sang a misogynist song that he and his roommates wrote, portraying one of the women as a conscienceless slut who slept with everybody. It was brutal, and totally incompatible with the Academy's goal of cultivating classmate loyalty and camaraderie."

"You're kidding," said Sarah. "Didn't anybody stop them?"

"That's the problem. Everybody just sat there, stunned. Our company officer was there, obviously uncomfortable, but he didn't say anything. I didn't, either. Now I feel bad, because I should have. I should have stopped them midsong."

"So should the company commander or company officer. If you had spoken up, they would have labeled you a bitch."

"I don't know. Anyway, later that night I called all the plebes into the wardroom and blasted them for their off-color behavior. I explained to them the importance of classmate loyalty and working as a team."

"Did they hear you?"

"I think most of them did, but I wish I had done it in front of the whole company. I guess I was afraid they might think I was siding with the women, and I've tried so hard to remain impartial to them."

"Me, too."

"It was kind of the same way last semester when I was conduct officer and had to decide how many demerits Drew was going to get for that 'hosebag' thing.

"He got fried for seventy-five and two for disrespect, but if I recommended seventy-five, the guys in my company were gonna be really pissed. If I didn't recommend seventy-five, all the women were going to be on my case. It was a no-win situation. So I ended up compromising and recommending thirty, which is what he got, and *everybody* was mad at me, the guys and the women. If he'd gotten seventy-five, he wouldn't have been able to go on the French Naval Academy foreign exchange."

"And I wouldn't have met him in the Caribbean."

"That's right. He would have had to restrict longer over Christmas."

"Well, although I wish he wasn't going to France, I'm thankful he got to go home on time for Christmas," Sarah said.

Friday, 21 March 1980

Kate and Gabe were in a print shop in Annapolis choosing wedding invitations. So far their efforts had been fruitless because they could not agree on the wording of the invitation. Kate wanted both their ranks to appear on the invitation, and Gabe wanted neither.

"We earned them," she argued.

"Who cares?" he countered.

"I bet it would be all right with you if we just listed *your* rank," she said caustically.

"No, that wouldn't be fair, Kate, although that's probably what *Service Etiquette* says is correct."

"Oh, right!" she fumed. "I doubt that *Service Etiquette* covers this situation. The copy we were issued was published back in the Dark Ages."

They argued for twenty minutes and finally decided to return to Bancroft Hall to check *Service Etiquette.* Kate knew it would not be in there, the book was so outdated. Why couldn't he just go along with her wishes? she wondered as they rode in his Corvette in silence.

They were to be married at 1500 the day after graduation, but there was so much to do. Another million things to coordinate with final exams, commissioning requirements, shipping arrangements for their personal goods, Commissioning Week visitors, and graduation. Kate wanted to cry. This should be one of the happiest times of her life, but she was completely stressed out.

She stared out the window. Gabe was so disagreeable lately. She would have thought he couldn't have cared less about something as trivial as the invitations. Something else must be bothering him.

Gabe turned the car into Gate One and found a parking spot along the sea wall.

"I take it we're done shopping," she stated belligerently.

"I'm not into it, Kate. Especially if we're just going to fight about everything."

She decided she had to swallow her pride and discover the source of his discontent. She turned toward him.

"Gabe, this is silly. We need to work together. There's so much to do yet."

"Okay, just drop the ranks then, Kate." He looked at her. His face held no emotion.

"Why? Are you embarrassed that I'm an ensign too?"

He bit his lip and looked out the driver's window. She had struck a nerve.

"You *are* embarrassed!"

"Kate, please."

"No, Gabe, I need to know. Are you embarrassed about my being an ensign too?"

"Of course not," he answered. "That's not it."

"Well, what is *it?*" she demanded. "Because if we don't fix *it,* we may not need any invitations."

He paused.

"There's more to this, isn't there?" she asked.

"Yes."

Oh, Lord. What had she done? "Tell me, then. I need to know." Her words were sharp and abrupt, and she regretted them the minute they were spoken. Why couldn't she have spoken gently? But it was too late.

"Kate." He spoke her name softly. Her stomach burned with apprehension. "Kate, maybe we should wait."

She quickly turned toward the passenger window, trying to squelch the sting in her eyes. She couldn't speak.

"Kate, honey, please. We need to talk about this. *I* need to talk about this."

"I'm listening," she said, staring out the window at a midshipman running sprints on Farragut Field.

"Kate, look at me."

"I can't, Gabe."

"Please."

She turned her head but stared at the gearshift, anxiously chewing the side of her mouth.

"Kate, there are some things that are really bothering me. Things that make me feel . . . well, different about us."

Kate inhaled deeply, and Gabe lifted her chin with his hand. Tears tumbled down her cheeks.

"Oh, babe, don't cry. Please don't cry. I don't want to hurt you. I love you. I do. Those feelings haven't changed."

"You just don't want to get married anymore," she whispered.

"I don't know. I mean, there's just so much going on with school and graduation right now that everything's a blur."

"But there's two of us. We can handle it, Gabe."

"I know we can. But there's other stuff. Like we aren't going to be stationed together for who knows how long."

"But we talked about that and agreed to make weekend trips."

"Kate, we'll need to study on the weekends. I've been talking to some of the other guys going air, and they've heard it's a tremendous amount of work. Sometimes you're scheduled to fly on the weekends."

"I suppose they also told you if you needed a wife, you'd have been issued one in your sea bag."

"Babe, it's not just that."

"Then what is it, Gabe? This is our future."

He paused. "Kate, why did you fry one of our classmates?"

"What has that got to do with anything?"

"After service selection, you fried that guy who—"

"—who bit me on the ass!"

"Yes."

"Why did I fry him? Because he was a jerk, and drunk or not, he shouldn't have done that. You agreed with me at the time."

"I agreed with you that he shouldn't have done it. I didn't agree that you should have fried him."

"That's not what you told me at the time."

"I didn't tell you anything at the time, Kate. I figured you could handle it."

"And I did handle it. Even so, the guy only got a warning."

"Doesn't that tell you something?"

"Yeah, it tells me that this 'boys club,' of which you are obviously a full-fledged member, continues to watch out for its own."

She could see that her words had angered him. She wished she had left out the 'member' part.

His jaw clenched. "You know, I have put up with more abuse, more ridicule, from the guys in my company over our relationship than I ever dreamed I could tolerate. I have justified the presence of women at the Academy until I am blue in the face because I honestly believe you girls deserve to be here. I've been called 'WUBA-lover,' 'slag-bagger,' 'bitch-lover,' and shrugged it off. I have stood up for you and backed you up on things that you have done that have been spread all over the brigade, and I have taken major grief for doing so.

"When you reamed that plebe out for not saying 'ma'am' in the hall, I stood behind you."

"No, wait! You interrupted the scene and jumped on my case!"

"At the time. But afterward I defended you to other guys who called you names I won't repeat."

The remark stung. Kate knew that Gabe had been harassed about their relationship. At first she had thought it would be the end of them. But he had always been so strong, joking about it as if it didn't bother him. She should have known better. It would have gotten to anybody after a while.

"So, frying our classmate was the last straw?" she asked, desperate to understand and fix their problem.

"No, Kate. Although I think you should have just talked to the guy about what he did, that wasn't the last straw."

"Talked to him?!" She couldn't let it go. Her voice rose in pitch. "I've tried to *talk* to them before, Gabe. I've *talked* to them when they cut the circuit breakers to my room during study hour. I've *talked* to them when they threw pies in my face. I've *pleaded* with them when they showed up on the edge of my bed in the middle of the night. Don't *talk* to me about *talking* to the guys. My getting bit on the ass may have not been the last straw for you, but it was for.me. I'm through with talking, because it stops nothing. The same shit continues again and again. I'm through with being treated like a second-class citizen. I've done nothing to deserve the way I've been treated. It's all been done because I'm a girl, and talking didn't get me anywhere."

"Neither did frying somebody."

"Only because the boys-will-be-boys attitude prevailed. It has to stop. They can't treat people like this and get away with it."

"Kate, mids treat guys badly, too. Mids can just be mean, sometimes. If they sense a weakness, they go after it."

"Oh, so being a girl is a weakness."

"I didn't say that."

"Yes, you did."

"Please, Kate. This is getting us nowhere. I know you've had a rough time here, but the issue right now is us and our future. With everything going on, I just think we should hold off the wedding part for now."

"Hold off or put off?" As soon as she had asked, she wished she hadn't.

"Let's just call it off for now, okay? See how things go over the summer."

She knew how things would go. He would go to Pensacola and have a blast. Probably meet someone new and forget about her. How could this be happening?

"I don't want to call it off, Gabe. I want to marry you in May. You've always been there for me, and I need you there in the future." She knew she was begging but didn't care. She couldn't lose him.

"I'll be there for you, Kate. I'll always be there for you. We've been through a lot, and you'll always be very special to me."

"Oh, Gabe, please don't call it off. Can't we talk about it later? Please." But she knew he had already made up his mind.

He held both of her hands. "Kate, it's how I feel. I can't help it. It's too much to deal with right now, and this is the one thing I feel I have some control over. Something I can slow down."

If he would just say it was a postponement. If they could just set a date next fall. But she knew better. He was trying to let her down gently. There was no need for her to make it any more painful.

"What'll we tell everybody?" she asked him softly.

"The truth," he replied.

"Oh, Gabe." Her tears began again as he took her in his arms and rocked her gently.

Friday, 28 March 1980

For the past two months Sarah had been stopping by Meredith Britain's room at least once each weekend to see if she needed anything. Meredith had been restricted to her room since the beginning of the semester after being fried.

Sarah wasn't clear on the details of Meredith's predicament, as Meredith had yet to open up to her. She did know that Meredith had been given a raw deal. Charged with unauthorized absence, for which a midshipman normally received seventy-five demerits and two months' restriction, Meredith had been awarded 150 demerits and six months' restriction.

Meredith had been caught by her company commander, a classmate, who initially reported the infraction as an honor offense. Sarah wondered how it had been reduced to a conduct offense and then ballooned into this ridiculous punishment, which would span the entire second semester of first-class year, the best time of their four years at the Academy.

As Sarah walked into Meredith's room, she noticed that her friend's face appeared bloated. She had put on weight. Meredith was always trying some fad diet. For a week or so she would only eat baked potatoes or grapefruit that she snuck out of the wardroom, skipping all other meals and exercising obsessively. It was not unusual for Meredith to work out for four hours a day. Sarah knew it wasn't healthy, but she shrugged it off as Meredith's way of coping with this absurd restriction. She couldn't begin to imagine what she was going through having to restrict at Main Office in uniform, every two hours, when other firsties were enjoying the privileges and liberty of first-class year.

"Hi, Toots! Come on in. My roommate's gone for the weekend. I just got back from restriction and have two hours of freedom until I have to go back. They inspect you every time you go down there."

"Hey, Mer!" Sarah bounced down on Meredith's rack.

"Whatcha been up to, Toots? How's Drew? How's Ryan?"

"Ryan's fine. Still at sea. I got a letter from him the other day."

"Does he know about Drew?"

"No. Not yet."

"You guys are getting pretty serious, aren't you?"

"Well, yeah, I really like him, and he asked me to his Ring Dance."

Meredith's eyes lit up. "Are you going?"

"Sure. Why not? Besides, Ryan and I agreed to date other people, so I don't feel like I need to tell him about Drew just yet."

"That's my Toots, burning the candle at both ends."

"Yeah, you should talk. Anyway, Drew's birthday was this week, so we're going out tomorrow night." The words were out of her mouth before she could catch them. Sarah hated talking about going out, when Meredith was stuck here. She tried to make up for it. "We'll stop by before we go, okay?"

Meredith turned to her and spoke with an atypical hint of disgust. "Look, Sarah, you can go out, and I can't. My being here isn't your fault, and I don't hold it against you, okay?"

"Sorry, Mer. I just feel so bad about it. I mean, I don't think it was your fault, either. You probably should have been punished, but this seems awfully extreme to me." Sarah's concern for her friend grew. Where once there had been an outgoing, sweet-natured person with no unkind words for anyone, Sarah now saw a cautious, more distant Meredith emerging.

"No, Sarah, I deserved 150 demerits for a mistake that would have cost anyone else 75," Meredith replied caustically. "I deserve to spend the entire second semester of my first-class year locked in my room while the rest of you are out partying."

"I'm sorry, Mer. Maybe I should go." Sarah stood to leave, unsure how to ease the tension between the two of them. She just didn't know how to make things better.

"No, Toots! Don't go! I'm sorry. I'm . . . I'm just going crazy being confined to this place! In another hour and a half I have to do it all over again. I don't know if I'm going to make it through the rest of the semester."

"Is there any chance they'll let you off early, for good behavior or something?"

Meredith didn't bother to answer, as Sarah knew that this was never the case at the Academy. Once a punishment was handed out, unless the president of the United States granted you clemency, you served your time.

"Meredith, I've never asked you, but just what was it that you did? How did this thing turn into such a mess?"

"James Webb did this to me, Sarah."

"James Webb? How?"

Meredith sat beside Sarah. "His article. It screwed me. I really believe that."

"Yeah, no kidding. It screwed all us girls."

"No, I mean the part in it where he wrote about the double-standard discipline. Some mid told him about a male midshipman and a female midshipman who were convicted of the same honor offense. The guy got thrown out, but the girl was put on probation. Webb wrote that those things happen all the time. Then this thing with me happened right after that article came out. So I think the administration wanted to show that that kind of thing *doesn't* happen, and they made me an example. How else do you explain the double punishment?"

"I don't know, Mer. I mean, what is it that you did, anyway? I never really understood."

"Last fall I was placed on an excusal list for one of my extracurricular clubs. I could miss the march-on to the football game but didn't have to be anywhere with the club, so I left for Florida to see Peter a couple of hours early." Peter was a member of the Class of 1979 whom Meredith had been dating. They had broken up shortly after Christmas. "You know, it's funny. We fought that entire weekend. It was the worst weekend I ever spent with him. Certainly not worth all of this.

"Anyway, since I was a platoon commander, I had left a note for my company commander stating that I wouldn't be at the march-on, since he received all the excusal lists. When I returned Sunday night, he came to my room and asked me where I'd been during the march-on. I told him I'd gone to Florida. He wanted to know if I had a legitimate reason to be on the excusal list and miss the game. Once again, I didn't lie. I told him probably not. Then he informed me that he was placing me up for an honor offense. He said I had lied to him in my note and I should've told him I was going to Florida instead. I discovered that at least one hundred other mids throughout the brigade were on similar excusal lists to miss the march-on with no scheduled club activity. In my own company, I knew of a few guys who were on phony excusal lists and were sleeping in their racks during the march-on.

"My company commander is the guy in my squad, plebe year, that I told you about. Mr. 'Plebe-of-the-Year,' who I honestly believes hates women. Especially women here. We never got along, and he hated being in a squad where the only other plebes were women. We've never been friends.

"Then he catches me in what he deems is an honor offense, and I could just see the glory in his eyes. So, I go before the Honor Board, which immediately dismisses the case, deeming it a conduct offense. The chairman of the honor committee said that the excusal list was legitimate but I shouldn't have been on it, I should have been at the game, so it was an unauthorized absence.

"I couldn't believe this whole thing was happening to me. I've always been in some kind of trouble since plebe year, but it was always little things, you know. Five demerits here, ten demerits there. Then all of a sudden I'm on the verge of being kicked out! After putting up with three years of this bullshit! I'm wondering how I'm going to call my parents and tell them this. Up till now, all I've ever told them was good. How am I going to tell them that now I've screwed up and they may kick me out and put me on a ship for two years to clean toilets?

"Well, after the commandant told me I was a piece of shit and awarded me 150 demerits and six months' restriction, I guess I was so relieved that I wasn't going to be thrown out that the full impact of his sentence didn't hit me until later.

"I mean, why would they do that, Sarah? Why would they double the normal award if they weren't trying to make an example of me?"

Sarah had no idea. What Meredith had done was pretty bold, but the punishment seemed too severe. Maybe Meredith was being used—being made an example the administration could point to to show that women weren't receiving preferential treatment.

"Meredith, I can't understand it. I think it's really terrible what's happened, and I don't know how to help. I want to come see you, but I feel bad about being able to go out into town and have fun while you're in here."

"Sarah, that's just the way it is. I try to concentrate on working out, and on my studies, because my grades are terrible. I have one B, one C, and the rest are D's. I may not graduate because of my grades. I try to go to the library, but by the time I check out of Main Office and get over there and back, I have only an hour and a half left to study. I mean, look at the clock now. I only have an hour until I have to be back down there. It's horrible living like this, hour to hour."

"What can I do?"

"Just stop by and see me every now and then. I'll be all right—I think."

Sarah was not convinced. "I'll stop by later, Mer. Hang in there, okay?"

"Yeah, Toots. Have fun. Have one for me. Have *lots* for me." Meredith smiled as Sarah departed solemnly. She saw the effects this ordeal was having on her friend, and she worried that Meredith would never be the same.

Wednesday, 9 April 1980

Sarah and her systems project partner, Marty Hack, had worked for two hours in the systems engineering laboratory in Maury Hall on their voice-operated telephone. Marty held the door open for her as they left the building to attend noon meal formation.

"So you understand what I'm saying, Sarah?" he asked.

"Yes," she replied. "We need to build a series of band pass filters, each set to a different range of frequencies corresponding to every spoken number zero through nine."

"Right."

"But then we'll only be able to build a phone operated by one person's voice," she said.

"Right again. So we'll program it to work for yours." Always the gentleman, Marty was tall and intelligent. His wire-rimmed glasses accented a peaches-and-cream complexion, reminding Sarah of a misplaced country boy.

"Sounds good to me," replied Sarah.

"Let's get together after study hour and work on the theory some more. Your place or mine?" he asked.

"I'll come down to your room," she answered.

As they crossed the parking lot adjacent to Stribling Walk, headed for noon meal formation, a television camera crew made a beeline toward them.

"Oh, no!" cried Sarah, ducking behind Marty. "I'm not talking to them!"

"Excuse me, miss. Miss!" The reporter was adamant, chasing Sarah with an outstretched microphone. Despite her attempts to walk faster, he caught up to her, and Sarah was forced to stop.

"We were just wondering, miss, what is your opinion of the recent proposal to reinstate the draft?" It was a proposal being bandied around Washington.

Sarah had an opinion on the subject, but she was not willing to share it with the press. Her plebe-year vow never to talk to them again remained intact.

"I have nothing to say to you guys," she answered firmly, turning away.

"Please, miss," the reporter pleaded, chasing after her like a puppy. "We just want to know how you feel about it."

She turned and faced him squarely. "Look, I know how this works," she said sternly. "I'll tell you what I think, then you'll edit it to your liking, and I'll get nothing but grief for the next four months from all the guys here."

"No, no," he said.

"Yes, yes," she interrupted. "You guys never get it right. You always misquote us, and then we pay the price. So get those cameras away from me. You want an opinion? Go ask him!" Sarah pointed vehemently toward Marty.

Frustrated, the reporter finally turned toward Marty and signaled the cameras to do the same. Sarah watched Marty's delight as the cameras rolled on him. He had a strong opinion, which he was thrilled to share with the Eleven O'Clock News.

Sarah watched from the sidelines, relieved that he had taken the spotlight. His words were faintly audible, but she could tell that he shared her view that it should be mandatory for everyone to participate in the armed forces for a designated amount of time. She waited until he was finished and then joined him again for the walk back to the Hall.

"Why didn't you talk to them?" he asked. "Be a star for a moment."

"No, thanks," she replied ardently. "It's like I told him: they'll show the parts they want, and I'll take the grief from the brigade. I've been in the *Log* enough lately."

Marty laughed.

"Salty Sam," in his last column, had awarded the "Stop the Car Award" to "the only female first class systems engineer, Midshipman Sarah 'BECKONS-THEM-ON.'" "When returning from a trip into town with some classmates," Salty wrote, "she spotted a visiting hockey team with the immortal 'Let me out, it's a team!' Now if only she had been kidding. . . .'"

"You know, you were one of the guys in that car with me," Sarah remarked. "I'm still not convinced you aren't the one who went to Salty with that piece of dirt. It's not even what I meant. I was pointing out that the hockey team had a game that night. One of the guys on the team is in my company."

"Right," Marty responded shrewdly. "That's not what *I* heard!"

Sarah punched him. "I know you were behind that Salty Sam award."

"Not me!" he told her. "But I do know who was, and I'll never tell." He loved stringing her along.

"It doesn't really matter, though, does it? The damage is done." Sarah didn't really mind. The incident was basically ridiculous.

The pair arrived at the bottom floor of Eighth Wing. "See you tonight, Marty."

"Okay," he called. "Twenty-three hundred."

Sunday, 13 April 1980

It seemed like she hadn't written to him in months, although she knew that wasn't true. Actually, she had been very faithful about writing, trying to send him a card every two weeks. Sarah couldn't imagine being stationed in the middle of the Mediterranean for months on end with no port calls, and Ryan had been at sea on the USS *Nimitz* since last September. His six-month deployment had been extended to nine because of the Iranian hostage situation, and distance was taking its toll. Her dad had been right. Absence makes the heart grow fonder—for somebody else.

She had spent Easter break in Virginia Beach with Drew at the home of one of her classmates. Over the holiday, Drew broke up with his girlfriend of four years. Now it was time for Sarah to do the same.

Several weeks ago she had sent Ryan an Easter card full of news about gymnastics, her upcoming engineer-in-training exam, and an offer from the Civil Engineer Corps to be the assistant public-works officer at a communication station in Nea Makri, Greece. She had no desire to start her career on a Greek island. She had visited Athens once when her family was stationed in Turkey, and although the location was beautiful, the groping and verbal harassment from the Greek men she encountered was enough to dissuade her from accepting the CEC offer. In August of this year she would report instead to the Naval Air Station at New Orleans as their assistant public-works officer. She couldn't wait.

But now she had to close a chapter in her life. She dreaded writing the letter she knew would end the relationship that had sustained her for the past four years. Ryan had always been there. Yes, she had dated others, but he had tarried in the shadows, always her number one. Looking back, she realized that he had also been her guide through plebe year. Although extremely risky, their relationship had helped her preserve a positive self-image during a time when shorn locks, masculine uniforms, and taunts about obesity and ugliness had permeated her existence. He found her attractive and boosted her self-esteem so that she had never found it difficult to consider herself a "real" girl. Now she could do it on her own, and now she was in love with Drew. It was time to say goodbye.

Alone in her room, Sarah leaned back against the headboard of her rack, balanced a systems engineering textbook against her knees, and spread a sheet of pink writing paper before her. Inhaling deeply, she began to write:

13 April 1980

Dear Ryan,

How are things on the big blue? Sure hope time is flying by. Only forty-eight more days until graduation! Yea!! Doesn't seem possible, but things are really busy as I count down the days. I picked up my uniform with ensign stripes the other day. I tried it on, and it felt great!

I don't know how to prepare you for what I am about to write, as this is very difficult for me, yet very necessary. I wish I could have waited until your return from deployment, but I can't. I have to clear this up before gradua-tion and all the craziness that goes with it. There's no easy way to say this, except that I feel our relationship is over. I think time and distance have finally taken their toll. I feel like I'm growing up and growing apart from you. Things that have happened in the past between us make me think that they're indicative of what a continued relationship would be like, and they are different from what I think they should be.

We can talk about them when you get back, but it's things like the time I called you last spring on a Friday night and wanted to drive down with Tammy to see you. I know it was very impromptu, but you told me not to come. Your words stung. I was really hurt, especially when you gave me no good reason. Maybe you had a date, I don't know, but I haven't been able to forget or forgive you. There are other things, but I'm not going into them now, and I feel certain that you know what they are.

I also won't lie and tell you there is no one else, because there is. I've only been seeing him since Christmas, but I like him very much. Don't worry, you don't know him.

I'm sorry it isn't going to work out between us, Ryan, and I'm especially sorry to have to write to you while you are at sea. I had really hoped to tell you in person, but the navy keeps messing that up. You are a huge part of my life and always will be. Times change, as do feelings, but you'll always be very, very special to me, and I want to never lose touch. I still hope you'll come to graduation if you get home on time. I'd love to see you, and I will always love you in a very special way. Take care out there.

Lots of love . . . always,
Toots

Tears were streaming down Sarah's face, yet despite the genuine feeling of loss, a weight had been lifted from her spirit. Ryan would take this hard, she knew, but she was also confident that they would remain friends. She cared too much about him for circumstances to be any different. And now there was Drew, whom she had grown to love very deeply.

After carefully addressing the matching pink envelope, she wiped her eyes and quietly left her room, turned right, and walked to the mail chute beside the elevator. She paused for only a second before softly sliding her note into the silver slot. As she watched her parting farewell fly down the clear chute, the butterflies in her stomach finally landed. It was over.

Monday, 12 May 1980

Denzel was leaning over her desk, writing a note, when Sarah walked into her room and startled him.

"Hi, Denzel!" The door closed behind her. "What are you doing here?"

He spun around. "Yo, Buns! You scared me!"

"Sorry, buddy. Whatcha writin'? A love note?"

"Yeah, a very passionate love note," he replied in his deep baritone. "No, really, I was packing some of my gear, and I started to get, well, sentimental, I guess." He paused as he balled up the piece of writing paper and took a shot at the wastepaper basket. His aim was good.

"I was writing you a note to come see me so we could chat. We've had some good times here, Sarah. And now, gettin' ready to leave. . . ."

"Are you getting soft on me, Denzel?" Sarah smiled, her eyes twinkling. "No, you're right. We've had some really good times. I can't even think about leaving, despite how much I want to graduate. Saying goodbye is gonna be really hard."

"Sarah," he drew in a breath before continuing, "you mean a lot to me. I remember when we met on I-Day. Remember?"

"How could I forget the hunk of a football player who was the first one to introduce himself?"

"Yeah, I remember your cute little haircut and cute little butt."

"Denzel!"

"I also remember all the clamor the media was making over the 'first' women. All you had to do to get on TV was stand next to a midshipchick and voilà, instant stardom."

"I remember," she replied.

"They really made a big deal about you guys. So did the firsties. They tried to establish esprit de corps right away with us, but they never let us forget the fact that our class was different because of the 'girls.'

"You know, invariably during a chow call or a come-around, I'd get comments or some sexual innuendo from the firsties about you. I guess they were just trying to rattle me, but your name usually came up when they were asking me rates. Even Schluntz would get in my face during a chow call and ask me how Miss Becker was. They must have sensed that I had a thing for you."

"Schluntz?! Oh, Denzel." Sarah blushed and looked at the floor, unsure that she could handle getting into this right now. Her emotions were so diverse this last week of school—excitement to be graduating, dread of the farewells.

"No, you know, I was impressed with you from the beginning," Denzel continued. "Especially at PEP. That's where you shined. I was really impressed with your ability to hang with the jocks and not let up. I respected you for that and admired your perseverance. I guess all of the guys respected you. You just bounced around with us, and of course, not looking your best in the morning didn't deter me!" He grinned slyly.

"You know, plebe summer was kind of a coming of age for me and I'm sure for a lot of other guys. Not just the experience of this place, but dealing with the women. I mean, I felt like I almost had to choose a side: A, be a WUBA lover, or B, not be a WUBA lover. I chose side A because I couldn't turn my back on you or Tammy. Being in the first class with women was a 'black eye,' in some minds. I just felt it was an excellent opportunity and was happy that I didn't go to an all-boys school!" He flashed her a wide smile.

She returned it with a friendly shove. "You're a nut, Denzel."

He grabbed her hand and held it tightly. "Sarah, I really thought we had something going plebe summer, and then came Nolde. I was pissed and extremely jealous that you would go out with him after all that we'd been through. I actually felt that he took you away from me, from the rest of the company, and that he had no right to do so. I don't think that I ever felt as angry toward you as I did then. Mitch told me that he thought it was a racial thing— that you couldn't handle my being black. That was a very trying time for me."

"Oh, Denzel," she said softly, looking down and then up at him. "I've always loved you. You know that, don't you?"

He took her in his arms, and Sarah spoke into his chest. "It's such a special love. Kind of like a brother, but more than that. I'm going to miss you so much." She started to cry. This was much harder than she had imagined.

"Oh, Buns. I'm going to miss you, too!" He held her tighter. "And I love you. I always will."

Sunday, 25 May 1980

Commissioning Week 1980 officially began Friday afternoon, 23 May 1980, with the Plebe Recognition Ceremony, but Sarah had begun celebrating the day before, when Drew returned from his three-week trip to France. They were joyously reunited at the Baltimore-Washington Airport, where she picked him up Thursday evening. Friday afternoon they watched the Class of 1983—among them, Drew's brother Steve—take two hours and forty-three minutes to climb

Herndon. Saturday night they danced past midnight at his Ring Dance in Dahlgren Hall after eating dinner at an expensive French restaurant in town, where he recounted his French Naval Academy exploits for her. His love of travel and adventure and his eagerness to share more with her strengthened her resolve to make theirs a long-distance relationship that worked.

Sarah's parents, brothers, sister, best friend, and grandparents arrived Sunday afternoon at the home of her battalion officer, now Lieutenant Colonel Bailey (previously Major Bailey of Thirty-fourth Company), who lived on Captains' Row behind Worden Field. Lieutenant Colonel Bailey had been good friends in Vietnam with Jim Becker's cousin, and he graciously offered the guest rooms of his home to the Becker family for Commissioning Week.

Sunday evening Sarah walked to Captains' Row to meet her parents for drinks prior to escorting them to the Superintendent's Garden Party. Approaching Colonel Bailey's house, she noticed her blue Toyota Celica, which she had lent to her parents for the week, parked beside the curb. Mounted on its roof was the biggest pink bow she had ever seen. As she advanced curiously toward the decorated car, her family shouted "Surprise!" from the Bailey's front porch and ran to greet her. Their outcry still mystified her. She had taken out a loan to purchase the car. It already belonged to her.

Finally, when her mother pointed to the title taped to the windshield, she understood. Her parents had paid off her car loan as a graduation gift. She was overwhelmed and began to cry as her mother hugged her tightly and other family members showered her with graduation gifts: a substantial sum of money from her grandparents, a diamond and emerald ring from her great-aunt.

Monday, 26 May 1980

Monday afternoon of Commissioning Week, Kate's family strained to view the awesome display of naval aviation performed directly above their heads. The Brigmans had arrived at Dewey Field at noon with a picnic lunch and plans to spend the afternoon tossing footballs and Frisbees while waiting for the Blue Angels' flight demonstration at 1530. They spread their blankets on the grass by the obstacle course. The weather could not have been kinder, and the Blue Angels flew flawlessly.

Running to catch a Frisbee, Kate noticed Gabe's family picnicking near the middle of the field. Obviously they had the same idea. Gabe saw her and waved. She waved back.

The last time the two had spoken was the day after Gabe disclosed his reluctance to get married. After sleeping on it, Kate had acquiesced, despite her disappointment and pain. They agreed over an ice cream cone beside Annapolis Harbor that with graduation, commissioning, and the subsequent training commands they both had to attend, waiting was the best thing. But Kate knew better, and so did Gabe. Their postponement was really a cancellation. They parted vowing to remain friends forever. However, with the ensuing scramble to organize upcoming events, they had found no time to spend together.

As the Blue Angels executed their impressive fleur-de-lis maneuver, Kate looked down the field toward Gabe. He was craning his neck toward the sky with the rest of the crowd.

"Be right back," she told her mom.

"Where're you going, honey?"

"Down the field, Mom. I'll be right back." Her parents, now divorced, had come "stag" to the graduation events, although she knew her dad had been dating someone. They had agreed to be civil to one another and to celebrate as a family, for which Kate was infinitely grateful. When she told them about her decision to postpone her wedding, they approved graciously, wishing only for her happiness.

Gabe saw Kate approaching and walked to meet her.

"Hi, Kate," he called in an unspoken "How have you been?"

"Hi, Gabe." Okay, her tone replied.

"They were really good, weren't they?" he asked, meaning the Blue Angels.

"Unbelievable. Might be you one day," she replied, smiling.

He shrugged. "I can dream. Excited about Wednesday?"

"Incredibly. Thanks for the card. It meant a lot." He had sent her a card congratulating her on graduating with a 3.28. She stood in the top 20 percent of the class.

"You're welcome. I'm proud of you, you know."

"I'm proud of you, too."

He inhaled deeply. "Hard to believe it's almost over, isn't it?"

"Yeah. Seems like yesterday we were out here running the O'Course."

"Really. I'm glad we'll never have to do that again. That's *one* thing I won't miss."

A pregnant pause hung between them. Gabe glanced toward the Severn River and then back to Kate.

"I'll miss *you,* though, Kate."

Oh, Lord. Why did he have to say that? Why couldn't he have kept it casual? Her eyes began to sting. She bit her tongue and nodded, meaning that she felt the same way but was afraid to speak.

"It's tough, isn't it?" he continued, hands in both pockets of his shorts. "Saying goodbye to everybody and moving out. This has been home for four years. I never thought I'd be sorry to say goodbye to 'Canoe U.'"

"Yeah," she sniffed. The tears were uncontrollable now. He held out his arms. She fell against his chest.

"I love you," he whispered gently in her ear. "I always will."

She nodded her head sharply, indicating that she knew and felt the same. Tears streamed down her face. She still couldn't speak. Saying goodbye was too painful. Especially to Gabe.

"We'll keep in touch, okay?" he told her.

She sniffed, pulled away from him, and wiped her nose with the back of her hand. "Of course." Her words were subdued. "Tell your parents I said hi, okay?"

"I will. Yours, too."

"And be careful in flight school."

"Thanks, I will. You be careful doing bumper drills."

She laughed. He could always make her laugh. "I will. Write to me, okay?"

"Sure. Hey, I'll look for you tomorrow."

"Okay. See you then." She turned to walk back to her family.

"Bye, Kate."

"Goodbye, Gabe."

Tuesday, 27 May 1980

Tuesday morning Sarah kissed Drew goodbye as he left for Norfolk to meet the USS *Santa Barbara* for his first-class cruise in the Mediterranean. After cruise, he would be a squad leader to the new gaggle of plebes arriving in early July. Sarah would not see him again until sometime in August. After graduation and her thirty days of leave, she would be reporting to the Civil Engineer Corps Officers School in Port Hueneme, California. She hated saying goodbye to Drew, but the excitement of graduation overshadowed her despondency, and they vowed to write to one another at least every week.

Hours after Drew's departure, Ryan arrived in Annapolis, having returned from his nine-month deployment on the USS *Nimitz* only days before. He had written that he planned on attending graduation despite their "new" relationship. He had received her "Dear John" letter on cruise and admitted that it could not have come at a worse time. The two of them had yet to find time to talk, but it was readily apparent that with the abundance of family and friends around and him staying at the Randolphs' house, their relationship would remain purely platonic for the next few days. She was thrilled that he had come for her special day, and the pride he felt for her radiated in his handsome, mustached smile.

Later that morning Sarah marched sharply at the front of Thirty-third Company in the Color Parade. She looked like a midget, positioned between two six-foot male classmates, but didn't care. She had earned the privilege finally to march in front instead of in the last row as a sandblower. All firsties marched in the front row.

After the parade the firsties made their traditional sprint to the Reflection Pool behind Mitscher Hall, where they jumped in, uniform and all, many pulling girlfriends in with them. In deference to modesty, because they wore white trousers and white T-shirts under their black jackets, the women midshipmen wore one-piece bathing suits under their uniforms.

Splashing and bouncing around in the pool, Sarah found Denzel, Kurt, and Meredith and gave each a huge, wet hug. Denzel dunked her underwater as her parents watched dryly from the edge of the pool, taking pictures of the debauchery. Freeing herself from Denzel's grasp, Sarah dragged her legs slowly through the thigh-high water, heading for her mom and dad. They were too dry!

Before her dad could move out of reach, she grabbed him in a hug and pulled him, with little resistance, into the fountain awash with first-class midshipmen and girlfriends. Her mom was next!

That afternoon, at the Prizes and Awards Ceremony, Sarah applauded loudly as Carrie Freeman became the first recipient of the Naval Academy Athletic Association sword as best woman athlete.

That night the Becker family and friends celebrated the following day's events at the Chart House Restaurant beside Annapolis Harbor. Before dinner, Jim Becker proudly and tearfully toasted his elder daughter. Embracing her with one arm and raising his glass with the other, his voice cracked. "Success is yours, my sweet. And unlimited pride, ours!"

CHAPTER FOURTEEN

Graduation Day

> Some of you are puzzling why I haven't made a big thing about this being the first class ever to count women among its graduates. Its seems to me it's about time we stop making firsts out of these young women. I am confident they're tired of it. They have met the test. . . . They have earned just as smart a salute and just as much respect as any other graduate.
>
> Adm. Thomas B. Hayward, Chief of Naval Operations,
> in his graduating address to the Class of 1980
> at the United States Naval Academy

Wednesday, 28 May 1980

The blue sky was flawless. At 1030 they mustered excitedly by companies in the driveway behind the Navy–Marine Corps Memorial Stadium sign. This would be their last march-on as midshipmen. After this time-honored ceremony, 938 midshipmen would march out as ensigns in the United States Navy or second lieutenants in the United States Marine Corps. Fifty-five of them were women, unaware that they actually outnumbered another minority of forty-six black male midshipmen also graduating today.

Sarah raised her hand to her forehead and searched for Thirty-third Company, squinting against the glare of light reflected from the large gathering of mids dressed in service dress whites, the women in skirts. The moment was reminiscent of Induction Day in Halsey Field House, when she had searched for Romeo Company's guidon. How far behind that day seemed.

They said we would be to the left of the sign, she recalled and headed in that direction, waving to friends in the class who responded with enthusiastic thumbs-up. To her left she heard Meredith Britain call.

"Toots, over here! Come on! They're taking a picture of all us girls."
Meredith waved her over. Sarah saw a group of about fifteen women already
gathered beneath the stadium sign.

"No, thanks, Mer. Not today. You know how I feel about girl-group stuff."

"Oh, Sarah, come on. I know what you mean, but it's just this once, and
it's for posterity."

Sarah shook her head. She was surprised at Meredith, who also typically
avoided any voluntary gathering of the girls. "Go ahead, Mer. I'm just not into
it." Meredith made a beeline for the photography session. There was no way
Sarah was going to be part of this group segregating themselves from the guys
the last day they would all be together. She didn't want that to be one of the
last impressions the guys had of them. It was bad enough that the press was
everywhere, ravenous to cover the historic graduation. Kurt Loper had
already pointed out the scaffold of media behind the rows of folding chairs
where the graduates would sit during the ceremony. The platform was teem-
ing with cameras, cables, and journalists. Behind them the bleachers pro-
gressively filled with families and friends of the Class of 1980. Sarah had yet
to spot her assembly of fans.

"Let's go! Line up!" called the officer in charge of this last formation.
Tammy squeezed Sarah's hand before falling in at the middle of Thirty-third
Company's line where she fit alphabetically.

"This is it, Tam!" Sarah called excitedly, tucking her midshipman combination cover under her left arm uniformly with the rest of her classmates. The
Class of 1980 marched under the stadium sign, across the brilliant green field,
toward the rows of folding chairs reserved only for them.

Kate squinted up at the bleachers filled with proud parents and friends, hoping to find hers before she got to her seat.

"Kate! Kate!" Someone was calling her name. It sounded like her sister.
She looked around, unable to pinpoint the source.

"Over here, Kate!" She caught a pair of arms flailing halfway up the
midsection of the bleachers and saw them all. Her family waved and
cheered.

She waved back until she had to navigate her way down Seventh Company's row of chairs. When the row was filled, the signal was given for them
to take their seats and place their covers under their chairs.

• • •

Sarah was seated on the end of the last row of the starboard seating area, right in front of the press platform. They were on her the minute she sat down. "Miss! Miss! What's your name? Where are you from? What company is this?"

She obliged them with brief answers but continued searching the bleachers for her family. She still hadn't found them. Wait! Was that her sister way up high, waving her arms crazily? It was! She found them, and despite orders to the contrary, she stood briefly to let them know so. The cameras clicked furiously, documenting her every move.

"Could you do that again, miss? Who are you waving to? Is that your mom? How 'bout another big smile for her?"

Initially having enjoyed the attention, she decided that this could get old.

"Look, guys, I'll give you all the pictures you want, just let me enjoy my graduation, okay?"

They agreed, and Sarah decided that it was time to disregard her plebe-year vow to ignore the media. Today she would relish the opportunity. She had earned it!

The procession of academic professors began, followed by honors for the chief of naval operations, who was giving the graduation address.

Sarah stood stiff at attention while one of her female classmates sang the "Star-Spangled Banner" and bowed her head when the invocation was given.

Ten rows ahead, Kate offered a silent prayer after the invocation. "Please help me to be a fair leader, Lord. Give me the strength to show them I can do it without being a flamer. And watch over Gabe as he learns to fly. Take care of him up there by you."

Admiral Lawrence, the superintendent, introduced the guest speaker, Adm. Thomas B. Hayward, the chief of naval operations. "You should anticipate a life of stress—for this is a stress-filled profession," Admiral Hayward told them. "A successful leader is one who has learned to deal with stress in a controlled, measured manner." Kate took his words to heart and prayed that she might do better in this area.

You are going to confront a whole host of complex situations—ranging from the seemingly small test of your backbone, when you watch one of your shipmates, officers as well as enlisted, take a drag on a joint, where the temptation may be strong to turn your back and let it ride, to some of those more character-testing situations where it might be up to you alone to chose between sacrificing lives or pressing on for the success of the overall mission.

He used the recent return of the USS *Nimitz* carrier group, which had stayed at sea for almost nine months, as an example of the extraordinary demands that might be put on them and the relentless hours of hard work they might be called upon to deliver out of "sheer joy of service to one's country and pride in doing so."

Sarah looked over her shoulder and up into the bleachers for Ryan. The cameras clicked again, but she thought she saw him wave.

About now, some of you are puzzling why I haven't made a big thing about this being the first class ever to count women among its graduates. It seems to me it's about time we stop making firsts out of these young women.

Applause boomed. Sarah and Kate both joined in.

"I am confident they're tired of it," he continued when the applause died down.

They have met the test. They have proven themselves in an environment that was far more stress-filled than that endured by most of their male counterparts. When they throw their hats into the air and put that gold bar on their collar, they have earned just as smart a salute and just as much respect as any other graduate.

"Hallelujah," Sarah whispered.

The academic dean and the superintendent conferred the degrees on the candidates before them, and the distribution of diplomas commenced. The first one hundred midshipmen, graduating with distinction, received their diplomas in order of merit, among them Elaine Richey, number thirty. Sporadic howls of congratulations burst from proud parents and families.

Ten minutes later Kate stood with the rest of her row as the row in front of her filled with confirmed graduates who sat down simultaneously, waving their diplomas in the air. She was shaking with anticipation. Seated on the starboard side, she would receive her diploma from the commandant of the Marine Corps, Gen. Robert H. Barrow. Graduates on the port side received theirs from the chief of naval operations.

Standing in line at the bottom of the blue-carpeted ramp, Kate listened as the names of classmates alphabetically before her were read. She found herself bouncing on the toes of her high-heeled shoes.

"Kate Ann Brigman." She bounded up the ramp, extending her right hand to shake the general's while accepting her diploma with her left. "Yes!" she cried with emotion, lifting her diploma in the air. "Thank you, God!"

Sarah waited anxiously, her enforced patience keeping her on pins and needles. She watched Carrie Freeman and Meredith Britain receive their diplomas, as well as the numerous male friends she had in companies numbered lower than hers, cheering for them all.

Finally her moment arrived, and her row was given the signal to rise. The Thirty-third Herd stood with a cheer. Sarah turned momentarily and called to her mother, "Mom! Here I go!" The cameras clicked wildly.

Sarah turned right and followed Dave Baker, practically skipping along the row of now empty seats. Unable to contain her excitement, she grabbed Dave's shoulders and bounced. "This is it, buddy!" she cried jubilantly. "We've made it!"

Used to Sarah's outbursts after being in the same company with her for four years, Dave did not try to squelch her elation. He turned and hugged her. "Yeah, baby! We're there!"

The line moved forward too slowly for Sarah, but eventually she was next to be called.

"Sarah Nicole Becker."

She took huge strides up the ramp toward General Barrow, unimpeded by her high heels. She accepted her diploma from the general with thanks and turned to face her family.

"Mo-o-om!!!" she screamed, holding both arms in the air. The cameras captured the unharnessed joy on her face. The photo was picked up by United Press International and printed the next day on the front page of newspapers across the country.

Sarah ran down the ramp, bumping into Kurt Loper now waiting in line to receive his diploma.

"Toots!" he yelled. "We made it! We did it!"

She leapt into his open arms and hugged him. Tammy was next.

"Congratulations, Sarah!" she cried. "Isn't it wonderful?!" They held hands and bounced up and down.

"Way to go, Buns!" Denzel called, still in line.

"Oh, Denzel, it's so great!" she said as he held her in a bear hug.

Back at her seat, the cameras took over. "Look up at your mother!" one ordered. "Wave to her!" Sarah obliged. She was on cloud nineteen!

The oath of office was administered by General Barrow and Admiral Hayward to those to be commissioned in the United States Marine Corps and Navy, respectively. After the singing of "Navy Blue and Gold" and the presentation of the class gift, the president of the Class of 1981 rose to lead a cheer for "those about to leave us." When the underclassmen cheered the graduating class, the president of the Class of 1980 took the microphone to lead the cheer for "those we leave behind."

"Hip-hip . . ."

". . . Hooray!"

"Hip-hip . . ."

". . . Hooray!"

"Hip-hip . . ."

". . . HOORAY!"

After the last salvo, the Class of 1980 tossed their covers into the air, creating a hail of headgear over the field and sending the camera crews ducking for cover.

Kate found her family at the edge of the field. They congratulated her over and over while posing for pictures. She looked for Gabe but never found him. It was okay. They had already said their goodbyes.

As she watched a small child scurry to grab a combination cover stuck under a chair (a traditional souvenir-hunting ritual), she suddenly recognized a voice behind her.

"Good job, Kate." She looked up at Dirk Walker, who held out his hand. She shook it graciously.

"Thank you, Dirk. Congratulations. It's been a long haul."

He nodded in agreement and turned to seek out his family. She stood stunned for a moment. His words had touched her deeply. It *had* been a long haul.

Sarah ran into Kurt and his family. They embraced in a tearful hug, releasing the day's pent-up joy and anticipation.

"I can't believe it's over," he told her. "I'll miss you so much, Toots."

"Me, too, Kurt," she replied wiping her eyes.

"See you back in the Hall?"

"You'd better. I want a goodbye hug."

Sarah left him to his family and turned to find hers. Her youngest brother found her first. "Come on, Sarah, let's peel these things off," he said, referring to the white strips of tape hiding the gold ensign stripes on each of her sleeves. As midshipmen the women wore shoulder boards with the service dress white uniform like their male counterparts, but women officers wore stripes on the sleeves of their service dress whites. So after striping the women's uniforms, the tailor shop covered the stripes with white tape to be peeled off after commissioning. Sarah had asked her two brothers to do the honors.

They peeled back the tape to reveal shiny gold braid at the end of each sleeve. She was almost official. Sarah had also asked her dad to personally administer the oath of office to her.

They walked together to the VIP platform, where Sarah raised her right hand and repeated the oath after her father. She promised to support and defend the Constitution of the United States against all enemies foreign and domestic and to obey the orders of the president and those officers appointed over her. She vowed that she took this oath without any mental reservation or purpose of evasion, so help her God.

It was official. She was an officer in the United States Navy. Her father grabbed her in his arms and squeezed. "I'm so proud of you," he told her. Jan Becker had them stand side by side for pictures, and then they moved off the stage for the next ensign's turn.

On the grass, Ryan hugged her tightly and told her how happy and proud he was. As Sarah posed with various family members, a newly promoted first-class midshipman waited her turn.

"Mary, come here!" Sarah called to her friend and teammate from gymnastics.

"Good afternoon, ma'am," Mary said politely, raising her right hand to her temple for what was to be Sarah's first salute. Sarah returned the salute smartly.

"Come here, you nut, and give me a hug!" Mary squeezed her tightly.

"Congratulations, Sarah!"

"Thanks, Mary. It's your turn next year. Let me tell you, it's a great feeling!"

"I can't wait. Good luck, Sarah. Keep in touch."

"I will." Mary turned to go. "Hey, here's your silver dollar." Sarah reached into her skirt pocket and performed the time-honored ritual of awarding a silver dollar to the individual who first saluted her after commissioning.

"Thanks, Ensign."

"Don't spend it all in one place," Sarah called. "Take care, Mary. Keep those gymnasts in line."

Mary smiled and waved.

Sarah turned to see her mother watching her and smiling. She moved toward her.

"I'm so proud of you, Sarah," she remarked gently, stroking her short hair. "I worried about you so much for so long, and now I see what a strong, confident person you've become. It means so much to me." Her mother's eyes flooded with tears. Sarah threw her arms around her and held her tightly.

"I'm really so proud of you, honey."

"You know, Mom, I'm proud of me, too."

AFTERWORD

Whether a woman stayed all four years or decided to go a different route was a difficult decision to make. The bottom line is, we were, and are, survivors. I am proud to be a member of the Class of 1980, but I am even more proud to be part of the group of women who made a difference.

Cdr. Tina D'Ercole, USNA Class of 1980

Friday, 23 May 1997

The Class of 1997, dressed in service dress whites, marched under the Navy–Marine Corps Memorial Stadium sign across the perfectly manicured grass to rows of folding chairs lined up in front of the stage with the blue backdrop. All hash marks and yard markers had been erased for this very special event. Some things never change, I thought. The plan had been much the same almost seventeen years before, when I graduated as a member of the Class of 1980. My name is Sharon Disher.

"Where's Lauren, Mom?" asked my daughter seated anxiously beside me.

"She'll be marching in soon," I replied, my camera poised. I sat in the bleachers with my husband, Tim, and our three children, waiting to see our friend and ex-neighbor Midshipman Lauren Taylor[*] graduate. As a young girl, Lauren used to babysit my children. Now she was about to become an ensign in the navy, following in my footsteps. It didn't seem possible.

As far back as I could remember, Lauren had always wanted to be a pediatrician. Her decision to attend the Naval Academy came as a huge surprise, but I was thrilled. Lauren was exactly the type of woman the navy needed: intelligent, confident, assertive, one who could keep up with the guys and show them that women could do it, too.

---

[*] Lauren Catherine Taylor is a pseudonym.

For service selection Lauren had elected to go surface nuclear power, a field newly open to women. The realization that women could now be assigned to nuclear-powered combatants made me feel that my four years of pioneering at the Academy had all been worth it. The presence of women over twenty years ago had made a difference for those who came after us.

When the National Anthem and invocation were over, the midshipmen took their seats. The superintendent introduced the secretary of the navy, who introduced the main speaker, the vice-president of the United States. Initially I listened but soon found myself lapsing into daydreams.

Two days before, I had received a call from my classmate, Cdr. Tina D'Ercole. Tina had been named by the Naval Academy superintendent to a committee of twenty distinguished Americans. The committee's purpose was to examine, evaluate, and make recommendations on Naval Academy programs in four specific areas: character development, professional development, intellectual development, and support programs. As a member, Tina had had occasion to speak with a number of women midshipmen.

"Please tell me it has changed," I had queried her. "Tell me things are better."

"In some respects, they are," Tina said. "When we were there, it seemed like 80 percent of the men didn't want us there, and the other 20 percent didn't know how they felt about us. Now I would say there is a majority of men who graciously accept the fact that women are there to stay. I attribute their acceptance primarily to the changing of the combat-exclusion law. Since women now *can* fight, they are taken more seriously.

"And the women midshipmen I met are refreshingly assertive and confident. Their response to the minority is 'It's the men's problem. They should get a life or leave.' Unlike us, they fight back. They don't let it get to them. One first-class mid bottom-lined it for me. She said, 'Ma'am, let me put it this way. The difference between my class and yours is that we wear our rings.'"

That statement almost knocked me over. Although I wear my class ring now, it was only two years ago that I put it on. For years after graduation, I would not wear it. I told myself that it was because it was too bulky, but the real reason was that I was afraid to wear it. Afraid because I never knew how individuals I met would react to the fact that I had attended the Naval Academy. Particularly my colleagues. Did they support the idea of women being there, or detest it? I was unwilling to take the chance of finding out. If it came up in conversation, I tried to skirt the issue. I told people I had gone to school in Maryland. When they found out it was the Academy, their faces immediately told me if I had a new friend or if I had to try and prove myself all over again.

Tina's voice continued in my mind. "The women also have role models, Sharon," she said. "Female role models. Remember, we had none. None who had been through what we had, anyway. And we didn't rely on each other. We didn't want to band together for fear of being seen as a 'sewing club.' But these women do band together, and they have female alumnae they look up to. They see professional naval officers who maintain their femininity as well. It's very rewarding to see. It tells me we made a difference."

"I know that now, Tina," I told her. "In March, when Lauren told me she was going to be a surface nuke, I almost cried. I know that sounds silly, but it really made it all worth it for me when I heard that. We've come so far."

"Yes, but we still have a long way to go," said Tina. "Attitudes are slow to change."

She was right. But some attitudes had changed, particularly those of our male classmates. At each Homecoming I attend, I feel more and more accepted. Female classmates have told me the same. Two of them confided to me that several guys in our class had apologized to them for the way they had behaved toward these women as midshipmen. Maybe with wives and daughters these men can now imagine how they would want their loved ones to be treated. Maybe we have all just finally grown up.

"Mom, can I get a Coke?" My youngest child brought me back to the present, and I asked Tim to take him. Of course, all three children wanted to go. I watched my husband and best friend gather three small hands and maneuver them to the edge of the bleachers and up the stairs.

The presentation of diplomas began. Those graduating with distinction went first. I watched with particular pride as the first midshipman graduate walked briskly up the ramp to receive her diploma: the number one graduate was a woman. It had happened before in years past, and the novelty of this achievement was diminishing. I looked at the program and counted at least nine other women among the top ninety-seven graduates. No one could question their achievements. This goal they had achieved all by themselves.

After graduation, I served my country for ten years in the navy's Civil Engineer Corps before deciding to stay home with my three children. It had been a difficult choice, but with a full-time job and a husband who was a routinely going to sea, I saw that my children were being short-changed. It was time to accept my responsibility to them. I did not have them to be raised by others.

I never regretted my choice. Now with them all in school, I work part time as a civil engineer and volunteer full time in their school, also taking time to coach their soccer and basketball teams.

My brood returned with their Cokes just in time.

"Lauren Catherine Taylor," the emcee announced. My family cheered and yelled. Tears sprang to my eyes.

Tim squeezed my arm. "Make you feel old?"

"No, just proud," I told him. He nodded. We watched the presentation of diplomas a while longer.

"Dad, when can we go get the hats?"

"I'll take them down now," said Tim. "You can stay here and watch."

I nodded. Yet watching them walk down the stairs, I realized that I wanted to be with them. Tim would need help keeping track of the kids in the throng that would assault the midshipmen once they threw their hats into the air.

As soon as the ceremony was over, masses of people attacked. I grabbed my daughter's hand and prayed that Tim had the boys. Searching under chairs, we found that the hats had already been scarfed up by others, but we continued searching.

"Mom! There's Lauren!" cried my daughter. I stood up and saw Lauren clambering over metal chairs to get to us.

"I can't believe I found you in this crowd!" she exclaimed. "Where's Tim?"

"Right here," he called. I sighed with relief when I saw our boys behind him.

I watched as my children grabbed Lauren and hugged her tightly. As I waited patiently for my turn, several reporters with a television camera approached Lauren and stole her next.

"Miss, we're with NBC. May we ask you some questions?"

"Sure!" she replied, casting a quick glance my way as if to ask, Should I? I nodded and mouthed, "It's your day."

I stood back and watched Lauren answer their biased questions with professionalism and confidence. "Do you think there is a double standard in the military?" they asked her at least three times.

"No," said Lauren. "We are all treated the same. There are specific qualifications and requirements that must be met before you are allowed to attain a certain rank or designator. They are applied uniformly across the board. I have never been treated differently from the men with whom I serve."

I beamed. The reporters weren't getting the answers they wanted. They moved on, and I finally got my hug.

"How'd I do?" asked Lauren.

"You've done great!" I told her. "Everything you've done has been great! I can't tell you how proud I am of you!"

About the Author

Sharon Hanley Disher is a native of Portsmouth, New Hampshire, and a 1980 graduate of the United States Naval Academy. After graduation, Mrs. Disher joined the Navy Civil Engineer Corps and initially served as the assistant public-works officer for the Naval Air Station, New Orleans. Subsequent tours of duty included staff civil engineer at the Naval Hospital, Charleston, South Carolina, and assistant resident officer in charge of construction, Charleston Naval Shipyard. In 1986, she received a masters degree in civil engineering from the University of Washington, after which she served as assistant resident officer in charge of construction at the Naval Station, Everett, Washington.

In 1988, she took charge as the Officer in Charge of Construction Battalion Unit 414 in New London, Connecticut, where she was the second woman in the navy to ever hold such a position. In 1990, she resigned her naval commission to raise her three children: Alison, Brett, and Matthew. She is married to Cdr. Timothy Disher of Virginia Beach, Virginia, who is a nuclear submariner.

Mrs. Disher currently resides with her family in Annapolis, Maryland.